THE GIANT BOOK OF
MYSTERIES

This Book Belongs
To
Maria Reekie
52 Hayfield Road
Kirkcaldy
Fife
Scotland

THE GIANT BOOK OF
MYSTERIES

Edited by
Colin Wilson, Damon Wilson
and Rowan Wilson

 ||| •PARRAGON• |||

This edition published and distributed by
Parragon Book Service Ltd in 1995
This edition first published by Magpie Books Ltd in 1995,
a division of Robinson Publishing
Magpie Books Ltd
7 Kensington Church Court
London W8 4SP

First published as *Weird News Stories, True Ghost Stories, Strange but
True and Strange Tales and Weird Mysteries in the World Famous
Series* by Magpie Books Ltd in 1994
Copyright © Magpie Books Ltd, 1994

ISBN 0 75251 000 2

A copy of the British Library Cataloguing in Publication Data is
available from the British Library.

Printed by Griffin Paperbacks, South Australia

Contents

THE GIANT BOOK OF
MYSTERIES

STRANGE BUT TRUE

Colin Wilson, Damon Wilson
and Rowan Wilson

STRANGE
VANISHINGS

*O*n a warm June Sunday in 1906, a youth named Harold Wilkins *was asked to join a search party for three missing children. That morning, the three had gone to play in a field near their home, a mile from Gloucester – a boy, aged ten, and his two sisters, aged three and five. When they failed to return home for lunch, their father, a railway brakeman named Vaughan, went to look for them in "Forty Acre" field; he found no sign of them, so he raised the alarm, and crowds of neighbours searched the area and the surrounding countryside.*

More than half a century later, Harold Wilkins told the story in a book called *Mysteries, Solved and Unsolved*: how he and many others had scoured the field, which was close to the locomotive-engine shed of the old Midland Railway, and had failed to find the slightest sign of the children. "Every inch was probed with sticks ... Had a dead dog been dumped there, he would certainly have been found." The police came to the conclusion that the Vaughan children had been kidnapped, and the following morning newspapers were full of the story. The Vaughan family received a great deal of sympathy, and cash donations and postal orders began to pour into the local post office. Vaughan himself seems to have been a rather coarse and brutal character, who when the local vicar called, closed the door in his face with the comment that he "didn't want no bloody parsons knocking at his door."

At six a.m. on the following Thursday morning, a plough-man starting work in a nearby field looked over a hedge and saw the three children fast asleep in a ditch. They were quickly restored to their parents, and newspaper readers awaited the solution of the mystery with interest. They were disappointed. The children had no idea of what all the fuss was about, and no idea that they had been missing for three days. The Superintendent of the Gloucester police, Nehemiah Philpott, took the view that the ploughman had kidnapped the children for ransom, and refused to hand over a penny of the reward money, which had been donated by readers of the *News of the World*. But local reporters only had to look at the labourer's cottage – in the nearby hamlet of Coney Hill – to see that this could not be true; it was tiny, and so close to neighbouring cottages that it would have been impossible to smuggle a cat in without being noticed. Besides, the plough-man had been gathering in the harvest at the time the children had vanished.

When Wilkins told the story in 1959, the eldest of the missing children was still alive, and verified that he did not have the slightest recollection of what happened in the four days during which hundreds of people were searching. It is true that the ditch where they were found might have been overlooked. But would three children sleep straight through four days?

Wilkins has his own theory about the mystery. He suggests that certain places on earth – places associated with witchcraft and ancient rites – are pervaded by strange unknown forces, and that such forces may not be limited by our normal space–time dimensions. But whether or not we can accept the "strange forces" theory, the fact remains that there have been hundreds of similar "vanishings" – so many that whole books have been devoted to them. And many cases involve people who have disappeared "into thin air". On 3 September 1873, an athletically inclined shoemaker named James Burne Worson bet three friends that he could run from Leamington to Coventry, in Warwickshire (a distance of forty miles). The friends followed him in a cart. A few miles along the road, Worson stumbled, fell headlong, and disappeared. His friends – including Burns, a photographer, and Wise, a linen-draper – insisted that he did not even touch the ground. Worson was never found. Neither was a seven-year-old boy named Denis Martin, who was walking within sight of his father and other adults in

the Great Smoky Mountains in the summer of 1969, when
he simply vanished.

These are two of the rare cases in which the vanishing was
witnessed. Far more frequent are cases like that of Sherman
Church, reported in the *Chicago Tribune* for 5 January 1900.

"Sherman Church, a young man employed in the Augusta
Mills (Battle Creek, Mich.) has disappeared. He was seated in
the Company's office, when he arose and ran into the mill. He
has not been seen since. The mill has been almost taken to
pieces by the searchers, and the river, woods and country have
been scoured, but to no avail. Nobody saw Church leave town,
nor is there any known reason for his doing so." This case is one
of many collected by an American historian of the weird and
inexplicable, Charles Fort, who – as we shall see – is the patron
saint of such events.

How could a human being vanish "into thin air"? The
American broadcaster Long John Nebel has a highly circumstantial account of how it happened before the eyes of a whole
audience, in New York's Paramount Theatre. During a Thursday afternoon matinee, Nebel's friend William Neff, a well-
known conjuror, stepped into a spotlight in front of the curtain
and began his patter. As Nebel watched, it seemed to him that
he could see light through Neff's body, as if he were turning
into frosted glass. Slowly, Neff became transparent, then
disappeared completely, although his voice continued to
sound perfectly normal. After a while, a faint outline "like a
very fine pencil sketch" began to appear; a few minutes later,
Neff was back again, looking perfectly normal. The audience
seems to have assumed that the vanishing was a part of his act.
As soon as the show was over, Nebel rushed backstage to ask
how Neff had done it. Neff seemed surprised; he was not aware
that he had "faded". But he admitted that the same thing had
happened three years earlier at a theatre in Chicago. Moreover,
it had happened only a few evenings before as he sat watching
television with his wife Evelyn. He had been alerted to the fact
that something was wrong when his wife had screamed. When
Neff went over and touched her, she screamed again and said:
"Who's touching me?" He then hastened from the room to get
her a glass of water, and when he returned, she flung her arms
round him and said: "I was so frightened – I couldn't see you
for a few minutes." Evelyn was so upset that Neff forbade
Nebel to question her about it. And Nebel, who tells the story in
his book *The Way Out World*, can offer no explanation.

Around the turn of the twentieth century, there were a number of theorists who thought they knew the answer. After the invention of non-Euclidean geometry by mathematicians like Riemann and Lobachevsky, many scientists became convinced that there must exist a "fourth dimension" at right angles to the other three (length, breadth and height), and that it is merely the limitations of the human mind that prevent us from seeing it. And a Professor Johann C.F. Zollner of Leipzig University suspected that this must be the answer to some of the more baffling questions of psychical research – for example, how the mysterious entity named the poltergeist (also known as the banging ghost) can sometimes throw objects *through* solid walls. (His suggestion was that the objects don't go "through", but into the fourth dimension and out again, just as a giant could step over a wall that would be unscalable to a tortoise.) In 1877, Professor Zollner convinced a large number of sceptics with an interesting experiment with a spiritualist "medium" named Henry Slade.

While the medium was in a trance, the "spirits" were asked to tie a knot in a circular piece of cord, and they obliged by doing so without breaking the cord. Unbelievers suggested that the medium had merely switched cords, but Zollner insisted that his test conditions were too tight for that.

A Russian philosopher named P.D. Ouspensky became so fascinated by the fourth dimension that he devoted most of his first book to this subject. And in *Tertium Organum*, he reports that Johan Van Manen, a scientist, described how, one night, as he lay in bed trying to visualise the fourth dimension, 'I plainly saw before me first a four-dimensional globe and afterwards a four-dimensional cube . . .'' Unless Van Manen was deceiving himself (although he claimed to be able to recall the globe with ease, and the cube with some difficulty) then our minds *are* capable of grasping that extra dimension. Ouspensky argued that the fourth dimension is the key to a proper understanding of the universe. For example, our three-dimensional understanding cannot grasp the idea of the universe having a beginning or an end, but insight into the fourth dimension would probably allow us to. Albert Einstein – who was unknown at this time – later argued that the fourth dimension is actually time, and spoke of the universe as being a kind of "finite yet unbounded" space which curves into the fourth dimension like a sphere.

Ambrose Bierce

Among all these speculations, Zollner's experiment stands out as a genuinely useful insight. For there can be no possible doubt about the real existence of poltergeists – there are literally thousands of recorded examples of these mischievous "spirits" that throw things and make appalling rackets. Many modern researchers are convinced that poltergeists are a strange effect of the unconscious mind – particularly, disturbed adolescents' minds – and they prefer to speak of "spontaneous psychokinesis" (i.e. mind over matter).

Others believe that poltergeists are some kind of spirit. But most accept the evidence that poltergeists can cause water to spill out of sealed pipes, and throw objects out of locked rooms through solid walls or doors. The existence of a fourth dimension is the only sensible hypothesis that can explain these phenomena.

In recent years, Harold Wilkins' "strange forces" theory has received some interesting support from students of terrestrial magnetism. Everybody knows that the earth is a magnet; nobody knows why. But zoologists have now established that birds migrate by following lines of the earth's magnetic force, and that animals use them too, for "homing".

"Dowsers" (water diviners) are also sensitive to these lines of

People in the Welsh town of Wrexham and the surrounding countryside were startled to see hay flying under its own power one ordinary summer day in the late nineteenth century.

According to an account carried in the newspaper, the event occurred at 2 p.m. on a calm July day.

Suddenly some haymakers on a farm saw about half a ton of hay sailing above them through the sky. They said it was higher than they had even seen a crow fly.

The flying hay moved in a northerly direction, which was somewhat surprising because it was going against the wind. Although the mass separated slowly as it covered more distance, it travelled at least five miles without falling apart entirely. It had risen from a field about five miles from Wrexham and had flown over that town at some point in its flight. As the article said, "it caused much consternation while passing over the town."

At the end of this flight of hay, wisps lay here and there along its route. One large clump fell in the middle of a field some distance from the point at which the half-ton mass had first taken to the sky.

"earth force". Soon after the Second World War, Guy Underwood, a retired solicitor, decided to devote his remaining days to exploring prehistoric sites with a dowsing rod. He quickly discovered that all prehistoric sites had at their centres "blind springs", from which streams radiated. The electrical forces of the earth in these places take the form of a huge spiral. (Significantly, "spiral" carvings can be found on all kinds of ancient stones at sacred sites.) Stonehenge, for example, presents a mass of these spirals and loops; the site was obviously chosen for a pagan temple because Stone Age priests could sense that there was something strange and powerful about the earth there. Moreover, when Christianity replaced paganism, Christian churches were deliberately built on sites of pagan temples, as if the builders were aware that the ground itself is "sacred".

One of the odd things about such sites is that the sites themselves seem to be able to "record" human emotions. It seems probable that many a "haunted" house is simply a house where a tragedy has taken place and where the earth forces have somehow "recorded" the negative emotions. Sensitive people often experience a "creepy feeling" in such places. One dowser, Paul Devereux, visited the Rollright Stones, near Oxford, after a black magic group had performed ceremonies there (including animal sacrifice); he said that the place positively reeked of "nastiness", which it took days of ceremonial cleansing to remove.

It has to be admitted that for some cases of mysterious "vanishings" there is a simpler explanation. One of the best known is that of a farmer called David Lang who, on the afternoon of 23 September 1880, strolled across a field by his home near Gallatin, Tennessee, in full view of his family, and vanished into thin air. A friend approaching the farm in a buggy saw Lang wave to him a second before he disappeared. Five people rushed to the spot where he had vanished, expecting to find a hole; but the ground was solid. Lang was never found, and the story, reported in many American newspapers, caused a sensation.

Unfortunately, the story was untrue. After reporting it in a book called *Enigmas and Mysteries*, I decided to try and get some more detail, and asked a friend in Tennessee to investigate. She did – and learned that a hardware salesman, Joe McHatten, having spent a boring day in Gallatin confined to his room by snow, had whiled away the time by writing his wife a letter in which he had invented the whole story.

Disappointing. But, according to an American historian of the bizarre named Robert Jay Nash (who recounts the case in *Among the Missing*), it was based on a real occurrence that took place a quarter of a century earlier. In July 1854, Orion Williamson, a farmer of Selma, Alabama, was strolling across a field to greet two friends who were approaching in a buggy, when he simply vanished. The friends, together with the farmer's frantic wife, searched the field without success. Later that day, three hundred men from Selma examined every inch of the field. They never found Orion Williamson. But the following spring, there was a fifteen-foot circle of dead grass at the spot where Orion Williamson had vanished.

Many years later, the story was retold in the *Cincinnati Enquirer*, where it was read by the American journalist Ambrose Bierce, famous for his horror stories and his mordant sense of humour; he made it the basis of a story entitled "The Difficulty of Crossing a Field". Bierce then went on to to achieve posthumous notoriety by vanishing into thin air – although not, in this case, in front of witnesses.

As Bierce approached the age of seventy – he was born in 1842 – he became increasingly cantankerous and restive. In his heyday he had been a famous wit and, virtually, the literary dictator of San Francisco; the thought of succumbing to decay enraged him. His life had been adventurous and tragic – one son had committed suicide and another died of drink – and there is evidence that he himself planned to die with his boots on. In 1913, he decided to revisit the battlefields of the Civil War – in which he had fought with distinction – then go on to Mexico, where there was also a civil war, and perhaps to South America. In fact, Bierce so impressed the Mexican bandit-turned-revolutionary, Pancho Villa, that Villa issued the writer with credentials to accompany him as a war correspondent. Bierce's last letter was written from Chihuahua, Mexico, on 26 December 1913. Then came silence. Ever since that time, "investigators" have produced "authentic" accounts of what happened. One declared that Bierce had lost his temper with Villa and told him he was nothing but a cutthroat, whereupon Villa had instantly ordered his execution. Another said that he had been killed in the siege of Ojinago, and that his death had been reported in Mexican army dispatches. One of his friends in Washington always insisted that he had blown out his brains on a high ledge of the Grand Canyon and them fallen into its depths ("an appropriate tombstone for his gigantic ego"). But the most bizarre story is that he had been captured by a wild tribe in southern Mexico and boiled alive, after which his shrunken remains had been worshipped. This is, clearly, the version that Bierce himself would have chosen.

THE MAN WHO LOVED MYSTERIES

C *harles Hoy Fort, the patron saint of the inexplicable, was a hermit and an intellectual rebel who died in New York City in 1932 at the age of fifty-seven.*

Charles Fort's father was a wealthy businessman who ruled his family with autocratic severity, often beating Charles with a dog-whip. An intelligent and strong-willed child, Fort grew up with a passionate hatred of authority and stupidity. He was always a maverick.

He had always wanted to be a naturalist, and was an eager collector of specimens. But in his teens he decided to be a writer and took a job on the Albany *Democrat*. He wrote novels – three and a half million words according to his own later estimate – but only one was published. It was a flop. Perhaps it was because Fort writes in a series of brief flat statements, often without verbs. To say that his style lacks flow and readability is an understatement.

In his late teens he travelled around the world on an allowance of $25 a month. After his trip, he married an English girl, and settled in a cheap apartment in New York. He made a poor living from journalism. Later, he received a small income from securities, but life was always a struggle. Fort was an eccentric and a recluse, obsessed by the mysterious and the unexplained from a fairly early age. He devoured books on Atlantis, the hollow earth theory, and the mystery of the pyramids. One of his own earliest books argued that our civilization is secretly controlled from Mars. He called this book simply X. Subsequently he wrote a book called Y, and planned another called Z.

Fort himself was no crank, however. He wrote X and Y with tongue in cheek, but later he attempted a closely reasoned statement of his beliefs in *The Book of the Damned*, published in 1919. By "damned" he meant phenomena that had been discredited and disregarded by orthodox science – enigmas, unsolved mysteries, the unexplained.

Here is a typical Fort entry:

Extract from the log of the bark *Lady of the Lake* by Captain F.W. Banner: . . .

"That upon the 22nd of March, 1870, at Lat. 5° 47' N., Long. 27° 52' W., the sailors of the *Lady of the Lake* saw a remarkable object, or "cloud", in the sky. They reported to the captain.

According to Capt. Banner, it was a cloud of circular form, with an included semicircle divided into four parts, the central dividing shaft beginning

An earthquake. A deluge of rain. Dead fish in dried up pools all over town. This weird sequence of events happened in Singapore in 1861. The description of it in *La Science Pour Tous* said the fish had not fallen with the rain. The local inhabitants of Singapore said they had. Charles Fort, American writer on the occult, supported the view that the fish had fallen from the sky. He thought "that a whole lakeful of them [fish] had been shaken down from the Super-Sargasso Sea."

Fort spent his life collecting scraps of information about odd, hard-to-explain occurrences everywhere in the world. He used such bits in his various books, which he wrote as his personal protest against modern science's failure to deal with psychic phenomena.

In *The Book of the Damned*, published in 1919, Fort talks about Singapore's puddles of fish as an example of things falling from the sky. He says that many such falling objects come from the Super-Sargasso Sea. According to Fort, this sea is a "region somewhere above the earth's surface in which gravitation is inoperative . . ." He goes on to say, "I think that things raised from this earth's surface to that region have been held there until shaken down by storms.

at the center of the circle and extending far outward, and then curving backward.

Geometricity and complexity and stability of form: and the small likelihood of a cloud maintaining such diversity of features, to say nothing of appearance of organic form.

Light gray in color, or it was cloud-color.

That whatever it may have been, it traveled against the wind . . .

For half an hour this form was visible. When it did finally disappear that was not because it disintegrated like a cloud, but because it was lost to sight in the evening darkness.

This might make the reader think at once of a flying saucer, especially since Captain Banner's description sounds like hundreds of other UFO sightings. But Fort recorded this account in 1918, thirty years before the start of the UFO craze. He was merely quoting from the *Journal of the Royal Meteorological Society*, an eminently respectable publication. He makes no attempts to draw conclusions from the report. It is simply one of hundreds of similar unexplainable occurrences that he quotes at length and in detail.

We can see immediately why Fort's contemporaries regarded him as mildly if not certifiably insane. Fort spent thirty years of his life in the New York Public Library, searching through piles of old newspapers and magazines for items like the one quoted above. He was particularly fond of tales of odd things falling from the sky – frogs, fish, blood, and snowflakes two-feet square. But what did it all add up to? Why should Fort spend a lifetime assembling a vast collection of tall stories and make no attempt to tie them together into a theory?

The flying saucer story above provides the answer. Fort could be described as a man of inspired intuition. He was also, by upbringing and training, a typical product of the age that believed in hard work, sound common sense, and respect for authority. All his instincts told him there was something wrong with the neat and orderly universe of science, and that the actual universe was a million times stranger than even the most brilliant scientist of his day could imagine. It was this instinct that rang a bell when he read the flying saucer story and dozens more like it – although he would have found it difficult to explain precisely why. In a sense, he wasn't even interested in explaining these phenomena. He felt there could be dozens of possible explanations, all equally at variance with scientific thinking, all equally exciting and fruitful.

Here is a typical example of the kind of thing that interested him. On 28 July 1860, fifteen years before Fort's birth, a great meteorite covered with ice crashed down in Dhurmsalla, India. The event was duly noted and described by a trustworthy authority, the British Deputy Commissioner in the area. An ice-covered meteorite is certainly strange, since most meteorites are white hot from tearing through our atmosphere. That was not all. On the next evening the Commissioner saw lights in the sky, some of them fairly low. They moved around like fire balloons. Nowadays we would probably assume they were the lights of airplanes, but this was long before the invention of the airplane. Fort also noticed from the Commissioner's report that other unusual events had occurred around the same time in India. Newspapers had reported a shower of live fish at Benares, a fall of some red substance at Farrukhabad, a dark spot observed on the sun, an earthquake, a lengthy period of darkness during daylight hours, and a luminous effect in the sky like the aurora borealis.

In the following year on 16 February 1861 there was an earthquake in Singapore, followed by a tremendous storm with three days of torrential rain. The odd thing was that in the pools of water formed by the rain, fish were seen swimming around; and when the pools dried up, dead fish were found on the ground. The most popular theory was that the heavy rain had caused a river to overflow, spreading the fish over a wide area. However, a reporter of the event recorded that fish were found in his courtyard, which was surrounded by a high wall that kept the water out.

Here Fort offers a strange, mixed mass of data, some baffling, some fairly straightforward. There is nothing unusual in a sun-spot, or in the aurora borealis effect that followed it. The lights in the sky could in fact have been fire balloons or ball lightning, although the Commissioner stated that he was sure they weren't. As to the rain of red substance and the falling fish, it seems just conceivable that they were carried aloft by a whirlpool or waterspout. Fort agrees that all these explanations could be true, but argues that there must be something more when so many strange events occur together. "My own acceptance is that either a world or a vast super-construction . . . hovered over India in the summer of 1860," he says. As to

Paul Trent of Oregon, photographed a flying saucer cruising silently over his farm in 1948.

the lights in the sky, his suggestion is: "Visitors." One of his general conclusions is that the earth has had many "visitors" at various times in its history. As to what kind of visitors: "I can think of as many different kinds of visitors to this earth as there are visitors to New York, to a jail, to a church – some people go to church to pick pockets."

Fort likes to keep all his options open. That is why he refuses to commit himself to any single theory to explain all the strange events he writes about. He always has half a dozen possible solutions for everything. Perhaps our earth passed through an area of space where there were shattered fragments of some other world. Perhaps "super-vehicles" have travelled through our atmosphere. (This seems to make Fort the inventor of the UFO hypothesis.) Perhaps there is some *other* world – a kind of twin to this one – in another dimension. Or perhaps all these theories are wide of the mark, and the truth is that "all things are phantoms in a super-mind in a dreaming state." Just as you are beginning to feel that perhaps Fort is building up to some plausible scientific theory after all, he reaches into his hat like a conjuror and produces some new and even more outrageous hypothesis. For example, he suggests that human beings may be "property" belonging to some invisible super-farmer. He seems to *want* his readers to lose patience and throw the book across the room.

As could be expected, most of Fort's contemporaries ignored him, and he repaid their neglect with contempt. When the writer Tiffany Thayer launched a Fortean Society in his honour, Fort firmly declined to become a member. He probably feared that his disciples would try to pin him down to a definite set of ideas and beliefs, and he had no intention of being pinned down.

For day after day and year after year, Fort continued his obsessive search through the world's newspapers, making endless notes on slips of paper which he kept in shoe boxes. After *The Book of the Damned* came *New Lands*, then *Lo!*, and finally *Wild Talents*. Fort became more and more of a hermit. He spent the morning in the library, and the afternoon at his desk, working in a small dark room that overlooked a courtyard. Almost his only recreation was going to the movies in the neighbourhood four or five times a week, and he said he went to keep his wife company. For himself, most films "bored him to death."

While Fort was writing *Wild Talents* his health began to break down – understandably, in view of his dreary and frustrating existence. He wrote desperately, often sending his wife to the movies alone and joining her later. The recluse became intensely resentful of all visitors, refusing to see anyone. He would not even consult a doctor. Finally, Fort became so weak that his wife had to send for an ambulance and take him to the hospital. But he had finished his book. When the publisher brought a copy of *Wild Talents* to the hospital, Fort was too weak to hold it. He died later the same day.

Fort was ignored in death as in life. Although the Fortean Society continued, it was composed of a small group of eccentrics. They admired Fort's fierce individualism, but if members of the general public picked up Fort's books, they soon dropped them again. Fort seldom bothers to tell a complete story. He breaks off halfway through some anecdote about giants or fairies or spontaneous combustion to denounce orthodox scientists or to hector the reader. He simply dumps his many facts like a cartload of stones, and leaves the reader to sort them out. This may be why Fort remained unread, and almost unremembered, for a quarter of a century after his death.

An event of 1947 led to Fort's resurrection. In that year an American businessman flying his private plane near Mount Rainier, Washington, saw nine gleaming disks hurtling at tremendous speed through the sky. Within months many more sightings of flying saucers had been reported, and within a few years there were thousands of reports from all over the world. Even then, few people remembered Fort, pioneer of the UFO idea. In France, however, Fort had at least one ardent admirer. This was Jacques Bergier, a student of philosophy and occultism. Bergier was fascinated by unexplained enigmas such as the riddle of the pyramids, the Easter Island statues, and evidence for highly evolved civilizations in the remote past. In the late 1950s Bergier teamed up with a brilliant journalist, Louis Pauwels, and together they produced the book that Fort had attempted to write all his life. They called it *The Morning of the Magicians*. When it appeared in Paris in 1960, it became an immediate best-seller. It contained a chapter about Charles Fort, and acknowledged its indebtedness to him. Published in Britain and the United States in 1963, it inspired hundreds of imitators. Secondhand works on Atlantis, magic, pyramidology, alchemy, and astrology began to get record prices. Publishers realized there was an "occult boom," and began to flood the market with titles like *World of the Weird* and *Nothing So Strange*. All Fort's books were reissued in paperback, and translations appeared all over the world. Recognition had finally arrived – half a century too late.

Many people now regard Fort as a prophet and a visionary, and many of his ideas have become part of the intellectual currency of our time. Today we freely discuss the possibility of a multidimensional universe in which other worlds could exist parallel with ours. The idea of visitors from other worlds has become commonplace in the past two decades. Arthur C. Clarke's *2001* suggested that human evolution may have been aided by beings from another galaxy – an idea that has become part of contemporary mythology. The Russian philosopher Georgei Gurdjieff, who has attained the status of a cult figure, liked to describe human beings as hypnotized sheep kept stupid and contented by some magician until it is time for the slaughter house. Another cult figure, the Argentinian writer and Nobel Prize winner Jorge Luis Borges, has often speculated that human beings are dreams in the mind of God – and that perhaps God himself is a dream in some even more civilized mind. In recent years, some scientists have suggested that there could be another universe of "antimatter" in which the atoms would be made up of antiprotons, antineutrons, and antielectrons. If ever such a universe were to come into contact with our own, there would be a dull explosion – and then Nothing.

Fort once said that every science is a mutilated octopus. "If its tentacles were not clipped to stumps, it would feel its way into disturbing contacts." Sixty years after the death of Charles Fort, it seems that we may at last be entering the age of what he called disturbing contacts.

MORE UNEXPLAINED DISAPPEARANCES

I n December 1937 China and Japan had been at war for six months, and the Chinese were getting the worst of the struggle. Shanghai fell, and in spite of the protests of the League of Nations, the Japanese advanced on the capital of Nanking.

South of the city, the Chinese commander Colonel Li Fu Sien decided to make a last-ditch stand in the low hills. An urgent request brought over 3000 reinforcements. The colonel disposed these troops in a two-mile line, close to an important bridge across the Yangtze River. They had a quantity of heavy artillery, and were prepared for a life-and-death struggle. The colonel returned to his headquarters a mile behind the lines, and waited for the Japanese attack. At dawn he was awakened by his aide, who told him that they were unable to contact the army. Had they been overrun by the Japanese in the night? The colonel and an escort drove cautiously toward the right flank to investigate. To their amazement the positions were deserted. The guns were still in position – but the men had vanished. Further investigation revealed that a small pocket of soldiers, about a hundred, were still encamped near the bridge. They had heard no sounds in the night. If the army had deserted or surrendered to the Japanese, they would have had to pass close to the camp. The sentries on the bridge also testified that no one had crossed the bridge in the night.

It was preposterous. Three thousand men cannot vanish into

thin air. Even if they had all deserted, such a mass exodus would have been bound to attract attention. Yet no one had heard or seen anything.

The Chinese had little time to ponder the problem. The Japanese army advanced across the river, and two days later Nanking fell. There followed one of the most horrifying and cruel massacres in history – the "rape of Nanking". The atrocities were so appalling that three Japanese commanders were recalled to Japan, as were many soldiers. The "vanishing army" ceased to be a matter of central importance to the Chinese generals. But it was generally expected that the mystery would be solved when peace returned – that perhaps the solution lay in the records of the Japanese

---

Walter Powell was an English politician who was the Member of Parliament for a Wiltshire area. On 1 December 1881 he became part of an unsolved mystery when he went up in a balloon with two of his friends. They came down on a beach in Dorset, the two got out, and Powell started to follow. Suddenly the balloon gave a violent jerk and went high up into the clouds again with Powell still on board. He was never seen again.

It seemed likely that he might have crashed into the English Channel, and a search was made for three days. The beaches on England's southern coast were combed for clues night and day. Nothing helpful turned up anywhere.

Right after Powell's disappearance, reports of mystifying lights and objects in the sky came from England, France, Scotland, and Spain. The day after Powell and the balloon had vanished, people in Dartmouth Harbor saw "two strange bright lights in the sky." Two days later an unidentified luminous object was seen traversing the sky over Cherbourg, France.

On 15 December a ship's captain saw a glowing object in the sky. He described it as the "gondola of a balloon, which seemed alternately to increase and diminish in size." That was in the east of Scotland. On the 16th, three Spanish coastguards reported seeing something that looked like a balloon in the sky. They climbed the nearby mountain to investigate, and saw it shoot out sparks as it vanished. The next day about seventy-five miles east of this sighting, a similar and strangely glowing object was reported.

Could these unusual sightings have had a connection with Powell's lost balloon?

army. In fact, the Japanese army reports contained no mention of the missing 3000 men. Today they are regarded as mysterious casualties of war. But no one knows what became of them.

Why has this mystery failed to excite more attention? The answer is probably that the misery and chaos of the Sino–Japanese war made it seem unimportant. The same seems to apply to an equally strange event that took place during World War I.

In April 1915 Allied armies landed on the Gallipoli Peninsula in European Turkey in an attempt to capture what was then the capital of the Turkish Empire (now Istanbul). They wanted to make contact with Russian allies through the Black Sea. It was bad strategy. Turkish resistance was stubborn, and the Allies were forced to withdraw nine months later, having lost hundreds of thousands of men.

Some of the bloodiest fighting in Gallipoli took place around a spot called Hill 60 near Suvla Bay. On the morning of 28 August 1915 a British regiment, the First Fourth Norfolk, prepared to attack Hill 60. The regiment consisted of more than a thousand men. It was a warm, clear day, but several observers remember noticing a group of curious low clouds over Hill 60. Although there was a breeze, these clouds seemed to remain stationary. The observers reported watching the regiment march uphill until the entire file of men disappeared into one of these "loaf shaped" clouds. Then the clouds moved away – leaving no sign of the army.

The disappearance of the regiment was duly reported to the British Government by the Commander-in-Chief of the Allied Expeditionary Force in Gallipoli. He made no mention of the mysterious clouds, but reported that the regiment had separated from the main body of troops and had vanished. The whole regiment was subsequently posted as "missing" – the assumption being that all its men had either been killed or taken prisoner. When the war ended in 1918 the British asked the Turks about their missing regiment. The Turks replied that they knew nothing about it. Their armies had never made contact with the First Fourth Norfolk.

In 1920 the bodies of a number of soldiers belonging to the First Fourth Norfolk were found in Gallipoli. It was assumed that these men must have died in battle after all, and that the remainder of the regiment probably perished in Turkish prisoner-of-war camps. Today it is generally accepted that the men of

Lights flying in formation above the air station, Salem, USA, 1952

the First Fourth Norfolk were victims of a bloody campaign in which all too many men were lost without trace.

Some people, however, have never accepted this explanation – particularly the witnesses who recalled the strange clouds over Hill 60. The French writer Jacques Vallée was sufficiently curious to investigate the matter, and included the incident in his book *Passport to Magonia*. He used a letter signed by three witnesses attesting to the curious disappearance of the whole regiment into a cloud.

Vallée is a scientist connected with Northwestern University in Chicago. He has also written one of the most balanced books on Unidentified Flying Objects, *Anatomy of a phenomenon*. Vallée puts forward the idea that the regiment marched into a cloud that concealed a UFO. This view is supported by the distinguished British ufologist Brinsley Le Poer Trench, now the Earl of Clancarty, who is Chairman of the International UFO Movement. Le Poer Trench cites another cloud disappearance in the curious case of Dr and Mrs Gerardo Vidal. They were driving home from a family reunion in Chascomus, Argentina, when they drove into a thick cloud of mist. They fell unconscious – and woke to find themselves on a road near Mexico City, 4500 miles away. On telephoning friends in Argentina, they discovered that they had apparently lost two days since they left the party.

This is not the only case in which couples have been *teleported* – that is, moved from one place to another by psychic means – to Mexico. Marcilo Ferraz, the owner of a sugar firm in Brazil, was driving with his wife from São Paulo to Uruguay. Near the border they drove into a white cloud; they woke up to find themselves in Mexico. In 1968 a Brazilian couple, driving through the state of Rio Grande do Sul on their honeymoon, suddenly became extremely drowsy. When they woke up, they were in Mexico.

At this point it is worth mentioning the strange experience of Betty and Barney Hill. It aroused widespread interest, and was the subject of a book, *The Interrupted Journey*, by John G. Fuller. Driving from Canada to New Hampshire in September 1961, the Hills saw a bright object like a star descending through the sky. Looking at the object through binoculars, Barney Hill thought it to be some kind of spacecraft. The couple drove off at high speed, but began to feel drowsy. They woke up an hour later, with no memory of what had happened in the meantime.

When they realized that they had apparently lost an hour – not to mention thirty-five miles – the Hills feared that they were going insane and began consulting doctors. Dr Benjamin Simons, a neurosurgeon, helped them recall what had happened during the lost hour by hypnotizing each of them. Their stories under hypnosis were the same. The engine of the Hills' car had failed on the approach of a UFO. They had been taken aboard the craft by beings unlike humans, and had each been subjected to a medical examination. Finally they had been put back in their car, further along the road, with the memory of what had taken place erased from their consciousness.

The story told by the Hills is supported by medical evidence, so it seems unlikely that they were lying. On the other hand, it is possible that the story they told under hypnosis may have been the product of subconscious fantasy – a kind of dream. A couple driving a long distance throughout the night are likely to become drowsy and it might seem to them to have lost minutes or even hours. It is true that the Hills were hypnotized separately; but it is conceivable that they had discussed the possibility of being kidnapped by extraterrestrial beings before they consulted Dr Simon, and under hypnosis produce a story based on their discussion. In short, the flying saucer theory remains no more than a hypothesis to explain these strange cases of teleportation even though it seems as plausible as any other hypothesis.

One curious aspect of teleportation incidents is that they so often involve couples. I have myself discussed such an experience with a couple that went through it – Dr Arthur Guirdham, former Consultant Psychiatrist to the Bath Medical Area in southwest England, and his wife Mary. The Guirdhams were taking a vacation on the Yorkshire moors, and were staying at a hotel in a small town. One day they visited a town some fifteen miles away. At the end of the outing, they started to drive back to their hotel. It was a warm pleasant evening, and they drove slowly. They had only been driving for five minutes when Guirdham noticed a signpost that indicated they were only three miles from their destination. This was clearly impossible unless they had been driving at more than a hundred miles an hour. They stopped to consult a map to see if they had taken a short cut or mistaken the distance. They had not. If the signpost were right, then they had covered twelve miles in less than five minutes. And the signpost was right. A few miles further on the Guirdhams entered the town where their hotel was situated.

There is a matter-of-factness about this story that argues for its truth. Guirdham did not attempt to draw any conclusions from the incident, or use it as the foundation for an argument about time. He simply recounted it as something odd that had once happened to him. His wife Mary confirmed it.

In this case, there was no question of lost time; it was only the distance that had apparently been telescoped. Which brings us to a fundamental question: is it conceivable that space and time could be stretched or compressed like a piece of chewing gum? This is a question that will be raised by many of the enigmas and mysteries recounted in this book, and it may be as well to consider it a little more closely.

In his famous book *An Experiment With Time*, first published in 1927, the British aeronautical engineer J.W. Dunne described how he began having dreams of the future. Among them were dreams of newspaper headlines that appeared the day after he dreamed them. Dunne decided to make a habit of jotting down his dreams when he awoke during the night because he was convinced that many interesting dreams are simply forgotten by the time we wake up in the morning. His records confirmed

---

It was a bright October morning in 1593. On the plaza in front of the palace in Mexico City there was the usual bustle of people and soldiers. One of these army men stood out. He wore a resplendent uniform unlike the others, and he carried a different kind of gun.

When questioned later, the strange soldier said that his orders that morning were to mount guard at the governor's palace in Manila, where he was stationed. "I know very well this is not the governor's palace – and evidently I am not in Manila," he said . . . "But here I am and this is a palace of some kind so I am doing my duty as nearly as possible." The soldier also told the authorities that the governor had been killed the night before.

The soldier couldn't believe that he was thousands of miles away from Manila, and everyone was baffled by his overnight transportation to Mexico City. The man with this incredible tale was put in jail.

Two months afterward a ship arrived from the Philippines. It brought news that the governor had been murdered – on the night before the soldier had appeared. The soldier was released and sent back to Manila. Some 400 years later his marvellous trip through space and time remains a mystery.

that he often dreamed of events which later happened. He persuaded others to write down their dreams, and they also found that they dreamed of future events that came true. As a result of these experiences, Dunne formulated his theory of "serial time". He suggested that there are several different kinds of time, and several different "me"s on different levels of being. For example, there is the superficial "me" who runs to catch trains, and chats with people at parties; a deeper "me" who appreciates music and poetry; and a still deeper "me" who may be aroused by some great crisis or challenge; and so on. Each of these "me"s, Dunne suggests, may have a different kind of time. A simple way to grasp this idea would be to imagine a carousel that contains several different carousels one inside the other, with each one going at a different speed: a different "you" exists on each of the carousels. Because of the speed differences, the "you" on an inner carousel may actually be ahead of the "you" on the outer carousel. Therefore you know what will happen tomorrow, or next week, or even next year.

Dunne's theory has been strongly criticized by many scientists and parapsychologists. Nevertheless it does seem to fit in with those strange glimpses into the future that provide such a challenge to investigators of psychic phenomena. A simple version of Dunne's theory is that time is like a phonograph record, and our human consciousness is like the needle that has to track it. Occasionally the needle can skip a groove, or even several grooves, and jump into the future.

There seems to be a likely possibility that time may be more complex than it looks. But how about space? All our experience tells us that space is the same everywhere. Things *in* space can change, but isn't space itself unchangeable?

The idea of unchangeable space was first challenged in the early years of the twentieth century by Albert Einstein. Although it has been said that only a handful of people fully understand Einstein's Theory of Relativity, its implications caught the imagination of the whole world. The first part of Einstein's theory, the Special Theory of Relativity, was published in 1905. It was concerned with bodies travelling at speeds that approached the enormous speed of light. At such speeds, Einstein suggested, measurements of distance and time would be altered: objects would shrink in length and time would slow down. For instance, a spaceship travelling at half the speed of light – about 93,000 miles per second – would have only about eighty-five per cent of its length when at rest, and clocks on board would run at eighty-five per cent of their normal rate. The crew inside the spaceship would even age more slowly because the clocks were slowed down. The crew would not be aware of these effects, however, because everything on the spaceship would be equally affected. On the other hand, the crew looking at the Earth would find that *it* was contracted, and would assume that Earth clocks were running slow compared with theirs. Time slows down on a moving object, and speeds, time intervals, and length are relative to the observer who is measuring them, said Einstein.

The effects of motion on the measurements of time and distance cannot be detected at everyday speeds, but it is impossible for a human being to move at anything like the speed of light. In 1961, however, scientists in Geneva succeeded in accelerating a tiny particle called a *meson* to three-quarters of the speed of light. The usual lifespan of this particle, when at rest, is only two-millionths of a second; but at three-quarters of the speed of light, the meson lasted three-millionths of a second, or half again as long. This experiment justified Einstein's conclusion that time slows down on a moving object.

. Einstein went on to develop the General Theory of Relativity with the aim of explaining gravitation. According to the General Theory, any mass tends to distort or "bend" space itself. The larger the mass, the greater the bending, so the distortion of space around a very large mass like a planet is considerable. As a result of such distortion, bodies tend to move towards each other in precisely the way bodies are attracted to each other by gravity. The General Theory demonstrated that gravity was a property of the "shape" of space itself.

This theory led to some surprising predictions. According to Einstein's reasoning, light rays ought to bend slightly as they pass close to a large mass like the sun. Many scientists dismissed this idea as absurd. Then in 1919 a total eclipse of the sun made it possible to measure light rays passing close to it from distant stars. It was discovered that light did bend in the sun's gravitational field.

Einstein saw space and time as being somehow bound together into a unity called space-time. If we were able to step outside our Universe and look in, we might see the Universe as a gigantic ball of space-time. Moreover, we would notice that it was more curved in the region of any large mass like a star or a planet.

The Theory of Relativity is extremely complex, and can only be fully understood with the aid of mathematical formulas. However, what matters from our point of view is that scientific research strongly suggests that the theory is correct, and that the space and time which we take for granted are far stranger than we think. A striking illustration of this is the recently advanced theory of so-called "black holes". This holds that certain stars burned themselves out like giant atom bombs, collapsed in on themselves, and became ever smaller and denser. Afterwards their gravitational fields got stronger. It is possible that the pressures exerted by a collapsing star could be so tremendous that it would go on collapsing forever, forming a black hole in space. The gravitational field would be so strong that not even light could escape from it. Anything that fell into a black hole would never get out again – any spaceship or planet that got sucked into this whirlpool of destruction could never escape.

Ideas like these fail to make sense in terms of the world we see around us. Yet there are certain spots on the surface of our Earth where we may be able to gain some impression of the strange effects of space-time. For example, on the banks of Sardine Creek, Oregon, there is a spot known as the "Oregon Vortex". It is about 165 feet across, and the force of gravity seems to be intensified towards its centre. Compasses and other instruments refuse to work in the vortex, and a photographer's light meter reveals a considerable difference in intensity between the daylight in the circle and that outside. There is a hut in the vortex – an old office abandoned long ago. It has slipped downhill, and is now at a slight angle towards the centre of the circle. People who step into the hut experience a weird sense of unbalance, as if they were in a hall of distorted mirrors at a fairground. This feeling is not entirely an illusion. A ball dangling from a beam in the ceiling of the hut seems to incline toward the centre of the vortex. Observations made from outside the vortex prove that this is so. Visitors feel pulled toward the centre of the circle, and seem compelled to lean backward at an angle. Cigarette smoke in the vortex spirals upward in a strange manner, and a handful of confetti whirls around as if caught in a twister.

It has been suggested that the phenomena of the vortex are due to electromagnetism, but they could equally be the manifestation of some eccentricity in the laws of gravity. Add to this the idea that "waves" of space-time are not fixed, but roll across the universe in a definite rhythm, and we begin to see how certain spots could be freakish and unpredictable. We cannot understand much about their mechanism, but we can see that such a space-time warp could have strange consequences for anyone who happened to get caught in it. Like Orion Williamson, who disappeared in full view of two friends. Like the Spanish soldier who was teleported from the Philippines to Mexico City. Or like Benjamin Bathurst, the British Ambassador to the court of Francis I of Austria, who, in the presence of his secretary and valet, strolled around the post horses that were to carry him back to London, and simply vanished. This happened on 25 November 1809 – and Bathurst was never seen again. The British suspected that their arch-enemy Napoleon was behind the disappearance, but Napoleon flatly denied knowing anything about it. He might have pointed out that even his secret police had no power to make a man vanish into thin air in front of two witnesses.

Charles Fort mentions the Benjamin Bathurst case, among many other strange disappearances, but has no explanation to suggest. In fact, the space-time warp idea might explain many of the strange phenomena recorded by Fort: the fish, frogs, coal, sand, and rain of blood that have fallen out of clear skies onto the earth. If a space-time warp could transport a Spanish soldier 9000 miles, it might just as easily transport fish from the depths of the sea to the midwestern plains of North America.

Fort mentions in passing a detail that modern researchers may find highly significant: the strange events he records are often accompanied by a failure of electric power in machines. Such an inexplicable power failure occurred in Cairo on 5 April 1923. It is linked by some with the famous "curse of Tutankhamun" because it coincided with the death of the Earl of Carnarvon, the man who sponsored the excavation of Tutankhamun's tomb. The same thing happened in Denver, Colorado, on 14 February 1963: all power failed, and engineers found the failure inexplicable. They were equally baffled when the lights came on again an hour and a half later. Flying saucer enthusiasts point out that similar failures seem to occur in the vicinity of UFOs. For example, on 17 August 1959 the Chief Engineer of the power station in Uberlandia, Minais Gerais, Brazil, saw a large flying object passing over the station. At the same moment, the automatic power switches kicked themselves open. The engineer closed them; they flew open again. The flying object passed over a substation a few miles away, and the keys there flew open in the same way. While the UFO hovered near the station, the keys refused to remain closed. When it flew off, everything functioned normally again.

Ufologists are inclined to believe that the motors of a UFO cause power failures. As far as I know, no one has yet suggested the more interesting hypothesis that UFOs may be associated with space-time warps, and that it is the warp that is to blame.

As the British scientist J.B.S. Haldane once remarked: 'The universe is not only stranger than we imagine; it is stranger than we *can* imagine.'

DEVIL'S GRAVEYARDS

*I*t is odd that we should call our planet the Earth. It would be far more reasonable to call it the Sea. Almost three quarters of this globe is under water, and if the polar caps melted, about half the remaining land would vanish. We human beings are little better than shipwrecked sailors living on tiny islands. The Pacific Ocean alone is larger than all the land areas of the world, and it is so deep that it could contain the whole landmass of the moon.

Because we have sailed all over the sea's surface, we believe that we know the sea. This is a fallacy. A mere two per cent of the ocean's floor has been charted. At its greatest depth, the Pacific Ocean is seven miles deep. As undersea explorer Jacques Cousteau has remarked, the sea is like a bowl of soup, and it gets thicker as you get deeper. It used to be thought that no life could exist at such a depth, but special deep-sea submarines – one of which reached a depth of almost seven miles – have revealed that this is an error. New marine species are always being discovered. In 1938 a fisherman in the Indian Ocean caught a coelacanth, a prehistoric fish that was believed to have died out sixty million years ago. There are reasonable grounds for believing that 100-foot long eels still exist in the ocean. The oceanographer Alain Bombard, making a one-man trip across the Atlantic in a rubber dinghy, was followed by an unknown sea creature he described as "a long, green sausage, about ten feet long and nine inches or so in diameter. It was not seaweed because it moved and wriggled . . ." The more we learn of the sea, the more obvious it becomes that we have scarcely begun to penetrate its mysteries.

To human beings the most frightening characteristic of the sea is its power to engulf them without trace. I am not speaking of straightforward drowning – the sea has a habit of yielding up its drowned – but of the strange disappearances at sea that are even more numerous and more baffling than those on land.

One of the more curious of the sea's minor enigmas is the mystery of the Eilean Mor lighthouse on the Flannan Islands off the west coast of Scotland. Ten days before Christmas in 1900, the lighthouse's 140,000 candlepower light was extinguished. Joseph Moore, the relief lighthouse keeper in the Outer Hebrides seventeen miles away, could not leave his post to investigate because wild storms of the North Atlantic had battered the coast for a week past.

Among the inhabitants of the Hebrides the Flannan Islands have the reputation of being haunted. Eilean Mor, the largest of the islands, has a fine green turf that is highly suitable for sheep, and farmers would sometimes take their sheep there for fattening. But nothing would persuade them to remain on the island overnight.

On 26 December the storm abated, and the steamer *Hesperus* set out for Eilean Mor with provisions. As the *Hesperus* circled the island, the crew observed that no preparations had been made for their arrival. There were no empty packing cases or mooring ropes on the jetty. A boat was let down, and Joseph Moore was the first ashore. The entrance gate and the main door of the lighthouse were closed. Moore went inside and shouted. There was no reply. The place was cold and empty. The clock on the shelf had stopped. Moore ran back to the jetty for help, afraid that he might find dead men in the lighthouse turret. Two men climbed the stairs with him. But there was no sign of life. The entire lighthouse was empty. In the sleeping quarters the beds were made, and everything was neat and orderly. The wicks of the lanterns had been trimmed, and they had been filled with oil ready to be lit after dark. The last entry on the record slate had been made at 9 a.m. on 15 December – the day the light had failed to appear.

At first it looked as if the mystery might be solved. Two of the three sets of oilskins belonging to the lighthouse keepers were missing. Investigators who landed on the island a few days later found that the west jetty had suffered severe storm

Early deep sea exploration vessel, the French Bathyscape reached depths of 4050 metres in 1954

damage. On a concrete platform sixty-five feet above the water stood a crane with ropes trailing from it. These ropes were usually kept in a tool chest, which was placed in a crevice more than a hundred feet above sea level. The chest was found to be missing. The astonishing conclusion was that some tremendous storm, with waves over a hundred feet high, seemed to have battered the island and carried away the chest – draping its ropes over the crane – and swept the three men to their deaths.

For that to have happened was well nigh impossible. To begin with, the day of the 15th had been relatively calm despite a week of storms. If this were not the case, all three oilskins would have been missing, whereas one had been left behind in the lighthouse. Furthermore, experienced lighthouse men would hardly be stupid enough to venture out onto a jetty in a storm.

It seems far more likely that the damage to the jetty had occurred in a storm the previous evening, and that the three men had gone out in calm weather to inspect it. And then what happened? One suggestion that gained wide general acceptance is that one of the three went insane, killed his two companions, and then committed suicide. But no weapons were missing. Hammers, axes, and knives were all untouched in their proper places.

Three men had set out for the west jetty of their lighthouse on a calm day – and vanished. No bodies were ever recovered. No plausible explanation has ever been put forward. Moore, left alone in the lighthouse for two days after landing, believed that he heard men's voices calling to him. Could they have been other than the cry of sea birds? Since 1900 no more disappearances have occurred, and the island has kept its secret.

As we examine some of the classic mysteries of the sea, a pattern begins to emerge. In case after case something frightened the crew into abandoning ship. No one has ever been able to suggest what that something might be.

The case of the Dutch schooner *Hermania* is typical. In 1849 a fishing vessel off the coast of Cornwall in southwest England found the ship drifting. She had been dismasted, evidently by a gale. Men went aboard and found that the schooner's lifeboat was still in its chocks. The property of the crew seemed to be intact, but every living soul aboard the vessel had vanished.

An even stranger mystery was encountered by another British sailing vessel, the *Ellen Austin*. In the summer of 1881 the ship was heading for St John's, Newfoundland. In the mid-

Atlantic, the crew sighted a schooner that seemed to be keeping a parallel course. As they came closer they realized that the ship was drifting. A boarding party examined the schooner. Everything seemed to be in order, and there was no sign of a struggle; but the crew was missing. The mate and several crew members from the *Ellen Austin* stayed on board to man the valuable prize, and for some time the two ships continued to sail parallel. Then a storm blew up, driving them apart. When the storm had cleared, the mystery ship seemed to be damaged. The captain saw through his telescope that there was no one on deck. He ordered a boat to be lowered, and went on board. The ship was deserted.

His crew went into a panic. It took the captain a great deal of talking – with offers of reward – to persuade a four-man crew to go aboard the derelict. Again, the two ships proceeded toward Newfoundland. The mystery schooner was faster than the *Ellen Austin*, and soon drew ahead. That didn't bother the captain, however, because he expected to find the ship in St John's when he arrived. But there was no sign of the schooner in port. It had vanished with the crew members.

In October 1917 the schooner *Zebrina* left Falmouth, England, for France – a fairly short voyage. Two days later, the *Zebrina* was found drifting and deserted with no sign of violence or anything else to indicate why the crew had left. In July 1941 the Portuguese lugger *Islandia* sighted the French cutter *Belle Isle* near the Gulf of Lyon. The sails of the cutter were set and undamaged. There was no one aboard, and no clue to the disappearance of the sailors was found. All these cases seem to have the same strange element in common – the mysterious something that caused panic, and left no clue behind.

The chief problem in most of these cases is lack of adequate documentation, which leads the critical reader to suspect the accuracy of most popular accounts. In at least two classic cases, however, we have accurate and detailed documentation. These are the mysteries of the *Mary Celeste* and the *Joyita*.

From the beginning, the American vessel *Mary Celeste* was an unlucky ship. Her first captain died a few days after taking command. On her first voyage she damaged her hull. In the Straits of Dover she collided with a brig and sank it. In 1867, only six years after her launching, she grounded on Cape Breton Island, Nova Scotia, and was assumed to be a write-off. A man who salvaged her went bankrupt.

In the autumn of 1872, with this history behind her, the *Mary*

Celeste set out from New York with a cargo of commercial alcohol. Captain Benjamin Briggs had his wife and two-year-old daughter on board, and there was a crew of seven. The *Mary Celeste* sailed for the Italian port of Genoa on 5 November. Ten days later, the British ship *Dei Gratia* also left New York bound for Gibraltar. Her captain was David Moorhouse.

On the afternoon of 5 December 1872 the *Dei Gratia* sighted the *Mary Celeste* in the North Atlantic, midway between the Azores and the coast of Portugal. She was obviously drifting. A boarding party found her deserted. The lifeboat was missing, indicating that the crew had abandoned ship in some kind of danger. But there was nothing noticeably wrong with the vessel. There were a few feet of water in the hold, but the ship's pumps proved to be working perfectly, and this was soon pumped out. The condition of the crew's quarters indicated that the ship had been abandoned in extreme haste. In the hold a few barrels of the commercial alcohol had broken open, and one was empty. The hatch of the hold was found on deck.

With some difficulty a skeleton crew sailed the *Mary Celeste*

In November 1964 Chuck Wakely, a pilot for a charter flight airline, had a narrow escape from being swallowed up by the unknown forces of the Bermuda Triangle. At the time of his frightening experience, he knew nothing about the perils of that area.

Wakely's brush with fate occurred on a return solo flight from Nassau to Miami. He climbed to 8000 feet, levelled off, and settled back for a routine run. Then he noticed a faint glow on the wings of his plane. He put it down to an optical illusion created by the cockpit lights through the tinted windows.

After about five minutes, however, the glow increased so much that Wakely found it hard to read his instruments. Soon he had to operate the craft manually because none of the electronic equipment was in working order.

He noticed that the wings glowed bluish-green and looked fuzzy. At that point he was in such operating difficulties that he had to let go of the controls and let the plane take its head. The glow became blinding, but then began to fade.

As soon as the glow had died down, the instruments began to work properly again. Wakely was able to make a normal landing at his destination.

He was one of the lucky ones.

to Gibraltar, arriving on 13 December. Right from the start they met with hostility. The British authorities in Gibraltar suspected that the men of the *Dei Gratia* were in collusion with the crew of the *Mary Celeste* to claim salvage money. The *Mary Celeste* was searched, and on 18 December an inquiry was heard in the Vice-Admiralty Court of Gibraltar. The Queen's Advocate, Solly Flood, who cross-examined the witnesses, concluded that there had been a mutiny aboard the *Mary Celeste*, and that the crew had killed the captain and his family. Searchers had found a cutlass under the captain's bed, and Flood maintained that certain stains on it were blood. The hull of the ship appeared to have been damaged, and Flood believed that the mutineers did this to make it look as if the vessel had struck rocks. The United States consul in Gibraltar disagreed hotly with this view. He insisted that there were no signs whatever of violence or mutiny aboard the *Mary Celeste*, and that the damage to the hull was natural.

The crew of the *Dei Gratia* was finally awarded £1700 salvage money – a mere fraction of the ship's value. And so the whole incident was forgotten – for eleven years. At that time an impecunious young doctor with ambitions to become an author wrote a story based on the affair. Entitled "*J. Habakuk Jephson's Statement*," the story appeared anonymously in *The Cornhill Magazine* in January 1884 with the ship's name changed to *Marie Celeste*. The story claimed that she had been taken over as part of what would now be called a Black Power plot. It also claimed that the vessel's lifeboat was still on board when she was found. When the identity of the author became known, he found himself launched on the road to fame.

The author was Arthur Conan Doyle, and his fictional version of the *Mary Celeste* mystery started a flood of books and articles on the subject. Most of them were speculation or pure fiction, and none of these accounts succeeded in throwing any light on the reasons for the ship's abandonment. One of the few plausible suggestions is that some of the alcohol on board exploded – which could account for the hatch being on the deck – and the captain decided that they should all climb into one lifeboat to be towed behind the *Mary Celeste*. At some point, the tow broke and everyone drowned. The only objection to this explanation is that there was no sign of an explosion in the hold.

The *Joyita* is often referred to as the *Mary Celeste* of the Pacific. It was a twin-screw ship that met with disaster in October 1955 some time after leaving Apia in Western Samoa. It was headed for Fakaofo in the Tokelau Islands, a mere 270 miles to the north. On 10 November, more than a month after she had set out, the *Joyita* was found abandoned and half foundering. But the ship was cork-lined, and therefore practically unsinkable. The captain, Dusty Miller, had known that perfectly well – in fact, he had often boasted of it. His officers knew it too. So why had they abandoned ship?

Stranger still, there were signs that two men had stayed aboard. An awning had been erected either to catch water or to keep off the sun. Where had these men gone?

There could be no doubt whatever that the *Joyita* had been in trouble. In fact, only one of the two engines was working, and the radio was defective. She was hardly seaworthy.

The ship was taken to Suva, Fiji, where she was dry-docked and pumped out. The basic cause of the trouble was soon apparent. A pipe under the boiler room floor had broken and flooded the vessel. Blood-stained bandages were found. This suggested that someone had been injured fairly seriously – probably the captain himself, since he would otherwise not have permitted the crew to abandon ship. It therefore seemed possible to reconstruct the tragedy. Somewhere out at sea, the *Joyita*'s engine stopped. The pipe burst and caused flooding. Captain Miller had somehow been badly injured, perhaps by being thrown from the bridge by a sudden listing. The crew and passengers had taken to the boats, and had perished at sea. Miller had remained on board, probably with a devoted attendant to look after him.

And then . . . what? At this point, we once again meet with a mystery. Did some new panic cause the captain and his companion to abandon ship? That is unlikely, since Miller knew that his ship was unsinkable. Even if the captain had died of his wound and was thrown overboard, surely his companion would have remained. One theory is that the drifting vessel encountered a pirate ship, and that Miller and his companion were murdered. It is true that some of the cargo was missing; but it seems likely that this was thrown overboard in the original panic to lighten the ship. In the two decades since it met disaster, the *Joyita* has joined the *Mary Celeste* as one of the unsolved mysteries of the sea. At this stage, it seems unlikely that the truth will ever come to light.

The cases described so far have occurred in many different parts of the world, but there are two small areas that have been

As a British steamer plowed its way through the Persian Gulf near Oman in the summer of 1906, an enormous wheel of light appeared. The vast wheel, seemingly bigger than the ship itself, was revolving in the sky not far above the surface of the water at that point. Vivid shafts of light emitted from the huge wheel and passed right through the steamer. But these beams fortunately did not interfere with the functioning of the boat in any way.

Since 1760 seamen have recounted sightings of unidentified flying objects in the form of a wheel. The Persian Gulf sighting of 1906 was one of eleven recorded reports between 1848 and 1910. Like most of the sea accounts of mysterious luminous wheels, this one remarked on the eery silence of the phenomenon. Also in common with most other such reports, nothing was said about humans or human-like beings in the wheels, even though the ascent and descent of these objects were obviously controlled.

Were such glowing wheels in the sky an early and less sophisticated form of flying saucer? Were they operated by beings from other planets who kept themselves hidden or were invisible? Were they just visions of mariners too long at sea? No one has found an answer.

responsible for more disappearances than the rest of the world put together. They are know as the "Bermuda Triangle" and the "Devil's Sea". One lies in the Atlantic off the east coast of the United States, the other in the Pacific south-east of Japan. Both have acquired a singularly evil reputation.

The term "Bermuda Triangle" was coined by the author of a book on sea mysteries, Vincent Gaddis, who also called it the "Triangle of Death". Gaddis was among the first to notice the incredible number of disappearances of ships and aircraft in this relatively small area off the coast of Florida. Well over a hundred such disappearances have been recorded, with the loss of more than a thousand lives. Most of these mysteries have occurred since 1945, and the disappearances have been total. Not a single body nor a fragment of wreckage from the vanished craft has ever been recovered.

A typical disappearance took place on 8 January 1962. A big United States Air Force Boeing Stratotanker took off from Langley, Virginia, and flew east for the Azores. Shortly afterwards the control tower received weak radio signals from the plane. When these ceased, the wide-scale search was launched. But no trace of the aircraft was ever found.

The long saga of disappearances in the Triangle begins in the year 1609. A ship called the *Sea Venture,* bearing English settlers to Virginia, was shipwrecked off the island of Bermuda. On 1 September the longboat of the wrecked vessel set out on the 500-mile voyage to the coast of the United States to bring help. With a fair wind in its sail, it passed beyond the horizon – and was never seen again.

In 1750 five Spanish treasure ships were caught in storms off Cape Hatteras. Three of them vanished completely, and no wreckage was found.

In 1800 two United States Navy ships vanished in the area. In his book on the Bermuda Triangle, Charles Berlitz lists twelve more cases of major vessels that have disappeared in the Triangle, and no less than seven cases of ships found drifting, like the *Mary Celeste,* abandoned but basically undamaged. His list begins with the *Rosalie,* a large French vessel found abandoned in 1840 with sails set and cargo intact, and ends with the total disappearance on 23 March 1973 of the 20,000-ton freighter *Anita.*

The disappearance of planes in the Triangle area began on 5 December 1945, when five United States Navy aircraft vanished on a routine training flight. Each plane should have been manned by an officer pilot and two crew members, but one of the crew members had a premonition of disaster and stayed away. The planes were Avenger torpedo bombers, and each had enough fuel for more than a thousand miles. Their projected flight was less than 500 miles. They took off from their base at Fort Lauderdale, Florida, at 2 p.m. At about 3.15 p.m., the control tower received a strange message from the flight leader. He reported that the planes seemed to be off course, and he could not see land. Asked to state his position, he said he didn't know. Clearly the aircrafts' compasses and navigation gear were not functioning. This was confirmed shortly afterward when control overheard conversations between the planes in which crew members referred to the instruments in all the planes as "going crazy". Each registered a different reading, they said. Meanwhile, heavy static had begun to obscure communications. The planes seemed unable to hear the base transmitter, and it became increasingly difficult for control to hear them. The last barely audible message from the planes was received at 4 p.m. It said again that the pilots could not be sure where they were.

Rescue planes were dispatched among which was a twin-engined Martin Mariner with a crew of thirteen. Shortly after takeoff, base also lost contact with the Martin Mariner. Like the five planes it sought, it was never heard from again. In spite of an intensive search involving over 300 planes and many hundreds of sailing vessels, no trace of the six missing aircraft was ever found.

In his book Charles Berlitz lists fourteen more planes that have disappeared in the Triangle area since 1945. In case after case, the same phrase recurs: "lost radio contact".

> In the summer of 1913 the British ship *Johnson* caught sight of a sailing vessel drifting off the coast of Chile. As they drew near they could see that the masts and sails were covered with green mold. On the prow, faded with the passing of many years, could still be seen the name *Marlborough*. The timbers of the deck had decayed so greatly that they crumbled as the boarding party picked a way across them. A skeleton was discovered beneath the helm, six more were found on the bridge, and 13 others elsewhere in the ship.
>
> It was later learned that the *Marlborough* had left Littleton, New Zealand, 23 years before in January 1890 with a cargo of wool and frozen mutton. There were also several passengers aboard, including one woman. Nothing had been heard of the ship since it had been sighted on the regular course passing through the Straits of Magellan 23 years before. What had happened? Where had the ship been to remain undiscovered for nearly a quarter of a century?

In April 1963 the crew of a Boeing 707 observed what looked like an atomic explosion in the sea. They saw the water rise up into a great mound, half a mile wide. The pilot later checked with the coast guard and meteorological agencies to find out if there had been an earthquake in the area, but he was told that no unusual occurrences had been reported.

The baffling element in most of these accounts is not the strange behavior of the compasses, but the loss of electric power. Compasses behave strangely if brought close to a large magnet or mass of iron ore, and there could well be some vast iron deposit under the seabed in the Triangle area. But there is no way known to science of draining a battery of its charge, or preventing a generator from producing electricity – if there were, it would be an invaluable weapon of war. Yet the force that operates in the area of the Bermuda Triangle seems to interfere with electrical circuits.

The evidence about sea disappearances, like those on land, appears to tie in with the notion of some disturbance of the gravitational field – an "antigravity warp" – in which the laws of gravity do not operate in conventional ways. However, such speculation only serves to emphasize how little we really know about gravity, and that we have no way of judging how it might be affected by local conditions. All we can say is that, *if* there is such a thing as an antigravity warp, the local conditions in the Bermuda Triangle would certainly appear to be an example of it.

The same observation may well apply to the "Devil's Sea" – an area in the Pacific 800 miles south-east of Japan between Iwo Jima and Marcus Island. Perhaps because this area is so far from the coast of Japan, its mysteries have never aroused the same excitement as those of the Bermuda Triangle. There had been occasional disappearances of ships and aircraft in the area over a long period; but between 1950 and 1954 no less than nine ships disappeared without trace. The Japanese government then became concerned, and declared it a danger zone. In 1955 the government sponsored an expedition to the area, and a group of scientists set sail aboard the *Kaiyo Maru No. 5*. The *Kaiyo Maru* itself vanished.

THE MAN WHO STUDIED GHOULS

T he nearest British equivalent of Charles Fort was a retired Cambridge don named T.C. Lethbridge, known to his friends as Tom. When he died in a Devon nursing home in 1971, his name was hardly known to the British public. Today, many of his admirers believe he was the single most important name in paranormal research. But unlike Fort, who was contented to collect weird phenomena in an attempt to confound scientists, Lethbridge's whole life was an attempt to understand "the unexplained".

Lethbridge was trained as an archaeologist and historian, and spent most of his adult life as the Keeper of Anglo-Saxon Antiquities at the University Museum in Cambridge. But even in this respectable setting, he was always upsetting his colleagues. They were particularly shocked at the rumour that he used a dowsing-rod or a pendulum to try to locate objects buried underground. Finally, he left Cambridge in disgust at the hostile reception of one of his books on archaeology. Together with his wife Mina, he moved into Hole House, an old Tudor mansion on the south coast of Devon. He meant to spend his retirement reading and digging for bits of broken pottery. In fact, the most amazing period of his eventful life was about to begin.

The person who was most responsible for this change of direction was an old "witch" who lived next door. This white-haired little old lady assured Lethbridge that she could put mild spells on people who annoyed her, and that she was able to leave her body at night and wander around the district – an ability known as "astral projection". Lethbridge was naturally sceptical – until something convinced him.

The witch explained to him one day how she managed to put off unwanted visitors. What she did was to draw a five pointed star – a pentagram – in her head, and then visualise it across the path of the unwanted visitor – for example, on the front gate.

Shortly afterwards, Tom was lying in bed, idly drawing pentagrams in his head, and imagining them around their beds. In the middle of the night, Mina woke up with a creepy feeling that there was somebody else in the room. At the foot of the bed, she could see a faint glow of light, which slowly faded as she watched it. The next day, the witch came to see them. When she told them that she had "visited" their bedroom on the previous night, and found the beds surrounded by triangles of fire, Tom's scepticism began to evaporate. Mina politely requested the old witch to stay out of their bedroom at night.

Three years later, the old lady died in peculiar circumstances. She was quarrelling with a neighbouring farmer, and told Lethbridge that she intended to put a spell on the man's cattle. By this time, Lethbridge knew enough about the "occult" to take her seriously, and he warned her about the dangers of black magic – how it could rebound on to the witch. But the old lady ignored his advice. One morning, she was found dead in her bed in circumstances that made the police suspect murder. And the cattle of two nearby farms suddenly got foot and mouth disease. However, the farmer she wanted to "ill wish" remained unaffected. Lethbridge was convinced that the spell had gone wrong and "bounced back".

But the old lady's death resulted – indirectly – in one of his most important insights. Passing the witch's cottage, he experienced a "nasty feeling", a suffocating sense of depression. With a scientist's curiosity, he walked around the cottage, and noticed an interesting thing. He could step *into* the depression and then out of it again, just as if it was some kind of invisible wall.

The depression reminded Lethbridge of something that had happened when he was a teenager. He and his mother had gone for a walk in the Great Wood near Wokingham. It was a lovely morning; yet quite suddenly, both of them experienced "a horrible feeling of gloom and depression, which crept upon us like a blanket of fog over the surface of the sea". They

The altar in most Christian churches is placed at the east end of the building. This is a tradition based on the idea that facing the direction of the sunrise symbolizes turning toward spiritual light.

This tradition, oddly enough, may account for the fact that the nave and chancel of many of the old churches in Great Britain lie at an angle to each other rather than in a straight line. In Oxfordshire alone, for example, there are eighty-one churches with crooked chancels (the part of the building housing the altar). Why were these and many other chancels throughout the rest of the country built at an angle?

The Reverend Hugh Benson of Plymouth, England, thinks it is because the churches were meant to face sunrise on the exact festival day of their particular patron saint.

According to his letter-to-the-editor of *The Times* of London in 1975, Reverend Benson has studied this matter over a period of years, and has examined nearly a thousand churches. After making careful calculations, he became convinced that a great many churches had in fact faced sunrise on their saint's day at the time they were built. There were only about half a dozen exceptions to this finding in the whole of his survey.

"Now it follows," he says, "that a church built in honor of St Mary, for example, and facing sunrise on 25 March, would after a century or so, owing to the Julian calendar, be found to be facing too far south. If then a new chancel was built, it would be set out to face the new sunrise position . . . The crookedness of the chancel, far from being due to carelessness, is due to a most scrupulous care."

hurried away, agreeing that it was something terrible and inexplicable. A few days later, the corpse of a suicide was found a few yards from the spot where they had been standing, hidden by some bushes.

About a year after the death of the witch, another strange experience gave Tom the clue he was looking for. On a damp January afternoon, he and Mina drove down to Ladram Bay to collect seaweed for her garden. As Lethbridge stepped on to the beach, he once again experienced the feeling of gloom and fear, like a blanket of fog descending upon him. Mina wandered off along the beach while Tom filled the sacks with seaweed. Suddenly she came hurrying back, saying: "Let's go. I can't stand this place a minute longer. There's something frightful here."

The next day, they mentioned what had happened to Mina's brother. He said he also had experienced the same kind of thing in a field near Avebury, in Wiltshire. The word "field" made something connect in Tom's brain – he remembered that field telephones often short-circuit in warm, muggy weather. "What was the weather like?" he asked. "Warm and damp," said the brother.

An idea was taking shape. *Water* . . . could that be the key? It had been warm and damp in the Great Wood. It had been warm and damp on Ladram beach. The following weekend, they set out for Ladram Bay a second time. Again, as they stepped on to the beach, both walked into the same bank of depression – or "ghoul" as Lethbridge called it. Mina led Tom to the far end of the beach, to the place she had been sitting when she had been overwhelmed by the strange feeling. Here it was so strong that it made them feel giddy – Lethbridge described it as the feeling you get when you have a high temperature and are full of drugs. On either side of them were two small streams.

Mina wandered off to look at the scenery from the top of the cliff. Suddenly, she walked into the depression again. Moreover, she had an odd feeling, as if someone – or something – was urging her to jump over. She went and fetched Tom, who agreed that the spot was just as sinister as the place down on the seashore below.

Now he needed only one more piece of the jigsaw puzzle, and he found it – but only years later. Nine years before Tom and Mina's experience of depression on those cliffs, a man had committed suicide there. Lethbridge wondered whether the "ghoul" was a feeling so intense that it had become timeless and imprinted itself on the area, casting its baleful shadow on those who stood there.

Whether from the past or from the future the feelings of despair were "recorded" on the surroundings – but how?

The key, Lethbridge believed, was water. As an archaeologist, he had always been mildly interested in dowsing and water-divining. The dowser walks along with a forked hazel twig held in his hands, and when he stands above running water, the muscles in his hands and arms convulse and the twig bends either up or down. How does it work? Professor Y. Rocard of the Sorbonne discovered that underground water produces changes in the earth's magnetic field, and this is what the dowser's muscles respond to. The water does this

'King Faria' of San Rafael, California, a water witch

because it has a field of its own, which interacts with the earth's field.

Significantly, magnetic fields are the means by which sound is recorded on tape covered with iron oxide. Suppose the magnetic field of running water can also record strong emotions – which, after all, are basically electrical activities in the human brain and body? Such fields could well be strongest in damp and muggy weather.

This would also explain why the banks of depression seem to form a kind of invisible wall. Anyone who has ever tried bringing a magnet closer and closer to an iron nail will know that the nail is suddenly "seized" by the magnet as it enters the force field. Presumably the magnetic field of water has the same property. And if it can "tape record" powerful emotions, then you would feel them quite suddenly, as you stepped into the field. Both Tom and Mina noticed that the ghoul on Ladram beach came to an end quite abruptly.

What fascinated Lethbridge so much was that he was beginning to discover *scientific* reasons for events that are generally labelled "supernatural". If the gloom of a suicide can "record" itself on the electrical field of water, would a dowsing rod provide more information about the nature of the field? In fact, many dowsers prefer a pendulum to a dowsing rod, believing that it is more sensitive. Now that Lethbridge had embarked on this weird study of witches and electrical fields, he decided to give it a try. He started by carving a one inch ball out of a piece of hazel wood, and threading it on a long piece of string, which he wound around a pencil. Next, he placed a silver dish on the floor, and held his pendulum over it. Then he carefully unwound the string. When it reached a length of exactly twenty-two inches, the pendulum stopped swinging back and forth, and began to go round in a circle. Lethbridge concluded that a pendulum of exactly twenty-two inches "reacts" to silver. Next, he tried it over a copper pot; this time it reacted at thirty and a half inches. He spent the rest of the day testing different substances to discover their "rates": sulphur, aluminium, gold, diamond, sand. He even tried holding the pendulum over organic substances like milk, oranges and apples. In each case, it reacted quite exactly at a definite length.

For his next experiment, he went out into the courtyard of his home – part of which had been built in the fourteenth century – and walked around slowly, holding the pendulum by its string.

After a short time, the back-and-forth swing of the pendulum changed to a circular motion. Lethbridge took a spade, and proceeded to dig cautiously at the point the motion had changed. Just under the turf he found a piece of seventeenth-century pottery, and six inches lower a piece of seventeenth-century Rhineland stoneware. But this was not what he was looking for. Twenty-two inches is the length at which the pendulum should be able to locate silver. Lethbridge held his pendulum over the heap of earth from the hole. It swung in a circle. He searched carefully through the heap of earth, but failed to find the expected silver. Finally, as he was filling the hole, he found another piece of old stoneware. He held the pendulum over it, and the pendulum swung with a violent circular movement. Then he remembered: old stoneware is glazed with lead salts, and lead is on the same "wavelength" as silver. The mystery was explained.

Any reader who is inclined to dismiss this as a typical crank theory should first of all try dowsing – an art that is thousands of years old. Take any kind of bead or bob and thread it on the end of a long piece of string. Now take a ruler, and measure off precisely twenty-four inches on the string. Ask any male of your acquaintance to lie down on the floor, and hold the pendulum over him. Start the pendulum swinging gently to and fro. After a few moments, this arc swing will change to a circular motion. If you hold the pendulum over a female, nothing will happen – the pendulum will continue to swing back and forth. However, if you increase the length of the string to twenty-nine inches, the pendulum will react over women, and will show no reaction for men. This is because twenty-nine inches is the so-called "female length". According to diviners, each substance has its own wavelength. Twenty-four inches will locate diamonds and males. Twenty-nine inches will locate gold, females, and anything colored yellow.

The behavior of a ball on the end of a piece of string may seem a far cry from the mysterious electrical or magnetic fields that can cause a ship's compass to spin wildly. However, it is significant that dowsers have insisted on the existence of such fields for centuries. Indeed, the dowser's ability to locate water, minerals, and other substances underground may be due to picking up the activity of these fields.

Lethbridge tells an interesting story about visiting an ancient stone circle called the Merry Maidens near Penzance, Cornwall.

This circle is believed to date from the same time as Stonehenge, about 1500 BC. Presumably it served some religious purpose, but nobody knows which. Lethbridge tried his pendulum close to one of the stones, setting it at thirty inches. This is the length that diviners use for testing the age of ancient monuments. As he held the pendulum, Lethbridge rested his free hand on the stone megalith. Almost as soon as the pendulum started to swing, the hand resting on the stone received a tingling sensation like an electric shock, and the pendulum began to circle so strongly that it was almost horizontal. Some very powerful force was apparently at work.

I have myself experienced the mysterious force at the Merry Maidens when dowsing with a friend who is interested in the subject. Although I had only tried dowsing once before – without success – on this occasion I obtained a powerful reaction. I was using a dowsing rod made of two thin springy strips of whalebone tied together at one end. As I walked toward the centre of the stone circle, holding the rod as directed by my friend, the rod began to push upward until

---

Experiments with dowsing led the British ethnologist T. C. Lethbridge to believe strongly in magnetic fields, or fields of force, as a possible explanation of ghosts. He tells this story about one ghost he saw.

According to Lethbridge, he was standing on a hill above a mill. A little stream ran nearby, vanishing into the slope of the hill. Below him, about 60 yards away, a woman stood near the mill. Her clothes were about forty years out of date. On investigation he discovered that no one remotely resembling the woman he had seen had been near the mill at the time. He had seen a ghost.

Lethbridge explained this by his field-of-force theory. Someone, he said, had once been on the hill, and had seen the figure he had seen. The sight caused such a strong emotion in the viewer "that a picture of her was impressed in the electromagnetic field of the streamlet." Lethbridge had caught sight of the original impression.

Later Lethbridge learned that the mill owner had seen a ghost on the hill. It was a man, dressed in the fashion of forty years ago. It was obvious to Lethbridge that his ghost and the mill owner's ghost had, when alive, been happy to see each other. Each had impressed a picture of the other on the one field of force.

it was pointing toward the sky. (For some people a dowsing rod reacts by pointing upward, for others it dips downward.)

I wondered if the strain on my fingers was causing the rod to point upward. I tried the experiment of making it dip down instead. It refused. I tried holding it so tight that it could not move. It was impossible. As I passed over the same spot, it twisted up so strongly that I could not hold it still.

The power was particularly strong in the centre of the circle. I asked my friend what this meant, and he said he did not know. It could mean water, but this was unlikely because we kept getting the same reaction all around the stone circle at a point just beyond the outer perimeter.

I do not know what this force is. All I can say, with complete confidence, is that it exists.

Lethbridge believed that these "earth forces" can be increased and intensified by generations of worship and religious sacrifice. This could explain why his hand began to tingle when he placed it on the stone.

The Merry Maidens is discussed by John Michell in his book *The Old Stones of Lands End.* Michell points out that this whole area is covered with *leys* – the "old straight tracks" or lines first observed by Alfred Watkins. The Merry Maidens is the focus of such a system of leys. You can draw neat straight lines from its centre through other local landmarks, like ancient *barrows* (prehistoric burial mounds) and other standing stones. Michell has suggested that leys are identical with the ancient Chinese dragon paths. If this is so, it seems just conceivable that when the dowsing rods twisted in my hands, I was experiencing the magnetic force of the dragon paths, and that the power which made the rods twist so violently at the centre of the circle springs from the union of several dragon paths at this point.

One of the first people to notice the alignment of ancient sites in the area of the Merry Maidens was the eminent British astronomer Sir Norman J. Lockyer, who wrote a book on Stonehenge and other British stone circles in the early years of this century. Lockyer's theory was that such monuments were not merely religious centres, but also sophisticated astronomical observatories. When certain stars came into alignment with a particular stone and the top of a burial mound, Lockyer suggested, the ancient priests would know that it was time for a certain religious ceremony or sacrifice.

When Lockyer first published his theory, it aroused scepticism and even downright hostility among scientists. Many objected that ancient cultures lacked the knowledge to construct anything so complicated. In recent years, however, Lockyer's theory has been revived by scientists like Alexander Thom, Professor of Engineering Science at Oxford University, and Gerald Hawkins, Professor of Astronomy at Boston University. As a result of their research, an increasing number of scientists now accept that Stonehenge, the Merry Maidens, and other megalithic monuments like Carnac in northwest France, were designed as astronomical observatories. Even more amazing was the discovery that astronomical measurements made in these observatories were of incredible accuracy. For example, the moon deviates from its regular course by an almost imperceptible amount – 0.9° over a long period. Yet when Hawkins and Thom studied the methods of observation used by the builders of Stonehenge and Callanish (a stone circle in the Outer Hebrides), they discovered that this minute deviation of 0.9° had been recognized more than 3000 year ago. It was not discovered by modern astronomers until the sixteenth century.

Why should prehistoric man want to observe the heavens so minutely? Why should he want to construct an observatory that is also a church? There can be no doubt that sites such as Stonehenge were used for religious observances. Of course, many modern churches are constructed so that the window behind the altar catches the light of the rising sun; but that is purely for dramatic effect. It would certainly cause comment if we installed computers behind the altars of our cathedrals, or used the towers to house astronomical telescopes.

The explanation almost certainly lies in the ancient science of astrology. It seems likely that the builders of Stonehenge and other such temples believed that there were certain times of the year when the stars were propitious for the performance of religious rites, and when the hidden forces of the earth could be harnessed for religious purposes. Our ancestors observed that the tides are affected by the moon, and that certain people become "lunatics" at the time of the full moon. They believed that the hidden forces of the earth also rise and fall according to the movements of the heavenly bodies. For example, an eclipse of the moon affects the level of the earth's magnetism; and this may have been why prehistoric astronomers attached particular importance to the prediction of eclipses. The very sacredness of a sacred place like Stonehenge would reach a maximum intensity at periods when the influence of the heavenly bodies on the earth's forces were strongest. These would be the obvious times for major religious rites.

The moon, being closer to the earth, has a greater influence on phenomena such as tides. Therefore we might expect our ancestors to be more concerned with the observation of the moon than of the stars. This, according to Professor Hawkins, is precisely the case.

Tom Lethbridge became convinced that there are at least three distinct varieties of magnetic field – one associated with water, one with mountains and one with deserts and other open spaces. The theory of water fields – or "naiad fields", as Lethbridge preferred to call them – came about as a result of the experience on Ladram Beach which has already been described. The "ghoul", he believed, was a kind of tape recording of the suicide's misery.

Lethbridge's theory could be the key to a mysterious death that occurred in England in 1939. On the morning of 10 May searchers found the body of Harry Dean lying at the foot of a boulder in an abandoned quarry on the slopes of Bredon Hill, Gloucestershire. On the previous evening, Dean had gone for a stroll on Bredon Hill. When he failed to return home his wife notified the police.

The strange thing was that there was no obvious cause for death. Since Dean was lying on the floor of the quarry, the likeliest explanation was that he had fallen from the surrounding cliff some fifty feet above; but the body was unbruised. A post mortem examination revealed the astonishing fact that he had been strangled by his own tie. The coroner concluded that Dean had climbed the three-foot-high boulder at whose foot he was found, and that he had slipped and displaced the cartilage of his leg. He had fainted and been choked by his tie.

There was never any suggestion that Dean had been the victim of foul play. Nothing was missing from his pockets, and there were no signs of a struggle. Yet it seemed extraordinary that an accidental fall from a boulder only three feet high could result in a man's death.

The sheer improbability of the coroner's explanation led local author Harold Wilkins to undertake his own investigation. He deliberately waited a whole year until May 1940 so that conditions would be as similar as possible to those at the time of Harry Dean's death. He then visited the quarry with his brother. The first thing Wilkins noticed about Death Quarry was that its floor had evidently been levelled many centuries before the site's use as a quarry, which archaeologists have dated at around 750 BC. On this flat floor at the four points of the compass, Wilkins noticed four weathered boulders. Dean's body had been found by the one at the south end.

Wilkins and his brother made their way out of the quarry, up a grass-embanked causeway with unopened Stone Age barrows, past two ancient obelisks known as the "King and Queen stones", to the Iron Age fort on the top of Bredon Hill. This fort dates from the fifth century BC, and excavations have uncovered the skeletons of fifty men who had died in battle and had been mutilated by the enemy. Their heads, arms, and legs had been chopped off. In one corner of the fort stands a strange cracked stone known as the Bambury Stone. Archaeological evidence suggests that this was once an object of religious worship, perhaps an altar for sacrificial victims. Wilkins clambered onto the Bambury Stone to be photographed by his brother. As he did so, both men heard a sudden thud, as if a heavy object had fallen on the grass above them. Intrigued and puzzled, they searched the ground. It was a still, clear day, but they were unable to find anything that could account for the noise. "Something eerie and sinister had demonstrated its presence and its objection to the photographing of this weird stone," says Wilkins. He goes on to suggest that Harry Dean was strangled by some "unseen entity" as he stood at the foot of the boulder. Wilkins points out that Bredon Hill forms a rough quadrilateral with other hills. In another corner stands Long Compton Hill with its circle of megaliths known as the Rollright Stones, used as the site of witches' sabbaths in the Middle Ages. In a third corner of the quadrilateral is Meon Hill, again associated with black magic and witchcraft, and also with the apparition of a black dog. Wilkins suggests that such sites are imbued with dark and violent forces associated with pagan religious rites. Significantly, the priests of ancient Britain held one of their most important rituals in early May – just when Harry Dean met his death.

It is impossible to say whether Harry Dean's death was simply an unusual accident. It is doubtful that Lethbridge would have accepted the theory that Dean's death was due to some unseen entity. But he might well have agreed that it was caused by a sudden and violent fear – a ghoul.

The chief problem concerning the enigmas discussed so far in this book is that they seem to have so little in common. What possible connection could there be between the disappearance of a British regiment into a cloud, the strange loss of electric power in the Bermuda Triangle, and a feeling of "something nasty" on a Dorset beach? Many of the writers on the Bermuda Triangle talk about "space-time paradoxes", and suggest that the disappearing planes and ships might have tumbled into another dimension. Link this with dowsing experiences and we may be getting somewhere. The whole idea of strange forces connected with fields – whether these are ancient Chinese dragon paths or Lethbridge's ghouls – might offer some *practical* possibility of investigation. There is nothing to prevent readers of this book from making themselves dowsing rods or pendulums, and checking whether these ideas have any basis in fact.

Lethbridge himself embarked upon such a careful course of experiment, and his results are startling and fascinating. I myself have performed some of the simpler experiments, and can confirm that they actually work.

In a book by Lethbridge called *The Monkey's Tail*, readers can find a whole table of "rates" for various objects and qualities – milk, youth, apple, iron, alcohol, and so on. But they may be puzzled to see that the table includes such concepts as north, east, south, and west, life, death, danger, and time. How on earth do you hold the pendulum above "time"? Lethbridge explains that all you have to do is to think about a concept clearly, and then lengthen the string of the pendulum, which can be wound on a bobbin, until it gyrates. For example, if you think of the concept of anger, the pendulum will gyrate at forty inches precisely, because forty inches is the rate for anger. This idea may be less absurd than it sounds. Whenever you "see" anything, you do so by *firing* your attention toward it, as you might fire an arrow at a target. For example, if you look at your watch while thinking of something else, you simply do not register the time. We have all had the experience of staring straight at an object we have been looking for, and not seeing it. In order to see it, we need to reach out toward it with an "intention." Lethbridge is merely saying that this intention is the essential element in the use of the pendulum. The force that makes the pendulum circle or the dowsing rod twist in your hand may exist "out there", but it connects up with something in your mind.

Lethbridge discovered that the rate for "life" is twenty

inches. The rate for death, which is twice that, appeared to be a limit, since all substances tested had rates between one and forty. There was, however, a curious paradox. Lethbridge found that if he went beyond the limit of forty inches, the pendulum reacted again when it hit a figure that was the sum of something's own rate plus forty. For example, when testing a male the pendulum reacted at twenty-four inches, but it also reacted at sixty-four inches – forty plus twenty-four. Similarly all the other substances reacted at their own rate, and at their own rate plus forty.

In making this discovery Lethbridge encountered an even stranger phenomenon. If you take an object such as a walnut salad bowl, place it on the floor, and hold the pendulum over it, you will get a reaction at the specified rate for walnut: ten and a half inches. If you lengthen the pendulum to fifty and a half inches, you again get a reaction, *but not in the same place*. It is as if there were another salad bowl at the side of the real physical object. Lethbridge declares that this is always so – as if the object had a second position in another plane.

Equally curious is the test for "time." The pendulum fails to give a reaction for time below forty inches. But if you lengthen the string, you locate time at sixty inches (forty plus twenty, or the rate for death plus the rate for life). Lethbridge makes the strange observation that the time thus located "appears to be static." (The pendulum gives different reactions for things that are static and things that are changing or in motion.) His conclusion is that time does not register in our physical dimension because it is always passing. But *beyond* our dimension – beyond the point of death – we encounter another kind of time that is somehow static. Lethbridge admits that he cannot begin to grasp this possibility, and that he may have reasoned incorrectly from the information supplied by the pendulum. But in that case, he has no doubt that the fault lies in him, not in the pendulum.

Admittedly, this reasoning sounds wildly absurd, and the sceptical reader will remain totally unconvinced. After all, it is only too easy to make a pendulum change its swing from an arc to a circle by tiny unconscious movements of the fingers. Yet most people will accept the reality of dowsing, which has been seen to produce results. According to Lethbridge, the use of a pendulum enables the mind to establish contact with the "other dimension". Yet most dowsers agree that dowsing consists of tuning in to a "field." Is it possible that there are spots on the earth's surface where such fields are created by freak condi-tions, manifesting themselves as a kind of whirlpool in our space-time continuum? If so, we might expect objects that pass too close to be sucked into the whirlpool and to reappear later, floating on the surface of our normal time-sea. And if this idea creates a slight sense of vertigo, that is perhaps what you might expect of a whirlpool in space-time.

UNINVITED VISITORS

L *ough Nahooin is a small brown-coloured lake in Connemara on
the west coast of Ireland. At seven o'clock on the evening of 22
February 1968 Stephen Coyne, a local farmer, was walking along the
shores of the lough. He was accompanied by his eight-year-old son and
his dog. Stopping beside a heap of peat, Coyne saw a black object in the
water, and assumed that his dog had gone for a swim. When he
whistled, however, the dog came running from the opposite direction
and, on seeing the black object began to bark furiously. The farmer
looked more closely and saw that the object was some kind of animal
with a long neck and shiny black skin. When it plunged its head under
the surface, two humps appeared. The farmer also caught a glimpse of
a flat tail. By this time the barking of the dog had attracted the
attention of the "monster"; it began to swim towards the shore, its
mouth open. Alarmed for the safety of his dog, the farmer hurried
toward the water. At this the creature turned and made off. The eight-
year-old boy ran back to the nearby farm, and brought his mother and
the four other Coyne children. The family stood at the edge of the
lough watching the monster until it became too dark to see. Describing it later to an investigator, F.W. Holiday, the Coynes said the
monster was about twelve feet long. It had no eyes, but there were two
horns like those of a snail on top of its head.*

Holiday was the author of a book on the famous Loch Ness
monster, which he believed to be some kind of giant slug. From
the descriptions of the Coyne family, he had no doubt that this

Lough Nahooin monster was another member of the same species. Since Lough Nahooin is a mere 100 yards long – compared with the twenty-four miles of Loch Ness – there seemed a reasonable chance of catching the Irish lake monster. Accordingly, Holiday's team brought nets, support-buoys, and 100 yards of heavy chain to Lough Nahooin. They stretched the nets across the middle of the lake, and then rowed around the lake firing a heavy rifle into the water to force the monster to rush into the nets. Nothing happened – except that Holiday developed a severe toothache. After several disappointing days, they abandoned the hunt. Nevertheless, Holiday remained convinced that the monster had been in the lake all the time – and is there still.

Holiday himself has acknowledged the obvious argument against his idea. Lough Nahooin is full of trout, and if a creature even the size of a crocodile lived there, the fish would all be eaten in a matter of weeks. Perhaps, then, the Coyne family mistook an otter or a large eel for the monster. Even if that were so in this case, there have been numerous sightings of some unknown species in many of the peaty lakes in the west of Ireland. Holiday gathered further evidence from Georgina Carberry, the librarian of Clifden in Connemara. In 1954 Miss Carberry and three friends drove to nearby Lough Fadda, a mile-and-a-half-long lake, to fish for trout. They settled down on a tongue of land to have a picnic. Then they saw the monster, which at first they took to be a man swimming. The creature moved toward them in a leisurely manner, and they could see two large humps and a forked tail. They also saw a huge sharklike mouth, although none of them noticed teeth. When they became alarmed and moved away from the edge of the lake, the creature turned and swam away. Georgina Carberry found the experience so unpleasant that she kept looking back as they drove away to see if the monster was following them. She suffered from nightmares for weeks afterwards, and one of her companions subsequently had a mental breakdown. Miss Carberry described the creature's movements as "wormy". Other witnesses who have reported seeing monsters in nearby lakes generally agree on an undulating worm-like movement.

Our original objection remains to all such monster sightings: how could creatures of the size described exist in these tiny lakes? Many writers on the Loch Ness monster have made the same point. It is true that Loch Ness is twenty-four miles long, but it is only a mile wide. There would have to be more than one monster for the species to survive, and a colony of monsters would soon eat all the fish and die of starvation.

A few months after his visit to Lough Nahooin, Holiday was browsing through a book on Babylonian history by Sir Wallis Budge. He came across a Babylonian creation myth that described how the god Anu had created marshes. According to the ancient text, "the marshes created the Worm. And the Worm said: '. . . Let me drink amongst the teeth, and set me on the gums, that I may devour the blood of the teeth . . .'" Holiday recalled the strange and persistent toothache that had begun as soon as he arrived at Lough Nahooin, and which vanished as soon as he left the area. He experienced a sudden absurd suspicion: could it be that the monster was not a creature of flesh and blood, *but some kind of a ghost*?

Of course, the idea sounds preposterous. But before we dismiss it, let us recall a point made by T.C. Lethbridge: a ghost is not necessarily a supernatural spirit. The image you see on your television screen is a kind of ghost. It is a mere "spectre" of something that may be happening in a studio many miles away. Lethbridge firmly believed that the ghost of the woman he saw near his home was some kind of tape recording. Carl G. Jung, one of the most eminent psychologists of our time, made a similar suggestion about flying saucers. He thought that the saucers could be *projections* of some deep unconscious need in mankind. Jung does not mean that UFOs are mere illusions, based on some form of wishful thinking; he means that some deep religious craving in the subconscious mind of the whole race may somehow project the image of UFOs so that they actually appear in the outside world.

Holiday reached the conclusion that UFOs and monsters share the characteristic of being less solid and real than they look. At least he can claim to have had experience of both. In his book *The Dragon and the Disk* he describes a number of sightings of UFOs and of the Loch Ness monster. The first UFO he saw, when fishing on the Welsh coast, resembled a cloud "of shiny blue-grey cotton wool", orbiting slowly in a circle. A week later, driving along a mountain road in Wales, he saw another such "cloud" and examined it through binoculars. The cloud was oval and about twenty-five feet long. Similar clouds have been described by witnesses over Loch Ness.

Holiday was fascinated by how often the two themes of "dragons" and "disks" appear in ancient cultures. He points

Loch Ness Monster

out that many Bronze Age barrows, when seen from the air, resemble flying saucers. Drawings of disklike objects are found all over the world in caves of the Palaeolithic period between 12,000 and 30,000 years ago. Equally common are drawing of worms or dragons. These also turn up frequently in carvings in old churches, and usually appear to symbolize the power of evil. Holiday's suggestion is that some of our remote ancestors worshipped disks, while others worshipped dragons or serpents. The disks usually seem to be associated with good, and the dragons are almost invariably evil.

Anyone who has ever taken an interest in UFOs knows that they have a curious habit of appearing and disappearing. Ivan Sanderson, who also wrote on the Bermuda Triangle, described a UFO he and his wife saw in 1958. It was an oval object that "was sort of flashing on and off, from almost total diaphaneity to complete solidity, at about three flashes per second." That is to say, it appeared solid one moment, and almost invisible the next. There have been dozens of reports of flying saucers that have "vanished into thin air" – giving rise to the theory that they have slipped out of our space-time into another dimension. Creatures like the Loch Ness monster seem to have the same irritating characteristic. For the past few years a Loch Ness investigation team has kept constant watch at the loch throughout the summer, with their cameras loaded. During that time the monster has been seen repeatedly – by members of the team and others – yet hardly ever photographed with any degree of success. Frustrated monster-watchers have sometimes wondered if the creature has a malicious sense of humor.

Many psychical investigators have entertained the same suspicion about ghosts and poltergeists. Holiday describes a case that he investigated in Wales. Some friends had leased a house that appeared to be haunted. Electric lights turned themselves on and off, footsteps walked down empty corridors, voices were heard, and a shadowy figure was seen in the house and the garden. The Society for Psychical Research was consulted. They suggested that the various phenomena might be due to the vibration of the tides *five miles away*. Careful experiment convinced Holiday that no amount of vibration could make a light turn itself on – as it did when he sat drinking tea with his friends. Nor could vibrations cause doorknobs to turn as they often did when no one was standing anywhere near them.

Anybody who has experienced such strange events at first

hand is bound to ask himself the question: where do ghosts or poltergeists come from? Are they projections of our subconscious mind or of someone else's subconscious mind? Are they actually here, in our world, but invisible except in special circumstances? Do they exist in some way outside our normal dimensions of space and time? If so, do they originate in that same world that many ufologists believe to be the home of flying saucers? In the present state of our knowledge, we cannot answer these questions; but we can go on asking them and trying to find the answers.

Holiday admits that his own case is far from complete. Some essential pieces of the jigsaw are missing. What he is suggesting – purely as a working hypothesis – is that there could be some connection between UFOs, lake monsters, and certain psychical phenomena. The dragon and disk symbolism that occurs in so many pre-Christian religions seems to indicate that the ancient priesthoods recognized the connection. We do not yet possess the knowledge to penetrate their secrets. But we do have an ever increasing mass of data about modern dragons and disks, some of which suggests a definite link between UFOs and psychical phenomena. Holiday cites the case of Annabelle Randall who, on the night of 7 October 1965, was driving her fiancé John Plowman back to his home near Warminster about fifteen miles from Stonehenge. Toward midnight they approached a railroad bridge near Heytesbury, Wiltshire, where there had been a number of fatal road accidents. In the beam of their headlights they saw a body sprawled at the roadside with its legs in the road. When they stopped the car and went to investigate, the body vanished. An hour later on her return journey, Miss Randall again passed under the bridge. As she did so, she saw a large orange ball that shot into the sky. At the same time, she saw two figures walking along the road toward her. They wore dark clothes and some sort of headgear, and the lower half of their bodies glistened as if wet.

A month later, a retired Royal Air Force Group Captain and his wife had a similar experience when driving about a mile from the bridge at one thirty in the morning. They saw a tall figure wearing a mask. Then a man staggered out of the hedge. He was covered in blood, and seemed to be an accident victim. By the time they had stopped the car and reversed, both men had vanished. The Group Captain told his story to the Features Editor of the *Warminster Journal* and to a BBC producer, but asked for his name to be withheld.

Holiday makes an interesting suggestion concerning such "phantom accidents". He observes that more UFOs have been seen in the area around Stonehenge than anywhere else in Britain. He adds that the first UFO he sighted over the Welsh coast moved away due east, towards the little mining village of Aberfan. It was there on 21 October 1966 – just thirteen days after his sighting – that a massive coal tip slid downhill, killing 128 children and sixteen adults. Holiday points out that in Celtic and Norse mythology, the souls of those who died in battle are conducted to the Underworld by special messengers of the dead, called *Valkyries* by the Norse. These messengers are usually represented as wearing unusual headgear – a kind of pointed helmet. Is it conceivable, Holiday asks, that the strange figures seen on the Warminster road were also "messengers of the dead", whose business is to perform some kind of psychic first aid on those who have died in violent accidents? And might the old legends of Valkyries and similar creatures have been based on the visitation of UFOs and their strange inhabitants?

Curiously enough, T.C. Lethbridge arrived independently at a similar theory shortly before his death in 1973. He published it in his last book, *The Legend of the Sons of God*. Lethbridge is careful to state that his conclusions are purely speculative, but they have a bearing on Holiday's Valkyries and it is worth examining what Lethbridge has to say on the subject.

Lethbridge's starting point is the mystery of ancient stone monuments like Stonehenge and the Merry Maidens. When he tested a stone at the Merry Maidens with his pendulum, the reaction was violent. Other prehistoric monuments produced a similar reaction. Lethbridge became convinced that the power that apparently emanates from such monoliths is a form of energy that comes from living creatures. He calls it *bio-energy*, or bio-electricity. He believes that such energy can be generated by the frenzied kind of dancing that forms part of many ancient religious rituals. This bio-energy, he maintains, can be stored in stone monoliths and in trees – and it was a vital link with visitors from other worlds.

In recent years, writers like Erich von Däniken have popularized the theory that the earth was visited by flying saucers in the remote past, and that accounts of these visits can be found in many ancient texts including the Bible. Lethbridge had already completed his *Legend of the Sons of God* when a friend sent him von Däniken's first book *Chariots of the Gods?*, containing this now-famous theory. Lethbridge's first reaction was to decide not to publish his own book. Then it struck him that many of his own conclusions differed so fundamentally from von Däniken's that it would have been a pity to consign them to the wastepaper basket.

Lethbridge had concluded that monuments like Stonehenge were intended to be signal beacons for some form of spacecraft. He suggests that the inhabitants of the UFOs understood the uses to which bio-energy could be put. They therefore encouraged the men of the Bronze Age to build these giant monuments, and to keep them highly charged with bio-energy to enable the UFOs to home in on them.

While we must admit that Lethbridge's theory sounds wildly speculative, we have to acknowledge that such monuments as Stonehenge present us with a baffling mystery. When modern engineers set about replacing one of the giant lintels at Stonehenge, they had the full benefit of modern cranes and lifting equipment, and the operation was still a difficult and costly one. Yet we know that our primitive ancestors not only succeeded in erecting these gigantic stones, but that they had transported them enormous distances across wild and rugged country. Either the ancient builders possessed a far higher degree of engineering knowledge than the traditional view of their culture suggests – or they were instructed and directed by beings from a more advanced civilization. The immense avenues of standing stones in Carnac, Brittany, present a similar problem. It is worth noting that their layout strongly supports the idea that they were aerial markers.

If the Earth had been visited by aliens in the distant past, where did these beings come from? There is a certain amount of evidence in ancient mythology – for example, in the legends of Easter Island – that suggests that the answer might be Mars or Venus or both. The astronomer Professor Carl Sagan believes that Mars could have been inhabited as recently as 1000 years ago. However, Lethbridge has another suggestion to make, based on the evidence of the pendulum. His suggestion indicates that there are other levels of existence beyond this one. If there are other levels, says Lethbridge, is it not conceivable that there are people living on them?

In addition to the evidence of the pendulum, Lethbridge produces many arguments in favor of these other levels based on out-of-the-body experiences and the power of certain mediums to foretell the future. He puts forward another fascinating idea. The pendulum appears to show that the other levels possess a higher rate of vibration than our earthly level, as if their energies were of a higher frequency. Yet the pendulum apparently enables us to establish some sort of contact with these levels. Perhaps, Lethbridge suggests, it might be possible for scientists to construct a machine that would alter our vibrational rate, and so make these levels directly accessible. Such a machine, he says, "would necessitate some kind of dynamo to produce a field of force around the experimenters . . ." Lethbridge would therefore seem to agree with F.W. Holiday and many ufologists that Unidentified Flying Objects could originate on some other plane of existence. Lethbridge also points out that if these other levels are characterized by a higher vibrational rate of energy, then creatures from these levels could actually be walking among us now – completely invisible to us. They would become visible only if their vibrational rate were suddenly slowed down. This can be grasped by means of a simple analogy. If a train on which you are riding goes through a station too fast, you cannot read the name of the station. If the train were travelling extremely fast, you would not even notice the station. On the other hand, to beings on other planes, we would appear to be travelling much more slowly than they – as if we were living in slow motion – and we would therefore be clearly visible to them. *They* could visit us by slowing down their vibrational rate, but we cannot at present visit them – except possibly by dying.

It is interesting to note that, if Lethbridge is right, our thought vibrations would have difficulty in grasping the nature of reality because they are too slow. But the faculty we call intuition seems to operate instantaneously, on a higher wavelength. This may explain why intuition has the power to grasp complex realities beyond the range of our everyday thought.

Lethbridge's machine for travelling to other planes sounds like pure science fiction. Yet there are many students of ufology who are convinced that such a machine has actually been built and tested. Unfortunately, one of the most important witnesses, the astronomer and mathematician Morris K. Jessup, is dead. Jessup taught at the University of Michigan, and was sent by the Carnegie Institute to study the Inca remains in Peru and the Aztec ruins in Mexico. The study of these ancient constructions led him to the conclusion that they might well have been erected with the aid of outer space visitors, whose aim was partly to create landing markers for spacecraft. He published his theory in 1955 in *The Case for the UFO*, one of the first great classics on the subject of flying saucers. In this book, Jessup also suggested that many of the strange disappearances of ships and planes in the Bermuda Triangle – and mysteries such as those of the *Mary Celeste* and *Ellen Austin* – could have been due to some kind of UFO activity.

After the publication of his book, Jessup was contacted by someone who claimed to be a survivor of an incredible experiment conducted by the U.S. Navy in 1943. Known as "the Philadelphia Experiment", it was supposed to have resulted in the death of some participants and the mental breakdown of others. When Jessup began to investigate the affair, the Navy asked him if he would be interested in working on a similar project. Jessup declined. In 1959 Jessup was found dead in his car, asphyxiated by exhaust gas. There are some who believe that his suicide was staged, and that he was killed before he could publicize ideas arising out of the experiment.

CURSES AND JINXES

*T he year was 1928. The city, Kobe, Japan. A middle-aged English
couple, the C.J. Lamberts, stood in front of a junk shop window.
"That's what I'd like," said Marie Lambert, pointing to a tiny
statuette of a half-naked fat man seated on a cushion. She recognized
the laughing man as Ho-tei, the Japanese god of Good Luck. "Let's
find out what he costs," said her husband, as they walked into the
shop. They were pleasantly surprised to find that the statuette was
cheap, even though it was made of ivory. It seemed almost too good to
be true. Back on their cruise ship, the Lamberts examined their
purchase closely. The statuette had the creamy colour of old ivory,
and was beautifully carved. As far as they could see, its only
imperfection was a small hole underneath. The carver had apparently
used the base of an elephant's tusk for the statue, and there was a tiny
hole where the nerve of the animal's tooth had ended. This had been
plugged neatly with an ivory peg. Altogether, the statuette seemed to
be one of those rare bargains that tourists dream about.*

Marie Lambert stowed the statuette in her luggage, and the
ship sailed to Manila. On the second day out, Mrs Lambert
began to suffer from a toothache. The ship's doctor prescribed
painkillers, but they did little good. The next twelve days were
miserable for both the Lamberts. In Manila, before Mrs Lambert
could visit a dentist, she and her husband contracted an
unpleasant fever whose chief symptom was pain in all the
joints. When Marie Lambert finally got to a dentist, his drill

slipped and drove through to the nerve of her tooth, increasing her pain instead of curing it.

On the next lap of the voyage, which took the ship to Australia, the god of luck figurine was somehow transferred to Mr Lambert's luggage. The following day, he was prostrated with an agonizing toothache. In Cairns, Australia, he went to a dentist, who told him there was nothing wrong with his teeth. In fact, the ache had stopped while he was at the dentist's. But it started again as soon as he got back to his cabin. Two days later, he consulted another dentist, and the same thing happened. In Brisbane, he ordered a dentist to start pulling out his teeth, and to keep on pulling until the pain stopped. When the first tooth came out, the pain went away. It started again as soon as Lambert returned to the ship.

In Sydney the Lamberts left their luggage in bond. The toothache ceased. On the voyage to New Zealand, the luggage was in their cabin only once, when they repacked; Lambert's toothache started again. Then the luggage went to the hold, and the pain stopped. In New Zealand, while on shore, he had no toothache. There was only one short bout of toothache on the continuing trip to Chile – when the Lamberts repacked their luggage in the cabin. In the United States, the couple visited Lambert's mother. She was so delighted with Ho-tei that they made her a present of the little god. When her excellent teeth started aching a few hours later, she handed back the gift saying that she felt it was "bad medicine." The Lamberts still did not connect Ho-tei with their toothaches.

Their first suspicion occurred on the way across the Atlantic to Britain. A fellow passenger who was interested in ivory borrowed Ho-tei overnight to show her husband. In the morning, she told the Lamberts that she and her husband had both had toothaches. The Lamberts thought about their own toothaches, and realized that they had always occurred when Ho-tei was in their cabin. Marie Lambert wanted to throw the statuette overboard. Her husband was afraid that the god might retaliate by rotting every tooth in their heads. So they took Ho-tei back to London with them. Lambert took the figure to an oriental art shop and showed it to the Japanese manager, who immediately offered to buy it. Lambert explained that he could not take money for the statuette, and he described the troubles it seemed to have caused. The manager sent for an old man in Japanese national costume, and the two men examined the figure carefully. From what they told him, Lambert gathered that Ho-tei was a temple god. In the East, the statues of such gods are sometimes given "souls" – small medallions hidden inside them. This probably explained the ivory plug in the base of the figure. The old Japanese man placed Ho-tei in a shrine at the end of the shop and lit joss sticks in front of it. Then, with an expression of awe, he bowed Lambert out of the shop.

In the end, C.J. Lambert derived some small profit from his uncomfortable adventure. He recounted it in a travel book that made good sales. But he never revisited the London art shop.

Lambert's understandable assumption was that the god of luck had been taking revenge on unbelievers who had removed

---

The home of Eugene Binkowski of Rotterdam, New York, had a hum that never stopped. The family wasn't sure when it had started, but became aware of it after a series of illnesses had afflicted each of them. Not only did they have frequent head-aches, earaches, and toothaches, but they also suffered from stiffness of the joints. Finally they realized that the source of the problems was a constant faint humming sound throughout the house. They reported the trouble to the police, who could not come up with any explanation.

It was natural that General Electric in nearby Schenectady should become interested in the sound mystery, so the next investigators were technicians from that firm. Using the latest equipment that they had at their command, they tested the house thoroughly. At the end of it, they claimed they could hear no sound of a peculiar nature in the house.

In desperation Binkowski wrote to the then President John Kennedy. A few days later some Air Force sound experts turned up with equipment designed to detect high frequency sounds. They could not trace the hum. The only bit of information they offered was that tests showed the whole family had especially acute hearing. It was possible, they said, for the Binkowskis to be hearing a sound at some unusual pitch. Despite the verdicts of the General Electric and Air Force experts, hundreds of visitors to the Binkowski home reported they could hear the hum. Some of them also felt the house to be mysteriously stuffy.

The Binkowskis endured the hum for about nine months without relief. They finally had to move out of the house and into a garage to escape it.

him from his temple. Yet there could be another explanation for this strange affair.

Around the Iron Age fort in Sidbury Castle in southern England, T.C. Lethbridge picked up many rounded flint pebbles of the kind commonly found on beaches. It seemed unlikely that the sea had transported the stones to the fort, which stands on the top of a hill three miles inland. However, the stones were like those used as slingshot in Iron Age times. Lethbridge tested the stones with a pendulum whose string extended to twenty-four inches – the male length. There was a strong reaction. He tested them again at forty inches – the rate for anger, war, and death. Once more the reaction was strong.

Lethbridge possessed some similar sling stones from the Iron Age camp in Wandlebury, south of Cambridge. These also gave the reaction for maleness, but not for war or anger. Stones of the same type collected from the beach gave no reaction either for maleness or war.

Lethbridge's conclusion was that the Wandlebury stones had only been used for practice shots – which seems likely, since Wandlebury had been an army camp in the Iron Age. The Sidbury stones had been used in actual warfare. Both groups of stones retained the impression of maleness caused by the men who had handled them. As a further test, Lethbridge took some of the stones from the beach and threw them against a wall. They then responded to the male rate of twenty-four inches. Stones thrown by his wife only responded to the female rate – twenty-nine inches. Some kind of thought energy – or biological electricity – had apparently impressed itself on the stones like a seal. And it seemed to last indefinitely.

According to Lethbridge, the pendulum can also reveal the *date* at which the thought field was implanted in an object. This is done by counting the number of times the pendulum revolves over the object before returning to its normal oscillation. Lethbridge established a date of 320 BC for all the Sidbury stones, and 220 BC for those from Wandlebury.

Lethbridge used a pendulum to establish who had last handled the stones. But there are certain human beings who can achieve the same result simply by contact with an object. They are called *psychometrists*. Two of the best-known modern psychometrists, Peter Hurkos and Gerard Croiset, have achieved considerable publicity by aiding the police in the investigation of crimes. By holding an object associated with the crime, such as a murder weapon, they have been able to describe the crime, and often the criminal.

In the 1840s the Frenchman Alexis Didier revealed similar powers. A report in the British *Medical Times* of 8 July 1844 tells how Didier was given a small leather case belonging to a certain Colonel Llewellyn. Didier placed the case against his stomach, and was then able to tell the owner that it contained a piece of bone – the colonel's own bone. He went on to describe in detail the incident in which the colonel had been wounded, even specifying the number of wounds he had received. The records of the Society for Psychical Research contain dozens of similar cases. These suggest that psychometry is a fairly common human faculty – as common perhaps as the ability to dowse, although less developed in most human beings.

What would have happened if Alexis Didier had held the statue of Ho-tei? He might have experienced some of the fear and agony of a dying elephant – and perhaps the appalling pain of having a tusk removed before death. For a man of Didier's sensitivity, the horror might have been almost unbearable. In less sensitive human beings, the tooth-fragment might have induced a milder form of psychic disturbance that manifested itself as severe toothache. If so, according to Lethbridge's theory, the statue of Ho-tei would still be capable of causing toothache in another thousand years.

It is worth recalling that F.W. Holiday complained of a severe toothache during his expedition to Lough Nahooin in search of monsters, and that he subsequently discovered a Babylonian text describing a supernatural worm whose activities include "devouring the blood of the teeth". Is it conceivable that certain negative psychic forces manifest themselves in the form of toothache?

If the idea sounds absurd, it is largely because we have ceased to think in terms of negative psychic forces. The peoples of primitive tribes say that a person who experiences continual misfortune is "accursed". We would call him "accident prone". Our classification implies that proneness to accidents arises from a person's own carelessness or nervous tension. We have all known people who seem to attract bad luck – the kind of people who happen to be walking past when the window-cleaner drops a bucket. These people appear to be suffering from other people's carelessness, or from plain undeserved misfortune. Yet we still have the feeling that there is some connection between this kind of ill-luck and the personality of the sufferer. There may be something about the attitude of such people – a certain expectation that the worst will happen. This raises the interesting question of whether the accident is somehow triggered by their subconscious attitude. Everything we learn about the power of the mind suggests that thought fields may be altogether more influential than we have hitherto recognized.

The psychic investigator and journalist Edward Russell has suggested that there may be a connection between negative thought fields and the "curses" that appear to surround certain objects like the statuette of Ho-tei. Like Lethbridge, he believes that thought fields can implant themselves in objects, rather as magnetism or static electricity does, and create the same kind of patterns that an electric field can produce on a magnetic recording tape. Lethbridge had advanced the theory that negative thought fields – or ghouls as he called them – can imprint themselves on the magnetic field of water, and there is some evidence that ghouls may also imprint themselves on objects. We have already seen that the *Mary Celeste* was dogged by bad luck from the moment of her launching, and few sailors doubt that there are such things as "jinxed ships". In his book on sea mysteries, *Invisible Horizons*, Vincent Gaddis writes, "There are happy, gay ships, and there are others so impregnated with evil that they must be destroyed by fire."

The particular evil ship that Gaddis had in mind was the German battleship *Scharnhorst*, launched in October 1936. When only half completed, the ship rolled onto its side, killing sixty workmen. Hitler and Goering arrived for the final launching only to discover that the ship had somehow launched itself the previous night, destroying several barges. In the *Scharnhorst*'s first major engagement – the attack on Danzig in 1939 – one of the guns exploded, killing nine men, and the air supply system broke down, suffocating twelve gunners. A year later during the bombardment of Oslo, the *Scharnhorst* was badly damaged and had to be towed away. In the dark, she collided with the ocean liner *Bremen*, which settled into the river mud and was bombed to pieces by the British. The *Scharnhorst* was repaired and set sail for the Arctic in 1943, but during the voyage she passed a British patrol vessel which her crew failed to notice. The vessel radioed a warning. Several British cruisers quickly located the *Scharnhorst* and bombarded her. The

Howard Carter and Lord Carnarvon outside the steps of the tomb thought to be cursed, the tomb of Tutankhamun

Scharnhorst fled, and it seemed she would escape her pursuers. But one British commander decided to try a last long shot on the off-chance of scoring a hit. The gamble paid. The *Scharnhorst* began to blaze, providing a target for more shells. The ship sank to the bottom with most of her crew. Yet the curse apparently lingered on. Weeks later, two survivors from the *Scharnhorst* were found on a beach. They were dead – killed by an emergency oil heater that had exploded when they tried to light it for warmth.

Misfortune also pursued the Lockheed Constellation airliner AHEM-4, starting on the day in July 1945 when a mechanic walked into one of the plane's propellors and was killed. Precisely one year later, on 9 July 1946, Captain Arthur Lewis died at the controls while the plane was flying in mid-Atlantic. Exactly one year after that, on 9 July 1947, a newly installed engine burst into flame shortly after takeoff. The captain, Robert Norman, extinguished the flames with a mechanical fire-extinguisher, but then found that the plane lacked the power to climb above the roof of an apartment building. Norman switched on the takeoff power and managed to climb out of danger. But when he tried to ease the power off again, the controls remained jammed. He and his copilot finally wrestled the controls back by sheer force, and landed the plane successfully.

July 1948 passed uneventfully. But on 10 July 1949 the airliner crashed near Chicago, killing everyone on board including Captain Robert Norman.

There are many records of houses, and even cars, that seem to bring disaster to their owners. A famous example is the car in which the Archduke Francis Ferdinand, heir to the thrones of Austria and Hungary, was assassinated in 1914 – a murder that precipitated the outbreak of World War I. The Archduke's wife died with him. Shortly after the start of war, General Potiorek of the Austrian army came into possession of the car. A few weeks later he suffered a catastrophic defeat at Valjevo, and was sent back to Vienna in disgrace. He could not stand this, and he died insane.

The next owner of the car was an Austrian captain who had been on Potiorek's staff. Only nine days after taking over the car, he struck and killed two peasants, and then swerved into a tree and broke his neck.

At the end of the war, the Governor of Yugoslavia became the owner of the car. After four road accidents in four months –

one of which caused him to lose an arm – he sold the car to a doctor. Six months later, the car was found upside down in a ditch. The doctor had been crushed to death inside it. The car was next sold to a wealthy jeweller who owned it for only a year before he committed suicide. After a brief spell in the hands of another doctor – who seems to have been all too anxious to get rid of it – the car was sold to a Swiss racing driver. He was killed in a race in the Italian Alps when the car threw him over a wall. The next owner was a Serbian farmer. He stalled the car one morning, and persuaded a passing carter to give him a tow. Forgetting to turn off the ignition, the farmer became the car's ninth victim when the motor started up, smashed the horse and cart, and overturned on a bend. A garage owner, Tibor Hirshfeld, was the car's final owner. One day, returning from a wedding with six friends, Hirshfeld tried to overtake another car at high speed. He and four of his companions were killed. The car then was taken to a Vienna museum where it has been ever since.

An example of a house that seems to bring bad luck to its tenants is the castle of Miramar near Trieste. It was built in the mid-nineteenth century by Emperor Franz Josef of Austria, but its first occupant was his brother the Archduke Maximilian. Maximilian died in front of a firing squad in Mexico, and his wife became insane. Empress Elizabeth was the next resident of Miramar, living there with her son Rudolph. In 1889 Rudolph and his mistress committed suicide, and in 1898 the Empress was assassinated by an Italian anarchist who believed in Italian liberation from Austria.

The next in line for the Austrian throne was Rudolph's cousin the Archduke Francis Ferdinand, who went to live in the beautiful castle. The Archduke and his wife were both assassinated in 1914 – the murder that contributed to bringing about World War I. At the end of the war the Duke of Aosta moved into Miramar. He died in a prison camp in British East Africa during World War II. After this war two British Major Generals became residents of the castle of Miramar. Both died of heart attacks.

It has not gone unnoticed that many jinxes appear to begin with a death or deaths: workers died building the *Scharnhorst*; a mechanic was killed by a propellor of the Lockheed Constellation airliner; the Archduke Franz Ferdinand and his wife were assassinated in their car. Many sailors are convinced that the spirits of the dead are involved in jinxes. To support their contention, they point to the two most notorious jinx ships of the nineteenth century: the British vessels *Hinemoa* and *Great Eastern*.

On her maiden voyage in 1892, the *Hinemoa* carried a ballast of rubble from a London graveyard. During the voyage four sailors died of typhoid. The ship's first captain went insane, the second ended in prison, the third died of alcoholism, the fourth died in mysterious circumstances in his cabin, and the fifth committed suicide – all, according to the crew, because of the bad luck brought by the bones of the four dead crew members.

The *Great Eastern*, built by the famous Victorian engineer Isambard Kingdom Brunel, was in her time the largest – and the unluckiest – ship in the world. Brunel collapsed with a heart attack on her deck, and died soon after. A riveter and his boy assistant vanished without trace during the ship's construction. The ship proved so heavy that she defied all attempts to launch her; it took three months and dozens of hydraulic jacks to move her from her berth. On her maiden voyage, a steam escape valve was left closed, resulting in an explosion that scalded five men to death. A full account of her subsequent misfortunes – explosions, collisions, and accidents at sea – would occupy many pages. Finally, a mere fifteen years after launching, she was brought back to Milford Haven in Wales, where she rusted and blocked the shipping lane. Breaking her up proved almost as difficult as building her. It was necessary to invent the wrecker's iron ball, suspended on a giant chain, to reduce her to scrap in 1889. Inside the double hull, the demolition experts discovered the skeletons of the riveter and his boy apprentice, who had vanished when the ship was being built. Few people doubted that they had discovered the cause of the ship's misfortunes.

The theory of thought fields provides a plausible alternative to the supernatural explanation. The sailors on board the *Hinemoa* knew that the ballast had been taken from a graveyard; the men who sailed the *Great Eastern* on her maiden voyage knew that a riveter and his assistant had vanished, and had possibly been sealed up in the hull. The crew of the airliner AHEM-4 knew that a mechanic had walked into the propeller and had been cut to pieces. The subsequent owners of Francis Ferdinand's car knew that the Archduke and his wife had met violent deaths in it. Therefore, assuming that in each vehicle the original tragic event itself created a negative thought field, or ghoul, does it not seem likely that their knowledge of the tragedy *predisposed* people to tune in to that field? In other words, the jinx may have been partly due to the negative thought field, and partly to the fear and nervous tension of the people involved.

Sceptics will object that fear and tension alone might have been to blame, and that the jinxes could have been entirely psychological in origin. This possibility cannot be completely ruled out. But it still leaves us with a residue of cases in which the victim knew nothing about the ghoul. C.J. and Marie Lambert had no reason to connect the statue of Ho-tei with their toothache, for example. Lethbridge put forward the theory of ghouls after he and his wife had independently experienced acute feelings of depression on an apparently peaceful beach. Lethbridge was even convinced that the field of a ghoul is sharply defined. He describes a ruined house where it was possible to step in and out of the affected area, as if there were a line drawn on the ground. The likeliest explanation would therefore seem to be that there is some sort of interaction between the negative thought field and the people who react to it.

ANCIENT FORCES

*A*t the Kofuku temple in Nara, Japan, a resentful priest named Kurodo decided to play an embarrassing trick on his fellow priests. At the side of a pond near the temple, Kurodo set up a placard that read: "On 3 March, a dragon shall ascend from this pond." The effect was just what he had expected. News of the placard spread far and wide, and people talked of nothing but dragons. On 3 March the pond was surrounded by thousands of people from all the neighbouring provinces. The day was sunny and peaceful. By noon nothing had happened, and the priests were beginning to feel worried. If no dragon appeared, they would lose face. Suddenly, a cloud drifted across the sky. A wind sprang up. The day became darker, and a storm broke. Rain fell in torrents and lightning flashed. Before Kurodo's startled eyes, a smoky shape like an enormous black dragon rose out of the pond and up into the clouds. This story may or may not be true. It was written by the great Japanese author Akutagawa, who probably based it on a tradition of the Kofuku temple.

If Akutagawa's tale sounds incredible, consider this story, which is certainly fact. In May 1727 François de Pâris, a young deacon of Paris, died of malnutrition and exhaustion. He was famous for his ascetic practices and for his charities to the poor, and his coffin was followed by hundreds of mourners. After it had been placed behind the altar of the church of St Medard, a line of mourners filed past. One small boy, accompanied by his father, limped awkwardly on a crippled leg. As he placed a bunch of flowers on the coffin, he suddenly fell to the ground, gasping and kicking. He was apparently suffering from a fit. A few minutes later, the fit passed off. The boy sat up, and was helped to his feet. A look of astonishment came over his face. Suddenly he began to dance and shout for joy. The crippled leg – twisted since birth – was straight. As the spectators stared in amazement, an old woman shouted: "I can use it!" She was waving her cured arm, which had been paralyzed for twenty-five years. Many fell on their knees around the coffin of the saintly deacon and prayed.

The miracles continued, and became more astounding. All kinds of sick people touched the coffin, went into convulsions, and were cured. After the body of the saintly priest had been buried behind the high altar, the miracles took place in the cemetery outside. They were so remarkable that it is tempting to dismiss contemporary accounts of them as pure exaggerations. Yet documentary evidence – some of it written by physicians – seems to show otherwise. A Mademoiselle Coirin had a cancer that had eaten away most of her breast, and the odour was so appalling that no one could go near her. After kneeling at the "saints'" tomb, not only was she cured, but the breast showed no sign of ever having had a cancer. This sounds absurd, but doctors examined it and testified that it was so.

Cripples walked; the blind were made to see; tumors vanished. Even odder manifestations began to occur. A young girl named Gabrielle Moler went into convulsions, after which she begged the spectators to beat her with sticks. She felt no pain and showed no bruises. She had seemingly acquired some of the curious powers possessed by Hindu fakirs. Strong men could pound her with hammers, and she remained unhurt. She would thrust her face into a blazing fire, and withdraw it unburned; she would leave her feet in the fire until the shoes and socks were burned away, and withdraw her feet unscathed. Another *convulsionaire*, the name given to those who experienced convulsions at the tomb, cured horrible sores and ulcers by sucking them. One man, who had been crippled, experienced the urge to spin on one leg at tremendous speed while reading from a holy book. He did this twice a day. Another convulsionaire could bounce six feet into the air, like a rubber ball, even when weighed down with heavy chains. Dozens of other visitors to the tomb rolled in convulsions or allowed spectators to beat them, without visible ill-effects.

Stonehenge, Wiltshire – the remains of a druid temple

A magistrate went to the churchyard convinced that the whole affair was a fraud. What he saw made him change his mind. He wrote books about it, and suffered imprisonment for his convictions.

The authorities were worried and embarrassed by the wild scenes at St Medard. François de Pâris, the young deacon who had started it all, had belonged to a religious sect known as the Jansenists. They denied free will and believed that people could only be saved by Divine Grace. The Jesuits, the most powerful religious order in Paris, detested the Jansenists. Through their influence, the churchyard of St Medard was closed down in 1732, five years after the miracles began. Convulsionaires were persecuted, and the miracles ceased. Jansenism was made illegal, and finally died out.

What happened at St Medard is similar to what happened at the Kofuku temple pond. A large number of people became deeply convinced that miracles were about to occur, and it seems likely that the united force of their subconscious minds *made* the miracles happen. The first people who followed François de Pâris's coffin already regarded him as a saint capable of producing miracles – and the initial cures strengthened their conviction. However, the story of the dragon in the pond suggests that there could be another explanation. In China and Japan, the dragon is a creature of deep religious significance – like the lamb in Christian countries. This recalls F. W. Holiday's observations about the dragon symbolism in ancient cultures and the association of dragonlike creatures with lakes.

It is also possible that the church of St Medard was built on a site where, like Stonehenge and other megaliths, dragon paths or ley lines meet. This would explain the concentration of magnetic powers there. Unfortunately, we know little of the religion that led our early ancestors to build great stone monuments in sacred places. But it seems clear that the stones themselves played some vitally important part in the worship. The gigantic granite blocks of Stonehenge, of Baalbek in the Lebanon, and of a hundred other ancient temples were not dragged into position merely to satisfy the whim of some all-powerful ruler. They were apparently intended to be giant accumulators of magic power. In some strange way, this force was used. It is even possible that it was used to raise the stones into position.

How was this power harnessed? The answer must surely

lie in some mysterious interaction between the forces of the earth and the powers of the subconscious mind. It may well be that a similar interaction occurred on a smaller scale in the cemetery of St Medard. Medical science cannot explain how Gabrielle Moler resisted the blows of strong men and the heat of a blazing fire. We know that hypnosis can render people insensitive to pain, but it could not prevent Gabrielle Moler from being burned when she thrust her face and feet into the flames. Hypnotism alone cannot explain how a man loaded with heavy chains could bounce six feet into the air. We know that yogis possess these kinds of powers, but they are acquired only after years of arduous training. All we can say is that whatever occurred at St Medard conferred extraordinary powers on the convulsionaires – or perhaps merely enabled them to make use of powers that all human beings possess.

Knowledge of the ancient religion of the forces of earth has been lost in the mists of time. Yet we have some fascinating clues to its nature. Anyone who wants seriously to follow them up should turn to an extraordinary and complex work called *The White Goddess*, written in the 1940s by the British poet Robert Graves. Graves describes how he was reading *The Mabinogion*, a collection of ancient Welsh legends, when he came across a curious and apparently meaningless poem called *The Song of.Taliesin*. Suddenly, in a flash of inspiration, he realized that some of the most baffling lines of the poem were a series of medieval riddles, and that these riddles contained clues to an ancient Celtic system of knowledge. As he pursued his research into this knowledge, he discovered that it was not confined to Wales. It could be found in the poetry and mythology of ancient Greece, Phoenicia, Scandinavia, India, and Africa. *And it was always closely linked with the moon.*

This was in itself a fascinating insight, and it tied in with a theory put forward twenty years earlier by the anthropologist Margaret Murray. In the early 1920s, Dr Murray had startled the academic world with a book called *The God of the Witches*. In it she had argued that what we now call witchcraft was actually an ancient pagan religion, whose chief deity was the moon goddess Diana. The ancient priests of Diana worshipped her by performing dances in which they wore animal skins and deer antlers on their heads. Christianity tried to stamp out this pagan religion, but it continued in secret. In Christian mythology, the antlered priest became the devil. In fact, he was a *shaman*, or magician-priest-doctor.

Graves came to an even more startling conclusion. He said that the ancients possessed a kind of knowledge based on intuition, on a certain oneness with Nature. This ancient knowledge sprang from the subconscious depths of the mind, and was symbolized by the moon.

When *The White Goddess* was published in 1948, many critics dismissed it as poetic fancy. Since then, however, an increasing number of scientific discoveries have supported Graves's ideas. Many scientists now accept that Stonehenge, Callanish, and other ancient monuments were intended as lunar observatories. The study of aboriginal tribes has confirmed the importance of the moon goddess and her connection with fertility rituals. In 1960 the anthropologist Charles Mountford studied tribes in the deserts of central Australia. He made a 300-mile journey with them to "centres of power", where certain rituals were performed. The ceremonies were designed to increase the life power of the worshippers, to stimulate the fertility of plants and animals, and to renew the sacred forces of the tribe. Mountford found that these centres of power lay on straight lines. Each tribe was responsible for looking after its own stretch of line, performing appropriate rituals to maintain its power. (According to students of dragon paths and leys, the lines of magnetic force do not remain permanently in the same place; they may change their location over the centuries, so that a holy place ceases to be holy.) Mountford observed that each centre of power was marked by a rock, and the Australian aborigines painted serpents – or dragons – on the rocks to symbolize the mysterious life force. However, the aborigines insist that it is not the painting that has magical or religious properties, but *the rock itself*.

Modern science is only just beginning to uncover the ancient systems of knowledge. It is therefore hardly surprising to find that there are dozens of strange and conflicting theories on the subject. The Austrian engineer and cosmologist Hanns Horbiger, who died in 1931, recognized the significance of the moon in ancient legends. He concluded that the earth has had several moons, all of which finally crashed into the earth and caused vast catastrophes like the biblical flood and the destruction of Atlantis. He was convinced that our present moon is a huge block of ice – a theory we now know to be untrue. The witchcraft revival of recent years is based on the belief that witchcraft is an ancient fertility religion, and that its forces can be tapped today through the rituals performed at *Sabbats*, or gatherings of witches.

T.C. Lethbridge thought that Stonehenge and similar monuments might be giant markers set up for the guidance of aircraft or spacecraft. He also speculated that the moon might have been the scene of a great war between two rival planetary races – perhaps those of Venus and Mars – and that its craters were formed by atomic bombardment rather than by meteorites. We know that many of the moon's craters were created by some kind of impact rather than by volcanic activity because they sometimes overlap one another.

Lethbridge's theory sounds absurd. Yet in 1966 two moon satellites – America's Orbiter-2 and the Soviet's Lunar-9 – both photographed groups of solid *structures* in two different places on the lunar surface. Ivan Sanderson writes: "The Lunar-9 photographs, taken on 9 February, 1966, after the craft had landed in the Ocean of Storms, reveal two straight lines of equidistant stones that look like markers along an airport runway. These circular stones are all identical, and are posi-

---

Does a place of worship have more intense thought fields than ordinary buildings? Can this explain the incredible case of the doll with human hair that keeps on growing?

The story comes from northern Japan and started in 1938. In that year Eikichi Suzuki took a ceramic doll to the temple in the village of Monji-Saiwai Cho for safekeeping. It had been a treasured possession of his beloved sister Kiku, who had died nineteen years before at the age of three. Suzuki kept it carefully in a box with the ashes of his dead sister.

Suzuki went off to World War II and didn't return for the doll until 1947. When he opened the box in the presence of the priest, they discovered that the doll's hair had grown down to its shoulders. A skin specialist from the Hokkaido University medical faculty said it was human hair.

The doll was placed on the altar, and its hair continued to grow. It is still growing, and is now almost waist length. The temple has become a place of pilgrimage for worshippers who believe the doll is a spiritual link with Buddha.

The priest of Monji-Saiwai Cho thinks that the little girl's soul somehow continues to live through the doll she loved so much.

tioned at an angle that produces a strong reflection from the sun, which would render them visible to a descending aircraft." The Soviet scientist Dr S. Ivanov notes that "the objects, as seen in 3-D, seem to be arranged according to some definite geometric laws."

The Orbiter-2 photographs, taken some 2000 miles away from the Soviet site, show what appear to be eight pointed obelisks. From the angle of the sun and the length of its shadow, the largest of these objects was estimated to be about seventy-five feet high and fifty feet wide at the base. This makes it sound more like a tall pyramid than an obelisk. Moreover, the Soviet scientist Alexander Abramov states that the distribution of the Orbiter-2 objects is similar to the plan of the Egyptian pyramids at Giza. A NASA official told Sanderson that the photographs were extremely clear, but explained that there had been "no speculation about them so far." He added that they had been filed.

On 26 November 1956 as American astronomer Robert E. Curtiss was photographing the moon's surface through a 16-inch reflector telescope, he was startled to observe a white cross near the ring plan Fra Mauro. Each arm of the cross was several miles long. Scientists have been unable to explain this phenomenon.

John O'Neil, science editor of the New York *Herald Tribune* observed a gigantic bridgelike structure in the Sea of Crises. The sun shone *under* it when it was at a low angle, making it clearly visible. Other astronomers have since confirmed the existence of this giant "bridge" on the moon.

These observations bring to mind the vast system of artificial lines that can be seen in the arid valleys near Nazca in Peru. These are a series of straight lines, interspersed with animal shapes and geometric patterns, that were scraped in the ground at some unknown date in the past. They look remarkably like landing strips for aircraft. They were not noticed until recent years because they can only be seen clearly from the air. The lines, which have been drawn in the rocky debris of the valleys, extend for over thirty miles, sometimes crossing ravines or stopping in front of small mountains and reemerging absolutely straight on the other side. The most puzzling question is how the lines were kept so straight by men working at ground level, presumably without guidance from the air. There are enormous designs of disks, flowers, spiders, and birds, which were only revealed by aerial surveys. On an aerial photograph they look like markings made in the sand by a child. The difference is that they must have taken hundreds of people hundreds of hours to construct. For what purpose? Von Däniken is convinced that they were markings to guide spacecraft; a likelier explanation is that they are connected with some ritual of the seasons.

If future astronauts can verify that there are artificial structures on the moon, built by intelligent creatures, it would certainly be one of the most exciting discoveries in the history of the human race. Yet even this would do little to solve the really baffling enigmas about our satellite. For thousands of years, people accepted that the human mind is influenced by the moon just as surely as the tides are. Our word "lunatic" stems from the age-old belief in a connection between the moon and madness. Then came the Age of Reason. Scientists and philosophers pointed out that the idea of a link between humans and the moon is absurd. How could a planetary body a quarter of a million miles away influence the human mind? It was a good point; but it was unsound. Modern research has shown that not only human beings, but also all kinds of animals, are affected by the moon. Oysters open and close their shells according to the rhythm of the tides, and it had always been assumed that this activity was the result of tidal movement alone. Dr Frank A. Brown, Professor of Biology at Northwestern University, found it to be otherwise. When he moved some oysters to a closed tank in the laboratory, away from the tidal influences, he discovered that they appear to open and close their shells in direct response to the movements of the moon.

The police have observed that crimes of violence tend to increase at the time of the full moon. One report from the Philadelphia Police Department stated that "people whose antisocial behaviour had psychotic roots – such as firebugs, kleptomaniacs, destructive drivers, and homicidal alcoholics – seemed to go on the rampage as the moon rounded, calming down as the moon waned." Nurses in mental institutions are familiar with the rise in violence and tension that occurs among their patients when the moon is full. Most family physicians in country areas, where the doctor-patient relationship tends to be closer and longer-lasting than in towns, can tell of people whose behaviour becomes eccentric at the time of the full moon. A doctor in the area where I live in Cornwall tells me he never expects to get an undisturbed night's sleep when the moon is full, and that there are far more cases of wife-beating and battered babies at that time.

How then, does the moon affect the human mind? The answer may lie in electrical forces. Scientists now know that the phases of the moon bring about modulations in the earth's electrical and magnetic fields. When Harold Burr of Yale University connected delicate voltameters to trees, he discovered that the electrical fields of the trees varied according to the seasons, to the activity of sunspots, and to the phases of the moon. The same delicate voltmeters connected to human beings are able to tell when women ovulate, and when people are suffering from cancer. It would therefore appear that human health is tied up with certain electrical forces in the body. The Chinese believe that these forces run in lines beneath the surface of the body, and the points at which they join are acupuncture points. Practitioners of acupuncture treat illness by stimulating these points with wooden splinters or metal needles. Western television teams have filmed surgical operations in China conducted on wide-awake patients who have been "anaesthetized" by means of one, or a few, needles inserted into the skin at acupuncture points. The patients appeared to feel no pain, and one of them smiled and joked as a tumor was removed from his stomach.

Acupuncture works, and it is gaining wider acceptance in the West. But Western science has not yet accepted the Chinese belief that the "meridians", or lines of force, that run through the human body are of basically the same nature as the dragon paths that extend over the earth. This seems altogether more difficult for the pragmatic Western intellect to acknowledge. After all, the earth is not a living creature.

Or is it? Sir Arthur Conan Doyle, the creator of Sherlock Holmes, once wrote a short novel called *The Day the Earth Screamed*. In it the hero, Professor Challenger, reaches the startling conclusion that the earth is alive. To prove his theory he drills a deep shaft through the earth's surface, and drops an enormous stake down it. The earth convulses and screams. In the light of modern knowledge, this idea is not so wildly improbable as it sounds. The earth has its fields of force just as human beings have. We speak of life-fields in human beings. Why not in the case of the earth? Perhaps the earth is not alive in the same sense that we are. But if some investigators are right, it often behaves as if it were.

This theory would offer an explanation of why certain spots

on the earth's surface seem to be blessed, while others are cursed. When sceptics read stories of miracles at holy places like Lourdes in France, Compostella in Spain, and Holywell in Wales, they are inclined to fall back on the explanation that faith, like hypnosis, can produce miraculous effects on the mind and body. Certainly most reports of amazing cures could be accounted for in this way. But some of the most astounding miracles involve things rather than people. Outside the old church of Arles-sur-Tech in southern France stands a marble sarcophagus that weeps – to the bafflement of modern science. It would probably be more accurate to say that the marble sweats. When the heavy lid of the sarcophagus is removed, water is seen to form in its inner surface. Usually the slab is held in place with iron bands. There is a small hole, large enough to insert a pipette, in the top edge of the sarcophagus. Through this hole the sarcophagus yields up on average about two pints of water per day. This water is reputed to have healing properties, and does not evaporate if left in an open vessel. In the past, the flow of water has amounted to many gallons at a time – more than the cubic capacity of the sarcophagus. There is no spring near the coffin, and the mystery cannot be explained by condensation. It is just another of those unsolved enigmas associated with holy places and objects.

The same is true of two bottles of blood that are kept in a small chapel next to Naples cathedral. It is the blood of St Januarius, who was martyred in 305 AD. Three times a year the blackened mass in the bottle changes color, and takes on the appearance of normal fresh blood. This has happened thousands of times – always on three religious feasts celebrated in May, September, and December. Careful investigation has revealed no evidence of trickery.

What is perhaps equally significant is that there have been occasions when the blood failed to liquefy. Why should that be so? The most plausible explanation is that the liquefaction somehow involves the faith of the worshippers, and that if this is insufficient to trigger the strange psycho-chemical reaction required, nothing happens. However, it is also possible that the earth forces that animate the spot are less strong at some times than at others. It would be interesting to have full astronomical data for the periods when the liquefaction failed to take place, and so be able to determine the exact position of the moon and the planets at the time.

But what would be most interesting of all would be to

understand the laws that govern the interaction between the vital forces of the earth and the vital forces of our subconscious. If we could discover that secret, we would have taken the first great step toward recovery of the lost knowledge of the ancients.

CREATURES FROM OTHER WORLDS?

*I*n February 1855 England was in the grip of an exceptionally icy winter. Even the West Country, where winters are seldom severe, was covered with a blanket of frozen snow. On the morning of 8 February Albert Brailford, the school principal of Topsham village in Devonshire, was intrigued to see a line of peculiar prints in the snow when he walked out of his front door. The prints were shaped like horseshoes, each about four inches long, and looked like they might have been made by a hoofed animal. The strange thing was that the prints were in a completely straight line, one in front of the other. It was as though the animal had been treading an invisible tightrope on its hind legs. Brailford followed the tracks along the street, and pointed them out to various acquaintances. The villagers agreed that the prints were unlike those of any known animal. As they tracked them through the fresh snow, the mystery deepened. The tracks stopped at a high garden wall, and continued on the other side. Yet the snow on top of the wall was undisturbed. It seemed that the creature had jumped the wall with one bound, or walked straight through it.

All along the South Devon coast for forty miles people discovered more of the mysterious tracks. In some places they went over rooftops. In one village they stopped at the door of a shed and reappeared at the back of it, emerging from a six-inch hole. The prints went up to a haystack, disappeared, and resumed on the other side. They stopped at one end of a drainpipe lying on the ground, and started again at the far end. The tracks always lay in a straight line, although they often doubled back on themselves.

News traveled slowly in those days. It was more than a week before Londoners learned of the sensational events in Devonshire. City sophisticates smiled at accounts of old ladies locking themselves in cottages while men armed with pitchforks and shotguns searched yards and barns for some unknown creature. They were amused at the country dwellers' belief that the tracks were the "Devil's footprints". To city dwellers it sounded like a typical rural storm-in-a-teacup. They surmised that the prints had been made by some animal, and that the superstitious country folk had interpreted them as the marks of the Devil himself. However, when more precise information began to appear, even Londoners had to admit that it was a strange story.

A Devon vicar and naturalist, who denied that there was a supernatural explanation, carefully measured the distance between the prints. He found it always to be exactly eight and a half inches. A fellow villager some distance away had measured the tracks in his garden, and also found them to be eight and a half inches apart. From this it appeared that there was only one creature involved. The oddest part was that the tracks extended over forty miles of coastline and, allowing for detours and deviations, extended for more than twice that distance. What small animal, if there was only one, could walk over eighty miles between dusk and dawn, climbing over roofs, and leaping over or walking through haystacks?

A famous naturalist, Sir Richard Owen, examined sketches of the tracks, and asserted that the prints had been made by a badger. Owen's badger presumably walked on its hind legs.

The likeliest explanation seemed to be that the tracks were made as a joke by some local prankster. But even supposing he wore special shoes with horseshoes attached to the soles, how did he vault walls, stride over rooftops, and cover eighty miles or so in a single night?

One of the correspondents of the *London Illustrated News* drew attention to a report made by the British explorer Sir James Ross in May 1840. Ross had anchored off the desolate Kerguelen Island in the Antarctic, and had been intrigued to find hoofprints in the snow. His party followed them for some distance until they vanished on rocky ground. There are no ponies on Kerguelen Island, or any other animal that could have made such prints.

The London *Times* for 14 March 1840 contains an account of mysterious tracks in the Scottish Highlands. They had been followed for twelve miles through the snow near Glenorchy, and they sound identical to the Devil's footprints in Devon. They were shaped like horseshoes, but gave the impression that the creature who made them had been bounding or leaping rather than trotting.

There are many accounts of Devil's hoofprints in old chronicles, but sceptical historians have been inclined to treat them as superstitious inventions. A typical example may be found in the *Chronicum* of the Benedictine monk Flavellus of Épernay, France. Describing a wild tempest that occurred in 943 AD he writes that, "demons or horses were seen at the height of the storm." Abbot Ralph of Coggeshall Abbey in Essex, England, records that after a tremendous storm in July 1205, "certain monstrous tracks were seen in several places, of a kind never seen before. Men said they were the prints of demons." No doubt many of these old stories are either inventions or exaggerations of an actual event. But couldn't some of these ancient chroniclers have been recording visitations similar to the one in Devon?

One explanation of the Devon prints was suggested by Morris K. Jessup, the ufologist mentioned earlier. Predictably, Jessup believed that the tracks were made by some kind of flying craft. He draws attention to the report of one observer that the prints were so clear-cut that they seemed to have been stamped into the snow "as if made by a drill or mechanical frame." Jessup suggests that the marks could have been made by a low-flying craft that maintained its distance from the ground by some kind of energy beam such as radar. This would certainly explain how the prints continued over rooftops and passed over walls and haystacks. Yet it fails to explain why the tracks often doubled back on themselves.

As we have seen, some ufologists have suggested that UFOs may originate in another dimension – a space-time world running parallel to our own. David Lang, the Tennessee farmer who disappeared without trace, may have fallen into this parallel dimension. If he could unwittingly fall into their dimension, why should not creatures from the parallel world accidently fall into ours? One of the most remarkable things about the Devil's footprints in Devon is that they wandered around for so many miles, as if the creature who made them were looking for something. They strayed over or through walls and across rooftops as if their owners were unfamiliar with our world.

It is interesting to note that the stories of demonic activity from Flavellus and Abbot Ralph both involve extremely violent storms, when electrical activity would have been unusually powerful. Remembering the strange behavior of compasses in the Bermuda Triangle and other Devil's graveyards, is it not conceivable that unusual magnetic fields might create a bridge between this world and a parallel universe?

It is now time to pause and survey some of the ground we have covered. As we look back over the mysteries considered in this book, we have to admit that no single explanation, or set of explanations, can accommodate all these strange phenomena.

On the night of 18 April 1962 at about 7.30 p.m. an explosion ripped across the Nevada sky. The flash was as bright as an atomic blast, and the noise shook the earth for miles. Was it an atom bomb test? A meteor? An enemy missile or aircraft? These logical questions were never answered by those who investigated the incident.

The first report of an odd UFO had come from Oneida, New York. Observers there saw a glowing red object moving west at a great altitude. It was too slow to be a missile, too high to be a plane. A meteor was ruled out because this object was tracked by radar, and meteors cannot be. As it moved west across the country, reports of it came in from the states of Kansas, Utah, Montana, New Mexico, Wyoming, Arizona, and California.

At some point the huge UFO landed near an electric power station in Eureka, Utah. Until it took off again, in its own time, the station was unable to operate at all.

The possibility that the explosion was from a nuclear test was denied by the Atomic Energy Commission. Its spokesmen said there was no atomic testing anywhere on the North American continent at that time.

Jet interceptors from the Air Defense Command pursued the UFO, but radar screens lost it about seventy miles northwest of Las Vegas. It was in that precise direction that the blast took place somewhere above the Mesquite Range.

Few people in the United States ever learned about this unusual event. Only the Las Vegas *Sun*, which was in the area of the explosion, carried the story. The news was otherwise suppressed by the Air Force.

Besides, there are many other types of enigmas that have not even been discussed. To touch briefly on a few, let us look first at poltergeist phenomena, about which I said a few words at the beginning of this book. In a famous case that took place in 1878 in Amherst, Nova Scotia, Esther Cox was the center of poltergeist manifestations. Objects flew through the air, spontaneous fires broke out, and an invisible spirit wrote on a wall: "Esther, you are mine to kill." Several witnesses were present with the young girl when the threat was written.

Then there is the closely related subject of demonic possession. When a possessed woman was exorcised by Theophilus Reisinger in Iowa in 1928, her body tore itself loose from the grip of several nuns who were trying to hold her down, rose through the air, and clung to the wall of the room close to the ceiling. Hundreds of similar cases have been recorded, some by modern psychologists. If these phenomena are caused by outside forces, it would certainly appear that such forces can sometimes be hostile to us human beings. It is of course possible that the forces originate in our own subconscious mind. In this case, the problem is equally baffling, because it suggests that a human being may possess several different personalities at different levels. There have been many astonishing cases of multiple personalities in which a person has suddenly lost his or her memory and been taken over by another personality. The second character has then performed actions that are completely foreign to the normal personality. In *Sybil*, a book by Flora Schreiber, the woman Sybil was taken over by no less than sixteen personalities. In which world do these personalities exist? Is the world of the subconscious mind one of the parallel worlds we have been discussing?

In a book called *Superminds*, the British physicist John Taylor discusses people like Uri Geller and Matthew Manning, who can bend spoons merely by stroking them and cause metal to fracture without even touching it. Taylor has observed many such psychics, including young children, in his laboratory. He has concluded that there is no trickery involved in their ability to bend metal or move objects at a distance. It is his opinion that their powers stem from some mysterious force, akin to magnetism, which is probably also involved in poltergeist activity. If the force of a child's mind can move small objects around Taylor's laboratory, is it not conceivable that a similar force might have been harnessed to raise the 1000-ton granite blocks of the temple at Baalbeck, or the immense monoliths of Stonehenge?

The hypothesis that we are simply dealing with unknown and impersonal forces that may originate in the human subconscious leaves far too many mysteries unexplained. It would not account for people vanishing without trace, nor the opposite of this – the appearance of mysterious strangers in our world.

In the eleventh century, two extraordinary children walked out of a cave at a place called Woolpit in Suffolk, England. The chronicler Abbot Ralph of Coggeshall describes them as follows: "They had all their members like those of other men, but in the color of their skin, they differed from all other mortals of our earth." Both children were green.

The boy grew sick and died, but the girl survived and slowly learned English. When she could talk, she explained that she and the boy had come from a land where there was no sunlight. One day they had wandered into a cavern while looking after sheep, and had lost their way. When they emerged into the unaccustomed sunlight of a strange world, they were terrified. The children had at first refused all food except green beans. The girl became used to other foods, however, and her skin slowly lost its green tint.

The most famous case of a strange person appearing in mysterious circumstances is that of Caspar Hauser. On 26 May 1828 a shambling teenage boy wandered into the Unschlitt Square in Nuremberg, Germany. Trembling and mumbling incoherently, he accosted a shoemaker and offered him a letter. When he was taken to the police station, another letter was found in his pocket. One letter purported to be from his mother, who said that the boy's name was Caspar, and that his father had been a soldier. The other was apparently from a poor labourer who had brought up the boy, and who asked that he be taken into the army. It was quickly established that both letters were fakes, written by the same person probably to cover up the boy's identity.

Asked to write his name, the boy wrote "Caspar Hauser." He was able to mumble a few words, but otherwise gave the impression of being imbecilic. It soon became clear, however, that Hauser was not an imbecile. Although he seemed totally ignorant of the world and of even the most everyday objects in it, he began to learn with a rapidity that proved he was highly intelligent. Within a few months, Caspar Hauser had learned enough German to explain what he knew of his former life. He said that for as long as he could recall, he had lived in a tiny cell. When he awoke, he found bread and water on the floor. Sometimes the water tasted bitter, and after drinking it he fell into a deep sleep. When he woke up, he had been washed and his nails had been cut. He was not unhappy because he knew no other way of life.

Handbills were sent out all over Germany to try to establish the boy's identity, but no one was able to throw any light on the mystery. Professor Georg Daumer, who became Hauser's guardian, discovered that the boy had an unusually acute sense of smell, could see in the dark, and found daylight painful to his eyes – all of which seemed to confirm his story.

In October 1829 Hauser was found unconscious and bleeding on the floor of Daumer's cellar. He had been attacked by an unknown assailant who had struck him down with a club, and possibly also tried to stab him.

During the next four years, Hauser had a number of guardians. Finally an Englishman, Lord Charles Stanhope, moved him from Nuremberg to the nearby town of Ansbach in Bavaria. On 14 December 1833 Hauser staggered into his house, bleeding heavily from a stab wound in his ribs. He explained that a labourer had brought him a message asking him to meet someone in the Hofgarten. There a man with dark whiskers and a black cloak had asked him, "Are you Caspar Hauser?" When he said yes, the man handed him a silk purse, and then stabbed him in the side. The purse was found in the Hofgarten, and contained an incoherent note signed MLO. It said that Hauser would be able to identify his assailant, who came from a place on the Bavarian border. The name of the place was illegible. Hauser died on 17 December 1833 without having been able to throw any light on the identity of his murderer.

From the moment of his appearance in Nuremberg, controversy had raged around Caspar Hauser. There were many theories as to his origins, but most people believed that he was the illegitimate son of some noble family, and had been kept a prisoner to conceal the dishonour until he became too big to remain locked away. Jacques Bergier, a French writer on the occult, has another theory that is shared by many students of enigmas. It would explain the mysterious appearance of the green children as well as that of Caspar Hauser. Bergier suggests that, for many centuries, the earth has been under study by certain extraterrestrial intelligences. "In my opinion," he says, "after the period of simply auditing and recording

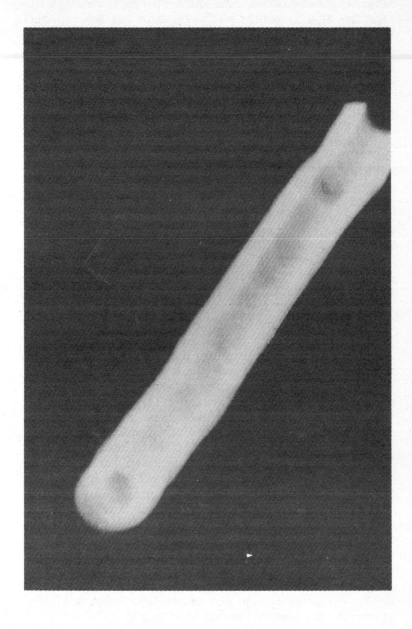

Unidentified flying object sighted over Palmero, Sicily 1978

what happened on earth, came another period, beginning a few centuries ago, in which the Intelligences began to conduct experiments. These experiments consist of introducing beings capable of arousing the most diverse reactions into our midst, and then studying the way we react – the way we study the behavior of rats in artificial labyrinths."

It is a suggestion worthy of Charles Fort. And, however great our revulsion at the idea of being treated as laboratory rats, it would certainly be hard to find a more all-embracing solution to the unexplained. Indeed, the chief objection to this theory is that it sounds *too* neat and easy. Any strange event can be explained by assuming that extraterrestrial intelligences wanted to study our reactions, and so deliberately engineered some incident that would baffle us.

There are, however, other mysteries that, if they do not contradict the extraterrestrial hypothesis, certainly challenge us to look for different possibilities. Two examples come to mind.

On 17 June 1908 an enormous meteor was seen to streak across the sky in Siberia. It struck the earth with a tremendous explosion near the Stoney Tunguska River. The explosion was heard for 600 miles around, and two villages were wiped out. But Siberia is a vast and barren land, and the government of the time had more to worry about than meteors – the country was seething with political discontent that led to the 1917 Revolution. In 1927 a scientific expedition penetrated the roadless terrain near the site of the explosion, and found that an area of 400 square miles had been devastated. The odd thing was that this meteor had not behaved like others. Instead of splitting into fragments as it hit earth, it had vanished like a huge bomb.

Later expeditions to the area also failed to solve the mystery. In 1975 a team of Soviet scientists concluded that the devastation had been caused by the tail of a comet that had struck the earth. However, students of enigmas point to an earlier finding that the soil in the devastated area was highly radioactive. It was as if a huge atomic bomb had exploded. Of course, atomic bombs do not streak across the sky. But UFOs do, according to all the evidence. Was it an atom-powered flying saucer that exploded over Siberia? If so, and if it was constructed by Bergier's extraterrestrial Intelligences, these beings are evidently less infallible than Bergier seems to suppose. Unless, of course, they created the explosion by some highly sophisticated means of remote control simply to see how people on earth would react.

If the aim of the extraterrestrials is to stimulate human beings for psychological study, it is hard to see what they achieved by disturbing a mausoleum on the island of Barbados. The Chase family tomb, which stands in a churchyard above Oistin's Bay, is constructed of stone blocks held together by cement, and is closed by a marble door. It was built in 1724 by a plantation owner, and his wife was the first to be entombed. It was not reopened until 1807, when the coffin of family member Thomasina Goddard was placed in it. The next year the massive marble door was opened again to receive the coffin of Mary Chase. She was the daughter of Thomas Chase, one of the most hated men in Barbados. In 1812 another of Chase's daughters, Dorcas, was buried in the tomb. According to rumor, Dorcas Chase had died through her father's ill-treatment.

A month later Thomas Chase himself died. When the tomb was opened to receive his body, some of the coffins were found to be disarranged. Mary Chase's coffin had been thrown across the tomb and stood upside down, and Thomasina Goddard's coffin was lying on its side. The family was indignant, assuming that hostile plantation workers were responsible. Other people were less certain. They knew it was unlike the superstitious Barbadians to disturb the dead. Besides, the marble door slab was heavy, and would have taken several men to remove it. Why would they have gone to all that trouble merely to overturn two coffins? The coffins were put in their proper places, and the vault was carefully sealed.

Four years later in 1816 the tomb was reopened for the interment of another child, Samuel Ames. It was discovered that all the coffins had been hurled about the vault. But the cement holding the great slab in place had been found undisturbed.

Two months later Samuel Ame's father died. A curious crowd accompanied the funeral procession to the tomb. When it was opened they were not disappointed. Once again the coffins had been thrown around the vaul – with the single exception of Mrs Goddard's. The Reverend Thomas Orderson conducted a careful search of the vault in an attempt to find the explanation. The tomb was dry and sound. There were no cracks either in the walls or floor. The seal of the door had not been broken.

The tomb was elaborately resealed. Three years later in July 1819 enormous crowds arrived to watch the interment of Mrs Thomasina Clarke. They saw five men chip off the cement from the slab, which was designed to open inward. Even when the cement had been removed, the slab seemed hard to move. The reason became clear when it had been shifted by main force. The leaden coffin of Thomas Chase lay against the door. The other coffins were once more in disarray – again with the exception of Mrs Goddard's.

After the vault had been searched in vain for any sign of intruders, the coffins were replaced, and white sand scattered all over the floor. The slab was again cemented into place, and then sealed with private seals.

During the following months visitors flocked to see the "haunted tomb". In April 1820 Sir Stapleton Cotton, the Governor of Barbados, became so curious about it that he decided to have it inspected. The seals were intact. But when the massive slab was moved, the usual disorder prevailed. Coffins had tumbled all over the vault. Mrs Goddard's coffin – now little more than a bundle of planks secured by wire – was the only one that was undisturbed. The sand on the floor bore no sign of footprints. The Governor decided that the strange affair was becoming a disgrace to the island. He ordered the coffins to be removed and buried. And from that day to this, the vault has remained empty.

None of the normal explanations is acceptable. An earthquake, to which the area is subject occasionally, would not account for the fact that Mrs Goddard's coffin always remained unmoved. A member of the Ames family believed that the answer lay in giant puffballs, a type of fungus that grows in caves in Honduras. These puffballs can reach a diameter of twenty feet, and can lift rocks by their thrust as they grow. On reaching their full growth they explode and disintegrate into powder. This explanation is improbable for many reasons. For one, Honduras is 2000 miles from Barbados. For another, puffballs had not been observed on the island. Finally, there were no cracks in the tomb for puffball spores to enter even if they had reached Barbados, and witnesses saw no sign of fungus between the stones.

It seems probably that, in this case, we are dealing with a mixture of poltergeist activity and haunting, centered around the coffin of the hated Thomas Chase. It would have been interesting to see what would have happened if Sir Stapleton Cotton had removed only Thomas Chase's coffin, resealed the tomb, and investigated it again later.

Clearly it seems unlikely that Bergier's extraterrestrials were involved in this curious mystery. But even as a haunting it was unusual. Normally poltergeist activities only take place in the presence of living human beings, as if they had to draw energy from a living person – or, as a psychologist might say, as if their energy originated in the subconscious mind. There have been cases in which poltergeists have persisted in the same house over a long period while a series of tenants have come and gone. This suggests that the poltergeist may be some kind of independent entity, a spirit, that needs to borrow energy before it can make itself heard or felt. There were plenty of human beings to supply energy for poltergeist activity in the area of the Chase family tomb. Many were simple peasants who were terrified of the phenomena. Their fear may have increased the psychic vibrations that led to the disturbances.

We must indulge in one more speculation in our attempt to formulate some general theory to cover enigmas and mysteries. The disappearance of Lang, Bathurst, and others suggest that there may be parallel worlds in our universe. Perhaps these worlds do not exist in other dimensions, but only on other

---

One day in August 1887 near the small village of Banjos, Spain, a boy and girl walked out of a cave. Some peasants working in a field saw them, and were utterly amazed. The two children had skin as green as grass!

When seen closer, the children were found to have almond-shaped eyes of an Asiatic type. They could not speak Spanish, and they wore clothes of a material never before seen in the Spain of the nineteenth century. No one could understand their language, and no one could analyze the fabric. For five days the boy and girl would not eat any of the various foods brought to them. Finally they began to eat beans. By then the boy was so weakened that he died, but the girl survived. The green color of her skin gradually faded.

After learning some Spanish, the girl described the country she came from and how she had left it. Her story only made the mystery deeper. She said her native land had no sun at all, and was separated from a sunny land by a river. One day a sudden whirlwind had lifted her and the boy and deposited them in the cave.

The green girl of Banjos lived for only five years more. The mystery of how she and the boy had appeared in Spain was never solved.

energy levels. Perhaps they can intermingle as the different levels of matter – solids, liquids, and gases – do in our world, as in a syphon of soda water, for example. If we look back over the scientific history of the past few hundred years – from Galileo to Einstein, from electricity to black holes – we cannot lightly dismiss Lethbridge's hypothesis that we live in a multi-level universe in which our reality is only one of many.

This book has been about the *interaction* of these levels of reality. Some people seem to have slipped through a "crack" in our reality into another world. Some phenomena – including poltergeists, UFOs, and lake monsters – seem to have slipped from some other level of reality into our world. It seems possible that certain types of powerful electrical phenomena are able to link the two worlds – and for all we know, the results may be as startling and incomprehensible to the inhabitants of these other worlds as they are to us. There is also a certain amount of evidence that some part of us – the psychic part – already has a bridge to other levels. This may be why certain people can foretell the future, or describe a crime simply by holding some object associated with it. Thought evidently has far more power than we give it credit for. It may be able to stamp itself on objects, leaving an imprint that remains for thousands of years. Some of the unknown forces we are trying to understand may be evil. Their thoughts may be able to evoke evil reality, as in the case of curses.

Imagine a book of unexplained mysteries written by a contemporary of Shakespeare. It might include the mystery of the falling stars that sweep through the sky foretelling disaster; the mystery of the Kraken, the giant sea devil with fifty foot tentacles; the mystery of monster bones, sometimes found in caves or on beaches. Such a book would be a curious mixture of truth and absurdity, fact and legend. We would all feel superior as we turned its pages and murmured: "Of course, they didn't know about comets and giant squids and dinosaurs." If *this* book should happen to find its way into the hands of our remote descendants, they may smile pityingly and say: "It's incredible to think that they knew nothing about epsilon fields or multiple psychic feedback or cross gravitational energies. They didn't even know about the ineluctability of time." But let us hope that such a descendant is in a charitable mood, and might add: "And yet they managed to ask a few of the right questions."

TRUE GHOST STORIES

Colin Wilson, Damon Wilson
and Rowan Wilson

THE INVASION OF THE SPIRIT PEOPLE

The "Exorcist" Poltergeist

The story of the haunted boy of Washington sounds like some absurd tale of medieval witchcraft; in fact, it is a true occurrence, and formed the basis of William Blatty's bestselling novel *The Exorcist*.

In January 1949, the Deen family, who lived in a suburb of Washington DC, began to wonder if they had a plague of rats; loud scratching noises came from the walls of the house and from the attic. But a company of rodent exterminators could find no trace of rats. The noises grew louder, until it was almost impossible to get a good night's sleep. Creaking sounds in the hallway sounded like cautious footsteps. Then the real "haunting" began. Dishes began to fly through the air, furniture moved of its own accord, a picture floated off the wall then floated back again, and fruit flew out of a bowl and smashed itself on the walls and floor.

By this time, the Deens realised they had a poltergeist. The word is German for "noisy ghost" – some of the earliest recorded cases occurred in Germany. Poltergeists seem to be the juvenile delinquents of the spirit world, and they delight in causing noise and confusion. The Washington poltergeist did more than that; within weeks, the whole family was on the point of nervous breakdown. But one thing was obvious: that the "spirit" centred its activities around their thirteen-year-old son, Douglass. The strange phenomena only occurred when he was in the room. And when he was out of the house, they stopped altogether.

Now the next stage began: Douglass's bed began to shake and tremble; it happened even when he was fast asleep. The distraught family asked the advice of their local minister, the Rev. Winston. He was inclined to be sceptical, but invited the boy to spend the night in his home; he set up a spare bed in his own bedroom. Douglass arrived at 9:20 on 17 February 1949, and at 10 o'clock he went off to bed. Within ten minutes, his bed was vibrating, and there were scratching noises from the wall. The minister hastily switched on the light, and saw that the boy was lying perfectly still, while his bed was shaking violently. He suggested that Douglass should sleep in a huge armchair, whose sheer size and weight should make it disturbance-proof. But as soon as the boy was tucked up in a blanket, the armchair began to move. First it rolled back against the wall, then it tilted until it shot the boy on to the floor. The minister was so curious that he tried sitting in the chair and making it tilt over; it proved to be impossible.

The boy finally had to sleep on a mattress on the floor. But even this slid about the room for the rest of the night, so that no one got much sleep. The next day the boy went into the George-town Hospital, a Catholic institution, for observation. Meanwhile, the minister gave a lecture to the Parapsychology Society, describing the amazing things he had witnessed.

When the hospital failed to solve Douglass's problem, they asked the help of the Jesuits. They decided that Douglass Deen was "possessed" by an "entity", and called upon the aid of a priest who specialised in exorcism, or the casting out of evil spirits. He spent several months fasting and repeating exorcism rituals over the boy, culminating in the words: "I command you, whoever you are, unclean spirit, that by our Lord Jesus Christ, you give me your name and the day of your exit . . ." For weeks this had no effect whatsoever; then Douglass began to shriek obscenities in a shrill voice, and to speak rapidly in Latin, a language he had never studied. It took until May 1949, but finally the "spirit" went away, and Douglass Deen became a normal teenager once more.

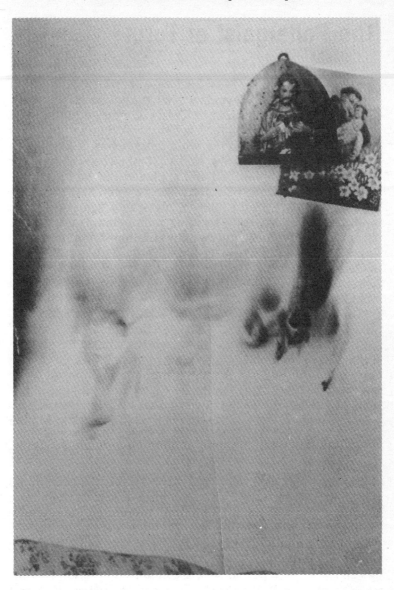

1972, this image of 'the Devil' appeared in Rome after an exorcism, according to a Roman Catholic Priest. He said the image resembling a malevolent goat seared on to a white plaster wall was accompanied by a series of savage blows on the wall which was suddenly enveloped in a sheet of flames, indicating that the Devil had left the young man being exerocised.

The Poltergeist of Turin

But *was* it an evil spirit? Most modern authorities on the subject would answer no. In November 1900, the famous psychologist – and sceptical materialist – Cesare Lombroso heard of a "haunting" in a tavern in the Via Bava in Turin. The proprietor took Lombroso down to the wine cellar, which proved to be covered with broken bottles. And as Lombroso stood there, six bottles floated off the shelf and exploded like bombs on the floor. Even as Lombroso left the cellar, he could hear the sound of breaking glass. In the kitchen, plates flew across the room and shattered, while in the servants' room, a brass meat grinder struck the wall so violently that it was flattened. If it had struck Lombroso, it would have killed him. The odd thing was that, in spite of its violence, the ghost never harmed anyone; heavy vases would miss people's heads by an eighth of an inch, and shatter against the wall.

Lombroso's first theory was that someone in the house was an unconscious "medium" – a person through whom "spirits" can express themselves. He suspected the wife of the proprietor, a skinny, neurotic woman, and suggested that she should go away for a holiday. But the disturbances continued while she was absent. Then Lombroso's suspicions fell on a tall, gangling thirteen-year-old boy, who was suffering from pimples and other physical effects of puberty; he was the only other person who was always present when the disturbances took place. The youth was sent away, and the disturbances instantly ceased.

Now the year 1900 was a time when the theories of Sigmund Freud were becoming known in medical circles. Lombroso reasoned that the turbulent sexual energies of adolescence were somehow responsible for the "poltergeist phenomena", but that the youth himself was totally unaware that he was to blame. In other words, the disturbances were caused by his *unconscious* mind. Of course, this still failed to explain how the unconscious mind can smash plates and bottles; but at least it seemed a step in the right direction. From that time on, most psychical researchers accepted the view that poltergeists are not real "ghosts", but some kind of bizarre effect of the unconscious mind.

Mind Over Matter

But *can* the unconscious mind move material objects? There is strong evidence that it can. In 1934, a professional gambler walked into the office of a psychical researcher named Dr J.B. Rhine and said he believed he could influence the fall of the dice. "Show me," said Rhine. So the two crouched on the floor, and the gambler began to "call his shots" with a remarkable level of success. Soon, dozens of researchers were investigating this strange possibility of mind over matter – it is known as psychokinesis or "PK" – in the laboratory. A Russian housewife named Nina Kulagina discovered she could make matchsticks move around simply by staring at them. And after seeing a film about her, an American researcher named Felicia Parise tried it. She had little success until one day she was told that her grandmother was dying. This gave her a bad shock, and when she reached out for a small plastic bottle, it moved away from her hand. The shock had somehow "shaken up" her unconscious mind, and from then on, she could move small objects simply by staring at them. And this, according to modern psychical research, is a mini-version of the "poltergeist effect", which happens to be far weaker because it is more or less *conscious*. For *really* powerful PK effects, the unconscious needs to operate spontaneously. That, at any rate, is the theory.

Freud's best-known disciple Carl Jung arrived at the same conclusion. He had a female cousin who, at the age of puberty, began to go into trances and speak with strange voices. One day when she was in the house the dining room table split in two with a loud report. There was also an explosion from the sideboard, and when they looked in the drawer, they found that a bread knife had shattered into several pieces. Jung decided that his cousin's unconscious mind was to blame. Jung called these occurrences "exteriorisation phenomena", another name for PK effects.

Years later, he was explaining his idea to the sceptical Freud, and becoming more and more irritated with Freud's stubbornness. Suddenly, said Jung, he experienced a curious burning sensation in his diaphragm, and there was a loud explosion in the bookcase which made Freud jump. "There," said Jung, "*that* is what I meant." "Bosh!" said Freud indignantly. "It is not bosh, and to prove my point, there will be another explosion in a moment." As he spoke, there was another explosion in the bookcase. Jung felt he had proved his point, but Freud always preferred to believe that the case was made of unseasoned wood, and that this was responsible for the cracking noises.

Another eminent Freudian psychiatrist agreed with Jung. He was a Hungarian named Nandor Fodor, and, like Cesare Lombroso, he had encountered poltergeists in the course of his work. He was so fascinated by them that he wrote a history of *The Poltergeist Down the Ages*, noting that the earliest recorded case took place in Bingen, in Germany, in 858 AD, and that the "spirit" showered the farmhouse with stones and shook the walls "as if men were striking them with hammers." It was apparently the farmer himself who was the object of the spirit's "malice", and it followed him around, making his life a misery, and even causing fires. (This is one of the poltergeist's more alarming and dangerous habits.) This poltergeist also developed a voice – which is unusual but not unique – and it denounced the farmer for adultery, and for sleeping with the daughter of his overseer.

And now, suddenly, we can begin to see the familiar pattern emerging. If the girl he seduced was on the verge of puberty, and if she lived in the same house as the farmer – which, in the overcrowded circumstances of the Middle Ages, is quite probable – then it would be understandable that the poltergeist would take out its annoyance on the seducer. Here is a case where Freudian sexual theory and modern psychical research seem to combine to indicate the solution. That, at any rate, was Fodor's view. He even went one further than the usual "unconscious" theory, and suggested something he called "somatic dissociation": "It means that the human body is capable of releasing energy in a manner similar to atomic bombardments. The electron shot out of its orbit . . . is like a bolt of lightning . . . The atom has no power to impart direction to it. A human being has." So, according to Fodor, a disturbed adolescent is like a miniature atomic bomb, with the additional power of *controlling* these strange energies. It is an impressive theory – but does it really cover all the facts?

The Hydesville Haunting

The most famous haunting in the world – and certainly the most influential in terms of its repercussions – took place in the middle of the nineteenth century. The strange case of the Hydesville haunting led to the launching of the movement called Spiritualism, and to the worldwide interest in ghosts and spirits that has persisted down to this day.

In fact, the Hydesville ghost belongs to the poltergeist type.

The Hydesville affair began on 31 March 1848, in a wooden frame house inhabited by a Methodist farmer named James D. Fox, his wife Margaret, and their two daughters, Margaretta, aged fourteen, and Kate, aged twelve. Hydesville is a small township not far from Rochester, New York. James Fox had moved into the house in the previous December. A previous tenant, Michael Weekman, had been disturbed by various loud knocks, for which he could find no cause.

The Fox family was also kept awake by various banging

During the 1930s the United Fruit Company cleared vast areas of Costa Rican jungle in order to create banana plantations. When the workers came to burn and hack the vegetation of the Diquìs Delta they were surprised to discover vast numbers of granite spheres, entirely buried in the foliage. They ranged from the small, about the size of a cricket ball and weighing a few pounds, to the enormous, eight feet in diameter and weighing sixteen tons. Many were rounded with astonishing accuracy, appearing to the eye to be perfectly spherical, yet their surfaces showed no sign of mechanical grinding. They were clearly man-made, not least because the granite from which they were cut did not occur naturally where they were found. Locals broke some open, believing them to contain treasure.

They remain entirely mysterious. Some were found over graves, others arranged in lines, curves and triangles. Pottery found underneath them dates from many centuries, the latest being the sixteenth. That they had some religious significance seems to be the only certain conclusion, for it is difficult to imagine a practical use for such an array of objects.

The more impressive of the balls now adorn the gardens of wealthy locals.

noises in the last days of March 1848; but since it was a windy
month, they were not unduly disturbed. On Friday 31 March,
the family decided to retire early to make up for lost sleep.
Mr Fox went round the house checking the shutters and sashes.
The children observed that when he shook the sashes, to see
how loose they were, banging noises seemed to reply like an
echo.

The whole family slept in two beds in the same room. Just
before the parents came to bed, the rapping noises started
again. Kate said cheekily, "Mr Splitfoot, do as I do", and
began snapping her fingers. To the amazement of the girls,
the raps imitated her. Margaret interrupted, "Do as I do", and
began to clap. Again, the sounds imitated her. Remembering
that the next day would be April the first, the children decided
that someone was playing a joke. In her account of what
happened, Mrs Fox wrote:

> "I then thought I could put a test that no one in the
> place could answer. I asked the noise to rap my
> different children's ages, successively. Instantly,
> each one of my children's ages was given cor-
> rectly, pausing between them sufficiently long to
> individualise them until the seventh [child], at
> which a longer pause was made, and then three
> more emphatic little raps were given, correspond-
> ing to the age of the little one that died . . ."

Now rather frightened – this was evidently no joke – Mrs Fox
asked if it was a human being who was making the raps; there
was no reply. "Is it a spirit? If it is, make two raps." Two
thunderous bangs followed, so loud that the house shook. She
asked if it was an "injured spirit", and again the bangs shook
the house. Further questioning revealed that the knocker was a
man who died at the age of thirty-one, that he had been
murdered in the house, and that he had a wife and five
children. Mrs Fox asked if the spirit had any objection to her
calling in the neighbours; the raps replied: "No."

The Foxs summoned in about fourteen neighbours. One of
these was a man called William Duesler, who assured his own
wife that the whole thing was ridiculous and that there could be
nothing mysterious about the noises. When he got there, some
of the neighbours were too nervous to go into the bedroom, but
Duesler was not worried. He went and sat on the bed, and was

astonished when Mrs Fox's questions were answered with a rapping noise that made the bed vibrate. (Later writers were to insist that the two children made all the noises by cracking their joints; but it is hard to see how the cracking of joints could make the house shake and cause a bed to vibrate.)

Duesler took up the questioning of the "spirit". By a code of knocks, he established that the entity was a man who had been murdered in the house, a pedlar named Charles B. Rosma, who had been attacked for the $500 he carried. The murder had taken place five years earlier, and had been committed by the man who was then the tenant of the house, a Mr Bell. A maid named Lucretia Pulver later confirmed that a pedlar *had* spent the night in the house, and that she had been sent home; when she returned the next day, the pedlar had gone.

As news of these amazing occurrences spread throughout the community, hundreds of people came to the house. On Sunday 2 April, Duesler learned from the murdered man that his body had been buried in the cellar. This seemed to offer a method of verification, and James Fox and his neighbours took shovels to the cellar – which had an earth floor – and proceeded to dig. At a depth of three feet they encountered water, and abandoned the attempt. But in July, when the water had gone down, they dug again, and at a depth of five feet found a plank; underneath this, in quicklime, there was some human hair and a few bones.

Mr Bell, on being heard that he had been accused of murder by a ghost, indignantly denied it, and produced a testimonial to his good character from his new neighbours in Lyon, New York. The spirit had already prophesied that the murderer would never be brought to justice.

In his account of the case in *Modern Spiritualism*, the sceptical Frank Podmore comments: "No corroborative evidence of the supposed murder, or even of the existence of the man supposed to have been murdered, was ever obtained." This was written in 1902. Two years later, in November 1904, a wall in the cellar of the Fox house collapsed, revealing another wall behind it. Digging between the two walls uncovered a skeleton and a pedlar's tin box. It looked as if someone had dug up the body from its original grave and interred it next to the wall, then built another wall to confuse searchers.

In those days immediately after the first manifestations, a committee was set up to collect the statements of witnesses. Not all the investigators were convinced that the sounds had a supernatural origin; but no one suggested that the Fox family could be responsible. With the family all together in the same room, it was obviously impossible that either the parents or the children could be causing the bangs.

What everyone soon noticed was that nothing happened unless the children were in the house – particularly Kate. A committee of sceptical Rochester citizens came to the house to investigate; they agreed that Margaret was certainly not responsible. A second and third investigation produced the same result. The children were stripped and searched to see if they had some mechanical device for producing the sounds; there was nothing. They were made to stand on pillows with their ankles tied; still the raps occurred.

The children were separated; Kate was sent to stay with her elder sister Leah in Rochester, and Margaretta with her brother

---

The *Watertown* was a large oil tanker owned by the Cities Service Company. In December 1924 a tragic accident occurred on board the ship. Two seamen, James Courtney and Michael Meehan, were cleaning a cargo tank while the ship was en route to the Panama Canal from the Pacific Coast. Both men were overcome by gas fumes and died. In true maritime tradition they were buried at sea on 4 December 1924.

The next day the phantom faces appeared. The first mate reported to the captain, Keith Tracy, that two faces were following the ship in the water. All the crew, as well as the captain, saw the faces of the two dead men, continually appearing day after day as the ship slowly made its way to the Panama Canal. When the ship docked in New Orleans the captain reported the bizarre events to officials of the Cities Service Company and J.S. Patton, of the company, suggested that the captain try to photograph the faces. The first mate owned a camera and Patton gave a sealed roll of film to the captain, who supervised the loading of the camera, hoping to procure a photograph of the faces.

The captain's hopes were fulfilled. When the *Watertown* set sail for its return voyage the phantoms again appeared. Six photographs were taken of the heads, but the film was not developed until the ship again docked in New Orleans. The film was delivered to J.S. Patton, who sent it to a commercial developer. Five of the photographs showed nothing, but a sixth revealed two heads very distinctly projected on the water dolorously following the ship.

David in Auburn. The "spirits" followed them both. Rapping noises were heard, and people felt themselves touched by invisible hands. In Leah's house, a lodger called Calvin Brown took a mildly satirical attitude towards the spirit, and it began to persecute him, throwing things at him. Mrs Fox's cap was pulled off and the comb pulled out of her hair. When members of the family knelt to pray, pins were jabbed into them. In brother David's boarding house, similar things were happening. It was clear that the murdered pedlar was not responsible for all this – he was back in the Hydesville house, making terrifying gurgling noises and sounds like a body being dragged across the floor. Mrs Fox's hair turned white. One spirit who communicated with Kate claimed to be a dead relative named Jacob Smith. Sister Leah Fish discovered that she could also communicate with the spirits, and began producing messages. One sixteen-year-old girl named Harriet Bebee, who visited the house in Auburn and witnessed the rapping noises, returned to her home miles away and found that the noises had followed her.

The Fox family moved to Rochester, but the manifestations continued. Sometimes the bangs were so loud that they could be heard miles away. Poltergeists had apparently taken over from the original "injured spirit". One day, a visitor named Isaac Post started asking the spirit questions, and was answered by a thunderous barrage of knocks. Then, by means of an alphabetical code, the "spirit" spelled out a message: "Dear friends, you must proclaim this truth to the world. This is the dawning of a new era; you must not try to conceal it any longer. God will protect you and good spirits will watch over you." And now began a series of manifestations that were to become typical of "Spiritualism". Tables moved and rapped with their legs; musical instruments were played by unseen fingers, objects moved round the room. The "spirits" intimated that they would prefer to manifest themselves in the dark – which confirmed the sceptics in their opinion. But other believers decided it was time to put the "spirit's" injunction into operation and "proclaim this truth to the world". On 14 November 1849, the first Spiritualist meeting took place in the Corinthian hall in Rochester.

Many people were convinced that the whole thing was a fraud. Passions rose to a fury, and one occasion, the girls were nearly lynched. But soon the tide began to turn in their favour. They went to New York in 1850 and sat in front of a committee of distinguished American intellectuals and public men for three days, producing rapping noises and messages from the dead, and the committee was convinced. They went on to become the most famous "mediums" in America. In 1861, Kate Fox produced even more remarkable phenomena. Sitting in a locked room, she caused the deceased wife of a banker named Charles Livermore to "materialise" in the room, so the husband could see her clearly, and even exchange a few words with her. While Kate's hands were held, the "spirit" of Estelle Livermore wrote messages on cards, and Livermore acknowledged that this was his dead wife's handwriting. He was so grateful that, as well as paying her generously, he paid for her to take a trip to England, where she became even more famous and successful.

Unfortunately, Margaret and Kate eventually fell on hard times. They quarrelled with their elder sister Leah, (who, unlike her sisters, was still a practising medium) and got together to try and ruin her. Both Margaret and Kate were drinking too much, and Margaret was living in actual poverty. In 1888 they gave interviews in which they claimed that they had made the raps themselves with their big toes, and by cracking their joints. This was obviously absurd, because the loud bangs and crashes in the Fox house could not have been caused by cracking the joints. But it caused a widespread scandal, and opponents of Spiritualism were delighted. But when Margaret was not paid as much money as she expected for these confessions, she withdrew them. Soon after that, both Margaret and Kate died from alcoholic complications. But by that time, Spiritualism had swept across America, and then across the world.

For whatever reason, the Fox sisters began a Spiritualist explosion. People discovered that all they had to do was to sit in a darkened room, preferably with a "medium" present – someone who had already established a communication with the spirits – and the manifestations would usually follow immediately. No apparatus was required, except possibly a few musical instruments. In the Rochester area, more than a hundred "mediums" appeared in the year 1850. In Buffalo, New York, two brothers and a sister named Davenport attended a seance at which the Fox sisters produced their manifestations, and decided to try it themselves – in fact, inexplicable raps and bangs had sounded in their home in the year 1846, two years before the Hydesville manifestations. When Ira, William and Elizabeth Davenport sat in a darkened room, with their hands on a tabletop, the table began to move, raps were heard all over the room, and when Ira picked up a pencil his hand began to write automatically. A few nights later, with witnesses present, all three children were seen to levitate into the air. At their fifth "seance," Ira was instructed – by means of raps – to fire a pistol in the corner of the room. As it exploded, it was taken from his hand, and by the light of the flash, a figure of a man was seen holding it. He vanished a moment later, and the pistol fell to the floor. The man introduced himself – through the code of raps – as John King; he was one of the first examples of a "control" (or master of ceremonies), who acted as intermediary between the medium and the "spirits". 'John King" was soon taking over the brothers directly and speaking through their mouths. The Davenport brothers went on to become even more famous than the Fox sisters.

In Dover, Ohio, a well-to-do farmer named Jonathan Koons discovered his own talents as a medium by sitting in a dark room and going into a trance. The "spirits" who spoke through him told him that all his eight children were gifted mediums. They instructed him to build a special house made of logs, sixteen feet by twelve, to be used exclusively for spiritualist activities. There were large numbers of musical instruments – drums, triangles, tambourines, a banjo, an accordion, a harp, a guitar, and so on. The room was dimly lighted by sheets of wet paper smeared with phosphorus. When the mediums – usually Koons and his eighteen-year-old son Nahum – were seated at a small table – with the audience on benches – Koons would play the violin, and the spirits would soon join in, producing the effect of a full orchestra. Witnesses also speak of a heavenly choir joining in. The racket was impressive, and could be heard a mile away. A voice would then deliver a homily, using a speaking trumpet, which floated in the air. A spirit hand floated round the room, touching people and shaking their hands. People came from all over the county to witness these marvels, and the spirits impressed everyone by producing information about strangers that none of the audience could have known.

This was, in fact, one of the most convincing things about the "spirits"; they seemed to have access to all kinds of information. In Boston, the wife of a newspaper editor, Mrs W.R. Hayden, startled the wife of the English mathematician, Augustus de Morgan, by giving her detailed messages from dead friends about whom she could not possibly have known. The result was that Mrs de Morgan invited her to England, where she held seances under "test conditions" in the de Morgans' home. She was loudly ridiculed by the English newspapers, who were convinced that this latest American craze must be based on fraud and deception (which the British were too sensible to swallow), but she convinced most of those who actually saw her. And respectable members of the British middle classes who tried "table-turning" to while away the long evenings were amazed to discover that it actually worked. One journalist wrote a few years later: "In those days you were invited to 'Tea and Table Moving' as a new excitement, and made to revolve with the family like mad round articles of furniture." Even Queen Victoria and Prince Albert tried it at Osborne, and the table moved so convincingly that the Queen had no doubt whatever that no trickery was involved – she decided that the answer must lie in some form of electricity or magnetism.

The initial reaction of scientists to these strange occurrences was incredulity, which slowly turned to fury; they found it incomprehensible that so many people could be "taken in" by this explosion of old-fashioned superstition. It took another twenty years before even the scientists had to recognise that this was more than an outbreak of mass hysteria. Then a group of scientists and intellectuals came together to form the Society for Psychical Research, and it was not long before most of them had to acknowledge that, whatever the explanation, ghosts and poltergeists were undoubtedly more than a figment of the imagination. It was something of an embarrassment to most of them. So when, in 1900, Lombroso propounded his own version of the "unconscious mind" theory, everybody heaved a sigh of relief. It looked as if poltergeists could be explained scientifically after all.

The Dodlestone Poltergeist

But is this true? If poltergeists were really nothing but "spontaneous psychokinesis", you would expect them to appear only where there are emotionally disturbed adolescents in the house, and to be limited to homes where there is a certain amount of misery and tension. In fact, poltergeist disturbances are far more frequent than is generally realised, and occur in all kinds of homes – there is probably one going on within twenty miles of where you are now reading these words; moreover, in many of them, there is not a disturbed adolescent in sight.

In a book called *Vertical Plane*, a teacher named Ken Webster describes how, in 1984, he and his girlfriend Debbie (aged nineteen) moved into a nineteenth century cottage in the village of Dodlestone, near Chester. One morning, as a friend named Nic was helping them paint the kitchen, a set of footprints was seen moving up the wall. A few days later, a stack of cat food tins was found on the kitchen floor. A blast of wind from under the kitchen door – connected to the living room – blew newspapers around like autumn leaves. The poltergeist's favourite activity was stacking things in piles – plates, crockery, cans of food.

Ken Webster had borrowed an old and rather primitive computer at this time, and when he used it in the kitchen, obscure words began to appear on the floppy disk – words he knew he had not typed. When a friend said, "Why not reply?", he at first felt rather silly – but decided it was worth trying. To his astonishment, it worked. The Fox family poltergeist had communicated in a code of raps; this one seemed quite happy to work on the word processor. It identified itself as a man called Thomas Harden, and gave the date as 1546. Oddly enough, he seemed to think that the present date *was* 1546. In fact, it became clear – and we shall find this in case after case – that the ghost *did not know it was "dead"*. One of his first questions was "Why are you breaking into my house?" As absurd as it seems, he seemed to think that Ken Webster was the poltergeist who was haunting *him*.

It all sounded like some kind of a spoof, and at first Ken and Debbie were half-inclined to take this view. What convinced them otherwise was that Thomas Harden used some rather odd words: for example, he said he had been "reethed" at night, and used words like "torablise" and "stincioun". Webster went along to a friend who had studied Middle English at Oxford, and discovered that "reethed" meant "disturbed", "torablise" meant "troubled", and "stincioun" meant "immovable".

The "spirit" showed an unexpected skill with the computer. Unfortunately, when the Society for Psychical Research sent someone to investigate, it became suddenly shy. But one day when the investigators had gone for a walk, and Webster himself was outside, it swiftly typed a message on the disk. The odd thing was that it left it on a part of the disc that took Ken *eight and a half minutes* to access (since this was an ancient model). Yet it did it in less than a minute, an apparent impossibility.

Fortunately, 'Thomas Harden" proved to be a fairly good natured soul, telling Ken that he didn't mind him being in his house. He continued to make his presence felt, throwing bits of metal pipe around when Ken and Debbie had visitors – they were warm when picked up – and making the upper floor of the house shake as if in an earthquake. He also bent the handle of a copper pan at right angles, then straightened it a day or so later. Oddly enough, although the handle was rusted, and might be expected to show signs of having been bent, it looks totally undamaged, as if Harden had some Uri Geller-like power over metals.

Finally, as if becoming bored with the whole thing, Thomas Harden went away. Or perhaps he got someone to come and exorcise his house and get rid of his strange twentieth-century intruders. At all events, Ken and Debbie still live in the cottage, and now all is peaceful.

We can see that the Dodlestone case seems to contradict the "disturbed adolescent" theory. Ken was twenty-nine, and although Debbie was only nineteen, she was certainly not "disturbed". But both Ken and Debbie felt oddly depleted and lethargic during Thomas Harden's tenancy, as if he was using their energy to manifest himself.

Harry Price, one of the most famous of pre-war investigators, disagreed with the "spontaneous PK" theory; he stated his conviction that poltergeists are genuine spirits or ghosts, who need to use the energy of human beings to manifest themselves. His view is now highly unfashionable. But cases like Douglass Deen, the Turin poltergeist and the Dodlestone manifestations seem to suggest that he could have been right after all.

The Bell Witch

In general, the poltergeist is harmless. Some heavy object big enough to kill a human being may fly within an inch of someone's head – yet it always misses. There have, however, been a few rare cases in which someone has been seriously hurt, or even killed. The best known of these is known as the Bell Witch.

It began in 1817, in the farm in Tennessee where John Bell lived with his wife and nine children; one of these was a twelve year old girl, Betsy, and it gradually became clear that she was the "focus" of the disturbances. These began in the usual way, with scratching noises and knockings (poltergeist effects always work their way up from small effects to large ones). There were sounds like rats in the walls and an invisible dog clawing at the floor. Then stones began to be thrown, and the bedclothes were whipped off beds; if the children tried to hold them on, they were slapped by an invisible hand. Strange whistling sounds gradually developed into a poltergeist voice which sounded not unlike a parrot with asthma. Whenever the disturbances were at their height, Betsy became pale, and often fainted (or went into a trance).

Now the "voice" – or rather, voices – developed, some of them quoting extracts from sermons, others using foul language. The major entity identified itself as a witch called Old Kate Batts. She declared that she was a tormented spirit who would make John Bell suffer and kill him in the end. And this is precisely what the poltergeist proceeded to do. It made his tongue swell until it filled his mouth; it struck him violently in the face; it sent him into convulsions. During all this time the "witch" shrieked with demonic laughter. On 19 December 1820, the long-suffering man was found unconscious in his bed. The "witch" declared that she had poisoned him, and in the medicine cabinet they found a bottle of a dark-coloured liquid which, when tried on the cat, killed it instantly. Bell died the next day.

In the following year, there was a loud explosion in the kitchen chimney, and the witch's voice shrieked: "I am going and will be gone for seven years." And so she was. Seven years later, the scratching noises started again; but this time they soon stopped, and the "Bell witch" was gone forever.

Nandor Fodor, the Hungarian psychologist who believed that poltergeists are explosions of "Freudian" energy, is convinced that John Bell had made an incestuous attack on Betsy, and that this was the cause of all the trouble; Betsy's repressed hatred finally exploded into attacks of "recurrent spontaneous psychokinesis". Yet there is one obvious objection to this theory. "Talking poltergeists" take considerable pleasure in embarrassing their victims, especially in public. If John Bell *had* committed incest – or even tried to – with Betsy, it seems unlikely that Old Kate Batts would not have said so in the most specific and crude language.

On the whole, the notion that poltergeists are spirits who do not know they are dead (psychical investigators call them "earthbound spirits") seems to fit the facts as well as any.

ANCIENT GHOSTS

Every country in the ancient world believed in ghosts: Babylon, Egypt, Israel, Greece, Rome, China, Japan. The trouble with the ghost stories that survive is that they are so fantastic and absurd that no sensible person can take them seriously. The Babylonians believed in a female ghost called Lamashtu, who snatched babies from their mothers' breasts, Namtaru, a plague demon who ruled the underworld, and "Rabisu the Croucher", who lurked in dark corners and leapt out to terrify unwary passers-by. It does not take much common sense to see that these were the inventions of ignorant and superstitious people who were afraid of the dark and had only the crudest ideas about medicine. The ancient Greeks believed in a kind of vampire-cannibal called the lamia, a beautiful girl who would lure men with her physical charms, then eat them. The ancient Chinese believed in vampires with red eyes, razor sharp claws, and green hair, who enjoyed eating dead bodies, and could re-create a body from a skull or a few bones. The Japanese were firmly convinced – and to some extent still are – of the existence of "were-foxes", beautiful female spirits who transform themselves into foxes.

Any modern investigator would dismiss these stories as pure superstition – possibly based on some grain of truth that has been so embroidered and distorted that it is now impossible to guess what it was. On the other hand, there are some ghost stories dating from ancient times that sound perfectly plausible – exactly like hundreds of other similar stories collected by the Society for Psychical Research.

The Unhappy Ghost of Pausanias

The Spartan general Pausanias took part in the great war between the Greeks and the Persians, which took place in the fifth century BC, and defeated the Persians in the great naval battle of Plataea in 479. That made him famous, and he went on to other successes. But according to the historian Thucydides, success made him conceited and arrogant, and after capturing Byzantium, he behaved so tyrannically that the Spartans asked him to come home and explain himself. This made Pausanias so furious that he approached the Persian king Xerxes and offered to betray his own people. Eventually, proof of his treachery came from a messenger who had kept a letter to a Persian go-between. (The letter had a PS: "Kill the messenger so he can't talk", and the messenger, wondering why previous messengers had failed to return, opened it up.) Pausanias fled to the temple of Athena, and took shelter in a small building next door. His pursuers walled him in, and allowed him to starve to death.

The result of this, according to an ancient chronicle, was that the ghost of Pausanias began to haunt the temple, and made such terrifying noises that the priestess was forced to send for a magician, who finally persuaded the ghost to go away.

And why is this story any more believable than stories about Greek vampires who eat men alive, and Japanese ladies who turn themselves into foxes? Because it sounds as if the ghost of Pausanias behaved exactly like a poltergeist. There are many stories of men and women who died under tragic circumstances, and who are not aware that they are dead – these are known as "earthbound spirits". There are also many examples of such spirits being persuaded to go away by a medium – we shall later discuss the case of the Enfield haunting of 1977 in which this happened. So there is nothing at all improbable about the story of the ghost of Pausanias.

The Chain-rattling Ghost of Athens

At which point, let us look at what is probably the very first story about a haunted house. It is told in a letter by the Roman author Pliny the Younger (61–114 AD).

According to Pliny, a certain large house in Athens remained permanently untenanted because it was haunted by the ghost of a filthy old man who rattled chains and made moaning noises. A few sceptics who spent the night in the haunted house were terrified out of their wits. Finally, the place began to turn into a crumbling ruin.

At this point, the stoic philosopher Athenodorus came on a visit to Athens and saw the house, and decided that it looked an ideal place for solitary study. On discovering that the rent was absurdly low, he decided to move in at once. The owners of the house told him frankly why it had remained untenanted, but Athenodorus said he was not afraid of ghosts. All he needed from them, he said, was a table and a few chairs, a bed and a lamp.

That same day he moved in. But out of curiosity – and possibly a little nervousness – he decided to spend the first night awake.

For several hours, all was quiet, and Athenodorus became absorbed in his writing. Then he heard the sound of rattling chains, which approached closer and closer. When he looked up, he saw the apparition of a filthy old man, who was beckoniong to him with his finger. Athenodorus waved his hand dismissively and went back to his writing. The ghost began to moan and rattle his chains. Finally, Athenodurus gave in – it was impossible to concentrate – and followed the old man down the dusty corridor and out into the garden. There the ghost walked as far as a dense clump of shrubs and vanished.

Athenodrus made a pile of stones to mark the spot, and went back to his room, where he slept peacefully for the rest of the night.

The next day he told the Athenian authorities what he had seen. Magistrates returned with him to the spot in the garden, and workmen began to dig. Several feet down they struck something hard. Cautiously clearing away the earth, they found a skeleton wearing rusty chains and shackles. These were so ancient that they fell off when the skeleton was moved.

The bones were buried in a proper grave with appropriate ceremonies, and the haunting ceased forthwith.

True or false? Most readers will unhesitatingly say: false. Why? Because there are so many improbabilities – to begin with, a ghost that moans and rattles chains, and a philosopher who is so cool that he ignores the ghost and goes on writing.

But now look at the story more closely. The philosopher Athenodorus died in the year 7 AD, about half a century before the birth of Pliny the Younger, and only sixteen years before the birth of Pliny the Elder, the latter's uncle and guardian. And since first-century Rome was full of Greeks, and every educated Roman regarded Athens as a spiritual home, the story was almost certainly passed on to Pliny by someone who was alive at the time it happened. In other words, it was not ancient history, but a fairly recent happening.

Second, some ghosts *do* make noises, as we have seen in the case of the Hydesville poltergeist, which declared it was a pedlar who had been murdered by the previous tenant. Whether the noise made by the ghost of the old man was really a rattling of chains or the usual banging and crashing of the poltergeist is another matter. What we *can* see is that if the ghost of the old man behaved like the Hydesville poltergeist, somebody would very quickly embroider the story to add rattling chains.

As to the main absurdity in the story – the coolness of the philosopher – it is easy to see that this would also be added soon after the event, probably the very next day. Perhaps Athenodorus added it – or at least, told the magistrates that he had kept his head and refused to panic. And, men being what they are, this would soon be converted into the story of the philosopher coolly waving the ghost away. In fact, no one would do such a thing, least of all a philosopher.

So altogether, we can see that the story of the haunted house of Athens is perfectly credible, and almost certainly happened. One more detail adds to its credibility. If it had been invented, its author would almost certainly have invented a reason for the old man being chained and shackled – he had been kept prisoner in the house by a wicked relative who had claimed his fortune, and who had told everyone that the old man had gone on a business trip and failed to return. But there is no such embroidery; the story is left unfinished because, in fact, no one could recall anything about the old man . . .

GHOSTS OR TAPE RECORDINGS?

The Cotgrave Colliery Ghost

In the autumn of 1989, a nineteen-year-old miner, Gary Pine, was working alone in a remote part of Cotgrave Colliery in Nottinghamshire when the moving conveyor belt began to make odd groaning noises. Gary assumed that something had got stuck in the roller and went to look; as he did so, he saw a man standing a few yards away, dressed in a black helmet and dark overalls, and realised with a shock that *he* was groaning. Gary's natural assumption was that somebody was playing a joke and trying to scare him; then, as he watched, the man walked through a pile of sacks and disappeared down a dead end. At that point, Gary realised he had seen a ghost – the shock was so severe that he had to take time off from work to recover. For weeks after the sighting, miners would only go into the "haunted" area in pairs.

Their attitude is understandable but – in the view of students of psychical research – quite unnecessary. No ghost in all the recorded history of sightings has ever been known to harm anyone (as distinguished from poltergeists – who, as we have seen, can *very* occasionally be harmful). In fact, according to the most widely held theory, they would be incapable of harming anyone because they are no more "real" than old films.

The Hampton Court Ghost

Consider, for example, the case of the haunted Long Gallery at Hampton Court, where the ghost of a woman with long flowing hair is reported. It is identified as Lady Catherine Howard, the wife of Henry the Eighth. This is what Peter Underwood, president of the Ghost Club, has to say about her in his *Gazeteer of British Ghosts*.

Perhaps the most famous ghost at Hampton Court is that of Lady Catherine Howard who came here in 1540, a lovely girl of eighteen, as bride of the fat, lame and ageing monarch. After little more than a year ugly rumours began to circulate and it was said that she behaved little better than a common harlot, both before and after her marriage. The night before she was arrested, her first step to the block, she broke free from her captors and sped along the gallery in a vain effort to plead for her life with her husband. But Henry, piously hearing vespers in the chapel, ignored her entreaties and she was dragged away, still shrieking and sobbing for mercy. As you go down the Queen's Great Staircase you can see on the right-hand side the low-roofed and mysterious corridor containing the room from which Queen Catherine escaped and to which she was dragged back, her screams mingling weirdly with the singing in the chapel. Her ghost re-enacts the grisly event on the night of the anniversary, running shrieking through what has come to be known as the "Haunted Gallery". Those who have heard and seen her ghost include Mrs Cavendish Boyle and Lady Eastlake, together with many servants at the palace. All the witnesses say the figure has long, flowing hair but it usually disappears so quickly that no one has time to observe it closely.

A hundred years ago the "Haunted Gallery" was locked and used as a storage room for pictures but adjoining chambers were occupied as a grace and favour apartment by a titled lady who has recorded that once, in the dead of night, she was awakened by

an appalling and ear-piercing shriek which died
away into a pulsating silence. Not long afterwards
she had a friend staying with her who was awakened by a similar dreadful cry which seemed to
come from the "Haunted Gallery". After the Gallery
was opened to the public an artist sketching some
tapestry was startled to see a ringed hand repeatedly
appear in front of it but he hurriedly sketched the
hand and ring. The jewel was later identified as one
known to have been worn by Catherine Howard.

All this sounds like a typical piece of absurd "spooky" gossip.
But the psychical investigator Joan Forman had a personal
experience of the manifestation. She had walked down the
Long Gallery and stood by the chapel door when she experienced a sensation "of utter misery and extreme physical
coldness". And when she received a letter from Mrs F. Kerridge of Towcester, she was fascinated to learn that
Mrs Kerridge had experienced it even more strongly.
Mrs Kerridge described how, as she reached the door of the
royal pew, she encountered "such an agony of distress" that
she stepped backwards. She tried to walk through the door
three or four times, and each time had the same experience.
"One went through a cloud – invisible but tangible to one's
senses. Two clouds really: one agony was at the door of the
antechamber, one in the Pew itself – with nothing between."
What she was "picking up", Mrs Kerridge believed, was the
misery of Catherine Howard as she battered at the door, and
the misery of the King who was seated inside, tormented by
guilt and his still-powerful attachment to her.

That sounds plausible – Catherine *was* beheaded the following year, and it seems a reasonable assumption that her spirit
might relive the traumatic experience. But Henry himself lived
on for another six years. Why should his spirit haunt the spot?
The answer, Joan Forman reasoned, is that it wasn't Henry's
ghost that Mrs Kerridge felt in the royal pew; it was a kind of
recording of his misery, just as the sense of agony at the door of
the pew was a recording of Catherine's agony.

In fact, the "tape recording" theory of ghosts was first put
forward around 1900 by the eminent scientist Sir Oliver Lodge.
He noticed the interesting fact that many people do *not* see
ghosts that are perfectly visible to other people – in some cases,
two people can be in the same room, and only one of them sees

the ghost. Why should that be? Perhaps, thought Lodge, for the same reason that some people can dowse for underground water with a hazel twig while others are completely insensitive to water. In other words, one of them is picking up "vibrations" like a radio set and the other is insensitive to them. Which in turn suggests that a ghost is some kind of "broadcast" or recording, not a real spirit. Lodge theorised that powerful tragic emotions, like those associated with murder or suicide, may be absorbed by the walls of houses in which such events have occurred, and sensitive people can "pick them up", just as bloodhounds can scent things that no human being would notice.

The Ghost in Hunting Kit

The same theory occurred to a retired Cambridge don, T.C. Lethbridge, more than fifty years later. When Lethbridge was a student at Cambridge, he was certain he had seen a ghost in the rooms of a friend. He had been about to leave, late at night, when a man wearing a top hat stepped into the room. Assuming he was a college porter with a message, Lethbridge said goodnight; the man did not reply. The next day Lethbridge asked his friend what the porter had wanted. His friend looked at him in amazement, and insisted that no one had entered the room. It was only then that Lethbridge recalled that the "porter" had been dressed in a kind of hunting kit – except it was not red, but grey. He concluded that he had seen the ghost of some previous occupant of the rooms.

Half a century later, Tom Lethbridge was sitting on a Devon hillside, looking down on the garden of his next-door neighbour, an old lady who claimed to be a witch. In the garden he could see the "witch", and a few feet away, a tall old lady dressed in grey, old fashioned clothes. He was so curious about her that he later asked his neighbour about her visitor. The old lady looked puzzled; and replied that she had been alone at the time. Then, as Lethbridge described the woman, she said: "Ah, you've seen my ghost."

Lethbridge's first idea was that the tall woman had been

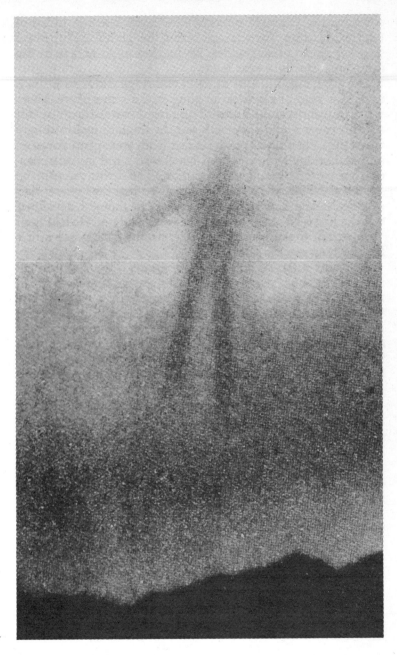

Harz Mountains, Germany – The Spectre of Brocken

some kind of "thought projection" – in other words a kind of television picture. Then, remembering that ghosts are supposed to reappear on anniversaries, he decided to go and sit at the same spot exactly a year later.

The ghost failed to appear. But Lethbridge and his wife both noticed a kind of electrical tingling in the atmosphere. There was a tiny underground stream running down the lane – under a drain cover – and they both felt the tingling most strongly when they stood on top of it. (In fact, both were good dowsers, and Lethbridge had even used his dowsing rod in his archaeological work, to locate volcanic dikes.) The stream ran past the "witch's" house, and Lethbridge realised that the "ghost" had also been standing directly over it. This, he thought, explained why he had seen the ghost and the witch had not. He had been "connected" to the spot by the underground stream, just as if it had been an electric wire.

And now it struck him that both ghosts – the "huntsman" and the tall lady – were probably "tape recordings" and that, for some reason, the picture had "recorded" in black and white instead of in colour, which is why both wore grey.

But what were they recorded *on*? Lethbridge concluded: the electrical field of water. His Cambridge friend's rooms had looked out on the river and were damp. Lethbridge came to believe that all "tape recorded" ghosts are seen in damp places.

At first the theory may sound far-fetched. But then, if you had told a contemporary of Shakespeare that one day sounds would be captured on tape, or on the wax bumps on a record, he would have thought you were insane. If we can accept the notion of sound (and video pictures) being captured on iron oxide tape, is it so unlikely that strong emotions could be captured on an electrical field of water?

So according to Lethbridge, the ghost of the coal miner at Cotgrave Colliery, and the spectre of Catherine Howard in the Long Gallery at Hampton Court (also close to a river) were "tape recordings". There can be no doubt that this theory fits many famous hauntings. Ghosts are often in "black and white", and they fade like a television being switched off.

The RAF Ghost

Yet it must be admitted that there are a few hauntings that are more difficult to explain. One of them was still going on in 1990 at RAF Linton-on-Ouse, Yorkshire, the main training school for jet pilots. The "spirit" – of an officer in flying kit – has been seen by many people in the control tower. Flight Lieutenant Mark Byrne was in there with twenty-one-year-old Brenda Jenkinson one night when both saw the figure – a man about six feet tall – walking across the room towards the approach room. It looked grey and shadowy, and vanished suddenly into thin air. The phantom has been seen by several other members of staff. But the RAF – which gave a press conference to talk about the ghost – believes it knows its identity. In 1959, Warrant Officer Walter Hodgson, from Hull, died at the age of thirty-eight, and his family got permission to put up a plaque in his memory outside the control tower. A few years ago, the plaque was moved inside. From then on, the "ghost" began appearing in the tower.

At the press conference, Squadron Leader Mike Brooks explained his own belief that the "spirit" of Walter Hodgson was upset about the removal of his plaque. But if he is right, then the ghost cannot be a "tape recording", which obviously couldn't care less whether a plaque were inside or out. Does this mean that Lethbridge was wrong about "tape recordings"? Not necessarily. Everyone who has studied hauntings knows that there seem to be be two types of ghost. One behaves like a tape recording or a television picture, fading away after a few moments; the other seems to respond to the presence of other people in the room, and often looks perfectly normal and solid, like a real person. Most of this latter type behave like people who do not know they are dead.

The Ghost in the Changing Room

The novelist Wilbur Wright had an experience with this kind of ghost. In 1941, when he was in the RAF at Hemswell, he returned from leave late one night and walked into a hangar to get some cigarettes from his locker. It was in darkness, and when he switched on the light, he saw a Leading Aircraftman named Stoker groping around in his locker. When Wright asked what he was doing, Stoker replied: "I can't find my bloody gloves." Wright located his cigarettes and thought no more of it.

The next morning at breakfast he asked if anything had happened in his absence, and was told that the bomber in which Stoker was a gunner had been shot down over Dortmund. "Stoker had a lucky escape then?" "Oh no – he went down with the rest. There was trouble before he took off – he couldn't find his flying gloves and kept moaning about it . . ."

Wright was so shocked that he reported sick and was unable to sleep for nights. It was only later that it struck him that the hangar had been in total darkness before he switched on the light and that he should have realised then that there was something odd about a man looking for his gloves in the dark.

It is, of course, possible that Stoker was a "tape recording". But Wilbur Wright's account makes it sound as if, like Warrant Officer Hodgson, Stoker was a real "spirit". In fact, cases of this sort – people who are "seen" by relatives or friends soon after death – make up the great majority of reported sightings of ghosts.

There are hundreds of similar recorded cases in the archives of the Society for Psychical Research. What follows is a small but typical selection.

Some Typical Cases

On 21 October 1893, Prince Victor Duleep Singh, a son of a maharajah, went to bed in a Berlin hotel, where he was staying together with Lord Carnarvon. Before switching off the light, he looked across the room at a framed picture that hung on the opposite wall. To his surprise, he saw the face of his father, looking at him with an intent expression. Thinking that the picture might resemble his father, he got out of bed to see; in fact, it showed a girl holding a rose and leaning on a balcony.

Prince Victor described the experience to Lord Carnarvon the next morning. Later the same day, he received a telegram announcing that his father had died of a stroke the previous day. The prince had seen his father's face at the time when the maharajah was lying unconscious after the stroke, a few hours before he died.

On the night of 16 October 1902, the wife of a railway guard woke up about 3 am for a drink of water. She was alone in bed, because her husband was on night duty, and the room was dimly lighted by a gas mantle. As she looked into the water, she saw a clear image of goods wagons smashing into one another, and observed which of them was most damaged. She was worried about her husband, in case he had had an accident. At nine the next morning he returned home, and she told him what she had seen. He told her that there *had* been an accident on the line that night, and it had happened just as she had seen.

The odd point about this case is that her husband had passed the scene of the accident twice: once at the time his wife had seen her "vision" in the glass of water, and again four hours later, when his train was on its way back. But when he passed it for the first time, it was dark and he could not see what was happening. At 7 am it was light, and he had then been able to see the scene clearly – as his wife had seen it in the water. Of course, her husband may have seen far more subconsciously than he was aware of seeing. But if this was telepathy, then he had managed to convey to his wife far more than he was aware of seeing.

The next case is perhaps one of the most famous ever recorded by the SPR. On 9 July 1904, the novelist Rider Haggard suffered such a bad nightmare that his wife shook him awake. In his dream, he had seen his daughter's black retriever dog, Bob, lying on its side among the undergrowth beside some water. Its head was at an unnatural angle, and it seemed to be trying to tell him that it was dying.

The next morning at breakfast Haggard told his daughter Angela about his dream. She was quite unworried because she had seen Bob the previous evening and he was safe and well. It was only later in the day that they learned that Bob was missing. Four days later, the dog's body was found floating in the nearby river. It had been struck by a train on the night Haggard had dreamed about it. He was able to work out the precise time the accident had taken place – a few hours before he had awakened from his nightmare.

On 19 March 1917, Mrs Dorothy Spearman was in her room in a hotel in Calcutta, feeding her baby son. Her little daughter was also in the room. She felt there was someone behind her, and looked round to see her half-brother, Eldred Bowyer-Bower, standing there; he was an officer in the Royal Flying Corps. He looked perfectly normal, and Mrs Spearman assumed he had been posted to India and come to see her. She told him that she would put the baby down, and then they could have a long talk. But when she had finished tucking in the baby, her half-brother had vanished. Her daughter did not appear to have seen anyone. She learned later that her half-brother had been shot down over the German lines at about the time she had seen him.

On 7 December 1918, Lieutenant J.J. Larkin, an RAF officer, was writing letters in the billet when he heard someone walking up the passage outside. Then the door opened, and his friend Lieutenant David McConnel shouted: "Hello boy!" Larkin turned and saw McConnel standing there, holding the doorknob in his hand. He said: "Hello, back already?" and McConnel replied "Yes, had a good trip". He had been ferrying a plane to a nearby aerodrome. Then McConnel closed the door with a bang and clattered off.

When Larkin learned several hours later that McConnel had crashed that afternoon, he assumed that it must have been after he had seen him. In fact, McConnel had been killed at roughly the same time that Larkin saw him at the door.

The next case has also become famous, and is regarded as one of the strongest pieces of evidence for survival after death. In June 1925, James Chaffin of Davie County, North Carolina, dreamed that his father stood by his bedside, wearing an old black overcoat, and told him: "You will find the will in my overcoat pocket." The father, James L. Chaffin, had died four years earlier, leaving his farm to his third son Marshall, and nothing to his wife or other three sons. The will had not been contested, since there seemed no reason to do so.

The next morning, James Chaffin hurried to his mother and asked about his father's old black overcoat; she told him it had been given to his brother John. He found the coat at John's house and examined it carefully. Sewn into the lining of the inside pocket – which his father had indicated in the dream – he found a roll of paper stating: "Read the 27th chapter of Genesis in my daddy's old Bible."

Taking a neighbour as witness, James Chaffin went back to

his mother's house, and unearthed the old Bible. In the 27th chapter of Genesis there was another will – made later than the one that left everything to Marshall – dividing the property between the wife and four sons. The first reaction of Marshall Chaffin was to contest the will, assuming it to be a forgery. But once he examined it, he had to admit that it was obviously genuine. Ten witnesses testified that it was in old Chaffin's handwriting. So the property was divided according to the wishes of the second will.

Like Marshall Chaffin's, the reader's first reaction is to suspect skulduggery. But the Canadian member of the SPR who heard of the case hired a lawyer to investigate it, and the genuineness of the will was established beyond all doubt. The significance of the 27th chapter of Genesis is that it contains the story of how Jacob deceived his blind father Isaac into granting him the inheritance of his brother Esau. This thought had apparently come to old Chaffin not long before his death, and he made the new will. But instead of having it properly witnessed, he inserted it in the Bible, no doubt expecting it to be found after his death – together with its implied criticism of his son Marshall. Unfortunately, the Bible was decrepit, and it may have been that the Chaffin family was simply not religiously inclined; so after four years, it seems the old farmer had to draw attention to his change of heart . . .

Mrs Crowe's *Night Side of Nature* has a whole chapter devoted to similar cases, in which important messages are delivered by dreams or apparitions. She tells, for example, of a butcher who dreamed that he was going to be attacked and murdered on his way to market by two men dressed in blue. He decided to go to market with a neighbour, and when he came to the place where the attack had taken place in his dream, saw the two men in blue waiting there . . . But all she tells us by way of detail is that the butcher's name was Bone and that he lived in Holytown. This can hardly be regarded as "confirmatory detail". The records of the SPR contain many equally melodramatic cases. But they took the trouble to get signed statements from all concerned, and the result is far more convincing. In a typical case of 1869, a couple, identified as "Mr and Mrs P", were lying in bed in a dimly lighted room when "Mrs P" saw a man dressed as a naval officer standing at the foot of the bed. Her husband was dozing, and she touched his shoulder and said: "Willie, who is this?" Her husband roared indignantly: "What on earth are you doing here, sir?" The naval officer said reproachfully, "Willie!", and, as

"Mr P" leapt out of bed, walked across the room, and disappeared into the wall. "Mrs P" said he looked like a solid human being, and that as he passed a lamp on his way across the room, he threw a shadow.

Realising that they had seen a "ghost", "Mrs P" began to wonder if it foreboded some disaster to her brother, who was in the navy. When she mentioned this to her husband, he said: "No, it was my father." "P"'s father had been dead for some years.

After this visitation, "Mr P" became seriously ill for several weeks. When he recovered, he told his wife that he had been in financial trouble for some time, and before seeing the apparition, he had decided to take the advice of a certain individual which, he now realised, would have ruined him and probably landed him in jail. He was convinced that the "ghost" had come to warn him not to do it.

Intrinsically, this case is no more convincing than that of Mr Bone of Holytown. But the SPR obtained signed depositions from "Mr and Mrs P", and from two friends to whom "Mrs P" had told the story immediately after it had happened. It is still possible to dismiss it as a dream or a "collective hallucination", or simply as a downright lie. But the signed statements make this seem at least unlikely.

An interesting point about the experience is "Mrs P"'s comment that the figure looked quite solid and normal – most "ghosts" do – and that it cast a shadow. This obviously suggests that it was made of some kind of solid substance, like the "materialisations" that appeared in the seance room.

In 1964 in a Detroit automobile factory a motor fitter suddenly lurched out of the path of a giant body press, which had been accidentally activated during the lunch hour. Shaken but uninjured, the man told his co-workers that he had been thrust out of the way by a tall black man with a scarred face, dressed in grease-stained denims. He had never seen the man before, but some of the older workers recognised the description. In 1944 a tall black man with a scarred left cheek had been decapitated while working in the same area of the shop floor. He had been pressing out parts for bombers. A subsequent inquiry had revealed that although the dead man was skilled at his job and totally familiar with his machine, long periods of overtime had made him sleepy and incautious.

A few weeks later, the mother died, "happy in the belief that she would rejoin her favourite daughter". Her son obviously took the view that the purpose of the apparition was to prepare her mother for her own death. This is another theme that runs fairly constantly through reports of apparitions and "death-bed visions" collected by the SPR. Sir William Barrett was later to devote a book to them, and its opening case is typical of the kind of thoroughness the SPR brought to its investigations.

Barrett's wife was an obstetric surgeon in the Maternity Hospital at Clapton in North London. A woman she calls "Mrs B" was in labour and suffering from heart failure. As Lady Barrett was holding her hands, she said: "It's getting dark." Her mother and husband were sent for. Then "Mrs B" looked at another part of the room and said: "Oh, lovely." "What is lovely?" "Lovely brightness – wonderful things." Then she exclaimed: "Why, it's father!" Her baby was brought in for her to see, and she asked: "Do you think I ought to stay for baby's sake?" She looked towards her "father", and said: "I can't stay." When her husband had arrived, she looked across the room and said: "Why, there's Vida!" Vida was her younger sister, who had died two weeks earlier. But the death had been kept from "Mrs B", so as not to upset her. She died soon after. Lady Barrett, the matron and the husband and mother all vouched that she seemed to remain conscious of the dead relatives up to the time of her death. With his usual thoroughness, Barrett obtained a letter verifying all this from the mother. It is the first of a number of cases cited by Barrett in which people on the point of death have "seen" relatives whom they did not know to be dead. Barrett points out that there is no known case of a dying person "seeing" someone who is still alive.

Sir Oliver Lodge, who was twice president of the SPR, was himself to supply one of the most convincing cases of "communication with the dead"; it is recorded in his book *Raymond*. On 8 August 1915, Sir Oliver Lodge received a message from a Boston medium, Leonore Piper, containing an obscure reference to a poem by the Roman poet Horace, about a tree being struck by lightning. Lodge interpreted this as a warning of some disaster. The message purported to come from Frederick Myers, who had been dead for fourteen years. A week later, Lodge heard that his youngest son Raymond had been killed in the Ypres campaign.

After this, a number of mediums relayed messages that

purported to come from Raymond, but Lodge remained un-convinced – most of them were of the "Having a lovely time" variety. But in the following month, Lodge's wife was taken by a friend to a seance by a remarkable medium, Mrs Osborne Leonard. Neither the medium nor Lady Lodge knew one another by sight, and they were not introduced. Neverthe-less, Mrs Leonard announced that she had a message from "Raymond", who stated that he had met many of his father's friends since death; asked to name one of them, Raymond replied "Myers".

Another "message" from Raymond was relayed to Lady Lodge via a male medium called Vout Peters; in it, "Raymond" spoke about a photograph showing himself in a group of people, and referred to a walking stick. The Lodges knew nothing about such a photograph. Two months later, the mother of one of Raymond's fellow officers wrote to say that she had a group photograph including Raymond, and offered to send a copy. Before this arrived, Lodge himself visited Mrs Leonard, and when her "control" "Feda" announced Raymond's presence, he took the opportunity to ask about the photograph. Raymond explained that it had been taken outdoors, and mentioned that someone had wanted to lean on him. When the photograph arrived a few days later, it showed a group of officers outside a billet. Raymond, sitting in the front row, has a cane resting on his leg, and the officer sitting behind him is using Raymond's shoulder as an arm rest.

Lodge's book gives many more examples of evidence of Raymond's "survival"; but, as he points out, this one is particularly convincing because it involves two mediums, both of whom spoke of the photograph before Lodge knew of its existence – thus ruling out any possibility of telepathy.

To conclude this chapter, here is a final example of a type of phenomenon so beloved by Mrs Crowe and other early writers on the "supernatural": the full-scale haunting.

In February 1932, the grandchildren of a chimney-sweep named Samuel Bull refused to go to sleep, insisting that there was someone outside the door of the cottage. (They were sleeping in a downstairs room, recovering from influenza.) Their mother, Mary Edwards, looked outside the door, but there was no one there. Soon afterwards, she and the children saw the figure of Samuel Bull – who had been dead since the previous June – walk across the room, up the stairs, and through the door of the room in which he had died. (This was closed.) They all screamed. This was the first of many appearances of the dead man at his cottage in Oxford Street, Ramsbury, Wiltshire.

The "ghost" was apparently aware of the presence of his family, for he twice placed his hand on the brow of his invalid wife Jane, and once spoke her name. Samuel Bull – who had died of cancer – looked quite solid, and could be seen so clearly that the children noticed the whiteness of his knuckles, which seemed to be protruding through the skin. They also noticed that the expression on his face was sad. After the first appearance, the family no longer felt alarmed – the children seemed "awed" rather than frightened. They assumed that the ghost was looking sad because of the miserable conditions they were living in – the cottage was damp and some rooms were unfit for habitation. On the last two occasions on which he appeared, Samuel Bull no longer looked sad, and Mrs Edwards assumed that this was because the family was to be re-housed in a council house.

The family was already on the move when the two investigators from the SPR arrived, but the local vicar had already interviewed the family and recorded their accounts of what took place. The investigators were understandably upset that they had not been told about the case earlier, but their conversations with witnesses, and the evidence of the vicar, left them in no doubt that the haunting was genuine.

On the whole, then, the evidence seems to suggest that while *some* ghosts are "tape recordings", others behave exactly like real people who do not realise they are dead.

chapter four

THE GHOSTLY "DOUBLE"

Soon after the Society for Psychical Research was formed in 1882, a three man team set about collecting accounts of what they called "phantasms of the living" – that is, people who are seen miles away from the place where they actually are at the time. Phantasms of the Living is a huge book – more than two thousand pages – and it contains hundred of accounts of strange sightings. Many of these do not involve the dead. For example, a Mrs Sarah Hall was sitting at her dinner table with her husband and another couple when all of them saw another Sarah Hall standing by the sideboard. Mr Hall said with astonishment: "Why, it's Sarah!" – at which the "phantom" Mrs Hall vanished. As far as is known, she never reappeared, and the story has no sequel. The phantom was of the type that psychical researchers call "doppelgangers" or doubles, and they seem to be – as Lethbridge suggested – some kind of "mental projection" or television picture.

The Doppelganger of a Girl in a Hurry

Doppelgangers are surprisingly common: in fact, I can personally vouch for a recent case.

During the time of the Napoleonic Wars, a German named Wesermann had been trying experimentally to send his apparition to various people. One night he decided to try instead to transmit the image of someone else. A lady who had died five years before was to appear to a Lieutenant N. in a dream at about 10:30 pm.

As it happened, Lieutenant N. had not yet gone to bed but was visiting a friend, Lieutenant S.. The two were chatting, and N. was just about to go to his room when the kitchen door opened and, in the words of S., "a lady entered, very pale . . . about five feet four inches in height, strong and broad in figure, dressed in white, but with a large black kerchief which reached to below the waist. She . . . greeted me with the hand three times in complimentary fashion, turned round to the left toward Herr N., and waved her hand to him three times; after which the figure quietly, and again without any creaking of the door, went out."

The case is interesting because the behaviour of the apparition was suited to the circumstances, which were not foreseen by the agent. He had expected N. to be asleep. The apparition behaved like a real person in greeting both men.

A few days ago, my part-time secretary, Pam, had a strange experience. Something had gone wrong with her car, making her late for her job at the local training college. When she finally arrived, a colleague asked her casually why she had gone away again. Puzzled, she asked him what he meant. "Well, you arrived half an hour ago, and now you're coming back again . . ." When she assured him that she had only just arrived, he looked at her as if she was joking.

Three more colleagues had also seen her, and assured her that she *had* arrived earlier, looking pale and distracted, and carrying the same folder that she always carried. One of them had spoken to her, but she had hurried past without answering.

Oddly enough, they had all seen her wearing her usual black coat. But on that day she was, in fact, wearing another coat for the first time.

Pam admitted that, as she was anxiously trying to start her car, she was thinking about the office. In some strange way, her anxiety had projected an image of herself which was seen by three colleagues at work. It was the Germans who gave such "projections" the name "doppelgangers" or "doubles", and

At the age of five Hoffman was a victim of a cholera epidemic in Germany. He was diagnosed as dead, and duly buried. The night after his burial his mother woke up to find the child's double standing at her bedside. He told her he was not dead, and begged her to recover his physical body from the grave. He said they would find him lying on his side with his right hand under his right cheek. The apparition returned on three successive nights. Though the father was reluctant to apply to have the grave opened on the dubious evidence of what was probably an anxiety dream, his wife finally prevailed upon him to do so. When the grave was opened the child was found in exactly the position his projected double had told his mother that he was in. Doctors were able to resuscitate him. The physical body had been in a state of suspended animation, just clinging to life, while the astral body went in search of help.

This young boy later became a well-known medium, the Reverend Max Hoffman.

there are hundreds of well-authenticated examples in the literature of psychical research.

The Doppelganger of John Cowper Powys

One of the most impressive concerns two novelists: John Cowper Powys and the American Theodore Dreiser.

One day in 1929, Powys had spent the early evening with Dreiser in his New York apartment. As he left he remarked: "You'll be seeing me later this evening." Dreiser thought he was joking, for Powys lived fifty miles away. But a few hours later, Dreiser looked across the room, and saw Powys standing inside the door. He jumped to his feet saying: "John! Come on in and tell me how you did it." But as Dreiser advanced towards him, Powys vanished.

Dreiser rushed to the telephone and rang Powys's number in upper New York State. Powys answered. And when Dreiser told him that he had just appeared in the room, Powys merely said: "I told you I'd see you later." Next time Dreiser saw him, he firmly refused to discuss the incident.

It is highly probable that the reason he refused to discuss it is that he had no idea how he did it. When he left Dreiser, he probably felt in a certain "mood", and was sure that he could do it. But he couldn't explain exactly how.

The Beard Case

One of the most famous incidents of "projection" occurred in the 1890s, and was studied by the Society for Psychical Research in London. A student named Beard was engaged to a girl called Miss Verity. One night, after reading a book on the unknown powers of the mind, Beard decided that he would

Harry Price, Psychic Researcher

try to "appear" to his fiancée. He sat in his armchair and tried to "will" himself to appear in her room. Suddenly, he felt as though he could not move his limbs. He "woke up" some time later sitting in the armchair. The next day, Miss Verity told him that she had seen him the previous evening in her bedroom. In fact, her younger sister had also awakened and seen him. A moment later, Beard had vanished.

Beard repeated this strange performance on a second occasion, when he not only "appeared" to Miss Verity's elder sister (who was staying in the house), but even touched her hair and took hold of her hand – apparently his own hand felt quite solid.

Beard made the interesting comment that he made a peculiar mental effort "which I cannot find words to describe . . . but which I can now at times set in motion at will." Obviously, Powys had also learned to make this mental effort. And my secretary somehow did it accidentally because she was worried about being late for work.

Perhaps one of the most interesting comments made by Beard is that when he was suddenly unable to move his body, he thought that this was because he had fallen into a "hypnotic trance".

Hypnosis seems to be able to release powers of which we are normally unaware. One student of the mystery said that it is as if we possess *two selves*, one of them the "normal everyday self", and the other a *deeper* self of which we are unaware – like the part of the iceberg below water. When a person is hypnotised, the "everyday self" goes to sleep, but the deeper self remains awake, and can do the most remarkable things. So it is quite possible that the "peculiar effort" made by Beard may have been a kind of self-hypnosis, and that he was then able to appear to his fiancée.

The Case of Emilie Sagée

In one famous case of a "doppelganger", a French school-teacher named Emilie Sagée kept losing her job because her "double" would appear and frighten the pupils. One day, when Emilie was in the school garden, she looked through a window and noticed that the schoolmistress had left the class for a moment, and that the girls were being noisy. Suddenly, the girls were amazed to see Emilie sitting in the schoolteacher's chair – while they could see the real Emilie standing out in the garden. One girl was brave enough to approach the "double" and touch her; she said that Emilie's flesh felt like muslin.

Poor Emilie was obviously incapable of controlling these "projections", and after losing job after job, she finally committed suicide.

One obvious explanation of the mystery is that it is some kind of telepathy. Most of us have had the experience of knowing what someone else is thinking, or conveying out thoughts to others. Perhaps we also have some mysterious power of conveying our *images* to others, like a television picture. Yet this seems to be contradicted by the fact that Beard was able to touch the hair of Miss Verity's sister, and hold her hand. Does the "telepathy" include an illusion of touch? Or is it possible that our "strange unknown powers" include the power to send our solid bodies elsewhere in the world?

Phantom Hitchhikers

In the 1970s, stories about phantom hitchhikers began to appear in newspapers all over the world. The story told by motorcycle policeman Mahmood Ali of Peshawar, India, is typical. He gave a lift to a pretty girl dressed in white. Before they reached the place to which she had asked to be taken, she had vanished from the back of his motorbike. Investigation revealed that the girl had been involved in a fatal accident at the spot where he had picked her up; he identified the photograph of the victim as that of his hitchhiker, "eyelash for eyelash".

Michael Goss is a respected psychical researcher who, in the early 1980s, was asked to look into the evidence for such cases, and his book *The Evidence for Phantom Hitch-Hikers* has a deeply sceptical tone; he points out the basic similarities in many of the stories, and argues that this is a typical example of the modern "folk legend". Yet he is forced to admit that a number of cases cannot be dismissed in this way. One concerns a twenty-six-year-old carpet-fitter named Roy Fulton, whom Goss himself interviewed on tape. On a Friday night in 1979, after playing in a darts match at Leighton Buzzard, Fulton drove back towards Dunstable through Stanbridge. In a dark lane he saw a man thumbing a lift, and pulled up; the man opened the door and got in. When Fulton asked where he was going, the man merely pointed ahead. Five minutes later, Fulton started to offer the man a cigarette, and found that he had vanished. He braked hard and looked in the back – there was no one there. So he drove fast to a pub in Dunstable, had a large scotch, then reported the incident to local Police Inspector Rowland.

Goss originally suspected that Fulton may have invented the story for the sake of notoriety, but a check with the local police, and with the publican who had served the badly shaken man the whisky, convinced him that it was genuine.

Are phantom hitchhikers ghosts, or simply doppelgangers projecting their "images" to another place? The obvious objection to this theory is that you would not expect a doppelganger – which seems to be some kind of mental image – to open a door. But then, when drivers offer a lift, *they themselves* usually lean over and open the door, often in order to ask the hitchhiker where he wants to go to. So where phantom hitchhikers are concerned, it is worth keeping an open mind.

VAMPIRES

Do vampires exist? The question sounds absurd – surely no sane person could take the idea seriously?

But then, the study of psychical research makes it clear that there are more things in heaven and earth than the average sceptic would be willing to grant. In the opening chapter of this book we considered the case of the "haunted boy of Washington", which seems to show fairly conclusively that some kind of "possession" can happen. We have also seen that the "Exorcist" case started with poltergeist effects, which seems to suggest that the "spirit" that claimed to be a demon was just an ordinary poltergeist telling lies. Poltergeists are like juvenile delinquents; they *love* causing trouble and confusion. And, as we shall see in this chapter, some stories about "vampires" make them sound very much like poltergeists operating according to slightly different rules.

It should be explained that the common idea of vampires, derived from films with Bela Lugosi and Christopher Lee, is almost completely mythical. *That* all started as recently as 1816, when Lord Byron was driven out of England by outraged public opinion, and began a lifetime of exile on the continent. He took with him his personal physician, a rather self-assertive young man named John Polidori. Most people have now heard the famous story of how Byron and Polidori, together with the poet Shelley and Shelley's wife Mary, stayed together in a villa overlooking Lake Geneva, and began talking about ghost stories. The result was that Mary Shelley wrote *Frankenstein*, and Byron began a tale called "The Vampyre". He wrote only a few pages, then gave up. But the competitive Polidori pushed on to complete his own tale "The Vampyre". This was about a sinister nobleman named Lord Ruthven (pronounced "Rivven") who charms his way into the affections of young ladies, only to leave their bodies drained of blood. It appeared in 1819 and caused a sensation – dozens of imitations immediately appeared, and it was turned into a popular opera by Marschner. Polidori's subsequent career was not a success, and he committed suicide two years later, at the age of twenty-five.

In 1849, a hack writer named James Rymer produced a vast serial novel called *Varney the Vampire*, which went on to become a bestseller. This improved on Polidori's formula, with its tall, cadaverous figure with eyes like "polished tin" and hideous fangs. This in turn was improved on by Bram Stoker in his masterpiece *Dracula* (1897) which has become the source of all modern stories about vampires. His Count Dracula was based on a real historical character, a king of Wallachia called Vlad the Impaler – the name derives from his unpleasant habit of impaling people on pointed stakes. Vlad was a sadist, and his death in battle in 1477 caused widespread relief.

But how did the legend of the blood-drinking vampire begin? The story first reached Europe soon after 1718, when Charles VI, Emperor of Austria, drove the Turks out of Eastern Europe, which they had dominated for the past four centuries, marching in and out of Transylvania, Wallachia and Hungary and even conquering Constantinople (1453). Don John of Austria defeated them at the great sea battle of Lepanto (1571), but it was their failure to capture Vienna after a siege in 1683 that caused the break-up of the Ottoman empire. During the earlier stages of this war between Europe and Turkey, Vlad the Impaler struck blow after blow against the Turks, until they killed and beheaded him in 1477. When the Turks were finally defeated, two hundred and forty-one years later, their conquerors were intrigued to hear strange stories about dead people who could cause death to the living. Such stories had been known to travellers in Greece down the centuries. There the vampire was known as the *vrykolakas*, and on 1 January 1701, a French botanist named Pitton de Tornefort had visited the island of Mykonos and been present at a gruesome scene of dissection. An unnamed peasant, of sullen and quarrelsome disposition, was murdered in the fields by persons unknown. Two days after burial, his ghost was reported to be wandering around at night, overturning furniture and "playing a thousand roguish tricks". Ten days after his burial, a mass was said to "drive out the demon" that was believed to be in the corpse, after which the body was disinterred, and the local butcher given the task of tearing out the heart. His knowledge of anatomy seemed to be defective, and he tore open the stomach and rummaged around in the intestines, causing such a vile stench that incense had to be burned. In the smoke-filled church, people began shouting "Vrykolakas" and alleging that some of the smoke poured out of the corpse itself.

Even after the heart had been burned on the seashore, the ghost continued to cause havoc, until the villagers finally burnt the corpse on a pyre.

De Tornefort takes a highly superior attitude about all this, convinced that it is simply mass hysteria. "I have never viewed anything so pitiable as the state of this island. Everyone's head was turned; the wisest people were stricken like the others." Although the year is only 1701, de Tornefort's attitude is that of a typical French rationalist of the eighteenth century.

Attitudes began to change after 1718, as the highly circumstantial accounts of vampires began to reach Western Europe – just how precise and circumstantial is illustrated by a report, known as *Visum et Repertum* (Seen and Discovered), which dates from 1732, and was witnessed by no less than five Austrian officers.

The vampire epidemic of 1730–35 seems to have started at the village of Meduegna, near Belgrade, through a young soldier named Arnold Paole, who returned from active service in Greece in 1727. He told the girl to whom he was betrothed that he had been attacked at night by a vampire in Greece, but had located its grave and destroyed it – which should have removed the curse. However, he died, and then was seen around the village after dark. Ten weeks later, after several people claimed to have seen him, or dreamed about him and felt strangely weak the morning after, his body was disinterred by two army surgeons and the sexton and his assistants. The body still had blood on its mouth. It was covered with garlic, which is supposed to be a protection against vampires, and a stake had been driven through the heart.

Six years later, there was an epidemic of vampirism at

Meduegna, and this time several distinguished doctors investigated; the medical report was signed on 7 January 1732, by Johannes Flickinger, Isaac Seidel, Johann Baumgartner and the lieutenant colonel and sub-lieutenant from Belgrade. They testified to examining fourteen corpses, all listed and described, including a girl of ten. Only two of the fourteen – mother and baby – were found in a normal state of decomposition, all the others being "unmistakably in the vampire condition". It is not recorded what was done, but presumably the corpses were burned or impaled.

There are even earlier accounts of the walking dead. The French expert on vampires, Jean Marigny, remarks:

"Well before the eighteenth century, the epoch when the word 'vampire' first appeared, people believed in Europe that the dead were able to rise from their graves to suck the blood of the living. The oldest chronicles in Latin mention manifestations of this type, and their authors, instead of employing the word 'vampire' (which did not yet exist) utilised a term just as explicit, the word 'sanguisugae' (Latin for leech, bloodsucker). The oldest of these chronicles date from the twelfth and thirteenth centuries, and, contrary to what one might expect, are not set in remote parts of Europe, but in England and Scotland."

He goes on to cite four cases described by the twelfth century chronicler William of Newburgh, author of *Historia Rerum Anglicarum*. These are too long to cite here (although they can be found in full in Montague Summers' *The Vampire in Europe*). The first, "Of the extraordinary happening when a dead man wandered abroad out of his grave", describes a case in Buckinghamshire, recounted to the chronicler by the local archdeacon. It describes how a man returned from the grave the night after his burial, and attacked his wife. When this happened again the following night, the wife asked various neighbours to spend the night with her, and their shouts drove the ghost away. Then the ghost began to create a general disturbance in the town, attacking animals and alarming people. That he *was* a ghost, and not a physical body, is proved by the comment that some people could see him while others could not (although they "perceptibly felt his horrible presence"). The archdeacon consulted the bishop, Hugh of Lincoln, who – on the advice of various learned men – suggested that the body should be dug up and burnt to ashes. Then he decided this would be "undesirable", and instead wrote out a

Devotees place flowers and a cross on the tomb of Sarah Ellen Roberts, the legendary 'vampire woman' of Blackburn, Northern England, she was buried in Peru in 1949 when her husband was unable to do so in England.

charter of absolution. When the tomb was opened, the body proved to be "uncorrupt", just as on the day it was buried. The absolution was placed on his chest and the grave closed again; after that, the ghost ceased to wander abroad.

One of William of Newburgh's other accounts sounds slightly more like the traditional vampire in that the ghost – of a wealthy man who had died at Berwick on Tweed – had an odour of decomposition which affected the air and caused plague. The body was exhumed (it is not recorded whether it was undecayed) and burned.

Stories like these have the touches of absurdity that might be expected from an ecclesiastical chronicler of that period; yet their similarity to the other chronicles cited suggests that they have some common basis. The same applies to another work, *De Nugis Curialium* by Walter Map (1193), also cited at length by Summers.

All these cases took place long before Western Europe heard tales of vampires from former Turkish dominions, and in only one of them is there is any suggestion of blood-drinking. But in most ways, the revenants behave very much like Peter Plogojowitz and the vampires of Medvegia. They haunt the living, climb into bed with people when they are asleep, and then throttle them, leaving them drained of energy. And when the bodies are disinterred, they are found to be undecayed. It seems very clear that there is no basic difference between the vampires of 1732 and the revenants of the twelfth century. And when we look more closely into the accounts of the vampires, we discover that they are energy-suckers rather than blood suckers. Peter Plogojowitz has fresh blood on his mouth, but it is merely a matter of hearsay that he sucked the blood of his victims – the account mentions only throttling. Otherwise, these earlier revenants behave very much like the paranormal phenomenon known as the poltergeist.

Two sixteenth century cases also bear a close resemblance to the later vampire legends. One is known as known as the Shoemaker of Breslau, and is to be found in Henry More's *Antidote Against Atheism* of 1653. This describes how, on 21 September 1591, a well-to-do shoemaker of Breslau, in Silesia – one account gives his name as Weinrichius – cut his throat with a knife, and soon after died from the wound. Since suicide was regarded as a mortal sin, his wife tried to conceal it, and announced that her husband had died of a stroke. An old woman was taken into the secret, and she washed the body and

bound up the throat so skilfully that the wound was invisible.
A priest who came to comfort the widow was taken to view the
corpse, and noticed nothing suspicious. The shoemaker was
buried on the following day, 22 September 1591.

Perhaps because of this unseemly haste, and the refusal of the
wife to allow neighbours to view the body, a rumour sprang up
that the shoemaker had committed suicide. After this, his ghost
began to be seen in the town. Soon it was climbing into bed
with people and squeezing them so hard that it left the marks of
its fingers on their flesh. This finally became such a nuisance
that in the year following the burial, on 18 April 1592, the
council ordered the grave to be opened. The body was complete and undamaged by decay, but "blown up like a drum".
On his feet the skin had peeled away, and another had grown,
"much purer and stronger than the first". He had a "mole like a
rose" on his big toe – which was interpreted as a witch's mark –
and there was no smell of decay, except in the shroud itself.
Even the wound in the throat was undecayed. The corpse was
laid under a gallows, but the ghost continued to appear. By 7
May, it had grown "much fuller of flesh". Finally, the council
ordered that the corpse should be beheaded and dismembered.
When the body was opened up, the heart was found to be "as
good as that of a freshly slaughtered calf". Finally, the body
was burnt on a huge bonfire of wood and pitch, and the ashes
thrown into the river. After this, the ghost ceased to appear.

Paul Barber, citing the case in *Vampires, Burial and Death*,
agrees that "much in this story is implausible", but points out
that so many details – notably the description of the body – are
so precise as to leave no doubt "that we are dealing with real
events".

But what are these "real events"? Before we comment further,
let us consider another well known case from the same year,
1592 (which is, of course, more than a century earlier than the
famous vampire outbreak in eastern Europe). This is also to be
found in More, and concerns an alderman of Pentsch (or
Pentach) in Silesia named Johannes Cuntze (whose name More
latinises to Cuntius). On his way to dinner with the mayor,
Cuntze tried to examine a loose shoe of a mettlesome horse, and
received a kick, presumably on the head. The blow seems to
have unsettled his reason; he complained that he was a great
sinner, and that his body was burning. He also refused to see a
priest. This gave rise to all kinds of rumours about him,
including that he had made a pact with the devil.

As Cuntze was dying, with his son beside the bed, the casement opened and a black cat jumped into the room and leapt on to Cuntze's face, scratching him badly; he died soon after. At his funeral on 8 February 1592, "a great tempest arose", which continued to rage as he was buried beside the altar of the local church.

Before he was buried, there were stories that his ghost had appeared and attempted to rape a woman. After the burial, the ghost began to behave like a mischievous hobgoblin, throwing things about, opening doors, and causing banging noises so that "the whole house shaked again" – on the morning after these events, animal footprints or hoofmarks were found outside in the snow. His widow had the maid sleeping in her bed; the ghost of Cuntze appeared and demanded to be allowed to take his proper place beside his wife. And the parson of the parish (who is mentioned as the chronicler of these events) dreamed that Cuntze was "squeezing" him, and woke up feeling utterly exhausted. The spirit was also able to cause a nauseating stench to fill the room.

The conclusion is much as in the story of the shoemaker of Breslau. Cuntze was finally disinterred on 20 July, five months after his burial, and was found to be undecayed, and when a vein in the leg was opened, the blood that ran out was "as fresh as the living". After having been transported to the bonfire with some difficulty – his body had apparently become as heavy as a stone – he was dismembered (the blood was found to be quite fresh) and burnt to ashes.

So the earlier vampire stories are very clearly about poltergeists, not blood-drinkers. And the Greek and Eastern European cases bear a strong resemblance to stories of "demonic possession".

If we can once concede the possibility of "psychic invasion", as well as the possibility of "spirits", then the notion of vampires suddenly seems less absurd. In *The Magus of Strovolos*, an American academic, Kyriacos C. Markides, has described his friendship with a modern Cypriot mystic and "magus", Spyros Sathi, known as Daskalos, who lives in Nicosia. Daskalos takes the actual reality of spirits for granted. It also becomes clear that Daskalos takes "possession" for granted, and Markides tells a number of stories, in some of which he was personally involved.

There are, Daskalos claims, three kinds of possession: by ill-disposed human spirits, by demonic entities, and by elementals (the latter being human thoughts and desires which have taken on a life of their own). And he goes on to describe a case of spirit possession of the first type. Daskalos was approached by the parents of a girl who claimed that she was being haunted by the spirit of her dead fiancé. Although they had lived together, she had refused to allow him to possess her until they were married. He died of tuberculosis, haunted by unfulfilled cravings. "Each night before she would go to bed he would semi-hypnotise her and induce her to keep the window of her room open. He would then enter inside a bat and would come to her. The bat would wedge itself on her neck and draw blood and etheric (energy)." The local priest told Daskalos how to deal with it. He must wait in the next room, and when he heard the bat entering, should go in and quickly shut the window; then, since the bat would attack him, he must stun it with a broom. Then he must wrap the bat in a towel and burn it in a brazier (stove). Daskalos did this, and as the bat burned, the girl screamed and groaned. Then she calmed down and asked: "Why were you trying to burn me?" The "haunting" ceased thereafter.

Daskalos told another story that has elements of vampirism. On a journey in southern Greece he had encountered another girl who was being haunted by a former lover. A shepherd who had been in love with her had died in a motor accident. Five years later, when looking for some goats, the girl saw the shepherd – whose name was Loizo – and he followed her, finally making her feel very sleepy so she felt obliged to sit down. He then "hypnotised" her, and caused her to experience intense sexual pleasure. When she reported the incident, she was medically examined and found to be a virgin. But three days later the shepherd came to her bed and made love to her. Medical examination revealed she was no longer a virgin. Daskalos noticed two reddish spots on her neck. "He kisses me there, but his kisses are strange. They are like sucking, and I like them."

Daskalos claimed that, two days later, he saw the shepherd coming into the house and greeted him. Loizo explained that he had wanted the girl for many years, and had never had sexual relations with a woman – only with animals like donkeys and goats. Now he was possessing her, he had no intention of letting her go. He refused to believe it when Daskalos told him he was dead. Daskalos warned him that if he persisted in possessing the girl, he would remain "in a narcotized state like a vampire". His arguments finally convinced the shepherd, who agreed to go away.

The doctor who examined the girl believed that she had torn the hymen with her own fingers; Daskalos seems to accept this, but believes that Loizo made her do this.

These two cases, taken in conjunction with the others we have considered, offer some interesting clues about the nature of the vampire. According to Daskalos, the "earthbound spirit" of the dead fiancé was able to enter an ordinary bat and then to suck her blood. This was an expression of his sexual desire, his desire to possess her. There had been many cases in the history of sex crime of so-called "vampirism". In the early 1870s, an Italian youth named Vincent Verzeni murdered three women and attempted to strangle several more. Verzeni was possessed by a powerful desire to throttle women (and even birds and animals). After throttling a fourteen-year-old girl named Johanna Motta, he disembowelled her and drank her blood. Verzeni admitted that it gave him keen pleasure to sniff women's clothing, and "it satisfied me to seize women by the neck and suck their blood". So it is easy to imagine that the earth-bound fiancé mentioned by Daskalos should enjoy drinking the girl's blood. But we can also see that his desire to "possess" her was also satisfied in another way – by somehow controlling her imagination. As the bat was burning, the girl cried out, "Why are you trying to burn me?"

Again, in the case of Loizo, we can see that the shepherd had entered the girl's body and taken possession of her imagination, enough to cause her to tear her own hymen with her fingers. This implies – as we would expect – that the lovemaking was not on the physical level, since Loizo possessed no body.

All this has an interesting implication. The act of lovemaking seems to involve a paradox, since it is an attempt at interpenetration by two bodies, an attempt which is doomed to failure by their separateness. Plato expresses the paradox in an amusing myth. Human beings were originally spherical beings who possessed the characteristics of both sexes. Because their sheer vitality made them a challenge to the gods, Zeus decided that they had to be enfeebled. So he sliced them all down the centre, "as you and I might slice an apple", and turned their faces back to front. And now the separated parts spent their lives in a desperate search for their other half, and they ceased to constitute a challenge to the gods.

It is also clear that, in its crudest form, the male sexual urge is basically a desire for "possession", and that the act of physical penetration is an act of aggression. (Most writers on *Dracula* have noted that it is basically a rape fantasy.) As a man holds a woman in his arms, he experiences a desire to absorb her, to blend with her, and the actual penetration is only a token union. So we might say that a "vampire" like Loizo is able to achieve what every lover dreams about: a possession that involves total interpenetration.

The notion of vampirism that begins to emerge from all this is simple and (provided one can accept the notion of "earthbound spirits") plausible. Daskalos told Markides that those who commit suicide may become trapped in the "etheric of the gross material world", unable to move to the higher psychic planes. A suicide dies in "a state of despair and confusion", and "may vibrate too close to the material world, which will not allow him to find rest". He becomes a "hungry ghost", wandering in and out of the minds of human beings like a man wandering through a deserted city. Yet he is incapable of influencing his involuntary host, or of making his presence felt, unless the host also happens to be on the same "wavelength" and to share the same desires.

Vampirism, then, involves the notion that "earthbound spirits" are attracted by the vitality of the human aura, and may do their best to share it. A book called *Hungry Ghosts*, by the journalist Joe Fisher, makes this point with great force. Fisher had written a book about reincarnation, in the course of which he had become convinced of its reality. One day, after being interviewed on radio in Toronto (where he lives), he received a phone call from a woman who explained that she had accidentally become a mouthpiece of "discarnate entities". She was being hypnotised in an attempt to cure her of leukaemia, and various "spirit guides" had begun speaking through her mouth. (Myers points out that a "spirit" can only enter a body when the usual "tenant" is absent, a point to note when considering that early accounts of vampires involve attack *during sleep*.)

The first time Fisher went to her house, a "spirit" named Russell spoke through her mouth with a reassuring Yorkshire accent, and told him that he had a female "guide", a Greek girl named Filipa, who had been his mistress in a previous existence three centuries earlier. This struck Fisher as plausible, since he had always felt some affinity with Greece. He began attending the seances regularly, and devoting some time every morning to relaxing and trying to contact Filipa. Eventually he succeeded; buzzing noises in his ears would be followed by a feeling of bliss and communication. Filipa was a sensual little creature who liked to be hugged, and Fisher implies that, in some sense, they became lovers. It broke up his current love affair; his live-in girlfriend felt she was no match for a ghost.

Other people at the seances were told about their "guides" or guardian angels. One guide was an ex-RAF pilot named Ernest Scott, another an amusing cockney named Harry Maddox. Fisher's disillusionment began when, on a trip back to England, he decided to try and verify Ernest Scott's war stories – with no doubt whatever that they would prove genuine. The airfield was certainly genuine; so was the squadron Ernest claimed to have belonged to; the descriptions of wartime raids were accurate; so were the descriptions of the squadron's moves from airfield to airfield. But there had been no Ernest Scott in the squadron, and a long search in the Public Record Office failed to throw up his name. Fisher went back to Canada in a bitter mood and accused Ernest of lying. Ernest strenuously denied it. Anyway, he said, he was due to reincarnate in another body, so had to leave . . . The "guide" Russell later told Fisher that Ernest had been reborn in England, and gave the name of the parents and date of birth. Oddly enough, when Fisher checked on this it proved to be accurate. He even contacted the parents, who were intrigued, but decided they had no wish to get more deeply involved.

With Russell's approval, Fisher tried to track down the farm in Yorkshire where Russell claimed he had lived in the nineteenth century. Here again, many of the facts Russell had given about the Harrogate area proved to be accurate; but again, the crucial facts were simply wrong. It seemed that Russell was also a liar. And so, upon investigation, was the lovable World War One veteran Harry Maddox. His accounts of World War One battles were accurate; but Harry did not exist.

Finally, Fisher took his search to Greece. In spite of his disillusion with the other guides, he had no doubt whatever that Filipa was genuine. She possessed, he states early in the book, "more love, compassion and perspicacity than I had ever known". The problem was that all his attempts to locate Theros – a village near the Turkish border – in atlases or gazetteers had failed. Yet that could be because it had been destroyed by the Turks in the past three centuries. But a town called Alexandroupoli, which Filipa had mentioned, still existed. After a long and frustrating search for the remains of Theros, Fisher went to Alexandroupoli, a city that he assumed had been founded by Alexander the Great. But a brochure there disillusioned him. Alexandroupoli was a mere two centuries old; it had not even existed at the time when he and Filipa were supposed to have been lovers . . . Like the others, Filipa was a liar and a deceiver.

In a chapter called "Siren Call of the Hungry Ghosts", Fisher tries to analyse what has happened to him. And the answer seems simple. He had been involved with what Kardec called "earthbound spirits", spirits who either do not realise they are dead, or have such a craving to remain on earth that they remain attached to it. These earthbound spirits or, in Tibetan Buddhist phraseology, *pretas* or "hungry ghosts", are individuals whose minds, at the point of physical death, have been incapable of disentangling from desire. Thus enslaved, the personality becomes trapped on the lower planes even as it retains, for a while, its memory and individuality. Hence the term "lost soul", a residual entity that is no more than an astral corpse-in-waiting. It has condemned itself to perish; it has chosen a "second death". He quotes Lt-Col. Arthur E. Powell, in a book called *The Astral Body*: "Such spooks are conscienceless, devoid of good impulses, tending towards disintegration, and consequently can work for evil only, whether we regard them as prolonging their vitality by vampirising at seances, or polluting the medium and sitters with astral connections of an altogether undesirable kind."

He also cites the modern American expert on "out of the body" journeys, Robert Monroe: "Monroe tells of encountering a zone next to the Earth plane populated by the 'dead' who couldn't or wouldn't realise they were no longer physical beings . . . The beings he perceived kept trying to be physical, to do and be what they had been, to continue physical one way or another. Bewildered, some spent all of their activity in attempting to communicate with friends and loved ones still in bodies or with anyone else who might come along."

The conclusion would seem to be that the vampire cannot be dismissed as a myth. But the reality of vampirism has very little in common with the Dracula legend. There is no fundamental difference between vampires and poltergeists – except that, fortunately, vampire phenomena seem to be far more infrequent.

PHANTOMS

The Phantom Drummer of Tedworth

The amazing story of the Phantom Drummer has become the most famous of British hauntings. It was recorded by an Oxford clergyman named Joseph Glanvil, who was so intrigued by the case that he went to investigate it personally.

The story begins in a day in mid-March 1661, when a magistrate named John Mompesson was visiting the small town of Ludgershall in East Wiltshire. While he was talking to the town bailiff, he heard in the street outside the noisy racket of a drum that almost drowned their conversation. When he asked what it was, the bailiff explained that it was an idle beggar who claimed he had a pass, signed by two eminent magistrates, giving him permission to attract attention to himself with his drum. He had also tried to use his pass to claim public assistance. The bailiff added that he thought the pass was a forgery, but had no proof. Since Mompesson knew most of his fellow magistrates, he sent the constable to bring the drummer to explain himself.

The beggar, a middle-aged man named William Drury, seemed perfectly confident of himself – in fact, rather arrogant. When Mompesson asked him by whose authority he plied his trade in Wiltshire, the man answered that he had good authority, and produced a pass signed by Sir William Cawly and Colonel Ayliff. A single glance told Mompesson that it was a clumsy forgery – he happened to know the handwriting of both men – and he ordered the beggar to hand over his drum. Then he told the constable to take him off to jail and bring him before the next sitting of the local bench.

Drury quickly lost his arrogance, and admitted that the pass was a forgery. And as the constable started to lead him away, he begged for the return of his drum. But Mompesson, who seems to have been an officious sort of man who enjoyed using his authority, told him that he could have the drum back if the local magistrate discharged him. And despite Drury's pleas, he refused to let him have the drum.

In fact, the local constable seems to have allowed Drury to escape. But the drum stayed behind.

A few weeks later, the bailiff of Ludgershall sent the drum to Mompesson's house in Tedworth. Mompesson was just on his way to London. When he came back he found the house in uproar. For three nights, there had been violent knockings and raps all over the house – both inside and out. That night, when the banging started, Mompesson leapt out of bed with a pistol and rushed to the room from which the sound was coming. It moved to another room. He tried to locate it, but it now seemed to be coming from outside. When he got back into bed, he was able to distinguish drumbeats among the rapping noises.

For the next two months, it was impossible to get to sleep until the middle of the night; the racket went on for at least two hours every night. It stopped briefly when Mrs Mompesson was in labour, and was silent for three weeks – an indication that the spirit was mischievous rather than malicious. Then the disturbances started up again, this time centring around Mompesson's children. The drumbeats would sound from around their beds, and the beds were often lifted up into the air. When the children were moved up into a loft, the drummer followed them. The servants even began to get used to it: one manservant saw a board move, and asked it to hand it to him; the board floated up to his hand, and a joking tug of war ensued for twenty minutes or so, until the master ordered them to stop. When the minister came to pray by the children, the spirit showed its disrespect by being noisier than usual, and leaving behind a disgusting sulphurous smell – presumably to imply it came from Hell. Scratching noises sounded like huge rats.

Things got worse. During the next two years lights were seen, doors slammed, unseen skirts rustled, and a Bible was burnt. The creature purred like a cat, panted like a dog, and made the coins in a man's pocket turn black. One day, Mompesson went into the stable and found his horse lying on its back with its hind hoof jammed into its mouth; it had to be pried out with a lever. The "spirit" attacked the local blacksmith with a pair of pincers, snatched a sword from a guest, and grabbed a stick from a servant woman who was trying to bar its path. The Reverend Joseph Glanvil – who wrote about the case – came to investigate, and heard the strange noises from around the children's beds. When he went down to his horse, he found it sweating with terror, and the horse died soon afterwards.

The phantom drummer seems to have developed a voice; one morning, there was a bright light in the children's room and a voice kept shouting: "A witch, a witch!" – at least a hundred times, according to Glanvil. Mompesson woke up one night to find himself looking at a vague shape with two great staring eyes, which slowly vanished. It also developed such unpleasant habits as emptying ashes and chamberpots into the children's beds.

In 1663, William Drury was arrested at Gloucester for stealing a pig. While he was in Gloucester jail, a Wiltshire man came to see him, and Drury asked what was happening in Wiltshire. When the man said "Nothing" Drury said: "What, haven't you heard about the drumming in the house at Tedworth?" The man admitted that he had, whereupon Drury declared: "I have plagued him, and he shall never be quiet until he has made me satisfaction for taking away my drum." This, according to Glanvil, led to his being tried for a witch at Salisbury and sentenced to transportation. As soon as Drury was out of the country, peace descended on the Mompesson household. But the drummer somehow managed to escape and return to England – whereupon the disturbances began all over again. Mr Mompesson seems to have asked – by means of raps – whether Drury was responsible, and it replied in the affirmative.

How the disturbances ended is not clear – presumably they faded away, like most poltergeists. Certainly they had ceased by the time Glanvil published his account twenty years later.

Why was the clergyman Joseph Glanvil so interested in the case? Because he was in the process of writing a book called

Saducismus Triumphatus, in which he argued that witchcraft was not a mere superstition, but a genuine "occult" power. By the time his book appeared in 1681, that view was by no means popular. In England, the "witchcraft craze" had come to a sudden end in 1646 with the discrediting and death of the evil "witchfinder general" Matthew Hopkins, who was responsible for more than a hundred executions, and now most educated people dismissed the belief in witchcraft with contempt.

What is a Poltergeist?

Yet Glanvil may not have been entirely wrong. One modern investigator, Guy Lyon Playfair, spent many years in Brazil, and became interested in psychical research. When he heard of a poltergeist that was causing disturbances in a house in Saõ Paolo, he offered his services to the Brazilian Society for Psychical Research (called the IBPP) to look into it. There

---

The Toby Jug restaurant in the Yorkshire village of Haworth can boast of a spectre of some distinction: poet and novelist Emily Brontë, a native of the village. According to the restaurant's owner Keith Ackroyd, Emily Brontë's ghost appears every year on December 19, the day she died. He once described for a reporter his first glimpse of the phantom in 1966 after taking over the Toby Jug. "I turned and saw this figure smiling and giggling," he said. "She walked across the room to where the stairs used to be and started to climb up to the bedroom." She was small, wore a crinoline and carried a wicker basket.

The ghost of such a famous writer might be considered an asset, but Ackroyd wanted to have it exorcized. He planned to sell the restaurant and feared that a spectre might be regarded as a liability. A curate from Leeds agreed to perform the rite, but was prevented by the Rector of Haworth who wasn't sure it was necessary. Perhaps, like many churchmen today, he takes a wary view of highly publicized exorcisms.

had been loud bangs and crashes, unexplained fires, and bedding soaked in water. Playfair witnessed many of these things, and was convinced of their genuineness. But what intrigued him was the signs that magic – or witchcraft – was somehow involved. A photograph with thread stitched through it had been found. The disturbances seemed to revolve around a girl called Nora, who had married the son of the house.

The Brazilian Society for Psychical Research tried having the house exorcised by a team of mediums. This worked for a few weeks, then the poltergeist came back. The Society then used its heaviest gun – a *candomble* specialist, or witch doctor. He performed various weird rites, and to Playfair's astonishment, the poltergeist left for good.

What surprised him was the assumption that seemed to be accepted by most Brazilians that a poltergeist can be conjured up by a witch doctor, and told to go and wreck somebody's house. But he soon realised that this view was not restricted to the uneducated masses. It was also accepted by Dr Hernani Andrade, the founder of the Brazilian Society for Psychical Research. And after a while, Playfair himself came to accept it.

Now witchcraft, which most of us regard as superstitious nonsense, is based on a belief in spirits. And this, as we have seen, is by no means an unreasonable belief. What strikes us as so strange is the idea that spirits can be persuaded to go and wreak havoc in someone's home. Yet the case of the Phantom Drummer of Tedworth suggests that William Drury possessed this power, and that he sent the "drummer" to make the life of the Mompesson family unbearable.

Was Drury a "medium"? Did he believe that the power lay in his drum, and was that why he pleaded so hard to have it returned? Unfortunately, we shall never know. Glanvil says that Drury had been a soldier under Cromwell, and had learnt magic "from some gallant books he had had of a wizard". Whatever the truth, Drury certainly obtained his revenge, for Mompesson became something of a laughing stock. Suspected of fabricating the whole story, "he suffered by it in his name, his estate and all his affairs".

The Cock Lane Ghost

The same sad fate was to overtake another household almost exactly one century later.

In November 1759, a woman named Fanny Lynes, who was lodging in the house of Richard Parsons, Clerk of St Sepulchre's Church in Smithfield, London, asked ten-year-old Elizabeth Parsons to sleep with her while her common law husband was away on business. All went well for a few nights; then the two were kept awake by scratching and rapping noises behind the wainscot. Now any modern investigator of poltergeists knows that, for some odd reason, many cases begin in this way. However, Richard Parsons had no reason to suspect that his house was haunted, and he told Fanny that it was probably the cobbler next door.

Soon afterwards, Fanny became ill with smallpox; she was six months pregnant, and her "husband" was understandably anxious. He and Fanny were unmarried only because she was his deceased wife's sister. William Kent had married Elizabeth Lynes two years earlier, but she had died in childbirth; now it looked rather as if the story were repeating itself. He moved Fanny into a house nearby, where, on 2 February 1760, she died of smallpox.

Meanwhile, the rappings in Richard Parsons' house were continuing; Parsons actually called in a carpenter to take down the wainscotting, but nothing was found. Meanwhile, the knockings got louder, and the story of the "haunted house" spread throughout the neighbourhood. They seemed to be associated with Elizabeth; they came from behind her bed, and when they were about to begin, she would begin to tremble and shiver – like Hetty Wesley in the Epworth case. Later that year, Elizabeth began to suffer from convulsions.

Like so many victims of poltergeist phenomena, Richard Parsons decided to call in a friend, the Reverend John Moore, assistant preacher at St Sepulchre's. And the Reverend Moore proceeded to communicate with the "spirit", asking it to answer his questions in the usual manner – one rap for yes, two for no. (They added a scratching noise to indicate it was displeased.)

By this means the spirit told its upsetting story. It was, it declared, the ghost of Fanny Lynes, returned from the dead to denounce her late "husband", William Kent, for killing her by poison. He had, it seemed, administered red arsenic in her "purl": a mixture of herbs and beer.

Richard Parsons was not entirely displeased to hear this story, for he was nursing a grudge against his late tenant. William Kent was a fairly rich man, having been a successful innkeeper in Norfolk, and he had lent Parsons twenty pounds, on the understanding that Parsons should repay it at a pound a month. Parsons, who seems to have been a drunkard, had failed to repay anything, possibly because he had discovered that Kent and Fanny were not married, and hoped to blackmail Kent into forgetting the loan. Kent had put the matter into the hands of his attorney.

If Parsons had been less anxious to believe the worst of his ex-tenant, he might have suspected the ghost of untruthfulness. To begin with, the knocking had begun while Fanny Lynes was still alive. And a publican named Franzen swore that he had seen a spirit in white one evening in December 1759, when Fanny had just moved from the Cock Lane house. Parsons apparently found it easier to believe that the earlier knockings had been caused by Kent's first wife Elizabeth – who was presumably also trying to denounce him for murder.

Throughout 1761, the house in Cock Lane acquired an increasing reputation for its ghosts, and the tale about Kent's supposed murders gained wide currency in the area. Kent himself heard nothing about it until January 1762, when he saw an item in the *Public Ledger* about a man who had brought a young lady from Norfolk and poisoned her in London. A few days later, another item about the Cock Lane ghost and its revelations led Kent to go along to see the Reverend John Moore. Moore, a respectable and well-liked man, could only advise Kent to attend a seance in Elizabeth's bedroom, and see for himself. Kent did this, taking with him the doctor and apothecary who had attended Fanny in her last illness. The small bedroom was crowded, and Elizabeth and her younger sister lay side by side in the bed. At first the "ghost" declined to manifest itself; but when the room had been emptied, Moore succeeded in persuading it, and they all trooped back. Now Kent listened with something like panic as he heard Moore asking the spirit if it was Kent's wife – one knock – if it had been murdered by him – one knock – and if anyone else was concerned in the murder plot – two knocks. Kent shouted indignantly, "Thou art a lying spirit!"

Now, suddenly, the ghost was famous all over London, and

Cock Lane was crowded with carriages. In February, a clergyman named Aldrich persuaded Parsons to allow his daughter to come to his vicarage in Clerkenwell to be tested. An investigating committee, including the famous Dr Johnson, was present. Inevitably, the ghost declined to manifest itself. Nor would the ghost rap on the coffin of Fanny Lynes in the vault of the church. Dr Johnson concluded it was a fraud. And this was the opinion of most of London.

On the day following this fiasco, Elizabeth was staying at the house of a comb-maker in Cow Lane when the bell of Newgate Prison began to toll – a sign that someone was to be hanged. The comb-maker asked the ghost whether someone was about to be hanged and whether it was a man or woman; the ghost answered both questions correctly. Later that day, a loose curtain began to spin on its rod – the only physical manifestation in the case.

The following day, as Elizabeth lay asleep, her father heard whispering noises; he carried a candle over to her bed, but she seemed to be asleep. The whispering continued, although the child's lips were plainly closed. In fact, the poltergeist seemed to be increasing in strength. Two nights later, the noises were so violent that their host asked them to leave. (Presumably she was sleeping away from home to avoid crowds.) Elizabeth and her father moved to the house of a Mr Missiter, near Covent Garden, and the manifestations continued, even when a maid lay in bed beside Elizabeth and held her hands and feet.

By now, the unfortunate Kent was determined to prove his innocence through the law; so the burden of proof now lay on Parsons and his daughter. Elizabeth was told that unless the ghost made itself heard that night, her father and mother would be thrown into prison. Naturally, she made sure something happened. The servants peered through a crack in the door, and saw her take a piece of board and hide it in the bed. Later, when there were people in the room, the knocking noises sounded from the bed. In fact, the listeners noticed that the knocks were coming from the bed and not, as usual, from around the room. The bed was searched and the board found. And the next day, the newspapers published the story of the "fraud".

On 25 February 1762, there appeared a pamphlet entitled: *The Mystery Revealed; Containing a Series of Transactions and Authentic Testimonials respecting the supposed Cock Lane Ghost, which have been concealed from the Public* – the author was probably Johnson's friend Oliver Goldsmith. A satirical play

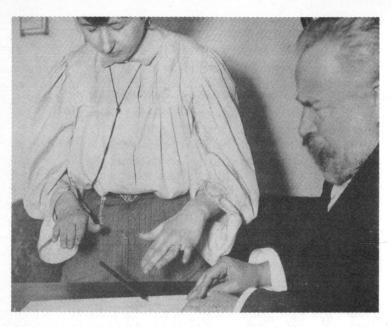

Unexplained talents, levitation by Stanislawa Tomczyk

called *The Drummer or the Haunted House* was presented at Covent Garden. And William Kent began legal proceedings against Richard Parsons. In July 1762, Mr and Mrs Parsons, and a woman called Mary Frazer – who had often acted as "questioner" to the ghost – appeared before magistrates in the Guildhall. Parsons was charged with trying to take away the life of William Kent by charging him with murder. The judges remained unconvinced by the evidence of neighbours who had heard raps resounding from all over the room, and who were certain that Elizabeth could not have made them. And finally, Parsons was sentenced to two years in prison, and to stand three times in the pillory; his wife was sentenced to one year, and Mary Frazer to six months. The Reverend Moore and one of his associates had to pay out £588 in damages to Kent. There was universal sympathy for Parsons, and when he stood in the pillory, the mob took up a collection for him – an unusual gesture for a period when malefactors were often badly injured in the pillory. (Later in the year a man convicted of sodomy was stoned to death in the same pillory.)

For more than two centuries, the Cock Lane ghost became a synonym for an imposture. When Andrew Lang wrote about it in 1894, he began his chapter: "If one phantom is more discredited than another, it is the Cock Lane ghost." Yet for anyone studying the case today, this view seems absurd. Nothing could be more obvious than that the Cock Lane ghost was a poltergeist like the hundreds of others that have been recorded down the ages. Unfortunately, it is now too late for us to discover certain essential facts that might help to explain it. For example, what kind of a girl *was* Elizabeth Parsons? She was rather younger than most poltergeist-children, but she may well have been sexually mature for her age. If her father was something of a drunkard and a spendthrift – as the records indicate – then it seems fairly certain that the Parsons household was not a happy one. The father of Christine Beauchamp – Morton Prince's famous case of multiple personality – was a similar type of person, and his daughter had severe psychological problems as a consequence. We know that Christine Beauchamp became fixated on her father's closest friend William Jones, and transferred to him all her adoration. It is conceivable that Elizabeth Parsons felt the same about William Kent. In which case, sleeping in his bed while he was away must have aroused morbid emotions – especially if she was aware that Kent and Fanny were "living in sin". The convulsions that began a year after the disturbances certainly suggest she was passing through a period of emotional upheaval. But since we know so little about Elizabeth, all these things must remain a matter for speculation.

Only one thing seems fairly certain: that the spirit itself was neither that of Elizabeth Kent nor of Fanny Lynes; it was the usual mischievous poltergeist, bent on creating as much havoc and confusion as possible. It seems to confirm G.K. Chesterton's remark that the only definite thing that can be said about such spirits is that they tell lies.

The Seeress of Prevorst

The Phantom Drummer of Tedworth and the Cock Lane Ghost demonstrate that the "Age of Reason" did not take kindly to ghosts. Dr Johnson, who was sure the Cock Lane ghost was a fraud, died in 1784, and his death signalled the end of an era. Not long after that, everything changed. Romanticism had arrived, and quite suddenly, everybody wanted to read about ghosts and haunted castles and vampires.

But all that, of course, was mere fiction. That is why, in 1828, a German book about real ghosts became an instant bestseller. It was called *The Seeress of Prevorst*, and was written by a rich and eccentric doctor called Justinus Kerner, who practised in Weinberg, near Heilbronn. In 1826, he was consulted by the relatives of a "haunted" woman called Friederike Hauffe, who was dying of a wasting disease. She had lost all her teeth and looked like a walking skeleton.

It seemed that marriage was responsible for her sad condition. Ever since childhood she had fallen into trances, seen visions, and conversed with invisible spirits. She could also accurately predict the future. When she was nineteen, she had married a cousin, and gone into depression; at twenty, her first child was born, and she began to develop hysterical symptoms. Every evening, she fell into a trance in which she saw spirits of the dead.

Kerner was at first inclined to be sceptical about her visions and spirits – he put them down to hysteria. Yet he found Friederike Hauffe a fascinating case for study. She claimed to be able to see into the human body, and certainly had a remarkably precise knowledge of the nervous system. She could read with her stomach – Kerner tested her by making her lie down with her eyes closed, and laid documents on her bare midriff; she read them perfectly. She could make geometrical drawings at great speed, even in the dark, and could draw perfect circles that looked as if they had been drawn by compasses. She claimed that her spirit often left her body and hovered above it.

Kerner tried ordinary medicines on her, but they had no effect. Friederike told him that if he placed her in a "magnetic trance" the spirits would instruct him on how to treat her, but he was reluctant to accept this advice. Eventually, he decided that he might as well try the effects of mesmerism.

Friederike reacted well to "magnetism", passing easily into a trance. But Kerner remained sceptical about the things she said in this condition. Then, one day, a remarkable experience changed his mind. Friederike declared that she was being haunted by an unpleasant man with a squint. From her description, Kerner recognised him as a man who had died a few years earlier. It seemed, according to Friederike, that the man was suffering from a guilty conscience. He had been involved in embezzlement and, after his death, another man had been blamed. Now he wanted to clear the man's name, for the sake of his widow. This could be done by means of a certain document, which would be found in a chest. The spirit "showed" Friederike the room where the document was to be found, and a man who was working there. Her description was so good that Kerner was able to identify him as a certain Judge Heyd. In her "vision", Friederike had seen Judge Heyd sitting in a certain place in this room, and the chest containing the document on the table. The document was apparently not in its proper numerical order, which is why it had not been found.

When Kerner told him about his patient's vision, Judge Heyd was astounded; he *had* been sitting in the position described on that particular day (Christmas Day), and the chest, contrary to regulations, had been left open on the table. When they searched, the document turned up where Friederike had said it would. The widow of the man who had been wrongly accused was able to obtain redress.

From now on, Kerner believed in Friederike's supernatural powers, and took whatever she said seriously. She told him that we are surrounded by spirits all the time, and that she was able to see them. These spirits often try to attract our attention in various ways: knocking, movement of objects, throwing of sand. And by way of convincing him, Friederike persuaded one of the spirits to make rapping noises, to make gravel and ash fall from the air, and to make a stool float up into the air. Kerner watched with amazement as the stool rose gently, then floated down again.

Friederike provided him with further proof of the accuracy of her visions when she succeeded in putting an end to a haunting. Kerner heard about a house where the ghost of an old man was frightening the inhabitants. He brought one of them, a woman, along to see Friederike; the seeress went into a trance and explained that the ghost was that of a man called Bellon, who was an "earthbound spirit" as a result of defrauding two orphans. Kerner made enquiries, but no one had ever heard of a man called Bellon. But since the ghost claimed that he had been Burgomeister, it seemed probable that some record existed. He claimed he had been Burgomeister in the year 1700, and had died at the age of seventy-nine. Armed with this information,

Kerner asked the present mayor to check the legal documents; they soon found that in the year 1700, a man called Bellon *had* been Burgomeister and director of the local orphanage. He had died in 1740 at the age of seventy-nine. After "confessing", the spirit took its departure.

While Friederike was in Kerner's house, there were constant poltergeist phenomena: knocks and raps, noises like the rattling of chains, gravel thrown through the window, and a knitting needle that flew through the air and landed in a glass of water. When Friederike was visited by a spirit one night her sister heard her say, "Open it yourself", then saw a book on the table open itself. A poltergeist tugged her boots off her feet as she lay on the bed, and threw a lampshade across the room. In the Kerners' bedroom, a table was thrown across the room. The poltergeist threw a stool at a maidservant who went into Friederike's room while she lay asleep. It extinguished a night-light and made a candle glow.

Friederike also produced what would later be called "spirit teachings", an amazingly complex system of philosophy in which man is described as consisting of body, soul and spirit, and of being surrounded by a nerve aura which carries on the vital processes. She spoke about various cycles in human existence – life cycles (or circles) and sun cycles, corresponding to various spiritual conditions. She also described a remarkable universal language from ancient times, said to be "the language of the inner life". (A mystical sect was founded to expound those doctrines after her death.)

All these mediumistic activities made Friederike more and more feeble, and she died in 1829 at the age of twenty-eight. Kerner's book *The Seeress of Prevorst* (the name of the Swabian village where she was born) created a sensation.

In the second half of the nineteenth century, as the scientific reaction against spiritualism increased, *The Seeress of Prevorst* ceased to be taken seriously by those engaged in psychical research, and by the twentieth century it had been virtually forgotten. Writing about it in his *Modern Spiritualism* (1902), the sceptical Frank Podmore – who believed that all poltergeists are due to naughty children – dismissed most of the evidence as second-hand, while another eminent researcher, E.J. Dingwall (writing in *Abnormal Hypnotic Phenomena*) seems to feel that Kerner was stupid to take her claims seriously, and that if he had remained sceptical and treated her simply as a case of hysteria, she would have lived longer. But reading Kerner's own account, it is difficult to see how he would have remained sceptical without being downright dishonest or blind; on one occasion, he saw a cloudy figure hovering in front of her, and although it had vanished when he came back with a lamp, Friederike continued to stare at the spot as though listening to it.

In fact, we can see that the case of the seeress of Prevorst is a thoroughly typical case of poltergeist phenomena caused by a medium. In detail after detail, it sounds like any number of other cases of "haunting". If anyone killed Friederike Hauffe, it was the spirits themselves, who must have been using her energy to manifest themselves. No doubt the poltergeist phenomena were unspectacular because Friederike was weak from the moment Kerner set eyes on her. (In a case cited by the novelist William de Morgan, a maidservant who was able to cause rapping noises gradually lost her powers as she became weaker from tuberculosis.)

In another of his books, Kerner describes another remarkable case with some of the characteristics of poltergeist haunting. He was asked to treat a "possessed" peasant girl in Orlach, near Stuttgart. For some reason which is not clear, she was persecuted by "spirits" from the age of twenty, and there were the usual bangs and crashes, movements of furniture, and even outbreaks of fire. Then, after five months of this, she saw two ghosts, one of a nun dressed in white, the other of a monk dressed in black. The nun asserted that she had been smuggled into the monastery disguised as a cook, and had had two children by the black monk, both of whom he had killed at birth. He also murdered three monks during the four-year period she was with him; and, when he suspected she was about to betray him, he killed her too. The black monk also spoke to the possessed girl, saying that he was the son of a nobleman from nearby Geislingen, and that as the Superior at the monastery of Orlach, he had seduced a number of nuns and killed the children they bore. He also confessed to killing monks. The bodies, he said, he threw into a hole in a wall.

The white nun told the girl that her sufferings would cease only if her parents agreed to their cottage's demolition. By this time they were so desperate that they agreed. On 5 March 1833 the house was finally demolished. Most of the walls were made of mud, but one corner was constructed of limestone, obviously part of a far older building. When this was pulled down, they found underneath it an empty well containing a number of human bones, including those of children. The girl's possession ceased from the moment the wall collapsed.

The story sounds like a typical invention of a German romantic novelist; but Kerner devotes a whole book to it, describing it in the same detail as his investigation of Friederike Hauffe. In spite of this, modern investigators are inclined not to take it seriously. Yet readers who are impressed by the clarity and detail of Kerner's reporting may feel that this case of the possessed girl of Orlach is one of the most convincing arguments for the close connection between poltergeists and spirits of the dead.

Ten years after publication of *The Seeress of Prevorst*, another doctor – this time of philosophy – produced an equally remarkable account of a case of possession, this time benevolent. In *Die Schutzgeister* (*The Guardian Spirit*, 1839), Heinrich Werner identifies his eighteen-year-old subject only as "R.O.". Like Friederike, she had been subject to all kinds of illnesses, then, at a certain point, found herself haunted by spirits. One day the girl fell into a trance; and from then on she was able to do so at will, and to supply Werner with all kinds of information obtained "clairvoyantly". She had a guardian spirit called Albert, who seems to have acted rather like the "spirit guide" of later mediums. And the spirit who caused her so much trouble was – again – a wicked monk. One day, when the girl claimed that the wicked monk was present in the room, Werner was puzzled to hear an odd sound coming from a small table – like a cup rattling on a saucer. This occurred a number of times, becoming steadily louder (a typical characteristic of poltergeist noises); R.O. said that the monk was producing the noise, and was delighted at Werner's astonishment – which also sounds typical of a poltergeist.

One day, Werner was startled to hear a loud crash from an empty room; he rushed in to find that two large flowerpots, which had stood on the window sill, had been hurled to the floor so violently that there was earth all over the room. The blind was closed and there was no breeze. One of the curtains had also been twisted around a birdcage. Later that day, Werner went to call on R.O., who went into a trance, and then told Werner that the black monk had been responsible for smashing the flowerpots (Werner had not mentioned this to her). Albert, apparently, had ejected him from the house.

Werner was greatly impressed by his patient's clairvoyant powers. She demonstrated these one day when she woke up from a trance and told him that she had seen herself driving in a green-lacquered chaise. Now Werner had, at the time, made some enquiries about a chaise that was for sale in a town some fifteen hours away, and he expected to get an answer in about a week. R.O. told him he would hear much sooner than that – in fact, the following afternoon; she also went on to describe the chaise, in some detail. The following afternoon, Werner received a message about the chaise, and discovered that the girl was right in every detail.

Her most dramatic piece of clairvoyance concerned her younger sister. One day, in a trance, she cried out: "Albert, help me! Emilie is falling down into the street." Then, after a short period, she said: "Thank God, help has already come!"

Asked what had happened, she explained that her little sister had been leaning out of a top-storey window, trying to grab a rope suspended from a winch above the window; she had been on the point of falling when her father had entered the room and pulled her back.

Werner contacted the father to ask if anything remarkable had happened on that particular day, and received a reply which Werner printed in his book. It said that the father had been sitting in his office when he had felt uneasy. He went home, and went upstairs, in time to find his daughter had leaned too far out of the window to catch the rope, and could not get back into the room; he grabbed her dress and hauled her back in. R.O. said that it was Albert, the guardian spirit, who had made her father feel uneasy.

The Haunting of Willington Mill

The cases described by Justinus Kerner and Heinrich Werner caused widespread interest all over Europe. A lady novelist named Mrs Catherine Crowe was so impressed by *The Seeress of Prevorst* that she decided to translate it into English. And after her translation had appeared in 1845, she went on and wrote her own bestseller, *The Nightside of Nature*, which was still selling on railway bookstalls at the end of the century. She collected stories about ghosts, poltergeists, premonitions of the future and haunted houses.

The following extract from her book will demonstrate why it remained a bestseller for more than half a century.

> But, perhaps, one of the most remarkable cases of haunting in modern times, is that of Willington, near Newcastle, in my account of which, however, I find myself anticipated by Mr Howitt; and as he has had the advantage of visiting the place, which I have not, I shall take the liberty of borrowing his description of it, prefacing the account with the following letter from Mr Procter, the owner of the house, who, it will be seen, vouches for the general authenticity of the narrative. The letter was written in answer to one from me, requesting some more precise information than I had been able to obtain.
>
> "Josh. Proctor hopes C. Crowe will excuse her note having remained two weeks unanswered, during which time, J.P. has been from home, or particularly engaged. Feeling averse to add to the publicity the circumstances occurring in his house, at Willington, have already obtained, J.P. would rather not furnish additional particulars; but if C.C. is not in possession of the number of *Howitt's Journal*, which contains a variety of details on the subject, he will be glad to forward her one. He would at the same time, assure C. Crowe of the strict accuracy of that portion of W. Howitt's narrative which is extracted from *Richardson's Table Book*. W. Howitt's statements derived from his recollection of verbal communications with branches of J. Procter's family, are likewise essentially correct, though, as might be expected in some degree, erroneous circumstantially.
>
> "J.P. takes leave to express his conviction, that the unbelief of the educated classes, in apparitions of the deceased, and kindred phenomena, is not grounded on a fair philosophic examination of the facts which have induced the popular belief of all ages and countries; and that it will be found, by succeeding ages, to have been nothing better than unreasoning and unreasonable prejudice.
>
> ["Willington, near Newcastle-on-Tyne,]
>   7th mo. 22, 1847."

"VISITS TO REMARKABLE PLACES.

BY WILLIAM HOWITT.

THE HAUNTED HOUSE AT WILLINGTON, NEAR NEWCASTLE-ON-TYNE.

"We have of late years settled it as an established fact, that ghosts and haunted houses were the empty creation of ignorant times. We have comfortably persuaded ourselves that such fancies only hovered in the twilight of superstition, and that in these enlightened days they had vanished for ever. How often has it been triumphantly referred to, as a proof that all such things were the offspring of ignorance – that nothing of the kind is heard of now? What shall we say, then, to the following facts? Here we have ghosts and a haunted house still. We have them in the face of our vaunted noon-day light, in the midst of a busy and a populous neighbourhood, in the neighbourhood of a large and most intelligent town, and in a family neither ignorant, nor in any other respect superstitious. For years have these ghosts and hauntings disturbed the quiet of a highly re- spectable family, and continue to haunt and disturb, spite of the incredulity of the wise, the investigations of the curious, and the anxious vigilance of the suffering family itself.

"Between the railway running from Newcastle- on-Tyne to North Shields, and the river Tyne, there lie in a hollow some few cottages, a parsonage, and a mill and a miller's house. These constitute the hamlet of Willington. Just above these the railway is carried across the valley on lofty arches, and from it you look down on the mill and cottages, lying at a considerable depth below. The mill is a large steam flour mill, like a factory, and the miller's house stands near it, but not adjoining it. None of the cottages which lie between these premises and the railway, either, are in contact with them. The house stands on a sort of little promontory, round which runs the channel of a water-course, which appears to fill and empty with the tides. On one side of the mill and house, slopes away, upwards, a field, to a considerable distance, where it is terminated by other enclosures; on the other stands a considerable extent of ballast-hill, ie, one of the numerous hills on the banks of the Tyne, made by the deposit of ballast from the vessels trading thither. At a distance the top of the mill seems about level with the country around it. The place lies about half-way between Newcastle and North Shields.

"This mill is, I believe, the property of, and is worked by, Messrs. Unthank and Procter. Mr Joseph Procter resides on the spot in the house just by the mill, as already stated. He is a member of the Society of Friends, a gentleman in the very prime of life; and his wife, an intelligent lady, is of a family of Friends in Carlisle. They have several young children. This very respectable and well-informed family, belonging to a sect which of all others is most accustomed to control, to regulate, and to put down even the imagination – the last people in the world, as it would appear, in fact, to be affected by any mere imaginary terrors or impressions, have for years been persecuted by the most extraordinary noises and apparitions.

"The house is not an old house, as will appear; it was built about the year 1800. It has no particularly spectral look about it. Seeing it in passing, or within, ignorant of its real character, one should by no means say that it was a place likely to have the reputation of being haunted. Yet looking down from the railway, and seeing it and the mill lying in a deep hole, one might imagine various strange noises likely to be heard in such a place in the night, from vessels on the river, from winds sweeping and howling down the gully in which it stands, from engines in the neighbourhood connected with coal mines, one of which, I could not tell where, was making, at the time I was there, a wild sighing noise, as I stood on the hill above. There is not any passage, however, known of under the house, by which subterraneous noises could be heard, nor are they merely noises that are heard; distinct apparitions are declared to be seen.

"Spite of the unwillingness of Mr Procter that these mysterious circumstances should become

quite public, and averse as he is to make known
himself these strange visitations, they were of such a
nature that they soon became rumoured over the
whole neighbourhood. Numbers of people hurried
to the place to inquire into the truth of them, and at
length a remarkable occurrence brought them into
print. What this occurrence was, the pamphlet which
appeared, and which was afterwards reprinted in
The Local Historian's Table-book, published by Mr M.A.
Richardson, of Newcastle, and which I here copy,
will explain. It will be seen that the writer of this
article has the fullest faith in the reality of what he
relates, as indeed vast numbers of the best-informed
inhabitants of the neighbourhood have.

"AUTHENTIC ACCOUNT OF A VISIT TO
THE HAUNTED HOUSE AT WILLINGTON.

"Were we to draw an inference from the number of
cases of reported visitations from the invisible world
that have been made public of late, we might be led to
imagine that the days of supernatural agency were
about to recommence, and that ghosts and hobgoblins
were about to resume their sway over the fears of
mankind. Did we, however, indulge such an apprehension, a glance at the current tone of the literature
and philosophy of the day, when treating of these
subjects, would show a measure of unbelief regarding
them as scornful and uncompromising as the veriest
atheist or materialist could desire. Notwithstanding
the prevalence of this feeling amongst the educated
classes, there is a curiosity and interest manifested in
every occurrence of this nature, that indicates a lurking
faith at bottom, which an affected scepticism fails
entirely to conceal. We feel, therefore, that we need
not apologise to our readers for introducing the
following particulars of a *visit* to a house in this
immediate neighbourhood, which had become notorious for some years previous, as being 'haunted'; and
several of the reputed deeds, or misdeeds, of its
supernatural visitant had been published far and
wide by rumour's thousand tongues. We deem it as
worthy to be chronicled as the doings of its contemporary *genii* at Windsor, Dublin, Liverpool, Carlisle,

and Sunderland, and which have all likewise hitherto failed, after public investigation, to receive a solution consistent with a rejection of spiritual agency.

"We have visited the house in question, which is well known to many of our readers as being near a large steam corn-mill, in full view of Willington viaduct, on the Newcastle and Shields Railway; and it may not be irrelevant to mention that it is quite detached from the mill, or any other premises, and has no cellaring under it. The proprietor of the house, who lives in it, declines to make public the particulars of the disturbance to which he has been subjected, and it must be understood that the account of the visit we are about to lay before our readers is derived from a friend to whom Mr Drury presented a copy of his correspondence on the subject, with power to make such use of it as he thought proper. We learned that the house had been reputed, at least one room in it, to have been haunted forty years ago, and had afterwards been undisturbed for a long period, during some years of which quietude the present occupant lived in it unmolested. We are also informed, that about the time that the premises were building, viz, in 1800 or 1801, there were reports of some deed of darkness having been committed by someone employed about them. We should extend this account beyond the limits we have set to ourselves, did we now enter upon a full account of the strange things which have been seen and heard about the place by several of the neighbours, as well as those which are reported to have been seen, heard, and felt by the inmates, whose servants have been changed on that account many times. We proceed, therefore, to give the following letters, which have been passed between individuals of undoubted veracity; leaving the reader to draw his own conclusions on the subject.

"(Copy, No. 1.)

'To Mr Procter,   17th June, 1840.

"Sir, – Having heard from indisputable authority, viz, that of my excellent friend, Mr Davison, of Low Willington, farmer, that you and your family are disturbed by most unaccountable noises at night, I beg leave to tell you that I have read attentively Wesley's account of such things, but with, I must confess, no great belief; but an account of this report coming from one of your sect, which I admire for candour and simplicity, my curiosity is excited to a high pitch, which I would fain satisfy. My desire is to remain alone in the house all night, with no companion but my own watch-dog, in which, as far as courage and fidelity are concerned, I place much more reliance than upon any three young gentlemen I know of. And it is also my hope, that if I have a fair trial, I shall be able to unravel this mystery. Mr Davison will give you every satisfaction if you take the trouble to inquire of him concerning me.

   "I am, Sir,

     "Yours most respectfully,

       "EDWARD DRURY

"At C.C. Embleton's, Surgeon,

 "No. 10, Church-street, Sunderland.

     "(COPY, No. 2.)

"Joseph Procter's respects to Edward Drury, whose note he received a few days ago, expressing a wish to pass a night in his house at Willington. As the family is going from home on the 23rd instant, and one of Unthank and Procter's men will sleep in the house, if E.D. feels inclined to come, on or after the 24th, to spend a night in it, he is at liberty so to do, with or without his faithful dog, which, by the bye, can be of no possible use, except as company. At the same time, J.P. thinks it best to inform him, that particular disturbances are far from frequent at present, being only occasional, and quite uncertain, and therefore the satisfaction of E.D.'s curiosity must be considered as problematical. The best chance will be afforded by his sitting up alone in the third story till it be fairly daylight, say two or three a.m.

 "Willington, 6th mo. 21st, 1840.

 "J.P. will leave word with T. Maun, foreman, to admit E.D.

 "Mr Procter left home with his family on the 23rd

June, and got an old servant, who was then out of place in consequence of ill-health, to take charge of the house during their absence. Mr P. returned alone, on account of business, on the 3rd of July, on the evening of which day Mr Drury and his companion also unexpectedly arrived. After the house had been locked up, every corner of it was minutely examined. The room out of which the apparition issued is too shallow to contain any person. Mr Drury and his friend had lights by them, and were satisfied that there was no one in the house besides Mr P., the servant, and themselves.

"(COPY, No. 3.)
'Monday Morning, July 6, 1840.

"To Mr Procter,

"DEAR SIR, – I am sorry I was not at home to receive you yesterday, when you kindly called to inquire for me. I am happy to state that I am really surprised that I have been so little affected as I am, after that horrid and most awful affair. The only bad effect that I feel is a heavy dulness in one of my ears – the right one. I call it a heavy dulness, because I not only do not hear distinctly, but feel in it a constant noise. This I never was affected with before; but I doubt not it will go off. I am persuaded that no one went to your house at any time more *disbelieving in respect to seeing anything peculiar*; now no one can be more satisfied than myself. I will, in the course of a few days, send you a full detail of all I saw and heard. Mr Spence and two other gentlemen came down to my house in the afternoon, to hear my detail; but, sir, could I account for these noises from natural causes, yet, so firmly am I persuaded of the horrid apparition, that I would affirm that what I saw with my eyes was a punishment to me for my scoffing and unbelief; that I am assured that, as far as the horror is concerned, they are happy that believe and have not seen. Let me trouble you, sir, to give me the address of your sister, from Cumberland, who was alarmed, and also of your brother. I would feel a satisfaction in having a line from them; and, above all things, it will be a great cause of joy to me, if you never allow your young family to be in that horrid house again. Hoping you will write a few lines at your leisure,

"I remain, dear Sir,
"Yours very truly,
"EDWARD DRURY.

"(COPY, No. 4.)
"Willington, 7th mo. 9, 1840.
"Respected Friend, E. Drury,
"Having been at Sunderland, I did not receive thine of the 6th till yesterday morning. I am glad to hear thou art getting well over the effects of thy unlooked-for visitation. I hold in respect thy bold and manly assertion of the truth in the face of that ridicule and ignorant conceit with which that which is called the supernatural, in the present day, is usually assailed.

"I shall be glad to receive thy detail, in which it will be needful to be very particular in showing that thou couldst not be asleep, or attacked by nightmare, or mistake a reflection of the candle, as some sagaciously suppose.

"I remain, respectfully,
"Thy friend,
"JOSH. PROCTER.

"P.S. – I have about thirty witnesses to various things which cannot be satisfactorily accounted for on any other principle than that of spiritual agency.

"(COPY, No. 5.)
"Sunderland, July 13, 1840.
"DEAR SIR, – I hereby, according to promise in my last letter, forward you a true account of what I heard and saw at your house, in which I was led to pass the night from various rumours circulated by most respectable parties, particularly from an account by my esteemed friend Mr Davison, whose name I mentioned to you in a former letter. Having received your sanction to visit your mysterious dwelling, I went, on the 3rd of July, accompanied by a friend of mine, T. Hudson. This was not

according to promise, nor in accordance with my first intent, as I wrote you I would come alone; but I felt gratified at your kindness in not alluding to the liberty I had taken, as it ultimately proved for the best. I must here mention that, not expecting you at home, I had in my pocket a brace of pistols, determining in my mind to let one of them drop before the miller, as if by accident, for fear he should presume to play tricks upon me; but after my interview with you, I felt there was no occasion for weapons, and did not load them, after you had allowed us to inspect as minutely as we pleased every portion of the house. I sat down on the third story landing, fully expecting to account for any noises that I might hear, in a philosophical manner. This was about eleven o'clock p.m. About ten minutes to twelve we both heard a noise, as if a number of people were pattering with their bare feet upon the floor; and yet, so singular was the noise, that I could not minutely determine from whence it proceeded. A few minutes afterwards we heard a noise, as if some one was knocking with his knuckles among our feet; this was followed by a hollow cough from the very room from which the apparition proceeded. The only noise after this, was as if a person was rustling against the wall in coming up stairs. At a quarter to one, I told my friend that, feeling a little cold, I would like to go to bed, as we might hear the noise equally well there; he replied, that he would not go to bed till daylight. I took up a note which I had accidentally dropped, and began to read it, after which I took out my watch to ascertain the time, and found that it wanted ten minutes to one. In taking my eyes from the watch they became rivetted upon a closet door, which I distinctly saw open, and saw also the figure of a female attired in greyish garments, with the head inclining downwards, and one hand pressed upon the chest, as if in pain, and the other, viz, the right hand, extended towards the floor, with the index finger pointing downwards. It advanced with an apparently cautious step across the floor towards me; immediately as it approached my friend, who was slumbering, its right hand was extended towards him; I then rushed at it, giving, as Mr Procter states, a most awful yell; but, instead of grasping it, I fell upon my friend, and I recollected nothing distinctly for nearly three hours afterwards. I have since learnt that I was carried down stairs in an agony of fear and terror.

"I hereby certify that the above account is strictly true and correct in every respect.

'North Shields.   EDWARD DRURY.

Mrs Crowe not only publishes the full correspondence between Dr Drury and Joseph Procter, but an account by a local historian, another by the owner of a local journal, and descriptions by four other people who had seen the ghost. In fact, there seemed to be more than one; there was also a man in a surplice who glided across a second-floor room at a distance of a few feet from the floor. The local historian adds to his account the information that Mr Procter has recently discovered an old book that states that similar hauntings had taken place in an older house that had been built on the same spot two hundred years before. Mrs Crowe ends her account by mentioning that Mr Procter has now decided to leave the house, and turn it into "small tenements" for his workpeople.

SOME TRANSATLANTIC CASES

The Phelps Case

The evil spirit in *The Exorcist* is apparently conjured up by a child playing with an ouija board. This is by no means as far-fetched as it sounds. It was an interest in ghosts that disrupted the home of the Rev. Eliakim Phelps in 1850.

The Reverend Phelps lived in Stratford, Connecticut, and had married a widow with four children. He was interested in clairvoyance, and attempted to treat illnesses by means of mesmerism. He was understandably excited by the news of the strange events at the home of the Fox family in 1849. And in March 1850, when he entertained a visitor from New York, the two of them arranged some kind of amateur seance, which was not particularly successful, although they managed to obtain a few raps.

A few days later, on Sunday March 10, the family returned from church to find the front door wide open and the place in disorder. Their first assumption was that they had been burgled; but inspection showed that nothing had been taken, and a gold watch left on a table was untouched. That afternoon, the family went off to church again, but this time the Reverend Phelps stayed behind to keep watch. He may well have dozed; at all events, nothing disturbed him. But when the family returned from church, the place again showed signs of an intruder. Furniture was scattered, and in the main bedroom, a nightgown and chemise had been laid out on the bed, with the arms folded across the breast, and a pair of stockings placed to make it look like a corpse laid out for burial. In another room, clothing and cushions had been used to make various dummies, which were arranged in a tableau, "in attitudes of extreme devotion, some with their foreheads nearly touching the floor", and with open Bibles in front of them. Clearly, the poltergeist had a sense of ironic humour.

From then on, the Phelps poltergeist practised its skill as a designer of tableaux. The astonishing thing was that these were done so quickly. One observer, a Dr Webster, remarked that it would have taken half a dozen women several hours to construct the "dummies" that the poltergeist made within minutes. One figure was so life-like that when the three-year-old boy went into the room, he thought his mother was kneeling in prayer, and whispered "Be still . . ."

That it *was* a poltergeist became clear the following day, when objects began to fly through the air. A bucket flew downstairs, an umbrella leapt through the air, and spoons, bits of tin and keys were thrown around. A candlestick jumped off the mantelpiece, then beat the floor violently until it broke. There were loud pounding noises as if someone was trying to demolish the house with an axe, and loud screams.

The poltergeist probably derived its strength from the fact that it had two "focuses" in the house – Harry, aged twelve, and Anna, who was sixteen. Harry was persecuted by the "spirit". When he went for a drive in the carriage with his stepfather, twenty stones were flung into the carriage. On one occasion he was snatched up into the air so that his head nearly struck the ceiling; he was thrown into a cistern of water, and tied up and suspended from a tree. In front of a visiting clergyman, the legs of his trousers were violently torn open from the bottom to above the knee.

After this, the poltergeist started to break glass; it smashed seventy-one window panes and various glass articles. Another of its favourite tricks was to write on sheets of paper; when the Reverend Phelps turned his back on his writing table, he heard the scratching of the pen, and found written on the paper: "Very nice paper and nice ink for the devil." (Typically, poltergeists seem to object to being watched while they do things like this; they wait until no one is looking.)

Phelps tried communicating with the "spirit" by means of

raps, and found that it would answer his questions. There seemed to be more than one spirit present; but the author of most of the mischief seemed to be a French clerk, who had handled a settlement for Mrs Phelps, and who had since died; he now claimed to be in hell because he had cheated Mrs Phelps. Her husband investigated this claim, and found that there *had* been a minor fraud; but it had hardly been as serious as the "spirit" seemed to believe. On another occasion the raps told Phelps to put his hand under the table; when he did this his hand was grasped by another hand, warm and human.

A well-known psychic named Andrew Jackson Davis visited the Phelps home, and put forward a theory very similar to that of Mrs Crowe. He said that the phenomena were caused by "magnetism" and by "electricity": the magnetism attracting objects towards the boy and girl, the electricity causing them to fly in the opposite direction. But Davis – the author of a bestselling work of "spirit dictation" called *The Principles of Nature* – also agreed that there were spirits present – he claimed to have seen five of them.

The poltergeist – or poltergeists – became increasingly destructive. Pieces of paper burst into flame, although always where they could be seen; sometimes, the ashes of burnt papers were found in drawers. All kinds of objects were smashed – Phelps estimated that the poltergeist had done about two hundred dollars' worth of damage. And the poltergeist also attacked the eldest girl, Anna. A reporter was sitting with the mother and daughter when the girl shouted that someone had pinched her; they rolled up her sleeve and found a severe fresh pinch mark on her arm. On another occasion, there was a loud smacking noise, and a red mark appeared on her face.

In October 1851, more than a year after the disturbances began, the mother and children went off to Pennsylvania and stayed there until the following spring. The poltergeist did not follow them; and when they returned to Stratford, nothing more happened.

It seems fairly clear that the Reverend Phelps made a mistake in attracting the attention of spirits to his home by holding the seance; they discovered that there were two excellent mediums in the house, and the result was one of the most spectacular cases of poltergeist disturbance on record. The assertion by one of the "spirits" that he was a French clerk, now in hell, need not be taken too seriously; another observer, the Reverend John Mitchell, also communicated with the "spirits" by means of raps, and received insulting replies in bad language. The Phelps poltergeists seem to have been the usual crowd of invisible juvenile delinquents.

The Dagg Poltergeist

It is rare for poltergeists to talk, but the "spirit" that haunted the farm of the Dagg family is a fascinating exception. The following account is from a book called *Ghosts and Poltergeists* by a Catholic priest, Father Herbert Thurston.

On 15 September 1889, the family of George Dagg, a farmer living in the township of Clarendon, Province of Quebec, began, we are told, to be troubled by some strange spirit of mischief which played havoc with their peaceful home and drove them to distraction. The family consisted of George Dagg, aged thirty-five years, his wife Susan, little Mary Dagg aged four, little

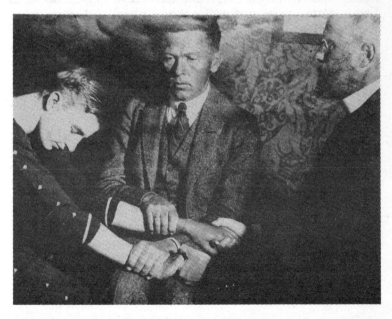

Willi Schneider, is tightly controlled during a seance, 1921

Johnny Dagg aged two, and Dinah Burden McLean aged eleven. This little girl Dinah, an orphan, was sent out from Scotland by Mr Quartier, and had been adopted from the Belleville Home by Mr Dagg five years earlier. Previously to the commencement of these troubles, she was a stout, rosy-cheeked Scotch girl. "Now," says the report, "her cheeks are sunken in, dark rings encircle her eyes, and she is a mere shadow of her former self." As constantly happens in such cases, the farmer folk of the surrounding country believed that some sort of witchcraft or magic must be at the bottom of the troubles, and a certain Mrs Wallace and her children fell under suspicion. The one fact which was a matter of observation was that when Dinah was away from the house the disturbances ceased.

The account of the case, which was printed in *The Recorder* of Brockville, Canada, was furnished by a certain Mr Woodcock, described as an artist well known in the Dominion, who had also lived in New York and in Paris. He visited the Daggs on Friday, 15 November, and spent most of his time with them until the Sunday evening. During these three days he made notes of what he could learn from the family and the neighbours, and seems to have convinced himself that the physical manifestations, alleged to have taken place during the previous two months, were unquestionably authentic. Among other things he was informed that on 15 September, Mr Dagg had brought home a five-dollar bill and a two-dollar bill and gave them to his wife, who placed them in a bureau drawer. In the morning a little boy named Dean, an orphan, who was employed by various farmers as "chore boy", and who was temporarily in the service of the Daggs, came down from his bed in the garret and proceeded to light a fire in the cooking stove. Seeing on the floor a five-dollar bill he took it at once to Mr Dagg telling him where he had found it. Mr Dagg, being suspicious, looked in the drawer and discovered that the two-dollar bill was also gone. So sending the boy out of doors to milk, he examined his room and found his missing bill in his bed. Although convinced that the boy was guilty, they said nothing until later in the day when, on returning from the milk house, Mrs Dagg found on the floor of her house from back to front a streak of filth. This, with the theft of the money, was too much for Mrs Dagg and she immediately ordered the boy Dean out of the house. The boy stoutly asserted his innocence, but had to go. Mr Dagg took the boy to Shawville before a magistrate, and while they were away the same thing hap-

During the presidency of Abraham Lincoln the vogue for the new Spiritualism was at its height among fashionable people. Even the President – a far from fashionable man – was drawn into it. Colonel Simon F. Kase, a lobbyist who had several times met Lincoln to discuss a railroad project with him, tells of encountering the President at a seance in the home of Mrs Laurie and daughter Mrs Miller. She was known for making a piano beat time on the floor as she played while in trance.

Kase said of the occasion that Mrs Miller began to play, and the front of the piano in truth rose off the floor and beat the time of the tune with heavy thuds. Kase asked if he could sit on the instrument so that he could "verify to the world that it moved". The medium composedly answered that he and as many others as wished could sit on the piano. Four men did: Kase, a judge, and two of the soldiers who were accompanying Lincoln. Mrs Miller again began to play and the piano – heedless of its load – began to rise and thump, lifting at least four inches off the floor. Kase concluded ruefully: "It was too rough riding; we got off while the instrument beat the time until the tune was played out."

pened again and filth was found in various places, in the eatables, in the beds, etc., showing conclusively that the boy was in no way connected with it. This continued for about a week and was accompanied by various other antics. Milk-pans were emptied, butter was taken from the crocks and put into the pans. As a precaution the milk and eatables were then conveyed to the attic for safety, but just the same annoyances occurred there as had happened before. This attic had no doors or windows and no entrance except by a stair which led up to it from the kitchen, and no one could enter the place without being seen, as these things were done in the daytime. The worry about eatables was succeeded by the smashing of windows, the outbreak of fires, the pouring of water and much other mischief. One afternoon little Dinah felt her hair, which hung in a long braid down her back, suddenly pulled, and on her crying out, the family found her braid almost cut off. It had to be completely severed. Incidents of this kind recurred during two months, and then a new type of manifestation developed. A gruff voice, which at first was heard by Dinah alone, began to be audible to all who were present.

THE PROJECTION OF ENERGY

In 1919 Bernard Kajinsky, a Russian electrical engineer, was awakened in the night by a ringing sound like that of a spoon hitting glass. The next day he learned that his closest friend had died of typhus. When he called on his friend's mother, he discovered that she had been about to give him a dose of medicine at the moment he died. Kajinsky, suddenly excited, asked her to show him exactly what she had done. She took a silver spoon and dropped it into a tumbler. It made the same ringing sound that had startled him awake.

Kajinsky was a scientist with no interest in telepathy or extrasensory perception. But he had no doubt that his friend had thought of him at the moment of death, and that the sound of the spoon striking glass had somehow been conveyed to him. He thereafter made an exhaustive study of telepathy and reached the conclusion that "the human nervous system is capable of reacting to stimuli whose source is not yet known."

On the Saturday morning of Mr Woodcock's visit, he tried to have a private talk with Dinah and took the child to an open shed at the back of the house where she declared she had seen something. Dinah said: "Are you there, Mister?" To Mr Woodcock's intense astonishment, "a deep, gruff voice, as of an old man, seemingly within four or five feet from him, instantly replied in language which cannot be repeated here." The visitor, recovering from his astonishment, said: "Who are you?" To which the reply came: "I am the devil. I'll have you in my clutches. Get out of this or I'll break your neck."

From these beginnings a conversational wrangle developed which went on, we are told, for several hours. The voice used foul and obscene language, but in deference to the remonstrances of Mr Woodcock and George Dagg, after a while showed more restraint. The account insists that the gruff voice could not have been that of the child, which was rather exceptionally high-pitched, and also that there was no possible place of concealment where a practical joker could have hidden himself. As Mr Woodcock had heard of writings having been found about the house, he challenged the spirit to write something. Putting a sheet of paper and a pencil on a bench in the shed he saw the pencil stand up and move along the surface. As soon as the pencil dropped, he stepped over, and examining the paper said: "I asked you to write something decent." To this the voice replied in an angry tone, "I'll steal your pencil," and immediately the pencil rose from the bench and was thrown violently across the shed.

In the report given of the dialogue between the voice and its questioners, we find passages like the following:

Mr Dagg: "Why have you been bothering me and my family?"

Answer: "Just for fun."

Mr Dagg: "It was not very much fun when you threw a stone and struck little Mary."

Answer: "Poor wee Mary! I did not mean to hit her, I intended it for Dinah; but I did not let it hurt her."

Mr Dagg: "If it was only for fun why did you try to set the house on fire?"

Answer: "I didn't. The fires came always in the daytime and where you could see them. I'm sorry I did it."

In the end a promise was obtained from the spook that it would say good-bye and leave the house for good on the following night, the Sunday.

News of this spread, and there was great excitement throughout the neighbourhood. People began arriving early in the morning, and all the afternoon the place was thronged. The voice was on its good behaviour, as had been promised, but it answered questions and made comments on different people as they entered the room. Some remarks were very amusing and displayed an intimate knowledge of the private affairs of many of the questioners. One of the visitors commented on the change for the better in the language used. The reply thereupon came: "I am not the person who used the filthy language. I am an angel from Heaven sent by God to drive away that fellow." This character was maintained for some time, but Mr Woodcock declares that the voice was the same as that which they had previously heard, and, as the day wore on and many questions were asked, the spook contradicted himself, and getting entangled, lost his temper, saying many things quite out of harmony with his supposed heavenly origin.

Before ending his visit on the Sunday, Mr Woodcock drew up the following report:

To whom it may concern: We the undersigned solemnly declare that the following curious proceedings which began on the 15th day of September, 1889, and are still going on on the 17th day of November, 1889, in the house of Mr George Dagg, a farmer living seven miles from Shawville, Clarendon Township, Pontiac County, Province of Quebec, actually occurred as below described.

1st. That fires have broken out spontaneously throughout the house, as many as eight occurring in one day, six being in the house and two outside; that the window curtains were burned whilst on the windows, this happening in broad daylight, whilst the family and neighbours were in the house.

2nd. That stones were thrown by invisible hands through the windows, as many as eight panes of glass being broken, that articles such as a water jug, milk pitchers, a wash basin, cream tub, butter tub and other articles were thrown about the house by the same invisible agency, a jar of water being thrown in the face of Mrs John Dagg, also in the face of Mrs George Dagg while they were being about their household duties, Mrs George Dagg being alone in the house at the time it was thrown in her face; that a large dining table was thrown down; a mouth organ, which was lying on a small shelf, was distinctly heard to be played and was seen to move across the room on to the floor, while immediately after, a rocking chair began rocking furiously; that a washboard was sent flying down the stairs from the garret, no one being in the garret at the time. Further, that when the child Dinah is present a deep, gruff voice, like that of an aged man, has been heard at various times, both in the house and out of doors, and when asked questions has answered so as to be distinctly heard, showing that he is cognizant of all that has taken place, not only in Mr Dagg's family, but also in the families in the surrounding neighbourhood; that he claims to be a disincarnated being who died twenty years ago, aged about eighty years; that he gave his name to Mr George Dagg and Mr Willie Dagg, forbidding them to tell it; that this intelligence is able to make himself visible to Dinah, little Mary and Johnny, who have seen him under different forms at different times, at one time as a tall, thin man with a cow's head, horns, tail and a cloven foot, at another time as a big black dog, and finally as a man with a beautiful face and long white hair dressed in white, wearing a crown with stars in it.

This document is signed by seventeen witnesses, beginning with the Daggs, all of them responsible people living in the district. No women's names are included, and Mr Woodcock declares that he might have had twice as many signatures had he wanted them.

Perhaps the most extraordinary feature of the story is the fact that the spook after all took his departure in a blaze of glory. Though Mr Woodcock left the house on the Sunday evening to return to his own lodging, a number of people seem to have remained behind with the Daggs, hoping to witness the promised leavetaking of the author of all the disturbance. By this time he had, so far as appearances went, completely changed his character. He suddenly laid aside his gruff tones, declared that he had only maintained this harsh accent because otherwise people would have believed that Dinah was doing it, and then proceeded to sing hymns in what is described as a very beautiful flute-like voice. The group of visitors present were enchanted, and completely convinced by this reassumption of angelic attributes. So far from hastening the departure of the spook, they pressed him to stay, and this strange seance was prolonged until 3 am. The spirit then said goodbye, but promised to show himself to the children later in the morning.

Early in the forenoon of the Monday Mr Woodcock himself came back to the Dagg's house to take leave. He describes how, as he got there, "the three children, who had been out in the yard, came rushing into the house, wild-eyed and fearfully excited." I can only copy the exact terms of the statement which follows:

"Little Mary cried out 'Oh, Mama! the beautiful man! He took little Johnny and me in his arms, and, Oh, Mama, I played on the music and he went to Heaven and was all red!'" They, the Daggs, rushed to the door, but nothing unusual was to be seen. On questioning the girls they both told the same story. Their accounts said it was a beautiful man, dressed in white, with ribbons and pretty things all over his clothes, with a lovely gold thing on his head and stars in it. They said he had a lovely face and long white hair, that he stooped down and took little Mary and the baby [Johnny] and said Johnny was a fine little fellow, and that Mary played on the music-thing he had with him. Dinah said she distinctly saw him stoop and lift Mary and Johnny in his arms and heard him speak to Johnny. Dinah said he spoke to her also and said – that man Woodcock thought he was not an angel, but he would show that he was, and then, she said, he went up to Heaven. On being questioned, she said he seemed to go right up in the air and disappear. He was in a kind of fire and the fire seemed to blaze up from his feet and surrounded him until he disappeared. No amount of questioning could shake their stories in the least."

What makes this case so interesting is that the poltergeist first declared itself to be the Devil, then an angel. It was obviously neither. We can also see that if the case had occurred a few centuries earlier, no one would have had the slightest doubt that they were dealing with real devils and angels. Is it possible that some of the stories about the devils and angels who appeared to saints in the Middle Ages were really about poltergeists up to their usual mischief?

The Esther Cox Case

But perhaps the most famous American haunting of the nineteenth century is the one that took place in Amherst, Nova Scotia, in 1878, and became known as "The Amherst Mystery".

A shoe worker, Daniel Teed, lived in a two-storey house with his wife and two sons, his wife's two unmarried sisters, Jane and Esther Cox, who were aged twenty-two and eighteen, his wife's brother William, and his own brother, John. (The house must have been grossly overcrowded.) All were Methodists. Jane, the elder sister, was pretty; Esther was short and rather stout. Nevertheless, Esther had a boyfriend, a local factory worker named Bob MacNeal.

In late August, Daniel Teed complained that someone had

been milking the cow; Esther was a suspect as she was unusually fond of milk. Esther was suffering from nervous tensions, and ran up from the cellar one night screaming that a rat had run over her leg. Her troubles were probably sexual in origin, as seems to be revealed by a dream she had at the time: hundreds of black bulls with bright blue eyes and blood dripping from their mouths tried to break into the house, while Esther frantically locked the doors . . .

The following evening, Esther and Bob MacNeal went out for a drive. Bob, who had a bad reputation locally, tried to persuade Esther to go into the woods with him, but she refused. He pulled out a gun and ordered her to get down from the buggy; he looked as if he might fire when the sound of an approaching vehicle distracted him. He leapt on to the buggy, drove back at a dangerous speed, let Esther off, then left Amherst for good. Esther cried herself to sleep, and for the next few days had red eyes.

On 4 September, a damp, misty evening, Jane heard Esther sobbing in bed. Then Esther screamed that there was a mouse in bed with her. They searched, but no mouse was found. The following night, both heard a rustling noise, and made a search. It seemed to be coming from a cardboard box containing patchwork, so Jane stood it in the middle of the room, expecting a mouse to run out. Instead the box jumped into the air and fell over. She stood it up, and it jumped again.

Daniel Teed came in to see what the noise was about, pushed the box under the bed, and told them to go to sleep.

The next night, Esther went to bed early. Soon after the light went out, she leapt out of bed shouting: "Jane, I'm dying." Jane lit the lamp and saw that Esther's face was bright red, and her hair was standing on end. Daniel Teed came in, together with the other two men. Esther got back into bed, but began to scream. Her body appeared to be swelling like a balloon. Suddenly, there was a loud report like a clap of thunder. The men rushed out to search the house, but found nothing. When they came back, Esther was back to normal and fast asleep.

Two days later, as Esther was getting into bed, she began to feel ill again. All the bedclothes flew off the bed, and landed in the far corner of the room. Jane fainted. Esther began to swell again. The men rushed in, and someone replaced the bedclothes; they promptly flew off again, and a pillow hit John Teed on the head; he left the house never to return. Again, there were some loud explosions. Esther stopped swelling, and fell asleep.

The following day, a doctor came to see Esther. As she lay in bed, the pillow under her head inflated, as if filled up with air, then collapsed, then re-inflated itself. Raps sounded around the room. The bedclothes flew off. There was a scratching noise above Esther's bed and, as they all watched, they saw writing appearing on the wall. It said: "Esther, you are mine to kill." A lump of plaster detached itself from elsewhere on the wall and flew across the room to the doctor's feet. Then rappings and bangs continued for the next two hours, while Esther lay, terrified, on her bed.

The following day, Esther complained of an "electric" feeling running through her body. The doctor gave her morphine; instantly, there was a series of bangs and crashes that seemed to go up to the roof.

These disturbances continued for another three weeks. Then, one night, Esther fell into a trance, became rigid, and told the story of what had happened with Bob MacNeal. When she recovered consciousness, she admitted it was true. When Jane said that Bob must be responsible for Esther's problems, loud knocks suggested that the "spirit" agreed completely. Jane remarked that it seemed to understand what she said, where-upon there were three distinct raps. The doctor tried asking the "spirit" simple questions, with one rap for no, two for "no answer", three for yes. But the doctor's attempts to get it to explain itself were a total failure.

Esther became a subject of controversy; the house was permanently full of people. When a minister called to see her, a bucket of cold water on the kitchen table began to bubble as if it was boiling.

In December, Esther developed a severe sore throat which turned to diphtheria. While she was ill, the manifestations ceased. Then she went away to convalesce. When she re-turned, the manifestations started immediately. Esther said she heard a voice telling her that the house was going to be set on fire. As she told the others about this, a lighted match fell from the air on to the bed, and the sheets caught fire. Jane quickly put it out. More lighted matches fell around the room, most of them going out immediately. The rapping noises started later, and when the family asked the "spirit" whether the house would be set alight, it replied that it would not be. At that moment there was smoke from under Esther's bed; they found that a dress had somehow transferred itself from the bedroom door, and had been set on fire.

Three days later, Mrs Teed smelled smoke coming from the cellar. They found a barrel of wood shavings burning vigorously and had some trouble putting it out.

The villagers were alarmed about this; if the Teed's house caught fire, half the village would probably be burned down. They suggested that Esther ought to be sent away. A neighbour named John White offered to take her in if she would do some housework. For two weeks, all went well; then a scrubbing brush flew out of Esther's hand, went up to the ceiling, and came down and hit her on the head.

White owned a restaurant, and Esther went to work there. An oven door refused to stay closed, and jumped off its hinges. Metal objects began flying at Esther as if she were a magnet, and a boy's clasp knife made her back bleed. When iron spikes were laid in her lap, they quickly became too hot to touch.

All this seemed to support the suspicion that Esther was somehow "electrified". They tried making her wear a special pair of shoes with glass soles; but these gave her headaches and made her nose bleed.

When furniture began to move around the restaurant, John White decided it was time for Esther to go home. Again, she left Amherst for a few months; first to stay with a man and his wife in New Brunswick, then to a farm three miles from Amherst. She told various visitors about the "voices" that spoke to her – voices which claimed to be the spirits that were causing the mischief. One of these spirits, "Bob Nickle", threatened her with fire and stabbing.

In June 1879, a stage magician named Walter Hubbell moved into the Teed's cottage as a paying guest; he had heard about the "haunting" and thought it might make the subject of a book. Within a few minutes of arriving, he had no doubt that this was no fraud. His umbrella sailed through the air, then a carving knife landed at his feet, then his bag was "thrown", then a chair shot across the room and hit his own so hard that he nearly fell on the floor. From then on, the chairs in every room he entered performed a dance. Esther told him he was unpopular with the spirits. Undeterred, Hubbell tried asking them questions by means of raps, and the spirits were able to tell him the number engraved on his watch, and the dates of coins in his pockets. Later, Hubbell lay down on the settee and closed his eyes; Esther came into the room, and Hubbell cautiously peeped at her, perhaps hoping that she would give herself away as a cheat. Instead, he saw a large glass paperweight float up across the room and rebound off the arm of the settee.

During the next few days the poltergeist put on a special show for Hubbell. Objects floated around, strange noises were heard – like sawing wood and drumming on a washboard – and Esther was attacked by "six spirits" who stuck no fewer than thirty pins in her. Small fires broke out – on one day there were forty-five of them – and the sound of a trumpet echoed through the house; they later found a small silver trumpet which no one had ever seen before. When Esther went to the local minister to pray, "Bob Nickle" attacked her viciously on her return, cutting her head open with a bone and stabbing her in the face with a fork.

Hubbell thought he saw a way of making money. He hired a hall and persuaded Esther to put on a "show" for the people of Amherst. Inevitably, the spirits declined to operate, and the audience demanded their money back.

Tired of the non-stop disturbances, Daniel Teed sent Esther off to stay with some obliging friends; Hubbell, who now had enough material for his book, went to St John to write it. It appeared in due course and went through several editions.

During Esther's stay with her friends, the spirits let her alone. She then took a job on a farm owned by people called Davidson. Her friends found that various articles were missing, and these were located in the Davidsons' barn. Esther was suspected of theft, but before the case could be investigated the barn caught fire and burned to the ground. Esther was accused of arson, and was sentenced to four months in jail. After this, the manifestations came suddenly to an end.

This abrupt termination of the "haunting" seems to favour the view that Esther's own unconscious mind was responsible. This is, in fact, the view I favoured when I described the case briefly in a book called *Mysteries*. Esther was sexually frustrated, and if Bob MacNeal had adopted a more gentlemanly way of seducing her, there would have been no "Great Amherst Mystery" (the title of Hubbell's book). Esther was a classic case of "the divided self": a part of her longing to give herself to her lover, while the inhibitions induced by her background and training made this impossible. So when she rejected his advances, and he vanished into the night, her unconscious mind said, in effect, "Now see what you've done, stupid!", and set out to punish her. As to the effects themselves, many of them fit the hypothesis I have suggested: that the "energy" comes from the earth. When Esther wore shoes with glass soles, the manifestations stopped but she developed headaches and nosebleeds. Her sensation of electric currents is also highly suggestive. There have been dozens of well-authenticated cases of "human electric batteries". Again, nearly all concern girls or boys at the age of puberty. Caroline Clare of Bondon, Ontario, began to lose weight at the age of seventeen (in 1877), then developed such powerful electric currents that people who touched her received severe shocks; pieces of metal stuck to her as if she were a magnet. Jennie Morgan of Sedalia, Missouri, became an electric battery at fourteen; when she touched metal objects, sparks flew. Frank McKinistry, also of Missouri, would develop an electric charge during the night and slowly lose it during the day. When highly charged, his feet would stick to the ground so that he had difficulty in walking – which sounds again as if the electricity comes from the earth. (Good dowsers receive a "tingling" sensation when they touch standing stones.) The Amherst minister, the Reverend Edwin Clay, was convinced that the secret of Esther's manifestations was electricity, and even delivered a lecture to that effect.

But how did Esther's unconscious mind know the number of Hubbell's watch and the dates of coins in his pocket – which no doubt he did not know himself? How did her mind scratch "Esther, you are mine to kill" on the wall above her head? How did it blow a trumpet all over the house? The truth is that the unconscious mind theory needs to be stretched so much that it loses the chief virtue of a good theory – simplicity.

But perhaps the strongest argument against the unconscious mind theory is simply that Esther's torment went on for so long. To actually read the case in detail is to feel that no one could get so angry with herself that she would continue relentlessly for more than a year. We may say, "Oh, I could kick myself," when we do something stupid; but no one has ever *done* it.

The fraud hypothesis also fails to stand up to close examination. If Hubbell's book was the main piece of evidence, then we might well feel suspicious, since he went to Amherst with the hope of writing it, and eventually made a great deal of money from no fewer than ten editions. But there are accounts in the *Amherst Gazette* that confirm everything Hubbell says. Moreover, in 1907, more than a quarter of a century after the events, the researcher Hereward Carrington went to Amherst and took various depositions from people who had witnessed the manifestations. By this time, Esther was unhappily married, and had turned into a sullen middle-aged woman, who agreed to talk to Carrington only on the payment of a hundred dollars; Carrington felt that such testimony would be valueless. But there could be no doubt that most of the people involved believed that the manifestations were genuine, including the farmer, Davidson, whose barn had been destroyed – he said that he had often watched Esther as she came downstairs and had noticed that she seemed to fly or float.

In the Middle Ages, levitation used to be one of the signs of possession by demons – another interesting piece of evidence for the suggestion that demons were really poltergeists.

THE HAUNTING OF GLAMIS

Glamis Castle, in Angus, Scotland, has a reputation as one of the most haunted houses in the country. The oldest castle in Scotland, it will be remembered by readers of Shakespeare as the place where Macbeth murdered Duncan. Many of the legends associated with it are too silly to be taken seriously – such as the room in the tower where two earls are doomed to play dice forever as a punishment for cursing God, and the secret room that housed the famous Glamis Monster, a horrible misshapen creature like a large soft egg, born to one of the Lady Strathmores around 1800, and confined there in secrecy for the rest of his life. But too many people have seen the little Grey Lady who haunts the chapel for this to be dismissed as fiction. No one knows who she is, but several members of the Strathmore family have seen her, often kneeling in one of the pews. Glamis also seems to have a poltergeist which causes a loud crash in the old wing at four in the morning.

Lord Halifax, whose *Ghost Book* has become a classic of its kind, wrote a chapter on Glamis, where he often stayed. His name was Charles Wood, and he was born in 1839. His grandfather had been Prime Minister of England, but Charles Wood was more interested in religion than politics, and spent most of his life working for a union of the Catholic Church and the Church of England. Although an avid collector of ghost stories, he never joined the Society for Psychical Research, and it must be admitted that this shows in his famous *Ghost Book*, in which obviously factual stories are mixed up with absurd tales involving the devil and other sinister entities.

But at least he was familiar with Glamis, of which his brother in law was the owner until his sudden death in 1865. So much of his chapter on "The Secret of Glamis" is first hand reporting.

> In 1870 we met Miss Virginia Gabriel, fresh from a long visit to Glamis and full of the mysteries which had assumed such prominence since the death of our poor brother-in-law in 1865. The Chapel had been cleaned and re-dedicated with great solemnity, and the gossip was that the ghosts were endeavouring to terrify Claude (Lord Strathmore) and his family from making the Castle their home.
>
> I will try to write down all that Virginia told us, much of which was afterwards confirmed by Lady Strathmore. It appears that after my brother-in-law's funeral the lawyer and the agent initiated Claude into the family secret. He went from them to his wife and said: "My dearest, you know how often we have joked over the secret room and the family mystery. I have been into the room; I have heard the secret; and if you wish to please me you will *never* mention the subject to me again."
>
> Lady Strathmore was too good a wife not to obey, but she talked freely to other people, and her mother, old Mrs Oswald Smith, was one of the chief propagators of stories which, of course, lost nothing in the telling.
>
> Claude made a good many alterations and improvements at the Castle, one being a staircase from the lower hall or crypt, as it was called, to the Chapel, which had previously been accessible only through the great drawing-room. One day, when the family were in London, a man working in, I think, the Chapel, came upon a door opening up a long passage. He went some way down it; then became alarmed and went back and told the Clerk of the Works. Immediately all the work was stopped and the head man telegraphed to Claude in London and to Mr Dundas, the lawyer, in Edinburgh. Both arrived by the earliest possible train and subjected the workman to a severe examination as to what he

had or had not seen, the end of it being that he and his family were subsidized and induced to emigrate.

It is unquestionable that for many years, after the revelation of the secret, Claude was quite a changed man, silent and moody, with an anxious scared look on his face. So evident was the effect on him that his son, Glamis, when he came of age in 1876, absolutely refused to be enlightened.

Virginia further informed me that in several of the bedroom cupboards there were stones with rings in them. Claude converted all these cupboards into coal-stores, with strongly boarded fronts, and ordered them to be kept always full, so that no inquisitive visitor might attempt an exploration. She told us a wonderful tale of the first housewarming – a dance in the new dining-room in November 1869. They had all been very merry and dancing went on until the small hours. The three sets of rooms on the Clock Landing were occupied by the Streatfields (Lady Strathmore's sister), Mr and Lady F. Trevanion (Lord Strathmore's sister), and Mr and Mrs Monro from Lindertis. The latter were in the Red Room, their little boy sleeping in the dressing-room, the outer door of which was rather stiff and difficult to open. In the middle of the night, Mrs Monro awoke with a sensation as though someone was bending over her; indeed, I have heard that she felt a beard brush her face. The night-light having gone out, she called her husband to get up and find the matches. In the pale glimmer of the winter moon she saw a figure pass into the dressing-room. Creeping to the end of the bed she felt for and found the matchbox and struck a light, calling out loudly "Cam, Cam, I've found the matches."

To her surprise she saw that he had not moved from her side. Very sleepily he grumbled, "What are you bothering about?"

At that moment they heard a shriek of terror from the child in the dressing-room. Rushing in, they found him in great alarm, declaring that he had seen a giant. They took him into their own room, and while they were quieting him off to sleep they heard a fearful crash as though a heavy piece of furniture had fallen. At that moment the big clock struck four.

Nothing more happened, and the next morning Mr Monro extracted a reluctant promise from his wife to say nothing about her fright, as the subject was known to be distasteful to their host. However, when breakfast was half over, Fanny Trevanion came down, yawning and rubbing her eyes and complaining of a disturbed night. She always slept with a night-light and had her little dog with her on her bed. The dog, she said, had awakened her by howling. The night-light had gone out, and while she and her husband were hunting for matches they heard a tremendous crash, followed by the clock striking four. They were so frightened they could not sleep again.

Of course this was too much for Mrs Monro, who burst out with her story. No explanation was offered and the three couples agreed on the following night to watch in their respective rooms. Nothing was seen, but they all heard the same loud crash and rushed out on to the landing. As they stood there with scared faces the clock again struck four. That was all; and the noise was not heard again.

We did not go to Glamis that year, but with our heads full of all these wonderful tales paid a visit to Tullyallan Castle, a large and comfortable modern house. It was inhabited by a most cheerful old couple, Lord and Lady William Osborne, and there was nothing about it to suggest a ghost. On the night of the 28th of September I dreamt I was sleeping in the Blue Room at Glamis, which Addy and I occupied during our memorable and delightful visit in 1862. The dressing-room has a well-known trap-door and a secret staircase leading to a corner of the drawing-room. I dreamt that I was in the park watching some horses when I heard the gong sound for dinner and rushed upstairs in a great hurry, begging the others not to wait for me. In the passage I met the housemaid coming out of the Blue dressing-room with her arms full of rusty bits of iron which she held out to me.

"Where did you find those?" I asked.

She replied that in cleaning the grate she had seen a stone with a ring in it which she had raised and in the hollow space below had found these pieces of iron.

I said, "I will take them down with me. His lordship likes to see everything that is found in the Castle."

As I opened the door of the Blue Room the thought crossed my mind: "They say the ghost always appears if anything is found. I wonder if he will come to me." I went in and there, seated in the armchair by the fire, I saw a huge figure of a man with a very long beard and an enormous stomach, which rose and fell with his breathing. I shook all over with terror, but walked to the fireplace and sat down on the coalbox staring at the ghost. Although he was breathing heavily I saw clearly that it was the face of a dead man.

The silence was unendurable, and at last I held up the pieces of rusty iron, saying, "Look what I have found" – an untruth, for the housemaid was the finder.

Then the ghost, heaving a deep sigh, said, "Yes, you have lifted a great weight off me. Those irons have been weighing me down ever since . . ."

"Ever since when?" I asked eagerly, forgetting my alarm in my curiosity.

"Ever since 1486," replied the ghost.

At that moment, to my great relief, I heard a knock at my door.

"That is Caroline" (my maid) I thought, "coming to dress me. I wonder if she will see this dreadful creature."

"Come in," I called and woke up.

It was Caroline opening my shutters, and the sun was streaming cheerfully into the room. I sat up in bed and found that my nightgown was quite wet with perspiration. I came downstairs very full of my dream, and still more of the fact, as I believed, that although the room was in all other respects exactly like the one I thought I remembered so well, the fire place was in a different corner. So persuaded was I of this that when next year I saw the room at Glamis and found that my dream memory was right and my waking memory wrong, I could scarcely believe my eyes. I even brought upon myself some ridicule by asking Claude if the fireplace had been changed, which would be neither easy nor likely in a house of that age and with walls of that thickness.

This part of my dream greatly interested Dr Acland and other Oxford dons as a striking confirmation of the theory that the brain receives impressions which are always accurate when it is undisturbed by outside influences. I wrote my dream down, but told it to very few people.

A year or two afterwards Mrs Wingfield, a daughter of Lord Castletown's, met my brother Eric at a water party and began asking him about my dream. She had had an odd experience of her own which unfortunately I can only relate second-hand, as I have never had the opportunity of meeting her.

So far as I could make out she was staying at Glamis for the first time during the same week, if not on the very same day, that we went to Tullyallan. She was occupying the Blue Room, but had heard none of the stories about Earl Beardie and his crew of ghosts. She went to bed with the usual night-light, which was so bright that she read by it before going to sleep. During the night she awoke with the feeling that someone was in the room, and sitting up in bed she saw, seated in front of the fire, a huge old man with a long, flowing beard. He turned his head and gazed fixedly at her, and then she saw that although his beard rose and fell as he breathed the face was that of a dead man. She was not particularly alarmed, but unfortunately made no attempt to enter into conversation with her visitor. After a few minutes he faded away and she went to sleep again.

Next morning, when Mr Oswald Smith began to tell her some of the tales of the Castle, she said, "Let me tell you first what I saw last night."

Whether she saw or dreamt it the coincidence was curious. Nothing came either of her dream or of mine, but some years afterwards, when we were driving from Glamis to Cortachy, my mother asked me if I had ever told my dream to Lady Strathmore. I replied that I had not thought it worth telling, but she insisted on my relating to Lady Strathmore just what I have written here. When I came to the date, Lady Strathmore gave a start, and turning to Fanny Trevanion, said, "Oh, that is too odd."

I said, "Surely that isn't the right date? I thought it was fifteen hundred and something."

"No," she answered, "it was in 1486, nearly four hundred years ago."

Of course I may have heard the date at some time, but have no recollection of it.

After 1870 we went to Glamis every year, nearly always spending my mother's birthday there. St Michael was the patron saint of the Chapel, people pretending that when it was re-dedicated he had been chosen for the purpose of keeping away evil spirits. I generally had a most ghostly little room, King Malcolm's Chamber, but never slept there, for my mother was so afraid of waking in the night and felt so nervous when she was alone that at Glamis I always slept with her.

We never saw or heard anything, and eager believers in the ghosts affirmed that this was because we had Lyon blood and the ghosts never appeared to any of the family. My mother's grandmother, Lady Anne Simpson, who was a Lyon, tried hard to see something and I often found her in her room with her face pressed against the window pane, straining her eyes for a glimpse of the White Lady, a most harmless apparition, who is supposed to flit about the avenue. One year on our arrival we found the whole house in great excitement as the White Lady had been seen by Lady Strathmore, her nieces and Lady Glasgow, from different windows at the same moment. Their descriptions were exceedingly vague and incoherent.

One more tale, related to me by old Dr Nicholson, the Dean of Brechin, I must put down. He said that once, when he was staying at Glamis, he had gone to bed in the room halfway up the winding stair. The door was locked, but he saw a tall figure enter, draped in a long, dark coat, fastened at the throat with a clasp. Neither spoke and the figure disappeared in the wall.

The Bishop of Brechin, Dr Forbes, who was also staying in the Castle, was very incredulous about this apparition and teased his friend by saying, "Now, Mr Dean, we all know you are the most persevering beggar in Scotland. I am sure you brought out your collecting book and laid the ghost by asking him for a subscription."

Next night, to the delight of Dr Nicholson, the Provost of Perth, who had joined the party, said he had had a similar mysterious visit the last time he slept in that room. The Dean at once hurried him off to the Bishop and made him repeat his tale to that sceptical prelate.

Bishop Forbes and Uncle Robert Liddell both offered to hold a service of exorcism in the Castle, but this was never done. I think Claude would have been afraid to have it. Unquestionably, there is something strange about the place. The Chaplain told me that he felt this more and more the longer he lived there, while the Factor, Mr Ralston, a dry, shrewd, hard-headed Scotsman, after he had been initiated into the secret could never be induced to sleep in the Castle. One winter evening, when he had come up for the theatricals, a sudden snowstorm came on and the road back to his home appeared impassable. However, he resolutely refused to spend the night on a sofa and insisted on rousing the gardeners and stablemen to dig out a path to his house nearly a mile off outside the Park. Lady Strathmore herself told me that she once disclosed to Mr Ralston her great curiosity about the mystery. He looked earnestly at her and said very gravely: "Lady Strathmore, it is fortunate that you do not know it and can never know it, for if you did you would not be a happy woman." Such a speech from such a man was certainly uncanny.

Many years afterwards, in September 1912, I visited Glamis with my daughter, Dora, for the first time after Claude's death. His son, the present owner, has no objection to talking about the ghost.

He and his wife were much interested in my dream and got me to give them a copy of my account of it. Lady Strathmore told me that on her first visit to Glamis after her marriage she and her husband occupied the Blue Room. During the night she dreamt that she saw a big man gazing at her from the other side of the bed; only he was thin, not fat like my ghost. She woke in a great fright and roused her husband, but of course there was nothing there. Two of her children, Rose, the second girl, and David, the youngest boy, often see shadowy figures flitting about the Castle. They are not alarmed by them, but Rose says she would not like to sleep in the Blue Room. Figures have been frequently seen by them and by a housemaid in the Oak Room, which my mother always had, but it has now been turned into an extra sitting-room. King Malcolm's Chamber, the little room where I used to dress, has also been dismantled and thrown into the passage. This is a great improvement, as it provides a better access to the great drawing-room and the Chapel.

BORLEY RECTORY

The most famous haunted house in England is undoubtedly Borley Rectory. And the man who made it famous is England's most remarkable ghost-hunter, Harry Price.

Price, ghost-hunter extraordinary, claimed that he was born in Shrewsbury, son of a wealthy paper manufacturer. A brilliant critical biography by Trevor Hall, *The Search for Harry Price*, reveals that he was, in fact, the son of an unsuccessful grocer, and that he was born in London in 1881. From then until he was about forty he seems to have supported himself by a variety of jobs, including commercial travelling, manufacturing patent medicines, journalism and giving gramophone concerts. What *is* certain is that his lifelong interest in stage magic began at the age of eight, when he saw an itinerant magician and patent medicine salesman, the Great Sequah, giving a public performance. Price began collecting books on magic, and became an expert magician. It may have been the interest in magic that led him to join the Society for Psychical Research in 1920 – the SPR was then, as now, much concerned with trying to detect fraud in mediums. E.J. Dingwall, who was then Research Officer for the Society, asked Price if he would care to come with him to Munich, to attend some seances of a remarkable German medium, Willi Schneider – one of two brothers. The man who arranged the seances was the German investigator, Baron von Schrenk-Notzing, a friend of Lombroso's, and the author of a sensationally successful book called

Materialisation Phenomena, which had aroused widespread scepticism in Germany when it appeared in 1914. Schrenk-Notzing himself was something of a flamboyant publicist, and Trevor Hall suggests that Harry Price took his example to heart, and decided that this was the way to achieve the fame he craved. (He admitted frankly that he had always wanted to get his name in *Who's Who*.)

The Schneider brothers, Willi and Rudi, the most psychic members of a psychic family, were born at Braunau-am-Inn and, according to one friend of the family, the phenomena began after they had spent an evening playing with a ouija board. Willi had then reached the age of puberty – in 1916 – and the family was disturbed by loud knocking noises. Then objects began moving around, and Willi saw a ghost in the sitting room. Neighbours became so alarmed about the racket that the family were on the point of vacating the flat. By means of the ouija board, they tried questioning the "spirit", which identified itself as a girl named Olga Lindtner, who claimed to be a reincarnation of the notorious Lola Montez. In due course, Willi went into a trance, and Olga spoke through him. In spite of doubts later raised by Harry Price – after he had quarrelled with the brothers – there can be no doubt that the phenomena were genuine. The novelist Thomas Mann attended one seance, and has recorded how, as he pressed Willi's knees tightly between his own, and two other people held his hands, a handkerchief floated into the air, a bell began to ring and then floated into the air, a music box played, and the keys of a typewriter were struck. Mann was convinced that deception was impossible.

Harry Price and E.J. Dingwall witnessed similar occurrences, and also saw a white hand which materialised in front of them; they had no doubt whatever of the genuineness of the phenomena, and said as much at a lecture to the SPR. But by way of keeping his options open, Price helped to edit and publish a book called *Revelations of a Spirit Medium*, in which a fake medium described the tricks of the trade.

The case with which Price's name has become most widely associated is, of course, that of Borley Rectory. And in spite of the debunking that has taken place since Price's death in 1948, it remains one of the most interesting hauntings of the twentieth century. After Price's death, a whole volume of the *Proceedings of the Society for Psychical Research* was devoted to *The Haunting of Borley Rectory*, "A Critical Survey of the Evidence", by

Dingwall, Trevor Hall and Kate Goldney. They allege that Price probably produced some of the "poltergeist" phenomena himself by tossing pebbles – which, from our knowledge of Price, must be admitted as possible. Their overall conclusion is that there are so many doubts that it would probably be simplest to regard the haunting of Borley as a fairy story. But this is to ignore the fact that stories of hauntings were common long before Price came on the scene, and have continued since he left it. Anyone who feels that the SPR survey proves that Price was a liar should read the long account of Borley in Peter Underwood's *Gazetteer of British Ghosts*, with Underwood's own firsthand reports from interviews with witnesses.

Borley Rectory was built in 1863 on the site of Borley Manor House, which in turn seems to have been built on the site of a Benedictine abbey. It was built by the Reverend H.D.E. Bull. It is difficult to pin down the earliest known "sightings", but it is clear that during Henry Bull's tenancy, a number of people saw the apparition of a nun. Henry Bull himself knew of the legend that a nun and a Benedictine monk had tried to elope, been caught, and had both been killed, the nun being bricked up alive. Bull's daughter Ethel confirmed in a letter to Trevor Hall in 1953 that she had awakened to find a strange man standing beside her bed, and had felt someone sitting down on the bed on several occasions; she also told Peter Underwood how, on 28 July 1900, she and her two sisters all saw a nun-like figure gliding along "Nun's Walk", apparently telling her beads. The other sister, Elsie, saw the nun, who looked quite solid, and went to ask her what she wanted; the nun vanished.

After the Reverend Henry Bull's death, his son, the Reverend Harry Bull, took over the rectory. He was interested in psychical research, and claimed that he saw many ghosts. His daughter told Price that he had seen a legendary phantom coach (in which the lovers were supposed to have fled) and that, one day in the garden, the retriever had howled with terror, looking towards some legs visible under a fruit tree. Bull, thinking this was a poacher, followed the legs as they walked towards a postern gate; at which point he realised that the "poacher" was somehow incomplete. The legs disappeared through the gate without opening it.

Harry Bull died in 1927, and the rectory was empty until 1928, when the Reverend Guy Smith and his wife moved in. One stormy night, there was a furious ringing of the doorbell;

Borley Rectory

when Smith arrived there, he found no one. It happened again later – a peal so prolonged that Smith was able to get to the door before it stopped; again, there was no one. After that, all the keys of all the rooms fell out of the locks overnight; later, they vanished. Then they began hearing slippered footsteps. Stones were thrown – small pebbles. Lights were switched on. One day, Mrs Smith thought she saw a horse-drawn coach in the drive. Mr Smith thought he heard someone whisper, "Don't, Carlos, don't", as he was walking into the chapel. The Smiths decided to contact the *Daily Mirror*, who asked Harry Price if he would be willing to go along with an investigator. They told Price their story, and gave him every facility to investigate. But within nine months, they had had enough of the place – perhaps because its plumbing left much to be desired – and moved to Norfolk. According to the SPR report, the Smiths only called the *Daily Mirror* because they were concerned about all the stories that the house was haunted, and wanted to reassure their parishioners by getting the place a clean bill of health. This story sounds, on the face of it, absurd. Moreover, there exists a letter from Mr Smith to Harry Price stating: "Borley is undoubtedly haunted." (It is true that Mrs Smith wrote a letter to the *Church Times* in 1929 saying she did not believe the house to be haunted, but this seems to have been a belated attempt to stem the flood of sensational publicity that followed the *Daily Mirror* story.)

In October 1930, the rectory was taken over by the Reverend L.A. Foyster, and his much younger wife Marianne. Foyster, oddly enough, had lived near Amherst at the time of the Esther Cox case, and the SPR survey makes much of this coincidence; however, it seems doubtful that the vicar would attempt to fake disturbances on the model of his earlier experience. Certainly, the Foyster incumbency saw the most spectacular exhibitions of the Borley poltergeist. Foyster kept a diary of the disturbances. Bells were rung, bricks thrown, footsteps heard and water out of a jug poured over the couple when in bed. Foyster was even awakened by a violent blow on the head from his own hairbrush. They saw a number of apparitions, including the nun and a clergyman who was identified as the Reverend Henry Bull, the builder of the rectory. Writing appeared on the walls, asking for a mass to be said, and asking for "Light".

There is much independent confirmation of all these events. A Justice of the Peace named Guy L'Estrange visited Borley at the invitation of the Foysters, and wrote a lengthy account of it.

As soon as he arrived, he saw a dim figure near the porch, which vanished as soon as he approached. Mrs Foyster had a bruise on her forehead – something "like a man's fist" had struck her the previous evening. The Foysters were telling L'Estrange about mysterious fires that kept breaking out in locked rooms when there was a loud crash in the hall; they found it littered with broken crockery. Then bottles began flying about. L'Estrange notes that they seemed to appear suddenly in mid-air. The bottles were coming from a locked storage shed outside. All the bells began to ring, making a deafening clamour – but all the bell wires had been cut. L'Estrange shouted: "If some invisible person is present, please stop ringing for a moment." Instantly, the bells stopped – stopped dead, as if each clapper had been grabbed by an unseen hand. Later, sitting alone in front of the fire, L'Estrange heard footsteps behind him; he turned, but the room was empty. The footsteps had come from a part of the wall where there had once been a door. In bed, L'Estrange felt the room become icy cold, and saw a kind of shape materialising from a patch of luminosity; he walked towards it, and had a feeling of something trying to push him back. He spoke to it, and it slowly vanished. He was luckier than another visitor who thought that the ghostly figure was someone playing a joke, and tried to grab it; he was given a hard blow in the eye.

The rector and others tried praying in the chapel, taking with them a relic of the Curé of Ars, and then went around the house making signs of the cross. Finally, they all spent the night in the Blue Room, where Henry Bull (and others) had died; they asked that the entity should stop troubling the inmates of the house; a black shadow began to form against the wall, then dissolved. But after this, temporary peace descended on Borley Rectory.

In 1935, the Foysters decided they had had enough, and moved. Price rented the rectory in 1937, and arranged for a team of investigators to go in. But the major phenomena were over. Even so, the chief investigator, Sidney Glanville, a retired engineer, became completely convinced of the reality of the haunting.

In March 1938, the team were experimenting with a planchette, which wrote the message that Borley would be destroyed by fire. This happened in February 1939, when the house mysteriously burned down. Yet the phenomena continued; a Cambridge team investigating the ruins heard footsteps, saw patches of light, and recorded sudden sharp drops in temperature.

In August 1943, Price decided to try digging in the cellars at Borley – which he had been advised to do by a planchette message which claimed to come from "Glanvil" – the same Glanvil who wrote the account of the Tedworth drummer. They found a cream jug, which had also been referred to by the planchette, and some fragments of a human skull. The jawbone showed signs of a deep-seated abscess – Peter Underwood speculates that this is why the phantom nun always looked miserable.

The SPR survey on Borley, which appeared eight years after Price's death, had the effect of seriously undermining his credit. Trevor Hall's *Search for Harry Price* (1978) completed the work of destroying his reputation. Yet although this leaves no doubt that Price lied about his origins – perhaps romanced would be a better word – and hungered for fame, it produces no evidence that Price was not exactly what he always claimed to be: an enthusiastic scientific investigator of paranormal phenomena. To assume that, because Price wanted to be thought a "gentleman", he was also dishonest as a paranormal researcher, is surely poor psychology. Price was one of those ambitious men who crave an outlet for their energies. He was forty years old before he found the opportunity he was looking for – a long time for a man of Price's impatient temperament. It came when Dingwall invited him to Munich to study the Schneider brothers. From then on, Price had discovered his vocation; at last, he had found the outlet he needed for his explosive energy and romanticism. And when a man as energetic and romantic as Harry Price finally finds what he is looking for, he does not risk spoiling everything with a little cheap skulduggery. It only takes one scandal to destroy a scientist's reputation. But to put it this way is to imply that Price disciplined his natural dishonesty solely to maintain his reputation and this is to miss the real point; that once a man has found his vocation, he pours into it all that is best about himself. Bernard Shaw has left an interesting description of the socialist Edward Aveling, who was Eleanor Marx's common-law husband; he was an inveterate seducer, and a borrower who never paid his debts, yet where socialism was concerned, he was fiercely sincere. Everything we know about Price reveals that, where psychical research was concerned, he was totally dedicated – although not above grabbing publicity wherever he could find it.

Unlike most automatic writers, who received their messages from the spirits, the nineteenth century British journalist William Stead got messages from the living – and saved them the bother of writing themselves. He would ask mental questions and his hand would write the answers automatically – sometimes learning more than the friends wanted him to.

Once he had arranged a lunch engagement with a woman who had been out of town over the weekend. He mentally inquired whether she had returned to London yet, and his hand wrote a long note. It described an unpleasant encounter she had had on the train. According to the message, she had found herself alone in a compartment with a strange man. He came over, sat close to her, and when she tried to push him away, attempted to kiss her. Struggling furiously, she thumped him with his umbrella, which broke. Then the train unexpectedly stopped and the man took flight.

When Stead sent his servant to his friend's house with a note condoling her on the assault, the woman was taken aback. She replied, "I had decided not to speak of it to anyone." She added, "The umbrella was mine, not his."

In short it would be of no advantage to him to pretend the Borley phenomena were genuine when they were not. His reputation was based on his scepticism as much as on his support of the reality of psychic phenomena. Possibly – like most of us – he was capable of stretching a fact when it appealed to his romanticism. But in the case of Borley, there was no need to stretch facts. The haunting of Borley does not rest on Price's evidence alone; there are dozens of other witnesses, such as Guy L'Estrange – or Dom Richard White-house, cited by Underwood, who witnessed just as many incredible occurrences: flying objects, ringing of bells, writing on walls, outbreaks of fire, materialisation of bottles.

And is there evidence that Price *did* stretch the facts? The SPR survey cites as an example of his dishonesty the episode of the pair of legs that Harry Bull saw walking through the postern gate. Price says, admittedly, that when the man emerged from behind the fruit trees, he was headless. But the report then goes on to cite Price's original notes, which read: "Rev. Harry Bull saw coach, Juvenal, retriever, terrified and growled. Saw man's legs rest hid by fruit trees, thought poacher, followed with

Juvenal, gate shut, but saw legs disappear through gate."
Clearly, what Bull saw disappearing through the gate was
not a complete man, or Price would not refer only to the
legs. It sounds as if the upper half of his body was missing
– in which case, headless is a fair description.

What seems clear from all accounts of the case is that the
"ground" itself is haunted, and continues to be so. Borley is a
"place of power", the kind of place that *would* be chosen for a
monastery, and that probably held some pagan site of worship
long before that. In the Rectory's early days, Harry Bull himself
– son of the Reverend Henry Bull – was probably the unconscious focus or medium; Paul Tabori says that he was probably
psychic. This is borne out by the fact that young Bull saw so
many of the "ghosts", including the coach and the nun. It is
important to realise that not all people can see ghosts. The
"ghost-hunter" Andrew Green describes, in *Our Haunted Kingdom*, a visit that he and other members of the Ealing Psychical
Research Society paid to Borley in 1951.

"One of the Society members grabbed my arm and, although

One night in early spring 1948, a young Swedish man awoke to
find a white-haired gentleman standing at his bedside. For some
reason the young man – whom we'll call Erson – wasn't
frightened. The stranger began to talk in a language Erson
couldn't understand, but thought must be English. He managed
to convey the information that his name was Price.

The mysterious Price began to appear fairly frequently, at
times in the morning, and he was seen not only by Erson but also
by his wife and daughter. The figure appeared solid and lifelike,
but when Erson tried to photograph it, he only got a few shadows
on the prints. Price seemed amused by these efforts to photograph him.

Finally Erson acquired enough English to understand that his
visitor had studied ghosts and related subjects when alive. It was
"Price" who urged Erson to go to a particular hospital in Lund to
take treatment for a health problem. While there, Erson told a
psychiatrist of his ghostly visitor. The doctor, having heard of the
famous English psychical researcher Harry Price, decided to find
out from the SPR when he had died. It was 29 March 1948 – just
about the time that Erson's spectral friend had made his first
appearance.

obviously terrified, proceeded to describe a phantom that he could see some thirty feet in front of him, standing at the end of the "Nun's Walk". It was of a Woman in a long white gown, and moved slowly towards the end of the neglected garden . . . the witness was perspiring profusely with fear and later with annoyance that I had failed to see the ghost."

Green had only *heard* the rustle of trees and bushes, as if something was walking through the undergrowth. We may assume, then, that if Green had been a tenant of Borley before its destruction, he would probably have seen no ghosts. Bull *was*, it seems, enough of a "medium" to see the ghosts. And Marianne Foyster was a far more powerful medium who changed the character of the haunting into poltergeist activity. (Most of the messages scrawled on walls were addressed to her.) The reason that the subsequent investigation of Borley (during Price's tenancy) was so unsuccessful was that there was no medium present to provide the energy.

Asked about the "ley system" of the Borley area, the ley expert Stephen Jenkins replied as follows: "Norfolk and Suffolk are a spider-web of alignments, many of which are linked to curious manifestations. Borley church stands at a node where four lines cross, one going from Asher church to Sproughton church . . ." After giving further details of the ley system, he goes on:

> My wife photographed me as I was standing with my back to the south wall of Borley churchyard, at ten o'clock on the morning of Saturday the 1st of September, 1979. Recently, this was borrowed for a magazine article, and the editor kindly sent me an enlargement. No less than three people, not one of them known to the others, have on separate occasions noted in the enlargement some odd – and not very prepossessing – faces among the trees close to the church. The same identifications have been made without possibility of collusion.
>
> More dramatic than unexpected faces in a photograph, which can always be explained away as "simulacra", or something wrong with the emulsion, is an incident of Sunday the 28th of August, 1977, on the road north of Belchamp Walter Hall. The time was precisely 12:52 pm, and we were driving south west along the minor road which marks the

north end of the Hall grounds, when on the road in front, in the act of turning left into the hedge (I mean our left, across the path of the car), *instantaneously* appeared four men in black – I thought them hooded and cloaked – carrying a black, old-fashioned coffin, ornately trimmed with silver. The impression made on both of us was one of absolute *physical* presence, of complete material reality. Thelma and I at once agreed to make separate notes without comparing impressions. We did so, and the descriptions tallied exactly, except that she noted the near left bearer turn his face towards her. I did not see this as I was abruptly braking at the time.

What I had seen as a hood, she described as a soft tall hat, with a kind of scarf falling to the left shoulder, thrown across the cloaked body to the right. The face was that of a skull.

The next day we returned to the precise spot at exactly the same time and took a picture. It is a Kodak colour slide. In the hedge near the gap where the "funeral party" vanished (there is a path there leading to Belchamp Walter churchyard) is a short figure, apparently cloaked, its face lowered with a skull-like dome to the head. A year later I returned searching the area where it had apparently stood. There was nothing, no post or stump that might have provided such an image, nor was there the slightest sign of the ground having been disturbed by the removal of anything that might have been rooted in it. The image is simply there on the film – we saw nothing wrong with the eye.

That minor road alongside the north edge of the Belchamp Walter Estate precisely coincides with a line passing through the node in the water west of Heaven Wood. That node itself linked with the node at Borley.

He adds a postscript: "I hazard a guess that the dress of the coffin-bearer is that of the late fourteenth century. There seems to be no local legend of a phantom funeral."

If Price invented the ghosts of Borley, he must have been in collusion with a remarkable number of people.

The English medium Rosemary Brown has produced quantities of music she claims has been dictated to her by the great masters of music, who have chosen this way to prove that their spirits survive. One of her special favourites is Beethoven, and the two of them are engaged on a project that is taking years: the Tenth Symphony. It is an enormous choral work, like the great composer's Ninth Symphony.

In writing this new work Beethoven will be able to hear it, according to Rosemary Brown. In her autobiography *Unfinished Symphonies*, she says that his deafness is gone. "Those human ills and frailties disappear once we reach the other side," she writes. The spirit Beethoven is a less stormy person than he was in life, but he is still awe-inspiring. Rosemary Brown was so much in awe of him at first that little conversation took place. She received his music by a kind of telepathy, slowly catching his ideas in writing.

Now Beethoven works much more directly, dictating several bars for one hand, and then going back to fill in for the other. "After all," says the medium, "they know already what they are going to tell me to write, and it is simpler to keep to one line at a time."

NEWS STORIES: WEIRD, FUNNY AND PECULIAR

Colin Wilson, Damon Wilson and Rowan Wilson

BELIEVE IT
OR NOT

Strange Animal Stories

A large accumulation of excreted methane gas in a pig shed near Verona in Italy was ignited by a spark from a fuse box. The resulting explosion destroyed the shed utterly and killed all 500 pigs. A witness said: "I saw pigs flying through the air, I thought it was Doomsday."

The *Big Issue*

In the *Cape Cod Times Restaurant Guide* an establishment called "The Sea Gull Café" is listed. According to the description, the café features American cuisine, outdoor dining, and an open buffet. It is open all year round. Unfortunately this pleasant eating place is a hoax played upon the paper: the address given is that of the city's rubbish dump.

The *National Enquirer*

The Anderson Hospital and Tumour Institute in Houston, Texas, has cell cultures of over 300 rare animals stored in liquid nitrogen in preparation for the day when gene science will allow them to be cloned into complete specimens.

Daily Courier Democrat

In August 1978 a strange rumour spread through Uganda, at the time ruled by the murderous dictator Idi Amin. According to whispered accounts, a tortoise had wandered into a small Ugandan village and explained to anyone that would listen that it must be taken to the town of Jinja, on the River Nile, near the country's capital Kampala. There, in the presence of the Regional Governor and the Police Commissioner, it would reveal its dark knowledge. The rumours did not reveal the reptile's news, but they did tell of the unfortunate creature's immediate imprisonment: it was not seen again.

This story was widely believed. It was brought to international attention when several departments of the Ugandan government held crisis meetings at which they strenuously denied the existence of the "politically imprisoned" tortoise. A spokesman commented that the Ugandan populace was "always drunk with rumours". But the story would not disappear. Finally Amin himself held a press conference at which he threatened to shoot anyone caught mentioning the animal again.

The *Guardian*

Among the many remedies available to sufferers of insomnia is a book entitled *Count Sheep*. On every page, the book features hundreds of photos of sheep, arranged in columns and rows for easy enumeration. In all, the home edition features 65,000 sheep; a travel edition is available featuring only 28,000.

LA Times

Vampire bats in Texas are being forced to change their diet. The South American, blood-drinking bats at the Houston zoological gardens in Texas have had their supply of beef blood ($1.20/gallon) cut off because of the meat shortage.

Curator Richard Quick explained that the meat packing firm that used to provide the bats' liquid diet had recently been forced to close down. Until the crisis is over the bats are being fed on *human* blood discarded by local hospitals.

Sunday Mirror

When BEA helicopter pilot Captain Dick Hensen set down in a field in Maldon, Essex, he paid little attention to a nearby herd of cows. However, when he returned from making a phone call a few minutes later he was horrified to see that the cows had licked most of the paint off the machine. One had even gouged a hole in the perspex cockpit windshield with a questing horn.

The helicopter was so badly damaged it had to be taken out of service.

Sunday Express

Farmer Ted Jewell arrived at the slaughterhouse in Eastleigh, Hants, yesterday, only to find that the back of his lorry was completely empty. The eleven stone pig he had loaded at the start of the journey had completely vanished. He said; "A pig jumping a over a five foot tailboard, then down six feet onto the road is almost as daft as a pig flying. But that's all that could have happened."

The People

"This is a very unusual case . . . pigs eating an aeroplane," remarked the prosecuting council at a recent case at Devizes Crown Court in Wiltshire. In the dock was Wilfred Grist, swineherd at Craymarsh Farm, Seend, which is owned by Mr Sam Cottle. Grist was accused of deliberately letting 968 pigs out of their sty with malicious intent.

The pigs celebrated their new found freedom by eating most of the fabric off an Auster aeroplane parked nearby. They went on to lunch on two and a half tons of hay, a straw rick, half a ton of cattle food and thirty asbestos sheets. They also uprooted three acres of pasture, damaged four farm gates and killed ten of their own number in fights.

In his defence, Grist claimed that Cottle had hit him. Then, he said, the farmer and his brother had forced him into a car saying that they were going to throw him into a slurry pit.

Mr Cottle did not deny the accusation, although he added that he had soon changed his mind . . . He decided that it would be much better to drop Mr Grist into the giant animal-food mixer instead.

Daily Mirror

While attempting the enormous project of constructing a dictionary of ancient Sumerian, scholars at the University of Pennsylvania in Philadelphia found that some of the phrases they encountered on ancient tablets remained semantically difficult no matter how they tried to interpret them. After weeks of work one example stubbornly refused to mean anything other than: "He put a hot fish in her navel."

Sunday Times

Snoopy, the philosophical beagle from the Charlie Brown comic strip, may have assumed a more historical, perhaps even religious significance.

Professor Filippo Magi, director of the Vatican's Archaeological Study and Research, reports a strange find at a dig beneath one of Rome's most historic churches: the papal Basilica of St Mary Major. Under the church are the remains of a huge, first century AD forum, or market, and among the crowded Roman graffiti on its walls is a perfect image of Snoopy the beagle.

Some Rome newspapers are reported to be showing a picture of the famous dog lying on the roof of his kennel thinking: "Suspirium! Aetate progredi, heu!" (Sigh! The years roll on alas!)

Daily Mail

San Francisco police were recently called in to apprehend a zebra making its escape from the Marine World zoo down a neighbouring six-lane freeway. After a high speed chase – up to 45 mph – the animal was finally cornered, but if the cops thought that was the end of it they were in for a shock.

The irate zebra kicked in two doors on a squad car, smashed a mudguard, climbed on the bonnet and chewed the steering wheel. It also bit two animal handlers before it could be returned to captivity.

Daily Mail

Mother Nature seems to have given up being subtle in warning us about the looming environmental crisis – from Albany in Jamaica comes a report of a doom-saying goat. Miss Adele Brown and her mother were out collecting pa fruit when they were approached by the animal. It prophesied that unless the Green Party came to power soon the planet's condition would take a drastic turn for the worse.

Much afraid, they asked what they should do. The goat replied: "There are no limits to creativity and no limits to subversion. Vote for any candidate opposed to the Year 2000 Party." Then it wandered into the forest.

The *Brisbane Telegraph*

From the recent *Lloyd's List* comes this environmental snippet: "The average seal rehabilitated after the Exxon Valdez oil spill had $80,000 spent on it. Two of the most expensive were put

back into the bay at a special ceremony. Within two minutes
they were both eaten by a killer whale."

The Observer

Detective Constable Bernard Startup, of Linden Avenue, Old-
ham, was disturbed at 9.30 p.m. on 5 August 1972 by a knock at
his door. The man on his step alerted DC Startup to the fact that
a huge hairy pig was eating the young fir trees in his garden. As
the pair watched, the alarming animal stretched too far in
search of food and fell into the fishpond. While it was thus
distracted, Startup blocked off the entrance to his garden with
his car, and phoned his colleagues. The animal was eventually
tranquillized by a vet.

This oddity became a mystery when it was discovered that
the 200 lb beast was a wild boar, a species supposedly extinct in
Britain for 400 years. The animal was taken to Marwell
Zoological Park when no collector or zoo claimed it as their
own.

Aldershot news

The death of thousands of goldfish in the ponds of Britain in the
spring of 1977 has been attributed to sex-crazed toads. That
spring, male toads found themselves in a ten to one majority
over female toads. The resulting dearth of breeding partners
left the males mating with anything, water-lilies, sticks, and
also pets. The grip of a mating male toad is easily sufficient to
crush an average goldfish.

Daily Mirror

Drivers on the M6 near Sandbach were surprised to find
themselves sharing the road with a sprinting pig. A police
car was despatched, but failed to find any trace of the animal
on the road. The sighting is made all the more mysterious by
the fact that no one in the area had reported losing such an
animal.

Daily Express

A magpie living on a golf-course in Aldershot is blamed for the
loss of £11 worth of golf balls. The bird had formed the habit of
swooping upon the balls as soon as they had landed, then
flying off and dropping them over the fence of a nearby high-
security aircraft establishment.

Daily Express

A London branch of the National Westminster Bank has been given the task of guarding a highly valuable – perhaps miraculous – fish. The five and a half inch Butterfly fish has Arabic writing on its tail spelling out: "Divine Universal. There none but God to be worshipped." (sic)

The fish was purchased in a Dar-Es-Salaam market eight years ago and an expert has said that the writing is natural and definitely not the work of fraudsters.

The quietly portentous creature has been exhibited around the world and is in the Nat West's keeping only until a suitably splendid permanent home can be provided.

London Evening News

Curious Laws and Law-suits

Two lawyers from Encino, California, were severely reprimanded by a judge for bringing the bar into disrepute. The pair were neighbours, and one sued the other for playing basketball noisily, thus interrupting his naps and lowering the value of his property. The other countersued for general damages on the grounds that his neighbour played loud rock music and had harassed him by filming his basketball games for evidence.

LA Times

The descendants of Jacob DeHaven are suing the US government for 141.6 billion dollars. They claim that this is equivalent, with interest, to the 450,000 dollars that their ancestor lent to the Continental Congress for the purpose of rescuing George Washington's troops at Valley Forge.

LA Daily News

In 1982 John Crumpton IV and Jane Berry robbed a bank in Los Angeles. While trying to escape, Crumpton was shot dead by the police and Berry was shot and seriously wounded. Subsequently, Berry decided that she would sue the police for not having arrested her on a previous warrant, thus indirectly causing her wounding.

LA Daily News

A grocery assistant, Tom Morgan, sued his co-worker, Randy Maresh, for $100,000 on the grounds that he was inflicting severe mental stress. Maresh was, allegedly, assaulting Morgan by farting at him. According to Morgan, Maresh would "hold it and walk funny to get to me" before evacuating himself. Maresh's attorney argued that flatulence was a form of free speech, and so covered by the First Amendment. The judge ruled that no law directly covered the subject of flatulence, and threw the case out.

Time

A bye-law passed in Cotton Valley, Louisiana, makes it an offence to play tennis while wearing a hat that might startle a timid person.

Tennis Magazine

In 1990, New York State was forced to pass laws to criminalize participation in two new and popular sports: Dwarf-bowling and Dwarf-tossing. In the former, a vertically challenged individual wearing a helmet is strapped to a skateboard and propelled towards an arrangement of pins. In the latter a similar individual, this time harnessed, is thrown at a padded target. It is not known if all concerned were willing participants.

LA Times

City officials of Toccoa, Georgia, have ruled that no public money is to be used as funding for Yoga classes on the grounds that this discipline is a form of Devil-worship.

LA Times

In 1990, the state of California decided that all personalized car numberplates featuring racial insults would have to be returned and renumbered in a less offensive manner. Among those recalled were DAGO ESQ, TOP WOPS, 14K WOP, FOXY DAGO and BBOP WOP. When the plates' owners complained, the state was surprised to find that they were nearly all Italian-Americans.

LA Times

A school in Florida has banned its pupil from reading the fairy tale *Snow White* after Christian parents complained of its "graphic violence".

Midweek

Aliens, Visitations and Psychic Occurrences

In 1976, on the back wall of Billsdown Hen House near Bournemouth, someone noticed what appeared to be an image of Christ crucified picked out in stains. The *Sunday People* heard the story and ran a feature article on the "miracle". They invited readers to examine a photograph of the wall, and then send in drawings of what they thought they saw. The next week some of the entries were printed. They included a jug, a candle, a group of four angels, a scene of rivers and trees, and Christ reclining on a sofa.

Sunday People

A block of flats in Hamilton, New Zealand, was the object of repeated assaults of hurled bottles. Among the projectiles were milk bottles, beer bottles and coffee jars. Despite a police surveillance set up to discover the source of the attacks, some of which lasted up to four hours, they remain a mystery. Maori elders explained the phenomena by saying that the building was erected on sacred land; the spirits of the land were showing that they were offended.

Sunday Express

Mrs Jean Hingley of Rowley Regis in the West Midlands reported a strange visitation to her local police. Answering her back door one night, she was faced with a blinding light. As her eyes became accustomed to it, she saw three figures with corpse-like faces and wings on their backs standing on her doorstep. Astonished and confused, Mrs Hingley entered into a "close encounter of the third kind" by asking the visitors if they would like some coffee. They refused, but said they would quite like some water. Formalities over, the aliens entered Mrs Hingley's house and enjoyed a glass of cold water. On their way out, they noticed some mince pies and decided to take them with them. They would, they said, be back sometime.

Daily Mirror

In July 1979, identical twin sisters Ruth Johnson and Allison Mitchell Erb were reunited. The pair had been adopted sepa-

Visitors from outerspace are always news, but these flying saucers in Brazil 1969 were only clouds

rately in New Hampshire twenty-six earlier, and had had no contact since that time. Both women were hairdressers. Both had daughters named Kristen. Both had watched a TV programme defending the right of adopted children to identify their families, and as a result each began the search for the other.

Daily Mail

A policeman called to the home of a man in Toledo and found the occupant in severe mental distress because of the invisible dwarfs that were overrunning his home. Obligingly, the policeman mediated: "I told the one dwarf in the kitchen to leave, then went to the cellar to tell the others . . . They didn't put up much resistance and left." Convinced, the man thanked the policeman profusely. The question is, how did he know that they were gone?

Toledo Blade

A farmer from Tout in France, reported to astounded police that a UFO had landed in one of his fields while he was

---

In 1975 three of the islands in the Comoro group, which lies between Africa and Madagascar, declared their independence from France. Soon afterwards a man named Ali Soilih declared himself dictator of the tiny state with the military help of a French mercenary, Bob Denard. Soilih proved to be a despot: he raised death squads, kidnapped and raped women and organized the destruction of all machinery on the islands.

Two years into his reign Soilih consulted a witch-doctor in order to know what the future held for himself and his descendants. The witch-doctor was encouraging: Soilih could only be killed by a man who owned a dog. Upon hearing this, Soilih acted as any dictator would and had his death squads kill all the dogs on the island.

Nevertheless, a year later he was dead, "shot while trying to escape" by the forces of his old comrade Bob Denard. The French mercenary had received a new contract, this time from one of Soilih's many enemies. And the witch-doctor had been right: among Denard's troops was his ever-present mascot, a large Alsatian dog.

Sunday Times

working. A man and a woman, both naked, had jumped out of the vehicle and proceeded to have sex three times. When the farmer tried to approach the copulating couple, he was thrown back by an inexplicable force. After the third time, the pair jumped back into the UFO and flew away.

News Of The World

Since 11 January 1976, a mysterious tree stump has been touring Ridgway, Illinois. The 500 lb stump appears in unlikely places, including inside a van and various people's houses. It stays for up to two days then disappears in an equally inexplicable way.

Lebanon Daily News

Bizarre Crimes

A twenty-three-year-old, bespectacled, Schools' Career Advisor named Graham Carter was arrested on 23 June 1977 at Oxford Circus in London. He was accused of being responsible for a wave of "clothes cutting" incidents. In the areas around Oxford Circus, Green Park and Piccadilly tube stations, over the previous six months, women had been finding that large circles of material had been removed from the back of their skirts with sharp scissors. Often the unfortunate victims went on their way unaware of the crime until either the draught or a considerate passer-by appraised them of their situation. Mr Carter admitted the offences, but while he was in custody a small number of snippings continued to occur. "There is certainly one other person, if not more, doing this sort of thing," commented Mr Carter's lawyer.

Daily Express

Rosana Vigil, aged sixty, was attacked by a man in the street in Denver, Colorado. The assailant prised her mouth open and removed her false teeth. Mrs Vigil told the police: "He said 'There aint no gold here, so here's your teeth', and he gave them back."

New York Post

In Tokyo, a twenty-six-year-old draughtsman was arrested for scratching the faces of twelve women with his tie-pin. He explained that travelling to and from work on crowded tube trains depressed him terribly, and that disfiguring fellow passengers helped him to relax. The man had a history of mental illness.

Straits Times (Singapore)

Mr Michael Douglas-Smith was driving back from a fancy-dress party when he was torn from his car by three large men and shoved into their vehicle. After having driven a few metres with their hostage, who was dressed as a fairy, the men had a change of mind. Mr Douglas-Smith was dumped by the side of the road and the assailants' car sped away.

Subsequently the three men were arrested and charged with assault. One commented: "There was a bit of confusion."

Weekend Magazine

In 1976, a man accused of squatting was dismissed from Brighton County Court because he was wearing a battery-operated flashing clown's nose.

The *Sun*

A young police recruit named Paul Williams decided to fake an assault upon himself. To this end, he stabbed himself repeatedly with a penknife and hit himself on the head with a brick.

After leaving hospital, Williams was given an award for his bravery in the "assault".

Unfortunately his fraud was detected: the emergency call for help, as well as other false alarms, were traced to his extension at the police station. Asked why he had done all this, he said

In both 1976 and 1978, British stuntman Eddie Shingler tried to organize his own crucifixion as a spectator event in Nottingham. Witnessing the actual nailing up of Mr Shingler was to cost three pounds whereas just watching him hang there would be a reasonable fifty pence. Both attempts were foiled by the police, who announced that they would arrest anyone trying to nail Mr Shingler to the cross on a charge of assault.

Daily Mirror

that he had expected police work to be more exciting than it was.

The *Sun*

Wendy Bergen, an award-winning news journalist for local television in Denver, planned a series of reports unmasking the vicious underground blood-sport rings in the area. The reports were to be big audience winners, broadcast during the stations "sweeps" week, a test week to establish average viewer numbers for the purposes of selling advertising space.

The problem was that, try as she might, Bergen could not find any illegal blood sports taking place in Denver. In desperation she organized one herself, a pit bull terrier fight, and filmed the violent results. Unfortunately for Ms Bergen, the police were aware of her activities, and she now faces up to ten years in prison.

Ann Arbor News

Three pilots for Northwest Airlines were arrested for drunk flying. One of the three, a captain, had a blood-alcohol level over three times the legal limit. He argued in his defence that, as a habitual drinker – indeed, an alcoholic – he had to drink far more than other people before he felt any benefit.

LA Times

One night in 1990 a woman of Van Nuys, California, stepped out of her bed and onto something large and apparently asleep on her rug. It turned out to be a burglar, who, overcome by the twenty beers which he had used to fortify his courage, had passed out.

LA Times

A man who had just robbed a petrol station in Taipei, Taiwan, before escaping took the precaution of performing a good luck

---

Arthur Gloria, a candidate for the Chicago police, was so determined not to let anything go wrong in his entrance test that he stole a car in order to be on time. When he arrived, he parked the car illegally. As he was dragged away by those he so wished to emulate, Gloria commented that he thought he had done well on the test.

Ann Arbor News

ritual to prevent his capture: following tradition, he dropped his pants and defecated at the scene of the crime.

Police arrived before the ceremony was complete.

China Post

In 1990, an Iranian student named Mehrdad Dashti took several hostages to protest against harassment by San Francisco police. One of his demands was that the chief of SFPD, Frank Jordan, should expose his genitalia on local television.

LA Times

In 1990 a Domino's Pizza delivery man of Balch Springs, Texas, was robbed by assailants brandishing only a snapping turtle.

LA Daily News

During 1976–7, a phantom spectacles-snatcher operated in South London, around the areas of Croydon and Norwood. The mugger, a man, began by running up to older women in the street and grabbing their glasses before they could get a good look at him. Of course the victims were not able to give a full description to the police. Eventually a crime was witnessed by someone with good eyesight, and a vague description was obtained. From then on the man committed his bizarre crimes with a bag or a cardboard box over his head. By this he apparently hoped to convince the police that he was a totally different madman stealing spectacles.

By 1977 the man was using violence, threatening his victims with a knife and sometimes hitting them on the head. A spokesman for the police said: "He must have a drawer full of spectacles at home. Heaven only knows what he does with them."

Daily Mirror

A man killed his friend in a fight in Thornburi, Thailand. The argument had arisen over the well-worn riddle: which came first, the chicken or the egg. The man left alive maintained that it was the chicken.

Sunday Times

Thieves made a lucky – if very slow – getaway from a building site in Lutterworth yesterday. They were stealing a sixteen ton, bright yellow, very noisy mechanical digger; but apparently nobody saw or heard them escape.

Daily Express

Psychiatrist Oscar Dominguez, forty-five, is facing a twenty-five year sentence for the murder of a female patient in São Paulo. She was telling him about her sex life when he grabbed a gun and shot her. "I couldn't take those nutcases any more," he explained to the court.

Daily Star

On 20 December 1976, a decomposed human right arm and partial rib-cage was found by builders in an attic in Falmouth, Cornwall. Instead of reporting the find to the police, the builders merely left the remains on their scaffolding with a note attached reading: "In case you need a hand . . ." The builders sent to take the scaffolding down discovered the grisly present, but they did not report it to the police either. They left it in the road. After five hours a passer-by discovered the limb and, eventually, the police became involved. The arm belonged to a woman and had been neatly sawed from its body. It was also partially mummified and its age (since severance) was guessed to be between 5 and 100 years. Neither the identity of its owner, nor her fate, could be discovered.

The West Briton

A woman from Buenos Aires in Argentina succeeded in obtaining a new trial after she had been imprisoned. She had been found guilty of killing a man, dismembering him, and boiling his head. Her new trial was granted on the grounds that her crime had been committed in self-defence.

Daily Express

As the final step towards casting out a demon that had supposedly possessed him, a young man of Arlington, Virginia, was told to bring all his money so that it could be blessed by his unofficial exorcist; unsurprisingly, she disappeared, along with the trusting young man's $16,000.

LA Times

Mistakes

Tom Field, from Turnditch in Derbyshire, was both baffled and annoyed to receive two £20 pound, fixed penalty tickets for illegally parking a steamroller in Edinburgh last December. Not only has he never owned or driven a steamroller, he has never been to Edinburgh.

Sunday Mail

A woman trying to accompany an elderly relative to the Gatwick Express train from Victoria found that it was not her day. She was forced to park her car illegally in order to get her relative safely onto the train. Luckily, a policeman agreed to watch over the vehicle during the five minutes her mission should take. Unfortunately, when the woman tried to leave the train, the station guard said "Oh no you don't!" and slammed the door. Stuck with an unwanted two hour round trip, the woman was faced with another guard demanding a ticket. "But I don't want to be on this train!" the woman screamed. "You're bloody lucky I don't give you a £200 fine," was the caring reply. He then sold her a £28 ticket. On her return to Victoria she found a £30 parking fine on her windscreen and a wheelclamp, that would cost £90 to remove, firmly installed. Worse still was the note left by the obliging policeman: "People like you are the pits of the earth. I put my trust in you and you betrayed that. You are the kind of person that makes our job a nightmare."

The *Big Issue*

990 graduates of the Navy's top educational establishment were surprised to learn that, according to their diplomas, they had been attending a Navel Academy.

LA Times

In its July 1991 edition, *Gourmet Magazine* published a recipe for mint sugar cookies. One of the ingredients that the magazine suggested was wintergreen oil, a toxin that can induce nausea, vomiting and in some cases death. *Gourmet* was forced to send 750,000 letters in an attempt to correct the error.

Ann Arbor News

Preparations for a ceremony at the public library in San Jose, California, were delayed when it was discovered that a banner that was supposed to read, in the Philippine language, "You Are Welcome!" actually translated as "You Are Circumcised!"

Parade Magazine

Freak Occurrences and Accidents

Doug Pitchard, a thirteen-year-old boy from Lenoir, North Carolina, was admitted to hospital for an unusual operation. Doctors removed a fully formed tooth, including root, from his foot, where it had been growing unseen.

Dallas Morning News

A man died while fishing on the banks of the Amazon tributary Rio Negro. Having been attacked by enraged bees after accidentally hitting their hive with his rod, he had sought sanctuary in the river, where he was eaten by piranhas.

Daily Telegraph

Thankamma Mathai fell dead during her wedding at Trivandrum, near New Delhi. Doctors examining her body found a snake bite on the back of her neck. They concluded that a snake must have fallen asleep in the bride's artificial hair bun during the previous night and had awoken confused and angry to find itself on the bride's head.

Sunday Express

A tabloid newspaper in the Philippines featured a story about a woman who had given birth to an adult mudfish. The parents of the animal were apparently quite content with this addition to their family; they put it to live in their bath. All seemed idyllic until disaster struck: the mudfish was eaten by the family dog.

LA Times

Between 1983 and 1988, five American servicemen were killed and thirty-nine injured by a hitherto unknown menace: soft drink vending machines. The accidents usually occurred when soldiers attacked the machines, either hoping to get a free drink, or trying to take revenge on the machine for eating their money without delivering the requisite refreshment. In most cases the machine then fell on the assailant.

Defense Week

Two thousand five hundred years ago, Cambyses II of Persia commanded an army of a thousand men into Egypt. They never arrived at their destination. There was no clue as to their fate until 1977, when Egyptian archaeologists digging in the Western Desert near Mount About Ballaasa began uncovering thousands of bones, weapons and Persian amphorae. The archaeologists believe that the army was on its way to the Amon temple at Siwa oasis when they were engulfed by a huge sandstorm.

Sunday Express

Rangers at the Mikumi game reserve in Tanzania have found a real-life Tarzan. After many sightings and several failed attempts at capture, they cornered him in a tree which he had apparently made his home. He seemed unable to talk and only whimpered like a terrified animal when questioned.

It appears that he has survived in the lion-infested park for some time, subsisting on a vegetarian diet of berries and fruit. At present he is being held in a police cell while they attempt to discover his identity.

Daily Mirror

Twenty-year-old waitress Pat Yearsley had a persistent itch in her throat. So she tried to scratch it with an eight inch dinner fork and to her shock swallowed the utensil whole!

Nobody at the Trefeddian Hotel in Lancashire, where she worked, would believe her. "Everybody thought I was joking. Even the hospital doctors did not believe it at first." She said later. "Then they took an X-ray and realized I was not having them on."

Doctors were forced to operate on Pat to remove the fork and she had to spend eleven days in hospital. Now all she has to remind her of the episode is an eleven inch scar across her belly; she was not allowed to keep the fork. "The surgeon wanted to keep it for his private museum. He said he was frightened I might swallow it again."

The Sun

Fourteen-year-old Mark Henderson had a rather shocking awakening yesterday. He yawned and opened his eyes only to find himself forty feet above his backyard, standing on the roof of his Burnley home. Apparently he had sleepwalked in his pyjamas right out of the tiny window of his attic bedroom. He then made his way, still fast asleep, down ten feet of slippery slates to the very edge of the roof. There, luckily, he came to a halt and stood snoozing.

Fortunately, the neighbours spotted him before he awoke and called the emergency services. Firemen arrived just in time to rescue him before he caught cold. He was returned to bed shaken, but otherwise unharmed.

Daily Mail

A Finnish vessel bound for London on 6 July reported seeing a twin-engine aircraft frozen inside an iceberg in Notre Dame Bay, Newfoundland. The bulk carrier "Burney" radioed the disturbing sighting to a lighthouse keeper who passed it on to the authorities.

Canadian armed forces personnel checked their records for any "Dakota-style" missing aircraft and searched the bay, but on both counts found nothing. They observed that a rapid thaw was taking place at the time and by mid-July the gruesome iceberg was assumed to have melted.

Windsor Star

A real-life story of Goldilocks and the three bears has been reported in former Soviet Yugoslavia. Five-year-old Goranka Cuculic wandered from her home in the village of Vranje and disappeared into the dense forest. Her parents and neighbours searched desperately for her well into the night, lighting their way with burning torches. Yet they could find no trace of the little girl and when some woodcutters told them they had seen bears near by, most gave up hope.

However, farmer Ivan Furian, Goranka's uncle, refused to stop searching and, armed only with a cudgel, pushed deeper into the forest. As in a good fairytale, his optimism was rewarded: he found his niece cold and hungry, but otherwise unharmed.

Back home and feeling much better she told everyone that she had met three bears in the forest after she lost her way . . . "One was big and fat, and the other two were quite small," she explained. "I played in a meadow with the two small ones and shared my biscuits with them. The big one licked my face . . . its tongue tickled. At night I snuggled between the cubs." The next day she lost them and had to spend a night cold and alone before her uncle found her.

There are quite a few documented cases of lost children being accepted and adopted by wild animals like wolves and bears so the story might not be complete bunkum – it is nice to believe it is true.

Daily Mirror

In 1922, a meteorite was seen to fall near Omsk in Russia. But when scientists tried to determine where the object had landed, they drew a blank. The rock was eventually located by Professor Dravert of the Omsk Mineralogical Institute. A local farmer was using it to weigh down the lid of the barrel in which he fermented his sauerkraut.

Sunday Express

Alexander Mitchell, a fifty-year-old bricklayer from King's Lynn in Norfolk literally laughed himself to death. During an episode of the BBC comedy series "The Goodies", Mr Mitchell laughed solidly for twenty-five minutes at a particular scene in which two men beat each other with large black puddings. He then slumped over, dead from heart failure. Doctors attributed the death to the fact that Mr Mitchell was laughing strenuously after a heavy meal. Mr Mitchell's widow, Nessie, commented: "I can still hear him laughing and it's a lovely remembrance. I shall write to The Goodies to thank them for making his last minutes so happy."

The Times

On 10 August 1972, a 100 ton meteor streaked through the air above Salt Lake City, Utah, at 33,000 mph. The object was observed by a US Air Force satellite: at its nearest point the thirteen-foot-wide rock was only thirty-six miles from striking the Earth's surface. If such a collision had occurred, the explosion would easily have equalled the destructive power of the nuclear weapon that destroyed Hiroshima.

Time

Peculiar Behaviour

On 25 August 1977, at 10 a.m., an unidentified man entered a petrol station in St Louis, Missouri, and asked the assistant for five dollars in change. He then walked to the drinking fountain and swallowed the money in handfuls, washing it down with gulps of water. After thanking the assistant, he left.

St Louis Post Dispatch

Until 1990 prison inmates in Texas were used as bait for training attack dogs. The practice was only halted after six injured prisoners sued the state. During an investigation, it emerged that the Vice Chairman of the Texas Board of Criminal Justice was one of the dog-handlers. So enthusiastic was the VC about his "hobby" that he even had jackets printed for himself and his fellow trainers featuring the slogan: "The Ultimate Hunt".

LA Times

An Arizona man decided to demonstrate his courage to his friends by kissing a rattlesnake that they had come across in the wild. The man picked up the snake and planted a kiss on its "lips"; unsurprisingly, he was bitten, on the tongue, by the shocked beast. In an effort to remove the venom, the man tried a drastic and unorthodox method. He attached his tongue to the battery of his car.

Arizona Republic

In 1990 La Cicciolina, Italy's porn queen turned MP, offered to defuse the increasingly tense situation in the Middle East by having sex with Saddam Hussein. She said: "I am willing to let him have his way with me if in exchange he frees the hostages."

LA Times

A department store in Japan will, for the equivalent of about £50, prepare a gourmet carry-out meal for your pet dog. A popular menu consists of premium rare beef, unsalted ham, sausages, cheese and white chocolate for dessert.

Wall Street Journal

The city of Concord, New Hampshire, decided to raise some

money by selling guns that it had confiscated from criminals. The money thus raised was to be used to buy bullet-proof vests for the local police.

Wall Street Journal

On 22 April 1990, a mass rally to raise awareness of environmental issues was held in New York's Central Park.

Fifty sanitation workers had to work all night to remove the 154.3 tons of litter that those attending the rally had dropped.

LA Times

British troops participating in the recent UN actions in the Gulf were forced to wear thick, green camouflage uniforms, obviously unsuited to the desert environment. This was because four years before the British government had sold all the army's desert uniforms to Iraq.

LA Times

The US Army has regulations concerning almost all aspects of a soldier's life. Here are some extracts from those regarding the baking of cookies: "They shall be wholly intact, free from checks or cracks . . . The cookies shall be tender and crisp, with an appetizing flavor, free from burnt or scorched flavor . . . They shall have been uniformly well baked with a color ranging from not lighter than chip 27885, or darker than chip 13711 . . . The color comparison shall be made under sky daylight with objects held in such a way as to avoid specular refraction."

Ann Arbor News

A New York company produces a small wooden device for the use of business managers who wish to say thank you to their employees. "The Congratulator" takes the form of a clip attached to a articulated wooden hand. Employees lucky enough to be awarded this prize clip the machine to their shoulder and, by pulling the string, can pat themselves on the back.

Wall Street Journal

In late 1977 the play-offs to determine who would play Anatoly Karpov in the Chess Championship of the World were taking place between Victor Korchnoi and Boris Spassky. After having lost three games in ten days, Korchnoi made an extraordinary claim. In front of the world's media, he alleged that the KGB were beaming him with microwaves while he was thinking about his moves, to confuse his thought and affect his play. He supported his claim by pointing out that Spassky got up and left the stage after each of his moves, evidently to get out of range.

Daily Mail

During late 1977 the front doors of four old people's bungalows at Castleton in Derbyshire were pelted with groceries night after night. Among the curious "gifts" were bacon, tomatoes, bread, eggs and black pudding. The attacks ceased when the police were called in. One of the bungalows' occupants, Mrs Ethel Bramley said: "It's unreal, weird! If people want to give us food why not wrap it up and leave it on the doorstep?"

Guardian

Two women presented themselves at the gaol in the early morning of Monday; their request was that they might be allowed, as a cure for sore necks, to be touched by the convict's hand, after his death by hanging!

West Briton

A doctor in Moscow has devised the ultimate cure for alcoholism. "I simply inject a special serum into the top of a patient's backbone," explained Dr Andronov. "Mixed with alcohol, it causes paralysis – one drink too many and you're a cripple." He claimed a 100 per cent success rate in the second half of 1992.

The *Guardian*

The public are respectfully informed, that Dr Taylor, the well-known water-doctor, from Manchester, who has performed so many cures in this neighbourhood, from the multiplicity of business in the vicinity of Bodmin and Truro, has not been able to attend to the patients as well as he could have wished, which has obliged them to remain all night, to their great inconvenience and additional expence; the doctor has now the pleasure to announce that, for the accommodation of his numerous patients, he will attend at the following places every market-day, where man, woman or child, bringing or sending their morning urine, may be told whether they are curable or not, free of any expense, as he charges nothing for his advice whatever.

Dr Taylor may be consulted at the New Inn, Falmouth, every Tuesday, at the White Hart, Truro, every Wednesday; at the Star Inn, Penzance, every Thursday; at the London Inn, Redruth, every Friday; and at the Fountain Inn, Liskeard, every Saturday . . .

West Briton

Police investigating strange cries in the night coming from the cemetery of St Mary's Church, Felling, Durham, found a full set of clothes and a pair of false teeth, but no sign of the owner. A senior officer commented: "There are no reports of anyone looking suspiciously undressed."

Daily Mirror

An ingenious individual of Liskeard, named Trethake, has for some time past been exhibiting himself to families in that town and neighbourhood, in a dress composed from top to toe of rat's skins, which he has been collecting for three and a half years. The dress was made entirely by himself, and consists of

An advert for Parker Pens, run in the *Newsweek* and *Time* magazines over past months, has caused something of a controversy in scientific and academic circles. The ad shows a well manicured hand writing a complex looking mathematical formula on a restaurant menu (presumably to suggest that Parker pens are the choice of sociable egg-heads).

Very soon the complaints were coming thick and fast. "We are getting letters from scientists and chemists who say they can't figure out the formula. Or that it is meaningless," said Gary Moss of the J. Walter Thompson advertising agency, who ran the campaign. In fact it is not meaningless: it's the formula for a martini. Translated it reads: three and half shots of gin, add half a shot of vermouth over four parts of water (taken down to freezing and cubed), then add three revolutions (stirs) . . . and there you go.

Only one person who wrote in had understood the hidden joke, and he was critical as well. He pointed out that it's no martini without an olive!

Milwaukee Journal

hat, neck-kerchief, coat, waistcoat, trousers, tippet, gaiters and shoes . . . The number of rats whose skins he has thus appropriated is 670, and when he is full dressed, he appears for all the world like one of the Esquimaux described in the account of Capt. Lyon's voyage; it should be mentioned that the tippet or boa (but not round like that worn by ladies) is composed of the pieces of skin immediately around the tails, and is a very curious part of the dress, containing about 600 tails and those none of the shortest.

West Briton

Geoffrey Wilson, eighteen, made a gruesome discovery while inspecting the roof of his East London home yesterday. Checking for damage after heavy rain, he happened to glance into his upstairs neighbour's window and saw a fully dressed skeleton lying on the bed. The police were called and identified the corpse as William Blackhally, the husband of the upstairs tenant.

Neighbours had noted that he had gone missing about ten years ago, but had assumed that he had left his spouse. In fact he had died of natural causes and she had simply left him where he was. Mrs Blackhally is receiving medical attention.

Daily Express

Family planners in South Australia recently hit on what seemed an excellent idea to help teach Aboriginal women about contraception. Since songs and singing are an essential part of the Aboriginal culture they composed a song full of helpful hints about avoiding pregnancy and taught it to the locals.

As they had hoped, the song had soon been spread near and far, but unfortunately something had been lost in the retelling. Many women were apparently under the impression that the song itself was all they needed to stop pregnancy.

Sunday Mirror

Many adults still have the teddy or doll that they had when they were children, but Harriet Lasky of Denver, Colorado, has something a little more idiosyncratic: she has kept the same piece of bubble gum for thirty-three years. Since she was seven years old she has been munching the gum by day and keeping it in a glass of water at night. "It gets better with age," she commented.

Sunday Mail

In July 1974, Chris Chubbock, a presenter on "Sarasota Digest", a local TV news programme on Florida's Channel 40, attempted suicide on air. During an unscripted apology for technical difficulties, Chubbock announced: "In keeping with Channel 40's policy of bringing the latest news in living colour, you are going to see another first attempted suicide." She then produced a .38 revolver from below the desk, aimed it at the back of her head and fired. A spokesman for the station commented that the attempt must have been planned, as Chubbock had left a script on her desk containing an item detailing her suicide to be used in the show. At the time of the report Chubbock was not expected to survive.

The *Sun*

On Friday last, the people assembled at St Austell market were surprised by the appearance of a man of advanced age leading a woman of about thirty, by a halter which was tied round her

Henri Rochatain, the man who walked 4,000 miles around France on a pair of stilts, has pulled off an even more amazing feat: for the last six months he has been living on a tightrope – literally.

For half a year he has eaten, exercised and even slept on a stretch of rope suspended eighty-two feet above a supermarket car park in St Etienne, France, without once coming down. His only articles of furniture were a covered toilet and a board bed. These were not attached to anything; while in use they were simply balanced on the rope. He had no defence against the elements and lived on a diet of seaweed soup, biscuits and tea.

Scientists were amazed by his endurance. "It is fantastic that he managed to sleep at all," said Dr Paul Monet, whose team monitored Rochatain's nervous system through electrodes attached to his skin. "He slept well even in thunderstorms and high winds. It is quite astonishing that he could rest, knowing that if he turned over in the night he would plunge off the rope."

M. Rochatain passed the time by walking up and down, doing stunts like standing on his head and occasionally pretending to fall off. He was not just in it for the thrills and the scientific discovery though. The owner of the supermarket over which he was perched paid him a large fee for attracting so many onlookers/customers.

Daily Mail

waist. The fellow is named George Trethewey, a labourer residing in the parish of St Stephens, in Branwell, and having become tired of his wife, he adopted this mode of leading her into the market, in order to dispose of her to the best bidder . . . Amongst those assembled were two itinerant tinkers, who travel in company; one of them offered two-pence for the woman, and after some time his companion doubled the sum, stating they were acting in partnership. The husband agreed to accept the last offer, when four-pence was handed to him, and the woman delivered to her purchaser, with whom she proceeded to a neighbouring pot-house, where they regaled themselves with a jug of ale. Meantime the collector of the market-tolls applied to the husband for a penny; the sum usually demanded for selling a pig, &c. This was at once paid . . . Trethewey then proceeded to select a replacement for his wife, and after a violent struggle with a man who laid prior claim to the woman chosen, made off with his new acquisition.

West Briton

A Scientific Experiment

"A remarkable experiment took place at the Scaramanga naval base, near Athens, yesterday. Its purpose was to discover if a legend over two thousand years old might, in fact, be true.

Sometime between 215 BC and 212 BC, the ancient Greek mathematician and inventor Archimedes is said to have destroyed the Roman fleet that was besieging Syracuse by using a "burning mirror". The tale is recorded in detail in Anthemius's sixteenth-century *Remarkable Devices* and there are also references in Polybius, Plutarch and Lucian's *Hippias*, but until now there has been no other evidence to support its actuality.

Dr Ioannis Sakkas has long held an interest in the fable and set about devising how the sage might have made a primitive laser with the technology of the time. "Archimedes may have employed flat bronze mirrors, the size of large shields, from the walls of the city to concentrate the solar energy and set the galleys on fire," Dr Sakkas said. "The flat mirrors are, for this purpose, the most practical as they can be handled by men obeying commands. You can visualize the scene: the Roman ships would hold as they converged on the sixty-foot-high walls of Syracuse within bowshot. The element of surprise was probably crucial, since the target had to be static. The defenders with their shield-like mirrors would focus the reflection of the sun on each galley and set it on fire in seconds."

At the Scaramanga naval base, Dr Sakkas used fifty or sixty sailors to wield mirrors made of bronze-coated glass, each measuring five feet by three feet. The men stood in a line along a narrow pier 130 feet from the target and moved their mirrors as ordered. The target was a six foot rowing boat with an outline of a galley made of tarred plywood – a slow burning material – attached to the landward side. "The reflective power would be about one-tenth less than the polished bronze Archimedes would have used, and the sun today is fairly weak," explained the doctor. Nevertheless, once all the mirrors were beaming at it, the galley cut-out was burning after only two minutes. "The heat generated today must have ranged between 280 and 340 degrees centigrade," estimated Dr Sakkas.

The Times

• chapter two •

ODD FACTS

The term "skid row" was first used in the lumberjacking days in Seattle. The logs were sent from a hilltop down a long chute and into the sea. Around the lower end of this chute there was a slum area where drunks and down-and-outs often slept in the gutter. This area became known as "skid row" after the logs that skidded down the chute.

Until the 1930s, no one knew why the sun shines. It was only then that it was understood that it is a vast nuclear furnace.

A cubic mile of seawater holds 150 million tons of minerals.

Benjamin Franklin suggested that clocks should be moved forward in spring to save daylight hours. He died in 1790, but his idea was not adopted in America and Europe until World War I, to save electricity.

In 230 BC, the Greek philosopher Eratosthenes worked out the size of the earth. He heard that the whole sun was reflected in the bottom of a deep well in Syene (now Aswan) at midday every midsummer, implying that the sun was directly overhead at that time and therefore that objects would cast no shadow. At midday on the summer solstice he measured the length of the shadow of a tower in Alexandria, whose height he knew. He also knew that the exact distance from Syene to Alexandria was 500 miles, having paid to have it paced out. With these figures in hand, he was able, by simple trigonometry to find out how much the earth curved in 500 miles, and therefore how much it would need to curve through a full circle, 360 degrees.

He calculated that the earth must be 24,000 miles in circumference – only 860 miles short of the true distance.

Mary Shelley's novel *Frankenstein*, written in 1816, was based on a real scientist, Andrew Crosse, whose lectures on electricity were attended by the poet Shelley and his wife in 1814. But twenty-one years after the novel was written, Crosse suddenly achieved notoriety when he announced that he had actually created life in his laboratory. In 1837, he decided to try and make crystals of natural glass; he made glass out of ground flint and potassium carbonate, and dissolved it in sulphuric acid. He then allowed the mixture to drip through a piece of porous iron oxide from mount Vesuvius which was "electrified" by a battery. After two weeks, tiny white nipples began to grow out of the stone, and these turned into hairy legs. When he noticed that they were moving he examined them through a microscope and saw what appeared to be tiny bugs. He thought there might be tiny insect eggs in the porous stone, so he sealed his carefully sterilized mixture into an airtight retort and passed electricity through it. In a few months, he again had tiny "bugs". A paper on his "discovery", read to the London Electrical Society, caused him to be violently denounced by clergymen as a blasphemer. Meanwhile the great Michael Faraday repeated Crosse's experiments and obtained the same "bugs". Crosse withdrew and led a hermit-like existence until his death in 1855. The mystery of the "bugs" has never been solved.

What has become known in zoology as "the Coolidge effect" – the fact that animals lose interest in females after sexual intercourse, but can be stimulated almost indefinitely by a variety of partners – was named after American president Calvin Coolidge. Coolidge and his wife were inspecting a government chicken farm, and were taken on separate tours. As she passed the chicken pen, Mrs Coolidge asked the man in charge if the rooster copulated more than once a day. "Dozens of times," replied the man. "Tell that to the President," said Mrs Coolidge. When President Coolidge visited the pen, the man passed on the message. "And does the rooster always choose the same hen?" asked the President. "Oh no – a different one each time." "Tell that to Mrs Coolidge," said the President.

The camel has never been "domesticated", in the sense of being friendly to man. It remains a sullen and aggressive creature.

The most literate people in the world are Icelanders, who read more books per capita than any other nation.

The first piece of science fiction was Kepler's story "Somnium", published after his death in 1630. Cyrano de Bergerac's *Voyage to the Moon* (published 1657), often cited as the first work of science fiction, is not only later, but fails to qualify because it is political satire rather than science fiction.

The first "best-selling" novel was Samuel Richardson's *Pamela, or Virtue Rewarded* (1740), which went into edition after edition, and was translated into most European languages. Rousseau's *La Nouvelle Heloise* (1760) surpassed it; it was so popular that lending libraries would lend it out by the hour. The first American best-seller was *Charlotte Temple* (1791) by an English-woman, Susanna Haswell Rowson, a melodramatic and badly written book that nevertheless went through 200 editions.

The word "gat" – American slang for a gun – was derived from the Gatling gun, the world's first machine-gun, which was invented during the American Civil War by Richard Jordan Gatling.

The practice of tapping a patient's chest was invented by an Austrian doctor, Leopold Auenbrugger, who used to watch his father – a wine manufacturer – tapping wine barrels to find out how full they were. Although he published the idea in 1761, it was ignored until his book was translated into French in 1808.

There were more opium addicts in America – per head of population – in 1865 than there are today. During the Civil War, opium was used as an anaesthetic during operations, and created 100,000 addicts in a population of 40 million. Today, with a population of 200 million, there are about 300,000 addicts.

The invention of transparent sticky tape was delayed for a long

---

George Asher of Joplin, Missouri, was obsessed by horses, which he felt to be superior to human beings. He had his hair cut like a mane, had his shoes shod with horseshoes, and had a harness made with which he pulled a wagon. In his prime he entered competitions against horses to prove he could pull heavier weights. He ate grass, beans, hay, bran and oats — although he supplemented this diet with other food. Asher died penniless in 1928.

time because of unsuccessful attempts to find a way of preventing the rubber-based gum from sticking to the back of the tape when it was wound into a roll. Finally, it was discovered that the experiments had been unnecessary: the gum has a natural tendency to remain only on one side of the tape.

Many clams in Australia's coral reef are ten feet long and weigh more than a ton.

The world hiccup record is held – as far as is known – by Vera Stong of Tennessee, who hiccupped continuously for fifty-eight days.

Mother Goose was a real person – the authoress of songs and jingles published in 1716. Her name was Elizabeth Foster, and she was born in 1665; she married Isaac Goose at the age of twenty-eight, and died in Boston – where her nursery rhymes were published – at the age of ninety-two.

In 1822, Thomas Dawson, ninety-one, and Michael O'Toole, eighty-five, engaged in fisticuffs to settle an argument and "fought to a finish" in Garford, Berks. O'Toole collapsed first, but ninety-one-year-old Dawson died a few hours later. The most tremendous contest in the history of wrestling was held between William Muldoon, the "Solid Man", and Clarence Whistler, the "Kansas Demon", in New York in 1880. They battled continuously for nine hours and thirty-eight minutes, until each collapsed with exhaustion.

A ton of gold would be worth less at the Equator than at the Poles. At the Equator, the centrifugal force of the Earth's spin counteracts the force of gravity, and would cause the gold to weigh fractionally less.

All the gold in the world could be placed under the curved base of the Eiffel Tower.

On 13 February 1746, a Frenchman named Jean Marie Dunbarry was hanged for murdering his father. Precisely a century later, on

---

In the early days of World War I, French airmen carried bags of bricks in their planes. Machine-guns were not then in use, since the problem of firing through the propeller had not yet been solved. The French tried to bring down German planes by throwing bricks into their propellers, and two planes are recorded as having been destroyed in this way.

13 February 1846, another Jean Marie Dunbarry, great-grandson of the other, was also hanged for murdering his father.

Big hailstones fall continually on the active volcano of Colima, in Mexico. The tremendous updraft from the boiling lava carries a column of air upward to cold regions where moisture turns to hail.

Local peasants gather the ice, wrap it in straw, and sell it in the villages.

The coldest place on earth is not the North nor the South Pole, but Verkovank in Siberia, where a temperature of 100 below zero has been registered. The North pole is about 60 below, while the South Pole often reaches 70 below. North Dakota has also registered 70 below.

According to *Encyclopaedia Britannica*, mules – the offspring of a horse and a donkey – are sterile. In the 1930, Old Beck, a mule owned by the Texas Agricultural and Mechanical College proved this wrong by giving birth to two offspring, one sired by a donkey, one by a horse.

Waves do not actually travel, in spite of appearances. The water only moves up and down; it is the force that travels. The simplest way to demonstrate this is to throw a stone into a pond with a paper boat in it . . . Although the waves appear to travel outwards, the boat merely bobs up and down.

Albert E. Herpin of Trenton, New Jersey, was a poor sleeper; in fact, he never slept at all during his lifetime. Born with a disorder that prevented him from falling asleep, Herpin lived

---

Ladak in Kashmir – high in the Himalayas – has the greatest temperature changes in the world. The temperature can drop from 160 degrees in the daytime to 45 degrees at night, and it is possible to experience a drop of 90 degrees by walking from the sunlight into the shade.

All Thoroughbred race horses in the world are descended from three Eastern horses imported into England in the early eighteenth century: the Byerly Turk, the Darley Arabian and the Godolphin Barb. Although 174 sires are mentioned in the first *General Stud Book*, these are the only three whose descent has remained intact.

to a ripe old age working as a gardener; at night, he read newspapers, an average of seven a night.

A man known as "Old Boots" in Ripon, Yorskshire, who lived in the middle of the eighteenth century, had such an upward curving chin and downward curving nose that he could hold a coin between his nose and chin.

On 5 December 1664, a man named Hugh Williams was the only survivor of a boat that sank crossing the Menai Strait – between Anglesey and Carnarvonshire in Wales. On 5 December 1785, the sole survivor of another such accident was also called Hugh Williams; sixty other passengers were drowned. On 5 August 1820, a man named Hugh Williams was again the sole survivor out of twenty-six passengers.

Both ice and steam are dry; ice is only wet when it melts, steam only wet when it condenses. Uncondensed steam is also invisible.

Siamese twins named Millie and Christina were famous singers, Millie a soprano and Christina a contralto. Born in Wilmington, North Carolina, in 1851, the twins had four legs but only one body. Either head could control the other's feet, so Millie could sing while beating time with Christina's foot, and Christina could sing while beating time with Millie's foot. They sang throughout America and Europe, and died in Wilmington in 1911, aged sixty.

Edgar Allan Poe received only $10 for his most famous poem, "The Raven". The manuscript was later sold for $200,000.

Alexander the Great, besides Alexandria, also built a city called Bucephala, named after his horse Bucephalus, which was killed in battle in 326 BC.

The largest statue of the Buddha in the world is in Pegu, Burma – it is 180 feet long and is in a reclining position. The statue was lost for 400 years: all records of it vanish around the middle of

---

It is possible to sail two hundred miles into the Atlantic and still remain in fresh water, by sailing out from the mouth of the Amazon, which disgorges over a million cubic feet of water a second into the sea. Ships far out at sea used to stock up with fresh water from this current – sometimes two hundred miles from land.

the fifteenth century, and it was not found again until 1881, when a railway was being built. The statue was covered with earth and vegetation.

There was one queen of England who never even saw her realm. She was the wife of Richard the Lionheart, Queen Berengaria, daughter of Sancho VI of Navarre. They were married in Cyprus in May 1191. The King's wanderings meant that she saw him only twice more; she lived in France and Italy and died in Le Mans, about 1230.

A gravestone in Sarajevo, Bosnia, has been almost entirely digested by human beings. It was believed that the pulverized stone, drunk in milk, would ensure pregnancy, so over the centuries most of the gravestone was chipped away. Finally, it was protected by a fence. The gravestone bears a medieval coat of arms, but the name of the owner has long since been swallowed.

The nearest relative of the elephant is the rock rabbit – the kinship is proved by the similarity of their skeletons. The rock rabbit mows its own hay and lets it dry in the sun, turning it over regularly, and then storing it for the winter.

The misplacing of a comma cost the United States treasury over a million dollars. In the Tariff Act of 1872, "fruit plants, tropical and semi-tropical" were exempted from tax. A clerk miscopied it: "fruit, plants tropical and semi-tropical." Importers contended that this meant that tropical and semi-tropical fruits should be exempted. The treasury disagreed and collected the tax, but finally gave way and refunded over a million dollars. The wording was then changed.

In Montana, snowflakes fifteen inches across and eight inches thick fell during a record snowstorm in the winter of 1887.

Little Jack Horner of the nursery rhyme was a real person. When Henry VIII was preparing to pillage the monasteries, the abbot of Glastonbury sent the title deeds of the abbey to the

---

Oswaldus Norhingerus, who lived in the time of Shakespeare, specialized in carving miniature objects out of ivory. He once carved 16,000 table utensils so small that they could be accommodated in a cup the size of a coffee bean. Each dish was almost invisible to the naked eye, yet perfect in every detail. Pope Paul V viewed them through a powerful pair of spectacles.

The 'Amorique market gardeners', Brittany, France are trying to tap into the growing market for exotic edible flowers

king hidden in a pie, and carried by Jack Horner. Horner extracted the "plum" deed of the manor of Mells, which remains in the Horner family.

The word "dunce" comes from one of the greatest of medieval philosophers, John Duns Scotus, born in 1265. Followers of Duns Scotus, knowns as "Duns men" or "dunces", opposed the new learning, and their opponents used the word "dunce" as a term of opprobrium, meaning someone who lacks learning.

The shrew, the smallest of all mammals, eats four times its own weight in thirty-six hours. It is also held to be the animal from which human beings descended.

Cobra venom is quite harmless to drink.

During the whole time he was world champion, boxer Jack Dempsey fought for only 138 minutes. This was because few opponents survived his savage style of fighting for more than a few minutes. On 8 February 1926, he knocked out four men in one round each, and repeated this stunt again four days later.

In 1644, Danish author Theodore Reinking was given the choice of eating his own book or being executed. King Christian IV of Denmark thought the book too democratic in sentiment. Reinking chose to eat the book torn up in his soup.

The bagpipe was first introduced into Scotland by the ancient Romans.

The average blonde has thinner hairs than redheads and black haired women. According to the *World Almanac*, the average blonde has 150,000 hairs on her head, while redheads and black haired women have respectively 30,000 and 110,000.

Francis Bacon was the father of the modern computer: in 1605 he developed a cipher using only *a* and *b* in five letter combinations, each representing a letter of the alphabet, demonstrating that only two signs are required to transmit information. Towards the end of the century, Leibniz developed the principle into the binary system which is the basis of modern computers. 0 and 1 can be combined to express any number.

Bacon died as a result of his passion for experimental science: in order to test the refrigeration of meat, he left his carriage to gather snow to stuff a chicken, and caught pneumonia.

chapter three

THE WEIRD AND THE SPOOKY

In the early 1970s, I was co-editor (together with the late Christopher Evans) of a series of volumes called The Unexplained. *One of my tasks was to unearth strange tales about ghosts, poltergeists, vampires, werewolves, zombies, UFOs, and various inexplicable psychic occurrences, which could be illustrated by an artist in a double-page spread; the stories themselves were printed in a "box" in the text. What follows is a brief – and far from complete – selection of these stories.*

C.W.

Seeing the Future

At the age of twenty-two the German poet Johann Wolfgang von Goethe had completed his studies in Strasbourg and was about to return home. While in Strasbourg he had fallen in love with the daughter of a pastor in a nearby village. He loved her but didn't want to be tied.

He paid one last visit to his Fredericka before leaving the town. "When I reached her my hand from my horse, the tears stood in her eyes and I felt sad at heart," he wrote in his autobiography. Then, as he rode away, he had a strange vision.

"I saw, not with the eyes of the body, but with those of the mind, my own figure coming toward me on horseback, and on the same road, attired in a suit which I had never worn – pike grey with gold lace. As soon as I shook myself out of this dream the figure had entirely disappeared . . . eight years afterward, I found myself on the very road, to pay one more visit to Fredericka, in the suit of which I had dreamed."

Although the phenomenon of seeing one's doppelgänger is traditionally regarded as a death omen, Goethe did not interpret his experience in that way. "However it may be with matters of this kind generally, this strange illusion in some measure calmed me at the moment of parting."

Air Marshal Sir Victor Goddard was lost. Flying over Scotland in a Hawker Hart biplane, he was caught in a heavy storm. He needed a familiar landmark to get his bearings, and so flew lower to see if he could sight Drem, an abandoned airfield whose location he knew. He did sight it – but instead of the deserted and dark scene he expected, he saw a busy scene in bright sunlight. Mechanics in blue overalls were hard at work on a group of yellow planes. He wondered that no one paid any attention to his low-flying plane, but, wondering, headed up into the clouds once more and went on toward his final destination.

That was in 1934 when Drem was indeed nothing but a ruin. In 1938, however, the airfield was reopened as an RAF flying school in the face of the war threat. Between these two dates, the colour of British training planes was changed from silver to yellow – a fact that Sir Victor could not have known at the time of his strange experience. Thus, in 1938, anyone flying over Drem would have seen exactly what Sir Victor had seen four years before it happened.

On an April night in 1865 – with the trials of the Civil War still heavy on his mind – President Abraham Lincoln lay asleep and dreaming. In his dream, he was asleep in his huge bed in the White House. Suddenly he was wakened by sobbing. Getting up and following the sound of the weeping, Lincoln found himself in the East Room. There he saw people filing past a catafalque guarded by soldiers. The men and women were paying their last respects to a body laid in state.

The face of the corpse was covered from Lincoln's view, but he could see that those present were deeply affected by the person's death. Finally, he went to one of the soldiers and asked who was dead. "The President," was the answer. "He was killed by an assassin." With that horrifying reply came a loud outcry of grief from the group near the catafalque – and Lincoln woke up.

This troubling dream, which Lincoln told his wife Mary and several of their friends, turned out to be a prophetic one. In that very month, Lincoln went to the theatre for a rare night away from his pressing responsibilities. Awaiting him there instead of a night of pleasure was a fatal bullet from an assassin's gun.

Eva Hellström, a Swedish psychical researcher, once dreamed that she and her husband were flying over Stockholm and saw a traffic accident. She wrote the vivid dream down.

"I looked down and thought we were somewhere in the neighbourhood of the Kungsträdgarden . . . I said to myself, 'The green [train] ran into [the tram] from the back . . .' I saw an ordinary blue tram of the Number 4 type, and a green train . . . run into the tram."

Eva Hellström also made a sketch of the accident as it had appeared in her dream. At the time there were no green railroad cars in service. But when some months later a few green cars were introduced, she was sure her dream was accurate. She then wrote in her diary:

"The accident will happen when the train from Djursholm [a suburb of Stockholm] and the Number 4 trolley meet at Valhallavägen [a Stockholm street]. This is a place where there have been accidents between autos and trains but so far as I know, never with a trolley . . ."

On 4 March 1956, nearly two years after her dream, a collision occurred at Valhallavägen between a Number 4 trolley and a green Djursholm train. The positions of the vehicles were exactly as in Mrs Hellström's sketch.

A foreboding dream saved Lord Dufferin, once the British ambassador to France, from possible death.

His dream was related by Camille Flammarion, French astronomer and psychical researcher.

Lord Dufferin dreamed that he went to the window of his room and looked out, compelled to do so by an overpowering apprehension. On looking down he saw someone walking by and carrying something. The figure looked up, and Lord

Dufferin saw a hideous face. At the same moment he realized that the figure was carrying a coffin.

Years later during his service as ambassador, Lord Dufferin attended a public dinner in Paris. A staff member led him to the lift that would take him up to the dining room. When he saw the lift operator's face, Lord Dufferin gasped in alarm. It was the face of his dream.

Instead of getting into the lift, Lord Dufferin went away to try to find out the operator's name. He had not gone far when he heard a crash, followed by screams and moans. The lift had fallen down the shaft. Everyone in it was killed or seriously injured. But the ambassador had been saved by his fear of the face he had seen in his dream.

"I dreamed that I had in my hands a small paper with an order printed in red ink, for the execution of the bearer, a woman . . . The woman appeared to have voluntarily brought the order, and she expressed herself as willing to die, if only I would hold her hand."

The dreamer, Dr Walter Franklin Prince, was an American psychical researcher. In his own account of his dream he wrote that the woman was:

> slender of the willowy type, had blonde hair, small girlish features, and was rather pretty. She sat down to die without any appearance of reluctance . . . Then the light went out and it was dark. I could not tell how she was put to death, but soon I felt her hand grip mine . . . and knew that the deed was being done. Then I felt one hand (of mine) on the hair of her head, which was loose and severed from the body, and felt the moisture of blood. Then the fingers of my other hand were caught in her teeth, and the mouth opened and shut several times as the teeth refastened on my hand, and I was filled with the horror of the thought of a severed but living head.

On the night after Dr Prince had his harrowing nightmare, a young mentally disturbed woman left her home on Long Island to pay a visit to her sister. The police later found her body near a Long Island railroad station. Her head had been cut off by a train. Near the body lay a note in which the woman stated that she was seeking decapitation in order to prove a theory that her body and head could live independently of each other. Her name was Sarah *Hand*.

On investigation Dr Prince learned that Sarah Hand, like the woman in his dream, was pretty, slender, and fair.

Bismarck, the Prussian statesman who unified the German states into an empire, fought three major wars to achieve his goal of unification. He became the chancellor of the German empire after the third of these, and King Frederick William IV of Prussia became Emperor Wilhelm I of Germany. Bismarck tells about one of his premonitory dreams of eventual victory in his book *Thoughts and Memories*.

In the dream he was riding on a narrow path in the Alps. On the right was a precipice, and on the left was smooth rock. The path got so narrow that his horse refused to go forward any further. Bismarck could neither dismount nor turn around in the space.

In this moment of trial, Bismarck struck the mountainside with his whip, and called upon God. Miraculously, the whip grew in length without end, and the "rocky wall dropped like a piece of stage scenery." A broad path opened out, giving a view of hills and forests that looked like the landscape of Bohemia. Prussian troops carrying banners dotted the area. They appeared to be victors of a bloody battle.

Three years later Bismarck was at war with Austria, and his troops marched through Bohemia on the way. They won – as in his dream.

In the third year of World War I on the Somme front, Bavarian and French troops faced each other in trenches across no-man's-land.

One day Corporal Adolf Hitler of the Bavarian Infantry woke suddenly from a fearful dream. In it he had been buried beneath an avalanche of earth and molten iron, and had felt blood coursing down his chest. He found himself lying unharmed in his trench shelter not far from the French front. All was quiet.

Nevertheless his dream worried him. He left the shelter, stepped over the top of the trench, and moved into open country between the armies. A part of his mind told him that he was being stupid because he could be hit by a stray bullet or shrapnel. But he went forward almost against his will.

A sudden burst of gunfire, followed by a loud explosion,

An Abominable Snowman, this picture was taken with a telephoto lens at a distance of 280 yards, May 1973

made Corporal Hitler fall to the ground. Then he hurried back to the shelter – but it was not there. In its place was an immense crater. Everyone in the shelter and that section of the trench had been buried alive. Only he survived.

From that day on, Hitler believed that he had been entrusted with a special mission which promised him a great destiny in world events.

Dr Edmund Waller, an Englishman living in Paris in the early 1900s, was having a sleepless night. He wandered downstairs, and, finding the crystal his father had just bought, gazed idly into it. There, to his surprise, he saw the image of Mme D., whom he had promised to look after during her husband's out-of-town journey.

The next day, Waller again looked into the crystal, and again saw Mme D. – with a man. He rubbed his eyes, and looked once more. The pair remained in view, this time at a racecourse outside Paris. Agitated by all these visions, Waller went to the racecourse the next day – and there met Mme D. with a man whom he took to be the one he had seen in the crystal.

Waller continued to see Mme D., her husband, and the other man in the crystal. One scene showed the illicit lovers in a particular Paris restaurant. On the husband's return, Waller told him about the visions. The two men went to the restaurant revealed by the crystal, and there found Mme D. with her lover.

There was a tragic aftermath to Waller's visions: Mme D. ended in an asylum, a broken woman after her husband had divorced her.

Seeing the Past

Arthur Guirdham is an English psychiatrist. For over forty years he was afflicted by a recurring nightmare in which a tall man approached him.

Then one day in 1962 a woman patient came to see him and described a nightmare similar to his own. Dr Guirdham did not tell her of his own dream; but oddly, it never recurred after that. As the woman, whom he calls Mrs Smith, continued treatment she revealed strange facts about her life: her ability to predict the future and her detailed dreams of life in the southern part of France during the Middle Ages as a member of a heretical sect called the Cathars. She did not at first tell the doctor that she immediately recognized him as her lover, Roger de Grisolles, in those dreams.

It is not unusual for a psychiatric patient to have sexual fantasies about the doctor. But Mrs Smith's recollections of medieval France, of the persecutions suffered by her co-religionists, and of being herself burned at the stake were extraordinarily detailed. Guirdham had details from them checked by medieval historians, and the most obscure of them were corroborated. Her memories struck a chord in the doctor's own psyche, and he is now convinced that he too lived as a Cathar in France.

Mrs Dolores Jay is an ordinary American housewife, married to a minister and the mother of four children. But when she is deeply hypnotized, Dolores Jay moves back through time past the time of her childhood and her infancy – deeper and deeper back until she whimpers in German. (When she is conscious, she neither speaks nor understands any German).

It is 1870. She is Gretchen Gottlieb, a sixteen-year-old Catholic girl, terrified and in hiding from anti-Catholic fanatics in a forest. "The man made my mother dead," she says. She complains that her head aches, she talks about a glittering knife, and then, desperately, evades questions. "Gretchen can't," she finally wails. And there it ends. Gretchen presumably was killed, and Mrs Jay remembers nothing until her own life began in 1923.

Dolores Jay herself can't account for it. She doesn't believe in reincarnation. She has only heard fragments of the taped hypnosis sessions, but she can't understand the language. She has never been to Germany. She has never heard of the little town of Eberswalde where Gretchen says she lived, and which exists in what is now East Germany close to the Polish border. But Eberswalde was the scene of Germany's last stand against the Soviet Union in 1945, and the town was almost completely razed. The records that once might have proved whether or not there was such a person as Gretchen Gottlieb have been destroyed.

Who can explain it? Not the modern middle-aged woman who, under hypnosis, becomes the young nineteenth-century

German girl – a girl who remembers her dolls, her home, and her own death.

Tina was born in 1940 in Brazil, but she has clear memories of a previous existence as a child in France and of her own murder by a German soldier early in World War II. She gave an account of her death to the Brazilian Institute for Psychical Research.

"I don't think there was anyone at home that day," she wrote, "because it was I who answered the door. It must have been about ten in the morning and the weather was cloudy." A soldier entered, wearing a round helmet and olive-green uniform. He carried what looked like a rifle and fired it at her heart.

"I remember," she continued, "asking for water before I died, but I don't remember if they gave me any. I can see myself lying on the floor on my back, wearing a light dress. I don't remember seeing any blood."

Tina has had from birth two distinct marks, on the front and back of her left side, precisely where a bullet aimed at the heart would have gone in and out. She has other memories too. In the interval between her death in France and her rebirth in Brazil she was present in the house of her parents-to-be. As soon as she could talk she correctly described all the furnishings in the house before her birth.

Out of the Body

"I neither drink nor take drugs, and all I brought to my bed was a considerable nervous exhaustion which sleep was required to restore." So begins William Gerhardie's description of his out-of-the-body experience in his semiautobiographical novel *Resurrection.*

When he became conscious in his astral body he was suspended in mid-air, light as a feather. Once on his feet he felt as if he were defying gravity. In appearance he seemed identical to his physical body on the bed, to which he was attached by a luminous cable.

When he tried to open the door, he found he could not turn the handle. Then he discovered that he could pass right through the door, and he moved around the apartment, making observations, lit by his own cord.

His new body responded to his thoughts and floated this way and that according to his whims. Part of him wished to fly to distant places, but part was afraid this might sever the link with the sleeping body.

When he awoke, he found that his earlier ideas of life after death had been shattered. It seemed to him that we already have a body stored away, rather like a diver's suit, in our own everyday bodies, "always at hand in case of death or for special use."

The biologist and author Lyall Watson was driving with a safari party through the bush of Kenya when suddenly the little bus skidded in the dust and overturned. It rolled over twice and then balanced on the edge of a gully.

A moment later, Watson found himself standing outside the bus looking at it. And yet he could see his own physical body slumped unconscious in the front seat of the bus. A more alarming sight was the head and shoulders of a young boy who had been pushed through the canvas top of the vehicle when it had come to a stop. If the bus fell into the gully – which seemed likely – the boy would be crushed.

The thought scarcely crossed his mind when Watson found himself regaining consciousness in the front of the bus. He rubbed the red dust from his eyes. The memory of what he had just seen was extraordinarily vivid. At once he climbed through the window of the bus and freed the boy, moments before the vehicle rolled over.

Telling the story in his book *The Romeo Error*, published in 1974,

---

"Having found, Sir, that the City of London should be sadly afflicted with a great plague, and not long after with an exorbitant fire, I framed these two hieroglyphics ... which in effect have proved very true." So spoke William Lilly, a seventeenth-century astrologer, suspected of intrigue in the Great Fire of London by a government inquiry committee in 1666. One of the astrologer's "hieroglyphics" of prophecy is a drawing of Gemini, the sign of the City of London, falling into flames, and it was done fifteen years before the fire that destroyed most of London. According to Lilly's report about the Parliamentary committee, he was released with "great civility".

Watson said "there is no doubt in my own mind that my vantage point at that moment was detached from my body," but he was unable to provide a scientific explanation for his experience.

The records of the Society for Psychical Research include the following account:

> One gray windy day in 1929 a man named Robert went for a swim in the ocean with a friend named Mildred. He had an extraordinary experience, which he related some years later.
>
> The sea was rough that day and the current extremely strong. He was about to head for shore when he heard a faint cry from a frightened young-ster clinging desperately to a board. Robert managed to reach him and hoist him onto the board just before he himself was overcome by a mountainous wave. He felt himself sinking.
>
> Suddenly, he found himself high above the water and looking down upon it. The sky, which had been gray and menacing, glowed with a glorious light. Waves of colour and music vibrated around him, and he felt an indescribable peace.
>
> Then below him he saw his friend Mildred in a rowboat with two men. Floating near them was a limp and ungainly object that he recognized as his own body. He felt a great sense of relief that he no longer needed it. The men pulled the body out of the water and lifted it into the boat.
>
> The next thing he knew, he was lying on the beach, cold and aching. He later learned that it had taken two hours to revive him. His help had saved the boy from drowning.

Few people have had the strange experience of seeing their own body from outside it. One man who did is a British Army colonel. It happened when he was desperately ill with pneumonia. Through the haze of his illness he heard his doctor say there was nothing more that could be done. The colonel, however, promised himself, "You *shall* get better." He then felt his body getting heavier and heavier, and suddenly discovered he was sitting on top of the cupboard in the corner of the room. He was watching a nurse tending his own unshaven, apparently unconscious body. The colonel was aware of all the small details of the room. He saw the mirror on the dressing table, the frame of the bed, and his inert body under the bedclothes.

The next thing he remembers he was back in his body, and the nurse was holding his hand and murmuring, "The crisis has passed."

During his convalescence he told the nurse what had happened to him, describing the exact motions she had made and the details of the room that had been so clear to him. She suggested that perhaps he had been delirious.

The colonel had a different answer. "I was dead for that time," he said.

Among the cases in the records of the Society for Psychical Research is the story of a distinguished Italian engineer. He wrote that one June, studying hard for his examinations, he had fallen into a very deep sleep during which he apparently knocked over his kerosene lamp. Instead of going out, it gave off a dense smoke that filled the room. He gradually became aware that the thinking part of him had become entirely separate from his sleeping physical body. His independent mind recognized that to save his life he should pick up the fallen lamp and open the window. But he could not make his physical body wake up and respond in any way.

Then he thought of his mother, asleep in the next room, and he saw her clearly through the wall. He saw her hurriedly get up, go to the window, and throw it open as if carrying out the thought in his mind. He also saw her leave her room and come into his. She came to his body and touched it, and at her touch he was able to rejoin his physical body. He woke up with dry throat, throbbing temples, and a choking feeling.

Later his mother verified that she had opened the window before coming in to him – exactly as he had seen it through a solid wall.

The Living Dead

William Seabrook avidly studied the spirit religions of the West Indies in the 1920s. In his book *The Magic Island* he relates a strange tale told to him by a Haitian farmer. It seems that there was a bumper sugar cane crop in 1918, and labourers were in short supply. One day Joseph, an old headman, appeared leading "a band of ragged creatures who shuffled along behind him, staring dumbly, like people in a daze." They were not ordinary labourers. They were zombies – dead men whom Joseph had brought back to life by magic to slave for him in the fields.

Zombies must never taste salt according to the farmer's tale, so Joseph's wife fed them special unseasoned food. But one day she took pity on them and bought them some candy, not knowing it was made of peanuts. As soon as the zombies tasted the salty nuts, they realized they were dead. With a terrible cry they set off for their own village. Stumbling past living relatives who recognized them in horror, they "approached the graveyard . . . and rushed among the graves, and each before his own empty grave began clawing at the stones and earth . . . and, as their cold hands touched the earth, they fell and lay there, rotting as carrion."

In 1837 in Lahore, India [in now Pakistan] the yogi Haridas was buried alive for forty days. British Colonel Sir Claude Wade, Dr Janos Honiberger, and the British Consul at Lahore all solemnly corroborated that he was locked in a box, placed in a sealed pavilion with doors and windows tightly blocked shut, and guarded day and night. After forty days, the box was opened.

Haridas had not gone into the tomb unprepared. For days before his burial he had no food but milk. On the burial day itself he ate nothing, but performed *dhauti* – a yoga purification practice that involves swallowing a long strip of cloth, leaving it in the stomach to soak up bile and other impurities, and then withdrawing it. Haridas then did another cleansing ritual. All the openings of his body were then sealed up with wax, and his tongue was rolled back to seal the entrance to his throat. Then he was buried.

When the box was opened the yogi's assistant washed him with warm water, removed the wax, and rubbed his scalp with warm yeast. He forced his teeth open with a knife, unfolded his tongue, and massaged his body with butter. After half an hour Haridas was up and about.

The Vampire

Do vampires still walk in Romania? In 1974 a gypsy woman told of her father's death when she was a girl. According to custom, she said, the body lay in the house awaiting the ceremonial final dressing by the family. After this ceremony it would be carried to the grave uncovered, so that everyone could see that the man was truly dead.

When the family lifted her father's legs to put them in his burial clothes, the limbs were not stiff. Neither were his arms nor the rest of his body. Rigor mortis had not set in. The family stared horrified at him and at each other, and the fearful whispering began.

The story spread among the villagers – people who remembered, or thought they remembered, the vampires that used to roam in the darkness of night. One unmistakable sign of a vampire is an undecomposed body, kept lifelike by the regular feasting on the blood of the living. Fear licked through the village, and the inhabitants soon came to the house armed with a wooden stake.

The family – bewildered, uncertain, and grief-stricken – fell back. The men tore off the corpse's covering sheet and, in the traditional manner, thrust the stake through the dead man's heart. The vampire – if such it was – was vanquished.

The nineteenth century diarist Augustus Hare recounts the following story:

> Croglin Grange was an English manor house that overlooked the nearby church in the hollow. It was rented by two brothers and their sister. One night as the sister lay in bed she became uneasily aware of something moving across the lawn toward the house. Mute with horror, she saw a hideous brown figure with flaming eyes approach. It scratched at her window with bony fingers, and one pane fell out. It reached in, unlocked the window, and before she could scream, sank its teeth into her throat.
>
> Her brothers were wakened by the commotion, but by the time they reached her room the creature had vanished and the girl lay unconscious and

bleeding. One brother tried to follow the attacker, but lost it.

The girl recovered and bravely insisted on returning to the house. Nearly a year later, she again woke to see the creature scratching at the window. Her brothers, who since the first attack slept armed, came running. They found the creature in flight. One brother fired and hit it, but it escaped into the churchyard. When the two men entered the churchyard vault, they discovered all the coffins broken open except one. In that coffin was the vampire – and it had a bullet wound in its leg.

Ape-man

In 1920 the Polish medium Franek Klusky had a series of sittings with the International Metaphysical Institue, among whose prominent members were the French investigators Professor Charles Richet and Gustave Geley. The seance circle sat with hands linked, and the expert researchers kept the medium under careful observation. Unlike many mediums, Klusky did not go into trance during a seance. He worked in a state of full consciousness, but with deep concentration.

Klusky was noted for a remarkable ability to materialize both humans and animals. His most electrifying seances were those in which strange forms loomed out of the darkness – on one occasion a great hulking creature halfway between human and ape. It was about the stature of a man, but had a simian face, long arms, and hair all over. It smelled, sitters said, like a wet dog. Once the big hairy head leaned heavily on a sitter's shoulder. Another sitter put out a hand, which the creature licked with a large soft tongue.

The scientifically minded sitters called Klusky's materialized apeman *Pithecanthropus*. Geley believed totally in the medium's psychic powers. On the other hand, British psychic researcher Harry Price doubted his abilities.

Werewolf?

By the admission of William Seabrook who tells the story, it was perfectly true that Nastatia Filipovna was not ordinary. A Russian aristocrat who had fled the revolution, she seemed slightly larger than life. She was tall and powerful with challenging tawny eyes. She had a fearful temper, but also charm when she chose to use it. She didn't like reality – it bored her – but although she fell into a self-induced trance easily, she didn't like that world either.

Then she decided to try the I Ching, the ancient Chinese method of opening the mind to future possibilities. For Nastatia Filipovna it seemed to open a door. "But it's opening into the outdoors!" she murmured. "Everything is white – everywhere snow. I am lying in the snow . . . I am lying naked in my fur coat . . . and I am warm."

She moved restlessly and muttered: "I'm running lightly like the wind . . . how good the snow smells!" She began to make unhuman sounds, like a wolf baying. Alarmed, her friends tried to rouse her. Her face changed. Her tawny eyes wide open, the wolf-woman sprang straight for a friend's throat. She fell short. Her companions snared her in blankets and held ammonia under her nose. She came out of it.

But Nastatia Filipovna remembered. And she liked it.

Monsters

Late in the eighteenth century a sailing ship off the coast of West Africa found itself becalmed in a placid ocean. The wind had dropped, and Jean-Magnus Dens, the Danish captain, ordered his crew to lower planks off the side from which they could scrape and clean the ship. Three men climbed onto the planks and began their work. They were scraping energetically when suddenly, out of the quiet sea around them, rose an immense octopus or squid. It seized two of the men and pulled them under the water. The third man leaped desperately into the rigging, but a gigantic arm pursued him, getting caught up in the shrouds. The sailor fainted from shock, and his horrified shipmates frantically hacked at the great tentacle, finally chopping it off. Meanwhile, five harpoons were being driven into the body of the beast in the forlorn hope of saving the two who had disappeared. The frightful struggle went on until, one by one, four of the lines broke. The men had to give up the attempt at killing the monster, which sank out of view.

The unconscious sailor, hanging limply in the shrouds, was gently taken down and placed in his bunk. He revived a little, but died in raving madness that night.

From the 1860 report of Captain William Taylor, Master, *British Banner*:

> On the 25th of April, in lat. 12 deg. 7 min. 8 sec., and long. 93 deg. 52 min. E., with the sun over the main-yard, felt a strong sensation as if the ship was trembling. Sent the second mate aloft to see what was up. The latter called out to me to go up the fore rigging and look over the bows. I did so, and saw an enormous serpent shaking the bowsprit with his mouth. It must have been at least about 300 feet long; was about the circumference of a very wide crinoline petticoat, with black back, shaggy mane, horn on the forehead, and large glaring eyes placed rather near the nose, and jaws about eight feet long. He did not observe me, and continued shaking the bowsprit and throwing the sea alongside into a foam until the former came clear away of the ship. The serpent was powerful enough, although the ship was carrying all sail, and going at about ten knots at the time he attacked us, to stop her way completely. When the bowsprit, with the jibboom, sails, and rigging, went by the board, the monster swallowed the fore-topmast, staysail, jib, and flying-jib, with the greatest apparent ease. He shoved off a little after this, and returned apparently to scratch himself against the side of the ship, making a most extraordinary noise, resembling that on board a steamer when the boilers are blowing off. The serpent darted off like a flash of lightning, striking the vessel with its tail, and striving in all the starboard quarter gallery with its tail. Saw no more of it.

A Russian hunter in 1918 was exploring the taiga – the vast forest that covers nearly three million square miles of siberia – when he encountered huge tracks in thick layers of mud by a lake in a clearing. They were about two feet across and about eighteen inches long, and appeared to be oval. The creature was obviously four-footed, and had wandered into the woods. The hunter followed the tracks curiously, from time to time finding huge heaps of dung apparently composed of vegetable matter. The tree branches were broken off about ten feet up, as if the animal's enormous head had forced its way through. For days he followed the tracks. Then he saw traces of a second animal, and a trampling of the tracks, as if the two creatures had been excited by the meeting. Then the two went on together.

The hunter followed. Suddenly, one afternoon, he saw them. They were enormous hairy elephants with great white tusks curved upward. The hair was a dark chestnut color, very heavy on the hindquarters, but lighter toward the front. The beasts moved very slowly.

The last of the mammoths are believed to have died more than 12,000 years ago, and the hunter knew nothing about them. But did he see mammoths?

In the decade after World War II Slavomir Rawicz, a Polish refugee living in England, wrote about his experiences in *The Long Walk*. In this book he claimed that he and six others escaped from a Siberian prison camp and walked 2,000 miles to freedom. During their gruelling journey to India they crossed the Himalayas. It was there, one day in May 1942, that he said they saw two massive Yeti.

"They were nearly eight feet tall and standing erect," Rawicz wrote. "The heads were squarish and . . . the shoulders sloped sharply down to a powerful chest and long arms, the wrists of which reached the knees." One was slightly larger than the other, and Rawicz and his companions concluded they were a male and female. The unknown creatures looked at the humans, but appeared completely indifferent. Unfortunately, the beasts were in the middle of the most obvious route for the refugees to continue their descent, and the men were disinclined to approach much closer in spite of the apparent lack of interest.

The refugee party finally moved off by another route. Behind them the Yeti watched their retreat with obvious unconcern, and then turned away to look out over the magnificent scenery.

Albert Ostman, a Canadian lumberjack, in 1924 combined a holiday with a bit of gold prospecting. He camped near the head of the Toba Inlet opposite Vancouver Island, spent a week exploring, and decided to stop in a lovely glade under some cypress trees. The second night there he awoke to find himself being carried away in his sleeping bag like a sack of potatoes. He saw a huge hand around the partly open neck of the bag.

When Ostman was later dumped out on the ground, he was in the middle of a family of four big-footed monsters – the Sasquatch or Bigfeet. They were all enormous and hairy: father, who had kidnapped him, mother, a nearly adult son, and a younger daughter. The father was eight feet tall, the mother about seven. For six days Ostman was held prisoner, though no harm was done him. He observed that they were vegetarians, eating the grass, roots, and spruce tips gathered mainly by the mother and son. The daughter and father kept an eye on Ostman, but grew increasingly trustful of him. Finally he got the chance to escape.

Fearing to be locked away as a madman, Ostman said nothing publicly about his adventure for many years.

The Poltergeist

The magistrate of Tedworth in Wiltshire, England, could not have imagined the consequences when he confiscated the drum belonging to William Drury – an itinerant musician caught in some shady dealings – and told him to leave the district.

That was in March 1662. Hardly had the culprit left Tedworth when the drum began to produce drumming noises itself. It also flew around Magistrate Mompesson's house, seen by several people besides the magistrate. After several sleepless nights, he had the drum broken into pieces. Still the drumming continued. Nor was that all. Shoes flew through the air, and chamber pots were emptied onto beds. Children were levitated. A horse's rear leg was forced into its mouth.

The possibility that the exiled drummer had sneaked back and was causing the trouble was fairly well ruled out when it was discovered that he had been arrested for theft in the city of

Gloucester and sent to the colonies. The Reverend Joseph Glanville, chaplain to King Charles II, came to Tedworth to investigate the phenomena. He heard the drumming himself, and collected eyewitness reports from the residents. No natural cause was found for the effects, which stopped exactly one year after they had started.

The manager and staff of the Co-operative Stores in the English village of Long Wittenham, Berkshire, were not amused in late 1962 when jam jars, cereal boxes, and other normally stationary objects began flying off the shelves and circling overhead. In fact, one sales assistant fainted. To add to the confusion, the invisible prankster switched the lights on and off. For some mysterious reason, the poltergeist concentrated on the bicarbonate of soda, transferring boxes of the substance from the shelf to the window ledge.

After a week of chaos, the local vicar offered his services and exorcized the shop. The ritual proved effective, and groceries stayed put at last. The exhausted manager and staff set about restoring the stock to order. Despite the apparent success of the exorcizing ceremony, however, they decided to take precautions with the bicarbonate of soda. They put it under lock and key.

This case is one of many in which possible natural causes, such as earth tremors or an underground river, fail to provide a satisfactory explanation for flying objects. If such natural vibrations were responsible, for example, the bicarbonate of soda would hardly have been given such special attention.

The Red Scratch Case

Mr F.G., a travelling salesman from Boston, had returned to his hotel room one afternoon. As he sat working he suddenly became aware of someone in the room. Glancing up he was astounded to see his sister, who had died nine years before. "I sprang forward in delight, calling her by name," he said, "and as I did so, the apparition instantly vanished . . . I was near enough to touch her, had it been a physical possibility . . . She appeared as if alive." Yet there was one noticeable change in her appearance: her right cheek bore a bright red scratch.

Disturbed by this experience, F.G. went to see his parents with the story. When he mentioned the scratch, his mother was overcome with emotion. She revealed that she had made the scratch accidentally while tending to her daughter's body. Two weeks after this, his mother died peacefully.

Psychical researcher F.W.H. Myers pointed out that the figure was not "the corpse with the dull mark on which the mother's regretful thoughts might dwell, but . . . the girl in health and happiness, with the symbolic red mark worn simply as a test of identity." He suggested that the vision was sent by the spirit of the girl to induce her brother to go home and see his mother.

Strange Powers

Wolf Messing was a stage mind reader who fled for his life from Poland to the Soviet Union during World War II. He had been in danger not only because he was a Jew, but also because he had predicted Hitler's death if the German dictator "turned toward the East." Hitler, a believer in fortune telling, put a price on Messing's head.

In the USSR Messing faced another dictator's challenge when Josef Stalin set a test for him. It was not an easy one. Messing was to enter Stalin's country house – a place bristling with guards and secret police – without a pass.

One day as Stalin sat working in the office of his country home, a man walked coolly into the grounds and then into the house. All the guards and servants stood back respectfully as he passed. He walked to the doorway of Stalin's study. When the dictator looked up, he was astonished. The man was Messing!

The celebrated psychic's explanation was this: by mental suggestion he had made the guards think he was Lavrenti Beria, the much-feared head of the secret police at that time. So strong were his powers that, even though Messing looked nothing like Beria, the guards were convinced it was he.

On another occasion, Stalin suggested to Messing that he rob a bank by telepathy.

Messing chose for the experiment a big Moscow bank in which he was not known. He calmly walked in and handed the teller a blank piece of paper torn from a school notebook. He placed his case on the counter, and mentally willed the clerk to give him 100,000 roubles.

The bank clerk looked at the paper, opened the safe, and took out piles of banknotes until he had stacked 100,000 roubles on the counter. He then stuffed the money into the bag. Messing took the case, walked out of the bank, and showed the money to Stalin's two observers to prove his success as a bank robber. He then went back to the clerk and began handing the bundles of banknotes back to him. The teller looked at him, looked at the money, looked at the blank paper – and collapsed on the floor with a heart attack.

Fortunately, Messing reported, the clerk recovered.

José Arigó was a simple man of little education who suddenly began to do skillful surgery in a small town in Brazil. His first operation was witnessed only by the patient. Arigó, who had been in a trance at the time, didn't believe the story himself when told about it. But his second operation took place in public.

It happened when an old woman lay dying, surrounded by her family, friends, and the Catholic priest who had just given her the last sacrament. Arigó was among the friends present. All at once he drew a large kitchen knife and ordered everyone to stand back in a strong German accent and voice that were not his own. He then plunged the knife into the woman's stomach. The onlookers, terrified that he had gone mad, stood transfixed. He slashed through the stomach wall, cut out a growth the size of an orange, and closed the incision by pressing the sides of the cut together. The incision closed immediately without a scar. A moment later he was himself again – the plain, somewhat bumbling man his neighbours knew. Arigó had no memory of the episode, though soon the woman who had been on the point of death was walking around the room, recovered.

Dr William Lang died in 1937, but he is practising today in a town just north of London – or so say many who have consulted him. Patients who come to see him meet him in a curtained room. He talks to them, diagnoses the complaint, and then, if necessary, operates on them. Because Dr Lang operates on the spirit body, the patient remains fully clothed. His hands move swiftly and surely, although his eyes are closed, to correct the difficulty in the patient's spirit body – and such correction enables the physical body to function properly.

Patients may have met the medium George Chapman before he went into the trance that allows Dr Lang to appear, but they report that he is quite unlike the formerly well-known surgeon. Dr Lang's voice is a little quavery and high-pitched, and his shoulders are stooped. Those who knew him in life say it is unmistakably Dr Lang.

Patients report that they can feel Dr Lang at work. During the operation his warm friendly manner sometimes grows sharp, and he snaps his fingers peremptorily to indicate which instruments he wants passed by his spirit assistants. Patients say they feel safe in Dr Lang's hands – though the hands are unseen.

St Joseph of Copertino became known as the "flying monk" because of the way he levitated during ecstatic states. Born Giuseppe Desa in 1603, he was a strange and sickly child. As a teenager with strong religious tendencies – and later as a monk – he tortured himself for penance. But in moments of rapturous joy, usually inspired by religious feeling, Joseph rose in the air with loud shouts and, sometimes, wild movements.

At the age of twenty-two Joseph became a Franciscan monk in the district of Copertino in southern Italy. He became known to the neighbouring people for his kindness and holiness, even though his noisy levitations disturbed his fellow friars. In fact, he was not allowed to join the rest of his brothers in the choir. One day he went away from the others into an obscure corner of the chapel to pray by himself. Suddenly he cried out with special intensity, rose straight up into the air and – to the astonishment of all present – flew to the altar. With another cry, he flew back to his corner in a kneeling position, and then began to whirl around in song and dance.

Joseph was investigated by the Church, but was acquitted of the charge of practising deception by false miracles.

Gerard Croiset Junior, son of the world-famous Dutch psychic who helped police solve many baffling cases, inherited his father's strange powers. He demonstrated this when he assisted in the case of two missing girls in South Carolina – and he did it from thousands of miles away. It all started when one of the girls' desperate mother, having heard about the Croisets' miraculous ability to locate missing persons, wrote to them in Holland with a plea for help. Croiset Junior replied.

The two teenage girls had gone for a walk on Folly Beach near Charleston, South Carolina, and they hadn't been seen since. In his reply to the mother, Croiset drew a map of Folly Beach – which he had never seen – including such details as a bus stop and a parked bulldozer. He also wrote a page and a half of comments. The accuracy of the map convinced sceptical police to take him seriously.

In the letter Croiset said: "The girls will be there [on the beach]; they will be together." The police found the girls where Croiset indicated. And they were together – buried in shallow graves in the sand. They had been murdered.

Two London mediums, Frank Herne and Charles Williams, were holding a joint seance with a respectable circle of sitters. The voices of the spirits John King and his daughter Katie were heard, and Katie was asked to bring something to the sitters – which she willingly agreed to do. One sitter perhaps jokingly suggested that Katie produce Mrs Guppy, a well-known medium of majestic dimensions. Katie chuckled and said she would. John King shouted out, "You can't do it, Katie," but she declared "I will." The sitters were all laughing when there came a loud thump on the table, and a couple of people screamed. Someone lit a match – and there was Mrs Guppy, her con-

---

Father Karl Pazelt, a Jesuit priest, came to the aid of a California couple in 1974 when they were troubled by a poltergeist. The couple, who reported their story to the *San Francisco Examiner* anonymously, believed that it was a devil.

The poltergeist pulled the standard prank of throwing shoes, but also plagued them by setting fires. At one point a plastic wastebasket caught fire and melted. Frightened for the safety of their two-year-old son as well as for themselves, they asked Father Pazelt to exorcize the malevolent force. In his opinion this was a case of "demonic obsession" – that is, the "devil is not *in* the people, but *around* the people." According to the couple, the devilish spirit made its presence strongly felt during the exorcism rite "by knocking both of us down."

siderable bulk deposited neatly on the seance table. She was in trance and held a pen and an account book.

When Mrs Guppy was gently awakened, she was somewhat upset. The last she remembered she had been sitting comfortably in her own home – about three miles away – writing up her accounts. Several sitters escorted the medium to her house, where an anxious friend waited. According to the friend, the two had been in Mrs Guppy's room together when, suddenly, Mrs Guppy was gone "leaving only a slight haze near the ceiling."

Latvian Edward Leedskalnin built his house out of local Florida stone. This stone is a very hard and dense form of coral. Leedskalnin worked without modern tools, using mainly timber and scrap metal to quarry and move the blocks of masonry he used, some of which weighed over thirty tons. Not only did he build a house totally without help, he also quarried twelve stone rocking-chairs, finely balanced upon their curved bases. He built stone astronomical instruments and a stone map of Florida. The door to his stone park was a nine-ton coral slab so finely poised upon its centre of gravity that it could be swung backwards and forwards at the touch of a finger.

He eventually decided to move all of his objects to a more accessible site and open a children's playground. He hired a lorry and moved it all himself. No-one knows how the slight four-foot eight man achieved all this on his own. No-one saw him move the objects, but move they did. Enquiries into Leedskalnin's secret brought a knowing look and oblique statements about having rediscovered the methods of the ancient pyramid architects.

He died in 1951, never having revealed his method.

On 3 October, 1984 a New Guinean giant fruit-bat, an animal with a three foot wing-span, was found clinging to the radiator of a car in Exeter, Devon. Its origins remain a mystery.

During his investigation of the powers of Eusapia Paladino, the Italian medium noted for highly eventful seances, Professor P. Foa tried to use a photographic plate to register radiations. Eusapia Paladino's spirits apparently resented the interference. As the medium sat in trance outside the curtained cabinet, a hand shot out and tried to snatch the plate. Dr Foa seized the hand as it retreated behind the curtains and felt the fingers, but the hand wriggled loose and hit him squarely.

The spirits then turned their attention to a table, which they sailed over the heads of the company. When one sitter attempted to approach it, the spirits whisked it behind the curtain where it began to break up noisily. Dr Foa saw the table turn over on its side, and one leg snap off. At that point it shot back out of the cabinet and continued to break up noisily under the fascinated gaze of the entire circle. One of the sitters asked for a handshake, and Eusapia Paladino invited him to approach the cabinet. He had hardly reached it when he felt himself attacked by hands and pieces of wood.

The entire circle heard the noises of the blows, and saw the hand moving in the ghostly half-light.

It was evening in Benares, India. The legendary Madame Blavatsky – the small, dumpy Russian mystic and medium with a strangely magnetic personality – was surrounded by several Indian scholars, a German professor of Sanskrit, and her devoted disciple Colonel Olcott.

The professor observed with regret that the Indian sages of old were supposed to have been able to perform amazing feats, such as making roses fall from the sky, but that people said the days of such powers were over. Madame Blavatsky stared at him thoughtfully. "Oh, they say that, do they?" she demanded. "They say no one can do it now? Well, I'll show them; and you may tell them from me that if the modern Hindus were less sycophantic to their Western masters, less in love with their vices, and more like their ancestors in many ways, they would not have to make such a humiliating confession, nor get an old Western hippopotamus of a woman to prove the truth of their Shastras!"

She set her lips together firmly, and made a grand imperious sweep of her right hand. With a swish, exactly one dozen roses came cascading down.

Madame Blavatsky returned calmly to her conversation.

Unlike most automatic writers, who received their messages from the spirits, the nineteenth-century British journalist William Stead got messages from the living – and saved them the bother of writing themselves. He would ask mental questions and his hand would write the answers automatically – sometimes he would learn more than the friends wanted him to.

Once he had arranged a lunch engagement with a woman who had been out of town over the weekend. He mentally inquired whether she had returned to London yet, and his hand wrote a long note. It described an unpleasant encounter she had

had on the train. According to the message, she had found herself alone in a compartment with a strange man. He came over, sat close to her, and when she tried to push him away, attempted to kiss her. Struggling furiously, she thumped him with his umbrella, which broke. Then the train unexpectedly stopped and the man took flight.

When Stead sent his servant to his friend's house with a note condoling her on the assault, the woman was taken aback. She replied, "I had decided not to speak of it to anyone." She added, "The umbrella was mine, not his."

UFOs

At 1.15 p.m. on 7 January 1948 the control tower of Godman Air Force Base in Kentucky got a phone call from the State Highway Patrol. They said that townspeople about eighty miles away had reported seeing a strange aircraft in the sky. Godman personnel checked and informed the police that there were no flights in the area. Not long afterward, however, the control tower saw the object, which no one could identify.

About an hour later, three F-51 Mustang fighters on a training exercise came into view. The Base commander asked Captain Thomas Mantell, the leader, to investigate the unknown flying object.

All the Mustang pilots knew that to go beyond 15,000 feet without oxygen was dangerous. Yet at 2.45 p.m. Mantell told the control tower that he was going to climb higher to get closer to the odd craft. When the others reached 15,000 feet, they could not contact Mantell, who was above them.

At 3 p.m. the control tower lost sight of the weird aircraft. A few minutes after that Mantell's plane dived, exploding in midair. The wreckage was found ninety miles away. The official explanation of Mantell's death was that he had been chasing Venus. Few believed this implausible reason – and the mystery remains.

The Stratoliner of the British Overseas Airways Corporation (now British Airways) was three hours out of New York on its run to London. At that point, Captain James H. Howard and his copilot noticed some strange uninvited company three miles off their left side: a large elongated object and six smaller ones. These UFOs stayed alongside for about eighty miles.

As the plane neared Goose Bay, Canada, for refuelling, the large UFO seemed to change shape, and the smaller ones converged on it. Captain Howard told the Goose Bay control tower what was happening. Ground control in turn alerted the USAF, which sent a Sabre fighter to the scene. When Captain Howard contacted the Sabre pilot, he said he was coming from twenty miles away.

"At that," said Captain Howard, "the small objects seemed to enter the larger, and then the big one shrank." He didn't find out what finally occurred because he had to leave Goose Bay on schedule.

These events took place in June 1954. The pilot and copilot described the UFOs as spaceships, and were confirmed in this belief by various passengers. However, in a 1968 report by a USAF-sponsored research team, this close-range sighting was dismissed as an "optical mirage phenomenon."

Hoaxers created new circles during the night, while scientists had their equipment trained on the area

E.A. Bryant, a retired prison officer who lived in southwest England near Dartmoor prison, was taking a walk on the evening of 24 April 1965. About 5.30 p.m. he arrived and stopped at an especially scenic spot. All at once he saw a flying saucer appear out of thin air about forty yards away. It swung left and right like a clock pendulum before coming to rest and hovering above ground.

Although he was frightened, Bryant was curious enough to overcome his fears and stay to watch. An opening appeared in the side of the spaceship and three figures, dressed in what looked like diving suits, came to it. One beckoned to Bryant, and he approached the strange craft. As he did so, the occupants removed their headgear. He saw that two had fair hair, blue eyes, and exceptionally high foreheads. The third – who was smaller and darker – had ordinary earthly features.

The dark one talked to Bryant in fairly good English. Bryant understood him to say his name was "Yamski" or something like it, and that he wished "Des" or "Les" were there to see him because the latter would understand everything. He also said that he and the others were from the planet Venus. After the UFO took off, some metallic fragments were left on the ground near the place it had been. Later some small pieces of metal were indeed found there.

When Bryant reported his experience, investigators were struck by the fact that George Adamski, author of the best-selling book *Flying Saucers Have Landed,* had died the very day before. His collaborator on this book had been Desmond Leslie. Was there a connection between "Yamski" and Adamski, and "Des" or "Les" and Desmond Leslie?

UFO enthusiasts were startled when the International Flying Saucer Bureau stopped all activity in late 1953. Although less than two years old, the organization founded by Albert K. Bender in Bridgeport, Connecticut, had been prospering. Why did it shut down?

The only person who could answer this question was Bender himself, and he was not talking. Not until seven years later did he talk – and his tale was one of contact with an "Exalted One" from space.

Bender claimed to have had a direct interview with the Exalted One, who warned him of instant death if he continued to delve into the mystery of UFOs. That's why he disbanded the IFSB. But he learned many interesting things during his interview, and he revealed all when he got the sign he could.

In his interview, for example, Bender asked the space being if his people believed in God. The reply was that they did not, because they did not have the desire to "worship something" as Earth people do.

Another topic Bender discussed with the space visitor was whether other planets were inhabited. The Exalted One said that there had once been life on Mars, but that it was destroyed by invaders. The Martians had built beautiful cities and developed a vast system of waterways, but had not been as technologically advanced at the time of their end as we now are. Venus was developing life, the being said.

One of the most interesting exchanges between Bender and the Exalted One was about the moon. Bender asked if the Earth people would ever reach the moon, and he was told yes.

Seven years after Bender wrote this, men were indeed walking on the moon.

Unidentified flying object seen by Hugo Vesa, Lima, Peru

One of the wildest UFO chases on record took place early in the morning of 1 April 1966. It started when Dale F. Spaur, deputy sheriff of Portage County, Ohio, stopped at a stalled car and spotted the brightly lit flying object that had been reported to his office. He was ordered to follow it. He and an assistant raced after it in their patrol car for about seventy miles, sometimes driving over 100 mph to keep it in their sight.

Forty miles east of the point at which he started, Spaur met Officer Wayne Huston of East Palestine after having talked to him by car radio. This officer saw the flying saucer too, and described it as "shaped something like an ice cream cone with a sort of partly melted top." The chase continued into neighbouring Pennsylvania, ending in Conway. Officer Frank Panzanella of that town came to the scene when he saw the other policemen, and told them he had been watching the shining object of the chase for about ten minutes. All four observers then saw the UFO rise straight up left of the moon, and disappear.

The United States Air Force Project Blue Book investigated the Spaur-UFO chase, and labelled it as a sighting of Venus. The four independent observers involved do not believe that was the right conclusion.

Miracles and Other Psychic Phenomena

Josephine Hoare, a healthy girl of twenty-one, had been married for only six months when she developed chronic nephritis, a serious inflammation of the kidneys. Her family was told that she had no more than two years to live. At her mother's suggestion, she was taken to Lourdes.

At the famous French shrine, Josephine braved the icy waters of the spring. Although she felt peaceful, she was not conscious of any change. When she went home, however, her doctor said in amazement that the disorder seemed to have cleared. Her swollen legs returned to normal size, her blood pressure became normal, and her energy increased. But she was warned that pregnancy would certainly cause a relapse.

Several years passed. Then Josephine and her husband had the opportunity to revisit Lourdes, and Josephine lit a candle of thanksgiving. Soon after they got home, she felt a sharp pain in her back. Fearful that nephritis was recurring, she went to her doctor. His diagnosis was simply that she was six months pregnant – and she had had no relapse.

Josephine Hoare had her baby, a son, and remained in good health. For her and her family, the spring of Lourdes had produced a double miracle.

In 1933 a six-year-old boy vanished from his home in Miège in the Swiss Alps. After an unsuccessful search for the boy, the town's mayor wrote to Abbé Mermet, who had often assisted police in locating missing people. The Abbé needed an article used by the missing person, a description of the last place he or she was seen, and a map of the surrounding area to do his work. He used a pendulum and a form of dowsing to find the missing person.

After the Abbé applied his pendulum to the problem of the missing boy, he reported that the child had been carried away into the mountains by a large bird of prey, probably an eagle. He also said that the bird – although enormous – had dropped its load twice to rest and regain its strength.

There was no trace of the boy at the first place the Abbé indicated. A recent heavy snowfall prevented a thorough search at the second place, but the conclusion was that Abbé Mermet had made a mistake.

When the snow melted two weeks later, however, a gang of woodcutters found the torn and mangled body of a small boy. It was the missing child. The bird had apparently been prevented from completely savaging the child's body by the sudden heavy storm that had also hidden the forlorn evidence.

Scientific investigation established that the boy's shoes and clothes had not come into contact with the ground where the body was found. He could only have reached the remote spot by air – the pitiful victim of the bird of prey. Later the boy's father apologized to the Abbé for having doubted him.

It was November 1971 in London on a day like any other. In one of the city's underground stations, a train was approaching the platform. Suddenly a young man hurled himself directly into the path of the moving train. The horrified driver slammed on the brakes, certain that there was no way to stop the train before the man was crushed under the wheels. But miraculously the train did stop. The first carriage had to be jacked up to remove the badly injured man, but the wheels had not passed over him and he survived.

The young man turned out to be a gifted architect who was recovering from a nervous breakdown. His amazing rescue from death was based on coincidence. For the investigation of the accident revealed that the train had not stopped because of the driver's hasty braking. Seconds before, acting on an impulse and completely unaware of the man about to throw himself on the tracks, a passenger had pulled down the emergency handle, which automatically applies the brakes of the train. The passenger had no particular reason for doing so. In fact, the Transport Authority considered prosecuting him on the grounds that he had had no reasonable cause for using the emergency system!

Eliphas Lévi, the nineteenth-century writer on theories of magic, seldom practiced what he wrote about. But when he was offered a complete magical chamber, he decided to try to evoke Apollonius of Tyana.

Lévi made his circle, kindled the ritual fires, and began reading the evocations of the ritual.

A ghostly figure appeared before the altar. Lévi found himself seized with a great chill. He placed his hand on the pentagram, the five-pointed symbol used to protect magicians against harm. He also pointed his sword at the figure, commanding it mentally to obey and not to alarm him. Something touched the hand holding the sword, and his arm became numb from the elbow down. Lévi realized that the figure objected to the sword, and he lowered it to the ground. At this, a great weakness came over him, and he fainted without having asked his questions.

After his swoon, however, he seemed to have the answers to his unasked questions. He had meant to ask one about the possibility of forgiveness and reconciliation between "two persons who occupied my thought." The answer was, "Dead."

It was his marriage that was dead. His wife, who had recently left him, never returned.

STRANGE TALES &
WEIRD MYSTERIES

COLIN WILSON
with
Damon and Rowan Wilson

• chapter one •

MAN INTO BEAST

In the year 1598, in a remote patch of forest in Western France, an archer and a group of armed countrymen came across the naked body of a boy. The corpse had been horribly mutilated and torn. The limbs, still warm and palpitating, were drenched with blood. As the Frenchmen approached the body, they caught sight of what appeared to be two wolves running off between the trees. The men gave chase, but to their amazement, they found they had caught, not a wolf, but what proved to be a man—tall, gaunt, clothed in rags, and with matted, verminous hair and beard. To their horror they noticed that his hands were still stained with fresh blood, and his claw-like nails clotted with human flesh. The man, it turned out, was a wandering beggar named Jacques Roulet, and he was brought to trial at the town of Angers in August, 1598. And if the discovery of Roulet was a shock to the people of Angers, the trial proceedings were shattering.

Roulet confessed to the court: "I was a wolf."

"Do your hands and feet become paws?"

"Yes, they do."

"Does your head become like that of a wolf?"

"I do not know how my head was at the time; I used my teeth."

In reaching their verdict the court had to decide whether Roulet was a werewolf, as he claimed, or a lycanthrope, which is related but different. A werewolf or werwolf is a living person who has the power to change into a wolf. The word comes from Old English *wer*, meaning man, and wolf. A *lycanthrope* is someone suffering from a mental illness that makes him believe he is transformed into a wolf. This word comes from the Greek for wolfman. In either case, Roulet could have faced execution. But the court showed a compassion rare for its time. Judging Roulet to be mentally sick—and therefore a lycanthrope—they sentenced him to a madhouse for only two years.

A true werewolf was generally believed to undergo an almost complete transformation into a wolf, unlike the werewolf of Hollywood movies who remains basically human in appearance. Much controversy arose in the past over people who were said to disguise the fact that they were wolves by wearing their fur on the inside. It was claimed that such people looked ordinary enough, but that their skin was inside out. When they were torn apart—as hundreds of innocent people were at various times in past centuries—the hair, or wolf fur, could be seen on the other side of the skin.

The werewolf and the vampire have much in common. In fact it was often assumed that a werewolf would become a vampire after death unless special precautions, such as exorcism, were taken. Anyone who ate the flesh of a sheep killed by a wolf was liable to become a werewolf. A person who ate a wolf's brains or drank water from his footprints was certain to become one. In some places, eating certain large and sweet smelling flowers or drinking from a stream where a wolfpack had drunk was a sure way to turn into a wolf.

Anybody with small pointed ears, prominent teeth, strong curved fingernails, bushy eyebrows that met over the nose, a third finger as long as the second on each hand, or even a lot of hair—especially on the hands and feet—was immediately suspect. However, if you are tempted to take a closer look at your friends next time you see them, remember that the eyes of a werewolf always remain human.

Like the belief in vampires, these beliefs stemmed from people's ignorant fear of anyone who was different. In some traditions it was easy to become a werewolf by accident. In others, you had to be especially evil to merit such a fate. Some tales suggest that a bestial person would return after death as a wolf. Ghostly werewolves, however, are extremely rare in folklore, which is where the werewolf differs most from the vampire. The vampire is akin to the ghost. The werewolf is very much a living person, and more akin to the witch in that he or she may actively seek to become a werewolf. This can be done by entering into a pact with a demon known as the Wolf Spirit or with the Devil himself.

THE BERMUDA TRIANGLE

On the afternoon of 5 December 1945 five Avenger torpedo-bombers took off from Fort Lauderdale, Florida, for a routine two-hour patrol over the Atlantic. Flight 19 was commanded by Flight Leader Charles Taylor; the other four pilots were trainees, flying what is known as a "milk run" that is, a flight whose purpose is simply to increase their number of hours in the air without instructors. By 2.15 the planes were well over the Atlantic, and following their usual patrol route. The weather was warm and clear.

At 3.45 the control tower received a message from Taylor: "This is an emergency. We seem to be off course. We cannot see land . . . repeat . . . we cannot see land."

"What is your position?"

"We're not sure of our position. We can't be sure where we are. We seem to be lost."

"Head due west," replied the tower.

"We don't know which way is west. Everything is wrong . . . strange. We can't be sure of any direction. Even the ocean doesn't look as it should."

The tower was perplexed; even if some kind of magnetic interference caused all five compasses to malfunction, the pilot should still be able to see the sun low in the western sky. Radio contact was now getting worse, restricting any messages to short sentences. At one point the tower picked up one one pilot speaking to another, saying that all the instruments in his plane were "going crazy". At 4 o'clock the flight leader decided to hand over to someone else. At 4.25 the new leader told the tower: "We're not certain where we are."

Unless the planes could find their way back over land during the next four hours, they would run out of fuel and be forced to land in the sea. At 6.27 a rescue mission was launched. A giant Martin Mariner flying-boat, with a crew of thirteen, took off towards the last reported position of the flight. Twenty-three minutes later, the sky to the east was lit briefly by a bright orange flash. Neither the Martin Mariner nor the five Avengers ever returned. They vanished completely, as other planes and ships have vanished in the area that has become known as "the Devil's Triangle" and "the Bermuda Triangle".

What finally happened to the missing aircraft is certainly no mystery. The weather became worse during the course of that afternoon; ships reported "high winds and tremendous seas". Flight 19 and its would-be rescuer must have run out of fuel, and landed in the sea. The mystery is *why* they became so completely lost and confused. Even if, the navigation instruments had ceased to function, and visibility had become restricted to a few yards, it should have been possible to fly up above the clouds to regain their bearings.

What seems stranger still is that this tragedy should have failed to alert the authorities that there was something frightening and dangerous about the stretch of ocean between Florida and the Bahamas – a chain of islands that begins a mere fifty miles off the coast of Florida. But then the authorities no doubt took the view of many more recent sceptics, that the disappearance was a rather complex accident, due to a number of chance factors: bad weather, electrical interference with the compasses, the inexperience of some of the pilots and the fact that the flight leader, Charles Taylor, had only recently been posted to Fort Lauderdale and was unfamiliar with the area.

Similar explanations were adopted to explain a number of similar tragedies during the next two decades: the disappearance of a Superfortress in 1947, of a four-engined Tudor IV in January 1948, of a DC3 in December 1948, of another Tudor IV in 1949, of a Globemaster in 1950, of a British York transport plane in 1952, of a Navy Super Constellation in 1954, of another Martin seaplane in 1956, of an Air Force tanker in 1962, of two Stratotankers in 1963, of a flying boxcar in 1965, of a civilian cargo plane in 1966, another cargo plane in 1967, and yet another in 1973 . . . The total number of lives lost in all these disappearances was well in excess of two hundred. Oddly enough, the first person to realize that all this amounted to a frightening mystery was a journalist called Vincent Gaddis; it was in February 1964 that his article "The Deadly Bermuda Triangle" appeared in the American *Argosy* magazine, and bestowed the now familiar name on that mysterious stretch of ocean. A year later, in a book about sea mysteries called *Invisible Horizons*, Gaddis included his article in a chapter called "The Triangle of Death". His chapter also contained a long list of ships which had vanished in the area, beginning with the *Rosalie*, which vanished in 1840, and ending with the yacht *Connemara IV* in 1956. In the final chapter Gaddis entered the realm of science fiction, and speculated on "space-time continua [that] may exist around us on the earth, interpenetrating our known world", implying that perhaps some of the missing planes and ships had vanished down a kind of fourth-dimensional plughole.

Soon after the publication of his book Gaddis received a letter from a man called Gerald Hawkes, who told of his own experience in the Bermuda Triangle in April 1952. On a flight from Idlewild Airport (now Kennedy) to Bermuda, Hawkes's plane suddenly dropped about two hundred feet. This was not a nose-dive, but felt as if he had suddenly fallen down a lift-shaft in the air; then the plane shot back up again. "It was as if a giant hand was holding the plane and jerking it up and down," and the wings seemed to flap like the wings of a bird. The captain then told them that he was unable to find Bermuda, and that the operator was unable to make radio contact with either the US or Bermuda. An hour or so later the plane made contact with a radio ship, and was able to get its bearings and fly to Bermuda. As they climbed out of the plane they observed that it was a clear and starry night, with no wind. The writer concluded that he was still wondering whether he was caught in an area "where time and space seem to disappear".

Now, all pilots know about air pockets, where a sudden change in pressure causes the plane to lurch and fall, and about air turbulence which causes the wings of a plane to "flap". What seems odd about this case is the total radio blackout.

This was an anomaly that had also struck students of UFOs or flying saucers, who had been creating extraordinary theories ever since that day in June 1947 when a pilot named Kenneth Arnold saw nine shining discs moving against the background of Mount Rainier in Washington State. The flying-saucer enthusiasts now produced the interesting notion that the surface of our earth has a number of strange "vortices", whirlpools where gravity and terrestrial magnetism are inexplicably weaker than usual. And if extra-terrestrial intelligences happened to know about these whirlpools, they might well find them ideal for collecting human specimens to be studied at leisure upon their distant planet . . .

Ivan Sanderson, a friend of Gaddis's and a student of earth mysteries, felt that this was going too far. His training had been scientific, so he began by taking a map of the world, and marking on it a number of areas where strange disappearances had occurred. There was, for example, another "Devil's Triangle" south of the Japanese island of Honshu where ships and planes had vanished. A correspondent told Sanderson about a strange experience on a flight to Guam, in the western Pacific, when his ancient propeller-driven plane covered 340 miles in one hour, although there was no wind – about 200 miles more than it should have covered; checks showed that many planes had vanished in this area.

Marking these areas on the map, Sanderson observed that they were shaped like lozenges, and that these lozenges seemed to ring the globe in a neat symmetry, running in two rings, each between

30°C and 40°C north and south of the equator. There were ten of these "funny places", about 72°C apart. An earthquake specialist named George Rouse had argued that earthquakes originated in a certain layer below the earth's surface, and had speculated that there was a kind of trough running round the central core of the earth, which determined the direction of seismic activities. Rouse's map of these seismic disturbance areas corresponded closely with Sanderson's "lozenges". So Sanderson was inclined to believe that if "whirlpools" really caused the disappearance of ships and planes, then they were perfectly normal physical whirlpools, caused, so to speak, by the earth's tendency to "burp".

Sanderson's theory appeared in a book entitled *Invisible Residents* in 1970. Three years later a female journalist, Adi-Kent Thomas Jeffrey, tried to put together all the evidence about the Bermuda Triangle in a book of that name, printed by a small publishing company in Pennsylvania. It was undoubtedly her bad luck that her book failed to reach the general public. For one year later in 1974 Charles Berlitz, grandson of the man who founded the famous language schools, once again rehashed all the information about the Bermuda Triangle, persuaded a commercial publisher, Doubleday, to issue it, and promptly rocketed to the top of the American best-seller lists. It had been twenty years since the disappearance of Flight 19, and ten years since Vincent Gaddis invented the phrase "Bermuda Triangle". But Berlitz was the first man to turn the mystery into a worldwide sensation, and to become rich on the proceeds.

Berlitz's *Bermuda Triangle*, while highly readable, is low on scholarly precision – it does not even have an index. One reason for its popularity was that he launched himself intrepidly into bizarre regions of speculation about UFOs, space-time warps, alien intelligences, chariots of the gods (à la von Däniken) and other such matters. And among the weirdest of his speculations were those concerning the pioneer "Ufologist" Morris K. Jessup, who had died in mysterious circumstances after stumbling upon information about a certain mysterious "Philadelphia experiment". This experiment was supposed to have taken place in Philadelphia in 1943, when the Navy was testing some new device whose purpose was to surround a ship with a powerful magnetic field. According to Jessup's informant, a hazy green light began to surround the vessel, so that its outlines became blurred; then it vanished – to reappear in the harbour of Norfolk, Virginia, some three hundred miles away. Several members of the crew died; others went insane. According to Jessup, when he began to investigate this story, the Navy asked him whether he would be willing to work on a similar secret project; he declined. In 1959 he was found dead in his car, suffocated by exhaust gas; Berlitz speculates that he was "silenced" before he could publicize his discoveries about the experiment.

And what has all this to do with the Bermuda Triangle? Simply that the Philadelphia experiment was supposed to be an attempt to create a magnetic vortex, like those suggested by Sanderson, and that (according to Jessup) it had the effect of involving the ship in a space-time warp that transported it hundreds of miles.

Understandably, this kind of thing roused sceptics to a fury, and there were suddenly a large number of articles, books and television programmes all devoted to debunking the Bermuda Triangle. These all adopted the common sense approach that had characterized the Naval authorities in 1945: that is to say, they assumed that the disappearances were all due to natural causes, particularly to freak storms. In many cases it is difficult not to agree that this is indeed the most plausible explanation. But when we look at the long list of disappearances in the area, most of them never even yielding a body or a trace of wreckage, the explanation begins to sound thin.

Is there, then, an alternative which combines common sense with the boldness necessary to recognize that all the disappearances cannot be conveniently explained away? There is, and it rests on the evidence of some of those who have escaped the Bermuda Triangle. In November 1964 a charter pilot named Chuck Wakely was returning from Nassau to Miami, Florida, and had climbed up to 8,000 feet. He noticed a faint glow round the wings of his plane, which he put down to some optical illusion caused by cockpit lights. But the glow increased steadily, and all his electronic equipment began to go wrong. He was forced to operate the craft manually. The glow became so blinding that he was dazzled; then slowly it faded, and his instruments began to function normally again.

In 1966 Captain Don Henry was steering his tug from Puerto Rico to Fort Lauderdale on a clear afternoon. He heard shouting, and hurried to the bridge. There he saw that the compass was spinning clockwise. A strange darkness came down, and the horizon disappeared. "The water seemed to be coming from all directions." And although the electric generators were still running, all electric power faded away. An auxiliary generator refused to start. The boat seemed to be surrounded by a kind of fog. Fortunately the engines were still working, and suddenly the boat emerged from the fog. To Henry's amazement, the fog seemed to be concentrated into a single solid bank, and within this area the sea was turbulent; outside it was calm. Henry remarked that the compass behaved as it did on the St Lawrence River at Kingson, where some large deposit of iron – or a meteorite – affects the needle.

Our earth is, of course, a gigantic magnet (no one quite knows why), and the magnetic lines of force run around its surface in strange patterns. Birds and animals use these lines of force for "homing", and water-diviners seem able to respond to them with their "dowsing rods". But there are areas of the earth's surface where birds lose their way because the lines somehow cancel one another out, forming a magnetic anomaly or vortex. The *Marine Observer* for 1930 warns sailors about a magnetic disturbance in the neighbourhood of the Tambora volcano, near Sumbawa, which deflected a ship's compass by six points, leading it off course. In 1932 Captain Scutt of the *Australia* observed a magnetic disturbance near Freemantle that deflected the compass 12°C either side of the ship's course. Dozens of similar anomalies have been collected and documented by an American investigator, William Corliss, in books with titles like *Unknown Earth* and *Strange Planet*. It was Corliss, who pointed out to me the investigations of Dr John de Laurier of Ottawa, who in 1974 went to camp on the ice-floes of northern Canada in search of an enormous magnetic anomaly forty-three miles long, which he believes to originate about eighteen miles below the surface of the earth. De Laurier's theory is that such anomalies are due to the earth's tectonic plates rubbing together – an occurrence that also causes earthquakes.

The central point to emerge from all this is that our earth is not like an ordinary bar magnet, whose field is symmetrical and precise; it is full of magnetic "pitfalls" and anomalies. Scientists are not sure why the earth has a magnetic field, but one theory suggests that it is due to movements in its molten iron core. Such movements would in fact produce shifting patterns in the earth's field, and bursts of magnetic activity, which might be compared to the bursts of solar energy known as sunspots. If they *are* related to earth-tensions and therefore to earthquakes then we would expect them to occur in certain definite zones, just as earthquakes do. What effects would a sudden "earthquake" of magnetic activity produce? One would be to cause compasses to spin, for it would be rather as if a huge magnetic meteor was roaring up from the centre of the earth. On the sea it would produce an effect of violent turbulence, for it would affect the water in the same way the moon affects the tides, but in an irregular pattern, so that the water would appear to be coming "from all directions". Clouds and mist would be sucked into the vortex, forming a "bank" in its immediate area. And electronic gadgetry would probably be put out of action . . .

All this makes us aware why the "simplistic" explanations of the problem – all those books explaining that the mystery of the Bermuda Triangle is a journalistic invention are not only superficial but dangerous. They discourage the investigation of what could be one of the most interesting scientific enigmas of our time. With satellites circling the earth at a height of 150 miles, it should be possible to observe bursts of magnetic activity with the same accuracy that earth tremors are recorded on seismographs. We should be able to observe their frequency and intensity precisely enough to plot them in advance. The result could not only be the solution of the mystery, but the prevention of future tragedies like that of Flight 19.

Atlantis, the fabled lost continent, is first mentioned in Plato's dialogues between *Timaeus* and *Critias* written around 350 bc. There it is described as an enormous island "beyond the Pillars of Hercules" (The Straits of Gibraltar). On this island, civilization flourished long before Athens was founded in 9600 bc. The inhabitants were great engineers and aggressive warriors, harassing early European and Asian civilization until the Athenians finally conquered them on their own territory. At that point great floods overwhelmed the island, and both the Athenian army and the Atlantian civilization disappeared beneath the ocean in a day and a night.

Plato describes their culture and territory in detail. The city was eleven miles in diameter, formed from concentric rings of land and water. The Atlanteans were fed by crops grown on a large plain 230 by 340 miles located behind the city. Plato describes their buildings and their habits, setting the pattern for all future Utopian literature; indeed that is all that his writings on Atlantis were considered to be for roughly two thousand years.

Then in 1882, Ignatius Donnelly, American senator and well-read theorist published a book suggesting that Plato's "fable" was based upon a real civilization. He pointed out that scientists were now relatively certain that continents do appear and disappear beneath the waves, and that earthquakes and volcanic activity are capable of terrible damage. Much of the minutiae of Donnelly's argument proves to be inaccurate on close examination, but the idea that there was an entirely lost civilization beneath the waves proved too romantic to be stifled.

Atlantis has been associated with Lyoness, the sunken area of land between Land's End in Cornwall and the Isles of Scilly. Regular patterns of stones and carvings found on the sea bed near Bimini in the Bahamas have been identified as Atlantean. More plausible in some ways is Professor Angelos Galanopoulos' theory that Santorini in the Mediterranean was the source of Plato's story. Santorini is a volcanic island whose last major explosion was in 1500 bc. The eruption ripped the island apart and sent a tidal wave out that devastated many surrounding islands. Only two problems exist with this explanation. Firstly Santorini is a great deal too small to be Plato's Atlantis. Galanopoulos explains this by positing an error in transcription that multiplied all the figures Plato gives by a factor of ten. Indeed if one does remove a nought from all of Plato's measurements a fair approximation of Santorini's size does appear. The second problem is more difficult to resolve: Santorini is on the wrong side of the Pillars of Hercules. Galanopoulos arguments on this score are more difficult to credit, as they place the Pillars of Hercules at the southernmost promontories of Greece. The area of Atlantean subjugation according to Plato does not marry well with this revision; Santorini is only marginally more likely as a sight for Atlantis then Cornwall.

The story of Atlantis still fascinates, but without more positive evidence it must be regarded as more a cautionary tale than a historical treatise.

THE DISAPPEARANCE OF AGATHA CHRISTIE

In 1926 Agatha Christie was involved in a mystery that sounds like the plot of one of her own novels. But unlike the fictional crimes unravelled by Hercule Poirot, this puzzle has never been satisfactorily solved.

At the age of thirty-six, Agatha Christie seemed an enviable figure. She was an attractive redhead, with a touch of grey, and lived with her husband, Colonel Archibald Christie, in a magnificent country house which she once described as "a sort of millionaire-style Savoy suite transferred to the country".

She was also the author of seven volumes of detective fiction, of which the latest, *The Murder of Roger Ackroyd*, had caused some controversy because of its "unfair" ending. Yet the authoress was hardly a celebrity; few of her books achieved sales of more than a few thousand.

Then on the freezing cold night of 3 December, 1926 she left her home at Sunningdale, in Berkshire, and disappeared.

At eleven the next morning, a Superintendent in Surrey Police was handed a report on a "road accident" at Newlands Corner, just outside Guildford. Agatha Christie's Morris two-seater had been found halfway down a grassy bank with its bonnet buried in a clump of bushes. There was no sign of the driver, but she had clearly not intended to go far, because she had left her fur coat in the car.

By mid-afternoon the Press had heard of the disappearance, and were besieging the Christie household. From the start the police hinted that they suspected suicide. Her husband dismissed this theory, sensibly pointing out that most people commit suicide at home, and do not drive off in the middle of the night. But an

THE DAILY MIRROR, Tuesday December 7, 1916

£100 FREE CROSS-WORD COMPETITION: SEE PAGE 4

Daily Mirror

THE DAILY PICTURE NEWSPAPER WITH THE LARGEST NET SALE

CAMPAIGN TO MAKE LONDON STREETS SAFER

No. 7,190   TUESDAY, DECEMBER 7, 1926   [24 PAGES]   One Penny

MYSTERY OF WOMAN NOVELIST'S DISAPPEARANCE

A thorough search in the woods near the spot where Mrs. Christie's car was found.

EARL'S DAUGHTER TAKES THE AIR IN A CAGE

Mrs. Agatha Christie, the missing woman novelist, with her daughter.

Jack Best at the place where he found the car abandoned.

Following an important clue received yesterday a special search will be made to-day for Mrs. Agatha Christie, the novelist wife of Colonel Archibald Christie, D.S.O., who disappeared after leaving her home at Sunningdale, Berks, in her car. The car was found abandoned near Newlands Corner, Surrey. (Daily Mirror photograph.)

The infant daughter of Earl and Countess De la Warr asleep in her perambulator inside a galvanised iron cage which her parents (inset) have had fixed outside the front of their home near Victoria. This enables her to take the air without risk. (Daily Mirror.)

extensive search of the area around Newlands Corner was organized and the Silent Pool, an allegedly bottomless lake in the vicinity, was investigated by deep-sea divers.

What nobody knew was that Agatha Christie's life was not as enviable as it looked. Her husband had recently fallen in love with a girl who was ten years his junior – Nancy Neele – and had only recently told her that he wanted a divorce. The death of her mother had been another psychological shock. She was sleeping badly, eating erratic meals, and moving furniture around the house in a haphazard manner. She was obviously distraught, possibly on the verge of a nervous breakdown.

The next two or three days produced no clues to her whereabouts. When it was reported that some female clothes had been found in a lonely hut near Newlands Corner, together with a bottle labelled "opium", there was a stampede of journalists. But it proved to be a false alarm, and the opium turned out to be a harmless stomach remedy. Some newspapers hinted that Archibald Christie stood to gain much from the death of his wife, but he had a perfect alibi: he was at a weekend party in Surrey. Other journalists began to wonder whether the disappearance was a publicity stunt. Ritchie-Calder suspected that she had disappeared to spite her husband, and bring his affair with Nancy Neele out into the open. He even read through her novels to see whether she had ever used a similar scenario. When the *Daily News* offered a reward reports of sightings poured in. They all proved to be false alarms.

Another interesting touch of mystery was added when her brother-in-law Campbell revealed that he had received a letter from her whose postmark indicated that it had been posted in London at 9.45 on the day after her disappearance, when she was presumably wandering around in the woods of Surrey.

In the *Mail* the following Sunday there was an interview with her husband in which he admitted "that my wife had discussed the possibility of disappearing at will. Some time ago she told her sister, 'I could disappear if I wished and set about it carefully . . .'" It began to look as if the disappearance, after all, might not be a matter of suicide or amnesia.

On 14 December, eleven days after her disappearance, the head waiter in the Hydropathic Hotel in Harrogate, North Yorkshire, looked more closely at a female guest and recognized her from newspaper photographs as the missing novelist. He rang the Yorkshire police, who contacted her home. Colonel Christie took an afternoon train from London to Harrogate, and learned that his wife had been staying in the hotel for a week and a half. She had taken a good room on the first floor at seven guineas a week, and had apparently seemed "normal and happy", and "sang, danced, played billiards, read the newspaper reports of the disappearance, chatted with her fellow guests, and went for walks".

Agatha made her way to the dinner table, picked up an evening paper which contained the story of the search for herself, together with a photograph, and was reading it when her husband made his way over to her. "She only seemed to regard him as an acquaintance whose identity she could not quite fix," said the hotel's manager. And Archibald Christie told the Press: "She has suffered from the most complete loss of memory and I do not think she knows who she is." A doctor later confirmed that she was suffering from loss of memory. But Lord Ritchie-Calder later remembered how little she seemed to correspond with the usual condition of amnesia. When she vanished, she had been wearing a green knitted skirt, a grey cardigan and a velour hat, and carried a few pounds in her purse. When she was found she was stylishly dressed, and had three hundred pounds on her. She had told other guests in the hotel that she was a visitor from South Africa.

There were unpleasant repercussions. A public outcry, orchestrated by the Press, wanted to know who was to pay the £3,000 which the search was estimated to have cost, and Surrey ratepayers blamed the next big increase on her. Her next novel, *The Big Four*, received unfriendly reviews, but nevertheless sold nine thousand copies – more than twice as many as *The Murder of Roger Ackroyd*. And from then on (as Elizabeth Walter has described in an essay called "The Case of the Escalating Sales") her books sold in increasing quantities. By 1950 all her books were enjoying a regular sale of more than fifty thousand copies, and the final Miss Marple story, *Sleeping Murder*, had a first printing of sixty thousand.

Agatha Christie divorced her husband (who wed Miss Neele) and in 1930 married Professor Sir Max Mallowan. But for the rest of her life she refused to discuss her disappearance, and would only grant interviews on condition that it was not mentioned. Her biographer, Janet Morgan, accepts that it was a case of nervous breakdown, followed by amnesia. Yet this is difficult to accept. Where did she obtain the clothes and the money to go to Harrogate? Why did she register under the surname of her husband's mistress? And is it possible to believe that her amnesia was so complete that, while behaving perfectly normally, she was able to read accounts of her own disappearance, look at photographs of herself, and still not even suspect her identity?

Lord Ritchie-Calder, who got to know her very well in later life, remains convinced that "her disappearance was calculated in the classic style of her detective stories". A television play produced after her death even speculated that the disappearance was part of a plot to murder Nancy Neele. The only thing that is certain about "the case of the disappearing authoress" is that it turned Agatha Christie into a best-seller, and eventually into a millionairess.

• chapter four •

THE LABORATORY
OF DR RHINE

Had the Bell Witch case occurred in the first part of the 20th century instead of 100 years earlier, we would be in a better position to evaluate it, both psychologically and psychically. Today psychical research is becoming more and more sophisticated. The Parapsychology Laboratory at Duke University, founded by Dr. J. B. Rhine, is perhaps the best equipped psychical research unit in the world. The staff members go to painstaking lengths in examining many paranormal phenomena, including cases of poltergeist activity. Dr. Rhine's assistant, J. Gaither Pratt, described some of the laboratory's methods in his book *Parapsychology*. In one chapter he tells of the Seaford Poltergeist, which troubled a middle-class Long Island family and was investigated by Dr. Pratt and William G. Roll, another psychical researcher, during February and March 1958.

Mr. and Mrs. James M. Herrmann lived with their two children James, age 12, and Lucille, 13, at their home in Seaford, Nassau County, New York. Over a period of two months, 67 recorded disturbances were investigated not only by the Duke University team but also by the Nassau County Police. The phenomena fell into two categories: the unscrewing of bottle caps followed by the spilling of the bottles' contents; and the moving of furniture and small objects.

Although Dr. Pratt states that no firm conclusion could be reached as to the cause of the Seaford poltergeist, he observes that nothing ever happened when all the family were out of the house, when they were fast asleep, or when the children were both at school. He also notes that the disturbances usually took place nearer to James than to any other member of the family.

Dr. Pratt's account is of interest mainly in showing to what lengths a psychical researcher must go before concluding that an alleged poltergeist is genuine. Between them Dr. Pratt, Roll, and Detective Joseph Tozzi first ruled out the possibility of hoax by one or more members of the family. Observing the tangible evidence of the force—the smashed objects and spilled liquids—they could quickly rule out collective hallucination. Next, they checked the possibility that the disturbances could be caused by high frequency radio waves, vibrations, chemical interference (in the case of the spilled liquids), faulty electrical wiring, drafts, water level alteration in a well near the house, possible underground streams, radio frequencies outside the house, and subsidence of the land under the house. They held a conference at nearby Adelphi College with members of the science departments, and they called in structural, civil, and electrical engineers from the Nassau Society of Engineers. They examined the possibility that takeoffs and landings at nearby Mitchell Air Field might be causing the events, and they checked the house's plumbing installations from top to bottom.

All of their findings were negative. After almost two months on the spot, Dr. Pratt tentatively gave his opinion that they were not dealing with the "kind of impersonal psychical force which perhaps sometime in the future will fall within the scope of physics. . . . If the Seaford disturbances were not fraudulent—and no evidence of fraud was found—they clearly make a proper claim upon the interests of parapsychologists." In other words, in his opinion some intelligence lay behind the disturbance.

Dr. Pratt did not overlook the fact that in the Seaford case, as in most poltergeist cases, adolescent children were on the scene. So far as he could tell during his short visit, neither of the Herrmann children had psychological problems. Perhaps no such problem is required; perhaps puberty itself can trigger off poltergeist phenomena as its energies react with other forces.

The existence of other forces can't be completely dismissed, for there have been some poltergeist cases in which no adolescents were involved. This was true in the case of the poltergeist phenomena at Killakee Arts Center in Ireland, which was also haunted by a phantom black cat. Margaret O'Brien, the only person who lived on the premises throughout the entire disturbance period—from the late 1960s to the end of 1970—is a mature and intelligent woman. Furthermore, she was absent from the house on several occasions when phenomena occurred. It's impossible, therefore, to link the trouble with any one person.

It does seem possible, though, that the Killakee poltergeist may have been goaded into activity—perhaps even created—by some amateur psychic investigators. It's worth remembering that the Bell Witch investigating committee helped to develop the phenomena by urging the presence to "smack its mouth" and make other noises. Old Jeffrey, the Wesley poltergeist, was encouraged to some extent by Kezzy following it from room to room, teasing it. A poltergeist may be an inhuman force, but it often seems capable of reacting to human interference.

After the appearance of a monstrous black cat during the renovation of Killakee House, several other apparitions were reported, though none of them was as vivid as the cat.

Following reports of these strange events in the Irish press, a group of show business personalities from Dublin persuaded Margaret O'Brien to let them try a seance at the house. They arranged letters of the alphabet in a circle on a table and used a glass turned upside down as a pointer that could be controlled by any psychic forces present. The results of the seance were inconclusive—although the lights failed, apparently without cause, at one point during the evening. Within a couple of days of the seance, however, serious disturbances began.

They began sporadically at first with bumps and rappings in the night, and lights being switched on and off. Then some of the artists living in the Center began to suffer sleepless nights, kept awake by the chiming of bells, although there were no bells in the neighborhood. The next stage of activity was more vigorous. Heavy pieces of furniture in locked rooms were found overturned, a stout oak chair was pulled apart joint from joint, and another solid chair was smashed to slivers.

For a few weeks after the chair smashing, peace descended. Then the disturbances began again. This time crockery was flung about and shattered, wide areas of the walls were smeared with glue, and several of the paintings were ripped to shreds.

Toward the end of 1970 the most peculiar of all the incidents occurred. They followed an attempt at exorcism by a Dublin priest.

At this time Mr. and Mrs. O'Brien were still making improvements to the premises, and had not yet installed a refrigerator. Consequently the milkman made use of a natural "icebox" in the form of a cool stream that runs through the grounds. He left the milk bottles standing in its shallow water. One morning when Mrs. O'Brien went to the stream to get a bottle, she found that the foil caps of all the bottles had been removed, though the milk inside was undisturbed. This continued for several days.

1 The Devil's Footprints, edited by G. A. Household, Devon Books 1985.

At first the O'Briens assumed that birds were pecking off the tops, although no trace of foil was ever found. To stop the nuisance Mr. O'Brien built a four-sided box of heavy stone on the stream bed, covered it with a massive slab of slate, and instructed the milkman to place the bottles in the box and replace the slate lid. Still the caps disappeared.

As if in compensation, though, other kinds of caps began to appear inside the house. In view of the various disturbances, the O'Briens naturally enough made a practice of locking all doors and windows before retiring for the night. Despite this, caps and hats began to appear all over the house. There were Derby hats and opera hats, children's knitted hats with woolly pom poms on top, and men's and women's straw sun hats. The pride of the collection was a lady's linen cap with drawstrings which was identified as 19th-century in style, although it appeared new.

This peculiar activity ceased suddenly at the end of 1970, and although occasional knockings and footsteps are still reported, Killakee Arts Center has settled down to a relatively quiet life. It was investigated at the height of its activity, but only in a limited way in the course of preparing a television program on the strange occurrences. It seems a pity that no thorough scientific investigation was conducted at Killakee, for it certainly ranks among the most fascinating poltergeist mysteries.

WAS DILLINGER SHOT?

Towards the end of his short life, John Herbert Dillinger was designated "public enemy number one", a distinction he shared with hold-up men like Baby Face Nelson, Pretty Boy Floyd and "Bonnie and Clyde". According to police records, Dillinger's sudden and violent end occurred outside the Biograph cinema in Chicago on 22 July 1934, when he was shot down by FBI agents. But since then there have been frequent doubts expressed about whether the man who died was actually the famous gangster.

John Herbert Dillinger was born on 22 June 1903, the product of an unhappy home life. When he was in sixth grade at school he was charged with stealing coal from the Pennsylvania Railroad's wagons to sell to residents of his Indianapolis neighbourhood. An angry magistrate shouted at him, "Your mind is crippled!"

When his father bought a small farm outside Mooresville, Indiana, Dillinger found country life intolerable. When a love affair went wrong he stole a car, drove to Indianapolis, and enlisted in the US Navy. During his four months as a sailor he was AWOL several times, and finally deserted in December. Back in Indiana, he married a sixteen-year-old girl and moved in with her parents. One day, after drinking in a pool hall, Dillinger and a former convict named Edgar Singleton concocted a robbery plan. They attacked a Mooresville grocer with a baseball bat, but the grocer fought back so vigorously that the would-be bandits fled. Dillinger was arrested on suspicion. When his father arrived at the gaol he admitted to the robbery, and the prosecutor promised his father that his son would receive a lenient sentence if he threw himself on the mercy of the court. It was Dillinger's bad luck to be brought before a severe judge, who fined him $200 and sentenced him to from ten to twenty years. Outraged at the broken promise, Dillinger made several unsuccessful attempts to escape from the State Reformatory at Pendleton. He also came under the influence of two determined bank robbers – Harry Pierpont and

Homer Van Meter. Dillinger, who had homosexual tendencies, also had a lover in prison.

Released in May 1933, after a petition from the residents of Mooresville, Dillinger set out to organize a mass escape for his former friends, who were then in the state prison in Michigan City. He began committing a series of bank robberies, in one of them netting $10,600. But a girl cashier in a bank at Daleville, Indiana, told the police that she felt that Dillinger – who wore a straw boater to commit the robbery – was anxious not to frighten her. His sense of impudent humour revealed itself when, in the World Fair in Chicago in the summer of 1933, he asked a policeman if he would snap a picture of himself and of his girlfriend Mary Longnaker.

In September 1933 Dillinger tossed three guns wrapped in newspapers into the athletic field at Michigan City prison, but other inmates found them and handed them over to the Warden. Next, Dillinger bribed the foreman of a thread-making company to conceal loaded guns in a barrel that was being sent to the shirt shop in the prison. But by the time his friends broke out of gaol Dillinger was already back in custody again – police keeping a watch on his girlfriend Mary had succeeded in arresting him. Ten men escaped. Shortly after, they rescued Dillinger from the Lima gaol, killing Sheriff Jess Sarber in the process. Eight days later, Dillinger and Pierpont walked into the gaol at Peru, Indiana, explained that they were tourists, and asked the police chief what precautions they had taken against the Dillinger gang. The police showed them their arsenal; Dillinger and Pierpont produced their guns, and left town with a car full of machine guns, shotguns and bullet-proof vests.

Now the "Dillinger mob" (as the press had already dubbed them) committed a whole series of robberies – the exact number is not certain – which made them notorious. When Dillinger was in a bank in Greencastle, Indiana, he saw a farmer standing at the counter with a pile of money in front of him. He asked, "Is that your money or the bank's?" "Mine," the farmer said. "Keep it," said Dillinger, and walked out with his sack full of the bank's cash. This kind of story brought Dillinger a reputation as a modern Robin Hood. The robbery brought the gang over $75,000. That winter they decided to move down to a warmer climate, and drove to Daytona Beach, Florida. But when they moved to Tucson, Arizona, their luck ran out: a fire broke out in their hotel, and a fireman discovered that their cases contained guns and ammunition. They were arrested and sent back to Indiana. Pierpont was charged with killing Sheriff Sarber.

On 3 March 1934 Dillinger made his spectacular escape from Crown Point gaol, Indiana, with a wooden gun that he had carved with a razor. The escape made him famous. (In fact, later investigation showed that Dillinger had somehow managed to get a real gun from somewhere.) Two weeks after the escape, Dillinger's fellow-escapee, Herbert Youngblood, was killed in a battle with

John Dillinger.

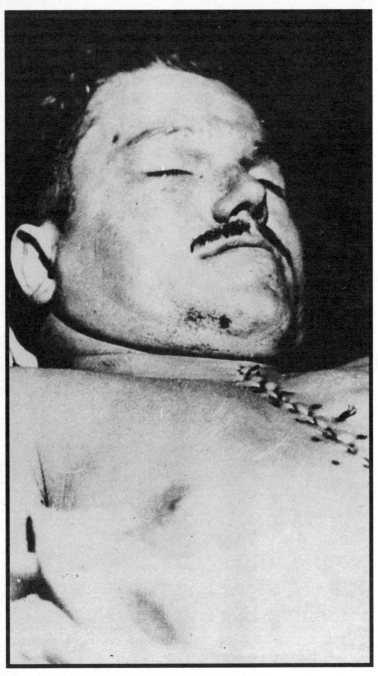

The man believed to be John Dillinger – in the morgue.

police. Dillinger quickly organized another gang, including Homer Van Meter and the short-tempered Baby Face Nelson (real name Lester Gillis). He also sent money for Pierpont's defence, but it did no good – Pierpont and another accomplice died in the electric chair. Soon after this Dillinger himself narrowly escaped death in a gun battle with police in St Paul, Minnesota. A month later police closed in around Dillinger's hideout at Little Bohemia Lodge, near Rhinelander, Wisconsin, but again the gang escaped. Only some innocent bystanders were shot. (The comedian Will Rogers joked that the only way Dillinger would get shot was if he got among some innocent bystanders some time.)

Under a plastic surgery operation to alter his face, Dillinger almost died, but the surgeon managed to pull his tongue out of his throat and got him breathing again.

With his new face, Dillinger had the confidence to go out into the open again. In Chicago he began to date a waitress named Polly Hamilton. Polly's room-mate was a forty-two-year-old woman called Anna Sage, who had served time for running a brothel. Anna was under threat of deportation, and when she learned Dillinger's identity it struck her that she might persuade the authorities to lift the deportation order if she betrayed him. Dillinger was now using the name James Lawrence.

So it came about that on the evening of 22 July 1934 Dillinger took his girlfriend Polly and Anna Sage to the Biograph cinema to see *Manhattan Melodrama*, starring Clark Gable. Anna Sage was wearing a bright red dress, in order to be easily identifiable. As they came out of the cinema FBI agent Melvin Purvis approached him and challenged him. The gangster pulled a Colt automatic from his pocket and sprinted for the nearest alleyway. Three agents fired, and Dillinger fell dead, with a bullet through his left eye; the man who had fired it was police detective Martin Zarkovich, of East Chicago. Later that day newsmen were taken to the morgue to see Dillinger's body. Foreign correspondent Negley Farson tells how the policeman pulled back the sheet over the naked body, and said grinning: "Well hung, isn't he?"

But was it Dillinger? The autopsy notes – made by Dr J.J. Kearns, the Cook County chief pathologist – reveal that the corpse's eyes were brown. Dillinger's were blue. The dead man possessed a rheumatic heart condition, chronic since childhood. Dillinger did not – he would not have been allowed to join the navy if he had. Lawrence was shorter and heavier than Dillinger, and had none of the scars and wounds or birthmarks that Dillinger was known to have.

Crime writer Jay Robert Nash has argued that the FBI was duped into believing that the dead man was Dillinger, and that J. Edgar Hoover was too embarrassed to admit the mistake afterwards. "Jimmy Lawrence", according to Nash, was a small-time hoodlum, who came from Wisconsin to Chicago about 1930 and was often seen in the neighbourhood of the Biograph cinema. If Nash is correct, then we may assume that the "lady in red" deliberately "set up" the small-time hoodlum in a plot to provide Dillinger with a permanent escape. A photograph taken from the handbag of Dillinger's girlfriend Billie Frechette some time before his "killing" shows her with a man who bears an amazing resemblance to the corpse of James Lawrence. It seems possible, therefore, that she was also involved in the plot to take the heat off her former lover.

Within months Dillinger's gang was wiped out. Homer Van Meter was killed in an alley and Baby Face Nelson died in a gun battle, after killing two FBI agents. Harry Pierpont attempted to escape from the death house in the Ohio State Prison by carving a gun out of soap, but the ruse failed. He was electrocuted in October 1934.

What happened to Dillinger? A fellow-gangster, Blackie Audett, who claims to have been in the Biograph cinema that evening, asserts in his book *Wrapsheet* that Dillinger married and fled to Oregon. He "disappeared" in the 1940s.

THE MYSTERY OF EILEAN MORE

The Island of Disappearing Men

In the empty Atlantic, seventeen miles to the west of the Hebrides, lie the Flannan Islands, known to seafarers as the Seven Hunters. The largest and most northerly of these is called Eilean More – which means in fact "big island". Like the *Mary Celeste*, its name has become synonymous with an apparently insoluble mystery of the sea.

These bleak islands received their name from a seventh-century bishop, St Flannan, who built a small chapel on Eilean More. Hebridean shepherds often ferried their sheep over to the islands to graze on the rich turf; but they themselves would never spend a night there, for the islands are supposed to be haunted by spirits and by "little folk". In the last decades of the nineteenth century, as Britain's sea trade increased, many ships sailing north or south from Clydebank were wrecked on the Flannans, and in 1895 the Northern Lighthouse Board announced that a lighthouse would be built on Eilean More. They expected construction to take two years; but rough seas, and the problems of hoisting stones and girders up a 200-foot cliff, made it impossible to stick to the schedule; Eilean More lighthouse was finally opened in December 1899. For the next year its beam could be seen reflected on the rough seas between Lewis and the Flannans. Then, eleven days before Christmas 1900, the light went out.

The weather was too stormy for the Northern Lighthouse Board steamer to go and investigate, even though the lighthouse had been built with two landing-stages, one to the west and one to the east, so one of them would always be sheltered from the prevailing wind.

Joseph Moore, waiting on the seafront at Loch Roag, had a sense of helplessness as he stared westward towards the Flannans. It was inconceivable that all three men on Eilean More – James Ducat, Donald McArthur and Thomas Marshall – could have fallen ill simultaneously, and virtually impossible that the lighthouse itself could have been destroyed by the storms.

On Boxing Day, 1900, the dawn was clear and the sea less rough. The *Hesperus* left harbour soon after daylight; Moore was so anxious that he refused to eat breakfast, pacing the deck and staring out towards the islands; the mystery had tormented him, and now he was too excited to take food.

The swell was still heavy, and the *Hesperus* had to make three approaches before she was able to moor by the eastern jetty. No flags had answered their signals, and there was no sign of life.

Moore was the first to reach the entrance gate. It was closed. He cupped his hands and shouted, then hurried up the steep path. The main door was closed, and no one answered his shouts. Like the *Mary Celeste*, the lighthouse was empty. In the main room the clock had stopped, and the ashes in the fireplace were cold. In the sleeping quarters upstairs – Moore waited until he was joined by two seamen before he ventured upstairs, afraid of what he might find there – the beds were neatly made, and the place was tidy.

James Ducat, the chief keeper, had kept records on a slate. The last entry was for 15 December at 9 a.m., the day the light went out. But this had not been for lack of oil; the wicks were trimmed and the lights all ready to be lit. Everything was in order. So it was clear that the men had completed their basic duties for the day before tragedy struck them; when evening came there had been no one on the island to light the lamp. But the 15th of December had been a calm day . . .

The *Hesperus* returned to Lewis with the men's Christmas presents still on board. Two days later investigators landed on Eilean More, and tried to reconstruct what had happened. At first it looked as if the solution was quite straightforward. On the westward jetty there was evidence of gale damage; a number of ropes were entangled round a crane which was sixty-five feet above sea-level. A tool chest kept in a crevice forty-five feet above this was missing. It looked as if a hundred-foot wave had crashed in from the Atlantic and swept it away, as well as the three men. The fact that the oilskins belonging to Ducat and Marshall were missing seemed to support this theory; they only wore them to visit the jetties. So the investigators had a plausible theory. The two men had feared that the crane was damaged in the storm; they had struggled to the jetty in their oilskins, then been caught by a sudden huge wave . . . But in that case, what had happened to the third man, Donald McArthur, whose oilskins were still in the lighthouse? Had he perhaps rushed out to try to save them and been swept away himself?

All these theories came crashing when someone pointed out that the 15th had been a calm day; the storms had not started until the following day. Then perhaps Ducat had simply entered the wrong date by mistake? That theory also had to be abandoned when, back at Loch Roag, Captain Holman of the *Archer* told them he had passed close to the islands on the night of the 15th, and that the light was already out . . .

Then what if the three men had been on the jetty on a calm morning – which would explain why McArthur was not wearing his oilskins – and one of them had slipped into the water? Perhaps the other two had jumped in after him and been drowned. But then there were ropes and lifebelts on the jetty – why should men leap into the water when they only had to throw in a lifebelt?

Suppose the drowning man was unconscious, and could not grab a lifebelt? In that case only one of his companions would have jumped in after him, leaving the other on the jetty with a rope . . .

Another theory was that one of the three men had gone insane and pushed the others to their deaths, then thrown himself into the sea. It is just possible; but there is not the slightest shred of evidence for it.

The broadcaster Valentine Dyall – the "Man in Black" – suggested the most plausible explanation in his book *Unsolved Mysteries*. In 1947 a Scottish journalist named Iain Campbell visited Eilean More on a calm day, and was standing near the west landing when the sea suddenly gave a heave, and rose seventy feet over the jetty. Then, after about a minute, it subsided back to normal. It could have been some freak of the tides, or possibly an underwater earthquake. Campbell was convinced that anyone on the jetty at that time would have been sucked into the sea. The lighthouse keeper told him that

---

In the late eighteenth century a traveller's tale was passed around London. It told of two Welsh missionaries who, having been captured by American Indians and sentenced to death, began lamenting to each other in Welsh. The tribe of Indians were astounded: they too spoke Welsh. The missionaries were freed and received the Indians heartfelt apologies.

The great Welsh Druid Edward Williams, or Iolo Morganwg, took the story so seriously that he raised backing for an expedition to investigate the Welsh Indians. The theory put forward for their existence traced their roots to the expedition of the Prince Madoc, who set sail westwards in the twelfth century and was never heard of again. Williams was eventually prevented from going on the expedition by failing health, but one of his followers, John Evans, did attempt the journey. He eventually died in New Orleans after many adventures, having been unable to locate the Welsh Indians.

this curious "upheaval" occurs periodically, and that several men had almost been dragged into the sea.

But it is still hard to understand how *three* men could be involved in such an accident. Since McArthur was not wearing his oilskins, we can presume he was in the tower when it happened – *if* it happened. Even if his companions were swept away, would he be stupid enough to rush down to the jetty and fling himself into the sea?

Only one thing is clear: that on that calm December day at the turn of the century, some accident snatched three men off Eilean More, and left not even a shred of a clue to the mystery.

DID JOAN OF ARC RETURN FROM THE DEAD?

On 30 May 1431 Joan of Arc was burnt as a heretic by the English; she was only nineteen years old. She regarded herself as a messenger from Heaven, sent to save the French from their enemies the English (who were in league with the Burgundians who captured her). At the age of thirteen Joan began to hear voices, which she later identified as those of St Gabriel, St Michael, St Marguerite and St Catherine. When the news of the encirclement of Orléans reached her little village in Lorraine, Domremy, her voices told her to go to lift the siege. Her military career was brief but spectacular: in a year she won many remarkable victories, and saw Charles VII crowned at Rheims. Then she was captured by the Burgundians, sold to the English for ten thousand francs, tried as a witch, and burnt alive.

But that, oddly enough, was not quite the end of "the Maid". "Now one month after Paris had returned to her allegiance to King Charles", writes Anatole France, "there appeared in Lorraine a certain damsel. She was about twenty-five years old. Hitherto she had been called Claude; but now she made herself known to divers lord of the town of Metz as being Jeanne the Maid." This was in May 1436, five years after Joan had died at the stake.

It sounds very obviously as if some imposter had decided to pose as Joan the Maid. But there is some astonishing evidence that suggests that this is not so. Joan's two younger brothers, Petit-Jean and Pierre, were still serving in the army, and they had no doubt whatever that their sister had been burnt at Rouen. So when they heard that a woman claiming to be Joan was at Metz, and that she had expressed a wish to meet them, the brothers hastened to Metz – Petit-Jean was not far away, being the provost of Vaucouleurs.

The burning of Joan of Arc, painted by the artist Lerepreu.

One chronicler describes how the brothers went to the village of La-Grange-aux-Ormes, two and a half miles south of Metz, where a tournament was being held. A knight in armour was galloping around an obstacle course and pulling stakes expertly out of the ground; this was the person who claimed to be their sister. The brothers rode out on to the field, prepared to challenge the impostor. But when Petit-Jean demanded, "Who are you?", the "impostor" raised her visor, and both brothers gaped in astonishment as they recognized their sister Joan.

In fact Joan was surrounded by various people who had known her during her spectacular year fighting the English, including Nicole Lowe, the king's chamberlain. If she was in fact an impostor, it seems absurd that she should go to a place where she would be sure to be recognised. (John of Metz was one of her first and most loyal supporters.) And the next day her brothers took her to Vaucouleurs, where she spent a week, apparently accepted by many people who had seen her there seven years earlier, when she had gone to see the local squire Robert de Baudricourt, to ask him to send her to see the Dauphin, the heir to the throne. After this she spent three weeks at a small town called Marville, then went on a pilgrimage to see the Black Virgin called Notre Dame de Liance, between Laon and Rheims. Then she went to stay with Elizabeth, Duchess of Luxembourg, at Arlon. Meanwhile her brother Petit-Jean went to see the king and announced that his sister Joan was still alive. We do not know the king's reaction, but he ordered his treasurer to give Petit-Jean a hundred francs. An entry in the treasury accounts of Orléans for 9 August 1436 states that the council authorized payment of a courier who had brought letters from "Jeanne la Pucelle" (Joan the Maid).

The records of these events are to be found in the basic standard work on Joan of Arc, Jules Quicherat's five-volume *Trial and Rehabilitation of Joan of Arc* (1841), which contains all the original documents. One of these documents states that on 24 June 1437 Joan's miraculous powers returned to her. By then she had become something of a protégée of Count Ulrich of Württemberg, who took her to Cologne. There she became involved in a clash between two churchmen who were rivals for the diocese; one had been appointed by the chapter, the other by the pope. Count Ulrich favoured one called Udalric, and Joan apparently also pronounced in his favour. But her intervention did no good; the Council of Basle considered Udalric a usurper, and the pope's nominee was appointed. The Inquisitor General of Cologne became curious about the count's guest (remember that this was at the height of the "witchcraft craze"), and was apparently shocked to learn that she practised magic, and that she danced with men and ate and drank more than she ought. (The magic sounds more like conjuring: she tore a tablecloth and restored it to its original state, and did the same with a glass which she broke against a wall.) He summoned her before him, but she refused to appear; when men were sent to fetch her the count hid her in his house, then smuggled her out of the town. The inquisitor excommunicated her. Back at Arlon, staying with the Duchess of Luxembourg, she met a nobleman named Robert des Armoires and – no doubt to the astonishment of her followers – married him. (The original Joan had sworn a vow of perpetual chastity under a "fairy tree" at Domremy.) Then they moved to Metz, where Robert had a house, and during the next three years she gave birth to two children.

Two years later, in the summer of 1439, the "Dame des Armoires" went to Orleans, whose magistrates gave her a banquet and presented her with 210 livres by way of thanking her for her services to the town during the siege. Oddly enough, these same burgesses had paid for Masses in memory of the Maid's death three months earlier; presumably they must have changed their minds in the meantime. After 1439 the Masses ceased.

After two weeks she left Orléans in rather a hurry, according to one chronicler, and went to Tours, where she sent a letter to the king via the Baillie of Touraine, Guillaume Bellier, who had been the Maid's host ten years earlier. Moreover, she soon afterwards went to Poitou, where she seems to have been given the nominal command of a place called Mans – presumably by the king she had enthroned. Then the king transferred this command to Joan's ex-comrade in arms, Gilles de Rais. Since the days when he had fought beside Joan before the walls of Paris, Gilles had begun to practise black magic – in an attempt to repair his fortunes, drained by his excesses – and had become a sadistic killer of children. In the following year, 1440, Gilles would be tried and condemned to be hanged and burned. Meanwhile – assuming he met the Dame des Armoises (which seems practically certain, since she had to hand over her command to him) – he seems to have accepted her as his former comrade-in-arms. He also placed her in authority over the men-at-arms.

In 1440 Joan finally went to Paris and met the king. And for the first time she received a setback; after the meeting the king declared her an impostor. It may be significant that he did so after the interview. Surely if he could see she was a fraud he would have said so at the time? He even attempted to practise on her the same trick he had tried at their first meeting eleven years earlier, concealing himself and asking one of his men to impersonate him. But as on the previous occasion Joan was not to be deceived; she walked straight up to the king and knelt at his feet, whereupon the king said: "Pucelle, my dear, you are welcome back in the name of God." It seems, to say the least of it, strange that he should then have decided she was an impostor.

And now, according to the journal "of a Bourgeois of Paris", Joan was arrested, tried and publicly exhibited as a malefactor. A sermon was preached against her, and she was forced to confess publicly that she was an imposter. Her story, according to the "Bourgeois of Paris", was that she had gone to Rome about 1433 to seek absolution for striking her mother. She had, she said, engaged as a soldier in war in the service of the Holy Father Eugenius, and worn man's apparel. This, presumably, gave her the idea of pretending to be the Maid . . .

But the whole of this story is doubtful in the extreme. To begin with, Joan then returned to Metz, and continued to be accepted as "la Pucelle". In 1443 her brother Pierre refers to her in a petition as "Jeanne la Pucelle, my sister", and her cousin Henry de Voulton mentions that Petit-Jean, Pierre and their sister la Pucelle used to visit the village of Sermaise and feast with relations, all of whom accepted her. Fourteen years later she makes an appearance in the town of Saumur, and is again accepted by the officials of the town as the Maid. And after that she vanishes from history, presumably living out the rest of her life quietly with her husband in Metz.

What then are we to make of the story that the king declared her an impostor, and that she admitted it publicly? First of all, its only source is the "journal of a Bourgeois of Paris". This in itself is odd, if she was involved in such a public scandal. Moreover, the "bourgeois" was hostile to the earlier Joan, in the days before her execution. Anatole France mentions that the common people of Paris were in a fever of excitement at the news that the Maid was still alive and was returning to Paris. The University of Paris was still thoroughly hostile to the Maid, who had been condemned as a witch. Her sentence could only be reversed by the pope, and he showed no sign of doing this, in spite of a movement to rehabilitate Joan. So as far as the clerks and magistrates of Paris were concerned, the return of Joan would have been nothing but an embarrassment. As to those authorities of the Church who were trying to have the Maid declared innocent (they succeeded in 1456, and Joan was finally canonized in 1922), they would have found the return of their heroine – alive, healthy and married – an obstacle to their patriotic campaign. The king must have found himself under intolerable pressure to declare Joan an impostor. After all, if *he* declared her genuine, then it was "official", and no one in France had a right to doubt her identity. Moreover, there would be some question of public recognition . . . On the other hand, if he expressed doubts about her, the whole scandal was defused. She could return home and drop out of sight. And everyone would be much happier. And that, it seemed, is precisely what happened.

Anatole France takes it for granted that the Dame des Armoises was an impostor. But then his biography of Joan of Arc is permeated with his famous irony, and takes the view that she was a deluded peasant girl; France was basically a disciple of Voltaire. The notion that she was an impostor is indeed the simplest explanation. But it leaves us facing the problem: why, in that case, did so many people who knew "the Maid" accept the Dame des Armoises as genuine? It is conceivable that her brothers may have decided that it would be to their advantage to have their famous sister alive, and so condoned the imposture. But why should so many old comrades have agreed to support the story?

The Dame des Armoises never as far as we know explained how she came to escape the flames. But then presumably she would not know the answer to this question. She would only know that she had been rescued, and that someone else had died in her place – perhaps another "witch". It is easy to see how this could have come about. We know that Joan was an extraordinarily persuasive young lady, and that dozens of people, from Robert de Baudricourt to the Dauphin, who began by assuming she was mad, ended by believing that she was being guided by divine voices. We know that even in court Joan declared that she could hear St Catherine telling her what to say. Even at her trial she had certain friends; a priest called Loyseleur was her adviser. When Joan complained about the conduct of her two guards the Earl of Warwick was furious, and had them replaced by two other guards – which suggests that the earl held her in high regard. So it would not be at all surprising if there was a successful plot to rescue her. And it is possible that the English themselves may have been involved in such a plot; when Joan was apparently burnt at the stake in Rouen the crowd was kept at a distance by eight hundred English soldiers, which would obviously prevent anyone coming close enough to recognize her. At the trial for her rehabilitation in 1456 the executioner's evidence was entirely second-hand, although three of Joan's comrades who were with her at the "end" – Ladvenu, Massieu and Isambard – were actually present. *If* Joan was rescued, presumably they also were involved in the plot.

The rehabilitation itself has its farcical aspects. It began in 1450, and Joan's mother was the person who set it in motion, supported by Joan's brother Pierre. We do not know whether Joan's mother accepted the Dame des Armoires as her daughter, but there can be no doubt that she lent credence to the claim by not denouncing her as an impostor. Yet now she and Pierre joined in the claim that was based on the assertion that Joan was executed by the English in 1431. But then the aim of the rehabilitation was financial; Joan had been a rich woman, thanks to the generosity of the king, and the wealth remained frozen while Joan was excommunicated. So, whether or not Joan's family believed that the Dame des Armoires was the Maid, they now had good reason to try to have her rehabilitated – even if it meant swearing that she was dead.

If the Dame des Armoires was genuine, she must have felt there was a certain irony in the situation. She had been an embarrassment to everyone during her first career as the saintly virgin warrior; now she was just as much an embarrassment as the heroine returned from the dead. It is thankless work being a saint.

THE LOCH NESS MONSTER

Loch Ness, the largest of British lakes, is twenty-two miles long and about a mile wide; at its greatest depth, it is 950 feet deep. It is part of the Great Glen, which runs like a deep crack right across Scotland, from one coast to the other; it opened up between 300 and 400 million years ago as a result of earthquakes, then was deepened by glaciers. At the southern end of the loch there is the small town of Fort Augustus; at the northern end, Inverness. Until the eighteenth century, the loch was practically inaccessible, except by winding trackways; it was not until 1731 that General Wade began work on the road that runs from Fort Augustus up the south side of the loch (although Fort Augustus was not so christened until 1742). But this steep road, which makes a long detour inland, was obviously not the shortest distance between Fort Augustus and Inverness; the most direct route would run along the northern shore. In the early 1930s a road was finally hacked and blasted out of this northern shore, and vast quantities of rock were dumped down the steep sides of Loch Ness.

The road had only just been completed in April 1933, and it was on the 14th of that month that Mr and Mrs John Mackay, proprietors of the Drumnadrochit Hotel, were returning home from a trip to Inverness. It was about three in the afternoon when Mrs Mackay pointed and said, "What's that, John?" The water in the middle of the loch was in a state of commotion; at first she thought it was two ducks fighting, then realized that the area of disturbance was too wide. As her husband pulled up they saw some large animal in the middle of the surging water; then as they watched, the creature swam towards Aldourie pier on the other side of the loch. For a moment they glimpsed two black humps, which rose and fell in an undulating manner; then the creature made a half-turn and sank from sight.

The Mackays made no attempt to publicize their story, but gossip about the sighting reached a young water bailiff, Alex Campbell, who also happened to be local correspondent for the *Inverness Courier*; he called on the Mackays, and his report went into the *Courier* on 2 May, more than two weeks after the sighting occurred. The editor is said to have remarked: "If it's as big as they say, it's not a creature it's a monster." And so the "Loch Ness Monster" acquired its name.

This was not, strictly speaking, the first account of the monster to appear in print. This distinction belongs to a *Life of St Columba* dating from about AD 565. This tells (in vol. 6, book 11, chap. 27) how the saint arrived at a ferry on the banks of the loch and found some men preparing to bury a comrade who had been bitten to death by a water monster while he was swimming. The saint ordered one of his own followers to swim across the loch. The monster heard the splashing and swam towards him, at which the saint made the sign of the cross and commanded the creature to go away; the terrified monster obeyed . . .

Other reportings down the centuries are more difficult to pin down; in his book on the monster, Nicholas Witchell mentions a number of references to the "beast" or "water kelpie" (fairy) of Loch Ness in old books between 1600 and 1800. And after Commander Rupert Gould published a book on the monster in 1934, a Dr D. Mackenzie of Balnain wrote to Gould claiming to have seen it in 1871 or 1872, looking rather like an upturned boat but moving at great speed, "wriggling and churning up the water". Alex Campbell, the water bailiff, reported that a crofter named Alexander MacDonald had seen the monster in 1802 and reported it to one of Campbell's ancestors. But hearsay reports like this inevitably led sceptics to suspect that local people, particularly hoteliers, had a financial interest in promoting the monster, so that by the mid-1930s "Nessie" (as she was soon christened in the area) had become something of a joke. In fact the first "modern" report of the monster had occurred in 1930; the *Northern Chronicle* reported that three young men who were out in a boat fishing on 22 July of that year, close to Dores, on the southern shore, saw a loud commotion in the water about 600 yards away, and some large creature swimming towards them just below the surface; it turned away when it was about 300 yards away. The young men commented that it was "certainly not a basking shark or a seal".

That summer of 1933 was one of the hottest on record, and by the end of the summer the Loch Ness monster was known to readers all over the British Isles; it was still to become a world-wide sensation.

By now the monster had also been sighted on land. On a peaceful summer afternoon, 22 July 1933, Mr and Mrs George Spicer were on their way back to London after a holiday in the Highlands. At about 4 o'clock they were driving along the southern road from Inverness to Fort William (the original General Wade road) and were on the mid-portion between Dores and Foyers. About two hundred yards ahead of them they saw a trunk-like object apparently stretching across the road. Then they saw that it was in motion, and that they were looking at a long neck. This was soon followed by a grey body, about five feet high (Mr Spicer said later "It was horrible – an abomination") which moved across the road in jerks. Because they were on a slope, they could not see whether it had legs or not, and by the time their car had reached the top of the slope it had vanished into the undergrowth opposite. It seemed to be carrying something on its back. They saw no tail, and the drawing that Commander Gould made later under their direction justifies Mr Spicer's description of a "huge snail with a long neck". When Gould heard of this sighting he thought it was a hoax; but after he had interviewed the Spicers in London he had no doubt that they were telling the truth. The Spicers still seemed shaken and upset. It was later suggested the object over the monster's shoulder could have been a dead sheep. In 1971 Nicholas Witchell interviewed Mrs Margaret Cameron, who claimed to have seen the monster on land when she was a teenager, during World War I; she said, "It had a huge body and its movement as it came out of the trees was like a caterpillar." She also described it as being about twenty feet long, and said that it had two short, round feet at the front, and that it lurched from side to side as it entered the water. She and her friends felt so sick and upset that they were unable to eat their tea afterwards. Witchell also interviewed a man called Jock Forbes, who claimed to have seen the monster in 1919, when he was twelve; it was a stormy night, and he and his father were in a pony and trap when the pony shied, and they saw something large crossing the road ahead of them, then heard a splash as it plunged into the loch.

In November 1933 "Nessie" was photographed for the first time. Hugh Gray, an employee of the British Aluminium Company, was walking on a wooded bluff, fifty feet above the loch, near Foyers. He had seen the monster on a previous occasion, and was now carrying a camera. It was Sunday 12 November 1933, a sunny morning, and Gray sat down for a moment to look out over the loch. As he did so he saw the monster rising up out of the water, about two hundred yards away. He raised his camera and snapped it while it was two or three feet above the surface of the water. It is not the clearest of all photographs – it is easy to focus attention on the dark shadow and to overlook the vague, greyish bulk of the creature rising from the water above it. This was only one of five shots; the others seem to have been even less satisfactory. Gray was so ambivalent about the sighting – afraid of being subjected to derision – that he left the film in his camera for two weeks, when his brother took it to be developed. It appeared in the Scottish *Daily Record* and the London *Daily Sketch* on 6 December 1933, together with a statement from the Kodak film company that the negative had not been retouched. But Professor

Graham Kerr, a zoologist at Glasgow University, declared that he found it utterly unconvincing as a photograph of any living thing. It was the beginning of the "debunking" of the monster, in which major zoologists were to be prominent for many decades to come.

And the sightings continued. The day after Hugh Gray had snapped the monster, Dr J. Kirton and his wife were walking down the hill behind the Invermoriston Hotel when they saw the monster swimming away from them. They saw a rounded back with a protuberance in the middle, "like the rear view of a duck in a pond". Gould lists this as the twenty-sixth sighting of 1933. A week later, on the 20 November, the monster was seen lying motionless in the water for some ten minutes by a Miss N. Simpson, near Altsigh; she judged its length to be about thirty feet. Then she saw it swim underwater to the centre of the loch "at about the speed of an outboard motor boat".

On 12 December 1933 a firm of Scottish film producers, Irvine, Clayton and Hay, managed to film the monster in motion for a few seconds; unfortunately, the film shows little but a long dark shadow moving through the water.

The most famous photograph of the monster was taken in the following April, 1934 – the celebrated "surgeon's photograph". On 1 April 1934 Robert Kenneth Wilson, Fellow of the Royal College of Surgeons, was driving northward with a friend; they had leased a wild-fowl shoot near Inverness, and meant to go to it and take some photographs of the birds. Wilson had borrowed a camera with a telephoto lens. It was early in the morning about seven and they stopped the car on a small promontory two miles north of Invermoriston. As they stood watching the surface they noticed the signs of "considerable commotion" that seem to herald the arrival of the monster, and the friend, Maurice Chambers, shouted, "My God, it's the monster." Wilson rushed to the car, came back with the camera, and managed to expose four plates in two minutes in such a hurry that he did not even look at what he was photographing. The serpentine head, not unlike an elephant's trunk, then withdrew gently into the water. Unsure as to whether he had captured anything, Wilson hurried to Inverness and took the plates to a chemist to be developed. They were ready later that day. Two proved to be blank; one showed the head about to vanish into the water. But the fourth was excellent, showing the dinosaur-like neck and tiny head.

Wilson sold the copyright of the photograph to the *Daily Mail* and it appeared on 21 April 1934, creating a sensation. It also aroused the usual roars of derision from the scientific establishment, who branded the photograph a fake, and pointed out that the "surgeon" (who had withheld his identity) could be an invention of the perpetrator of the fraud. In fact, Wilson soon allowed himself to be identified, and his name appeared in Commander Gould's book

The Loch Ness Monster and Others, which came out later the same year, with the "surgeon's photograph" as a frontispiece. (The fact that the photograph was taken on 1 April may have increased the general scepticism.) Many years later another monster-investigator, Tim Dinsdale, held the photograph at arm's length and noticed something that convinced him of its authenticity. When viewed from a distance, a faint concentric circle of rings is visible around the monster, while there is another circle in the background, as if some other part of the body is just below the surface. No one, Dinsdale pointed out, would take the trouble to fake a detail that is almost invisible to the eye. Another piece of evidence in favour of its authenticity emerged in 1972, when the photograph was subjected to the computer-enhancement process at NASA; the improved picture showed signs of whiskers hanging down from the lower jaw.

In July 1934 a team of fourteen men was hired by Sir Edward Mountain, at a wage of £2 per week per man, to spend five weeks standing on the shores of the loch, armed with cameras. Five promising photographs were taken; four of them only showed a dark wake, which could have been caused by a boat; the fifth showed a head disappearing in a splash of spray. After the watchers had been paid off, Captain James Frazer, who had been in charge of the expedition, succeeded in shooting several feet of film from

The Loch Ness Monster photographed on the 19th April 1934 by London Surgeon R. K. Wilson. *Fortean Picture Library.*

a position just above Castle Urquart. It showed an object like an upturned, flat-bottomed boat, about fifteen feet long; it disappeared in a spume of spray. Zoologists who viewed the film said that the creature was a seal. Captain Frazer later admitted that he had to endure a great deal of ridicule.

Sightings continued, and more photographs were taken; but the general public had ceased to be deeply interested in the monster. After the initial excitement, most people were willing to accept the view of sceptics that the monster had been a cynical invention of people involved in the Highland tourist business; if so, it had certainly succeeded, for Loch Ness hotels were crowded throughout the summer. One of the most interesting sightings of 1934 went virtually unnoticed. On 26 May Brother Richard Horan, of St Benedict's Abbey, was working in the abbey boathouse when he heard a noise in the water, and saw the monster looking at him from a distance of about thirty yards. It had a graceful neck with a broad white stripe down its front, and a muzzle like a seal's. Three other people corroborated his sighting. In the December of the following year, a Miss Rena Mackenzie also saw the monster fairly close, and noted that its head seemed tiny, and that the underside of its throat was white. A man named John Maclean, who saw the monster in July 1938, saw the head and neck only twenty yards away, and said that it was obviously in the act of swallowing food, opening and closing its mouth, and tossing back its head "in exactly the same manner that a cormorant does after it has swallowed a fish". When the creature dived Maclean and his wife saw two humps. They described it as being about eighteen feet long, and said that at close quarters its skin was dark brown and "like that of a horse when wet and glistening". Each of these sightings enables us to form a clearer picture of the monster. And in July 1958 the water bailiff Alex Campbell had a sighting which confirmed something he had believed for many years – that there must be more than one of the creatures; he saw one lying quietly near St Benedict's Abbey while another (visible as a large black hump) headed across the loch, churning the surface of the water. (Many accounts indicate that the animals can move at high speed.)

During World War II interest in the monster (or monsters) waned, although sightings continued to be reported. In 1943 Commander Russell Flint, in charge of a motor launch passing through Loch Ness on its way to Swansea, reported a tremendous jolt that convinced the crew that they had struck some floating debris. In fact, they saw the monster disappearing in a flurry of water. His signal to the Admiralty, reporting that he had sustained damage to the starboard bow after a collision with the Loch Ness monster, earned him in response "a bit of a blast".

In November 1950 the *Daily Herald* ran a story headed "The Secret of Loch Ness", alleging that dozens of eight-foot-diameter mines had been anchored on the floor of the loch since 1918, some at a depth of a mile. (The *Herald* stated that at its greatest depth, the loch is seven miles deep.) The story apparently had some slight basis in fact; mines *had* been laid in 1918 by HMS *Welbeck* – Hugh Gray, who later took the first monster photograph, was on board – but when a vessel went to collect them in 1922, only the anchors remained. The mines, which were designed to have a life of only a few years, were probably at the bottom. Certainly none of the photographs looks in the least like an eight-foot mine, even one with horns.

In the following year another monster photograph was taken by a woodsman named Lachlan Stuart. He was about to milk a cow early on 14 July 1951 when he saw something moving fast down the loch, so fast that he at first thought it was a speedboat. He grabbed his camera, rushed down the hill, and snapped the monster when it was only fifty yards offshore. The result was a photograph showing three distinct humps.

Four years later a bank manager named Peter Macnab was on his way back from a holiday in the north of Scotland, and pulled up his car just above Urquhart Castle. It was a calm, warm afternoon – 29 July 1955 – and he saw a movement in the still water near the castle; he hastily raised his camera, and took a photograph which has joined the "surgeon's photograph" and the Lachlan Stuart photograph as one of the classic views of the monster. But he was so anxious to avoid ridicule that he released the picture only three years later, in 1958.

Before that happened, interest in the case had been revived by the best book on it so far – *More Than a Legend*, published in 1957. The author was Constance Whyte, wife of the manager of the Caledonian canal, who became interested in the monster after she was asked to write an article about it for a small local magazine. Mrs Whyte interviewed every witness she could find, and produced the first overall survey of the evidence since Rupert Gould's book of 1934. *More Than a Legend* aroused widespread interest, the author was deluged with correspondence, and once again the Loch Ness monster was news. What Mrs Whyte had done, with her careful research, was to refute the idea that the monster was a joke, or the invention of the Scottish Tourist Board. No one who reads her book can end with the slightest doubt that the monster really exists, and that it shows itself with a fair degree of frequency.

The immediate result was a new generation of "monster-hunters". One of these, Frank Searle, was a manager for a firm of fruiterers in London; he bought Constance Whyte's book, and in 1958 decided to camp by Loch Ness. From then on he returned again and again. In June 1965 he was parked in a lay-by near Invermoriston and chatting to some hitch-hikers when he saw a dark object break the surface, and realized he had at last seen the monster. His excitement was so great that in 1969 he gave up his job and pitched his tent by Loch

Ness, where he was to remain for the next four years. In August 1971 he saw the tail at close quarters as the monster dived; his impression was of an alligator's tail, "seven feet long, dark and nobbly on top, smooth dirty white underneath". In November 1971 he got his first photograph of the monster – a dark hump in a swirl of water; he admitted that it was "inconclusive". But in the following five years he obtained at least ten of the best pictures of the monster taken so far, including one showing the swan-like neck rising out of the water, and another showing both the neck and one of the humps; these were published in his *Nessie: Seven Years in Search of the Monster* in 1976. During that time his tent had become a "Mecca for visitors" – mostly directed to him by the Scottish Tourist Board – and in 1975 he estimated that he had seen twenty-five thousand in eight months. On 7 June 1974, together with a girl visitor from Quebec, he had a memorable sighting. As they approached a barbed-wire fence near Foyers, they noticed a splashing sound. They crept up and peered over the fence, "and saw two of the strangest little creatures I've ever seen. They were about two feet in length, dark grey in colour, something like the skin of a baby elephant, small heads with black protruding eyes, long necks and plump bodies. They had snake like tails which were wrapped along their sides, and on each side of the body, two stump-like appendages." When he tried to get through the fence the small creatures "scuttled away with a kind of crab-like motion" and were submerged in the loch within seconds.

But in his book *The Loch Ness Story* – perhaps the best comprehensive account of the hunt for the monster – Nicholas Witchell comments: "It is a regrettable fact which can easily be proved that these 1972 photographs have been tampered with. Mr Searle has also produced another series identical with the original shots in all respects except that an extra hump has been added to them by some process of superimposition or by rephotograph." And he adds: "Because of the highly suspicious content of some of Mr Searle's photographs and the inconsistencies of the facts surrounding the taking of them, it is not possible to accept them as being authentic photographs of animate objects in Loch Ness."

In 1959 an aeronautical engineer named Tim Dinsdale read an article about the monster in a magazine called *Everybody's*, and was intrigued. He spent most of that winter reading everything he could find; it was in the following February that (as already described) he looked at the surgeon's photograph, and noticed the circle of ripples that convinced him that it was genuine. In April that year Dinsdale went off to Loch Ness to hunt the monster. But after five days he had still seen nothing. On the day before he was due to return home he was approaching his hotel in Foyers when he saw something out in the loch; his binoculars showed a hump. He snatched his 16-mm ciné-camera and began to film as the creature swam away. Then, almost out of film, he drove down to the water's edge; by the time he got there the creature had vanished. But Dinsdale had fifty feet of film showing the monster in motion. When shown on television it aroused widespread interest and – as Witchell says – heralded a new phase in the saga of the monster.

That June, 1960, the first scientific expedition to Loch Ness embarked on a month-long investigation, with thirty student volunteers and a Marconi echo-sounder, as well as a large collection of cameras. A ten-foot hump was sighted in July, and the echo-sounder tracked some large object as it dived from the surface to a depth of sixty feet and back up again. The expedition also discovered large shoals of char at a depth of a hundred feet – an answer to sceptics who said that the loch did not contain enough fish to support a monster; the team's finding was that there was enough fish to support several.

But Dr Denys Tucker, of the British Museum of Natural History, who had organized this expedition, did not lead it as he had intended to; in June he was dismissed from his job – as he believed, because he had publicly expressed his belief in the existence of the monster.

Dinsdale became a close friend of Torquil MacLeod, who had seen the monster almost out of the water in February 1960. MacLeod had watched it for nine minutes, and admitted being "appalled by its size", which he estimated at between forty and sixty feet. It had a long neck, like an elephant's trunk, which kept moving from side to side and up and down, and "paddles" at the rear and front. In August 1960 MacLeod had another sighting from the shore, while a family in a motor yacht belonging to a company director, R.H. Lowrie, saw the monster at close quarters for about a quarter of an hour, taking a few photographs. At one point they thought the monster was heading straight for them and about to collide; but it veered away and disappeared.

It was also in August 1960 that Sir Peter Scott, founder of the Wildfowl Trust, and Richard Fitter of the Fauna Preservation Society approached the Member of Parliament David James and asked for his help in trying to get government assistance for a "flat-out attempt to find what exactly is in Loch Ness". In April 1961 a panel decided that there was a prima facie case for investigating the loch. The result was the formation of the Bureau for Investigating the Loch Ness Phenomena, a registered charity. In October 1961 two powerful searchlights scanned the loch every night for two weeks, and on one occasion caught an eight-foot "finger like object" standing out of the water. In 1962 another team used sonar, and picked up several "large objects"; one of these sonar recordings preceded an appearance of the monster on the surface.

In 1966 Tim Dinsdale's film was subjected to analysis by Air Force Intelligence, which reported that the object filmed was certainly not a boat or a submarine, and by NASA's computer-enhancement experts, who discovered that two other parts of the body also broke the surface besides the main hump.

In 1972, a team of investigators led by Dr Robert H. Rines took some remarkable underwater photographs, one of which showed very clearly an object like a large flipper, perhaps eight feet long, while a 1975 photograph showed a long-necked creature and its front flipper; this was particularly impressive because the sonar evidence – waves of sound reflected back from the creature – made it clear that this was not some freak of the light or a piece of floating wreckage.

Yet in spite of this, monster-hunters in the 1970s and 80s began to experience an increasing sense of frustration. When Commander Gould had written his book in 1934 the solution of the problem seemed close; then it receded. Constance Whyte's book revived interest in the mystery, and when the Loch Ness Phenomena Investigation Bureau began to co-operate with the team from the Academy of Applied Science, and to use all the latest scientific equipment, it began to look as if the mystery was about to be solved once and for all. Yet at the time of this writing – eleven years after that remarkable underwater picture of the monster – there has still been no major advance. Nicholas Witchell triumphantly concludes his book *The Loch Ness Story* (1975) with a chapter entitled "The Solution", in which he describes his excitement when Rines telephoned him from America to describe the colour photograph of the monster; it contains the sentence: "With the official ratification of the discovery of the animals in Loch Ness, the world will lose one of its most popular mysteries." And he declares that it would be ignoble now to gloat about the short-sightedness of the scientific establishment for its sceptical attitude towards Loch Ness.

It is now clear that Witchell was premature. Most people still regard the question of the monster's existence as an open one, and the majority of scientists still regard the whole thing as something of a joke. In 1976 Roy Mackal, a director of the Loch Ness Investigation Bureau and Professor of Biochemistry at the University of Chicago, published the most balanced and thoroughgoing scientific assessment so far, *The Monsters of Loch Ness*. He turns a highly critical eye on the evidence, yet nevertheless concludes that it is now proven that "a population of moderate-sized, piscivorous aquatic animals is inhabiting Loch Ness". If the scientific establishment was willing to change its mind, this book should have changed it; yet it seems to have made no real impacts.

When the "monster" is finally identified and classified it will undoubtedly be something of an anticlimax, and Loch Ness will probably lose most of its tourist industry at a blow. Half the fascination of the monster lies in the notion that it is terrifying and dangerous. In fact all the evidence suggests that like that other legendary marauder the "killer" whale, it will turn out to be shy, amiable and quite harmless to man.

THE MYSTERY
OF THE
MARY CELESTE

On a calm afternoon of 5 December 1872 the English ship *Dei Gratia* sighted a two-masted brig pursuing an erratic course in the North Atlantic, midway between the Azores and the coast of Portugal. As they came closer they could see that she was sailing with only her jib and foretop mast staysail set; moreover, the jib was set to port, while the vessel was on a starboard tack – a sure sign to any sailor that the ship was out of control. Captain Morehouse of the *Dei Gratia* signalled the mysterious vessel, but received no answer. The sea was running high after recent squalls, and it took a full two hours before Morehouse could get close enough to read the name of the vessel. It was the *Mary Celeste*. Morehouse knew this American ship and its master, Captain Benjamin Spooner Briggs. Less than a month ago both vessels had been loading cargo on neighbouring piers on New York's East River. The *Mary Celeste* had set sail for Genoa with a cargo of crude alcohol on 5 November, ten days before the *Dei Gratia* had sailed for Gibraltar; yet now, a month later, she was drifting in mid-Atlantic with no sign of life.

Morehouse sent three men to investigate, led by his first mate Oliver Deveau, a man of great physical strength and courage. As they clambered aboard they saw that the ship's decks were deserted; a search below revealed that there was not a living soul on board. But the lifeboat was missing, indicating that Captain Briggs had decided to abandon ship.

There was a great deal of water below decks; two sails had been blown away, and the lower foretop sails were hanging by their corners. Yet the ship seemed seaworthy, and was certainly in no danger of sinking. Then why had the crew abandoned her? Further research revealed that the binnacle, the box containing the ship's compass, had been smashed, and the compass itself was broken. Two cargo hatches had been ripped off, and one of the casks of crude alcohol had been stoved in. Both forward and aft storage lockers contained a plentiful supply of food and water.

The seamen's chests were still in the crew's quarters, an indication of the haste in which the ship had been deserted. But a search of the captain's cabin revealed that the navigation instruments and navigation log were missing. The last entry in the general log was dated 25 November; it meant that the *Mary Celeste* had sailed without crew for at least nine days, and that she was now some 700 miles northeast of her last recorded position.

Apart from Captain Briggs and a crew of seven, the *Mary Celeste* had also sailed with Briggs's wife Sarah and his two-year old daughter Sophia Matilda. Faced with the mystery of why they had abandoned ship for no obvious reason, Morehouse experienced a certain superstitious alarm when Deveau suggested that two of the *Dei Gratia*'s crew should sail the *Mary Celeste* to Gibraltar; it was the prospect of £5,000 salvage money that finally made him agree to Deveau's scheme.

Both ships arrived in Gibraltar harbour six days later. And instead of the welcome he expected, Deveau was greeted by an English bureaucrat who nailed an order of immediate arrest to the *Mary Celeste*'s mainmast. The date significantly was Friday the 13th.

From the beginning the *Mary Celeste* had been an unlucky ship. She was registered originally as the *Amazon*, and her first captain had died within forty-eight hours. On her maiden voyage she had hit a fishing weir off the coast of Maine, and damaged her hull. While this was being repaired a fire had broken out amidships. Later, while sailing through the Straits of Dover, she hit another brig, which sank. This had occurred under her third captain; her fourth accidentally ran the ship aground on Cape Brenton Island and wrecked her.

The *Amazon* was salvaged, and passed through the hands of three more owners before she was bought by J. H. Winchester, the founder of a successful shipping line which still operates in New York. Winchester discovered that the brig – which had now been renamed *Mary Celeste* – had dry rot in her timbers, and he had the bottom rebuilt with copper lining and the deck cabin lengthened. These repairs had ensured that the ship was in excellent condition before she had sailed for Genoa under the experienced Captain Briggs – this helped to explain why she had survived so long in the wintry Atlantic after the crew had taken to the lifeboat.

British officials at Gibraltar seemed to suspect either mutiny or some Yankee plot – the latter theory based on the fact that Captain Morehouse and Captain Briggs had been friends, and had apparently dined together the day before the *Mary Celeste* had sailed from New York. But at the inquiry that followed, the idea of mutiny seemed to have gained favour. To back this theory the Court of Inquiry was shown an axe-mark on one of the ship's rails, scoring on her hull that was described as a crude attempt to make the ship look as if she had hit rocks, and a stained sword that was found beneath the captain's bunk. All this, it was claimed, pointed to the crew getting drunk, killing the master and his family, and escaping in the ship's boat.

The Americans were insulted by what they felt was a slur on the honour of the US Merchant Navy, and indignantly denied this story. They pointed out that Briggs was not only known to be a fair man who was not likely to provoke his crew to mutiny, but also that he ran a dry ship; the only alcohol on the *Mary Celeste* was the cargo. And even a thirsty sailor would not be likely to drink more than a mouthful of crude alcohol – it would cause severe stomach pains and eventual blindness. Besides, if the crew had mutinied, why should they leave behind their sea-chests together with such items as family photographs, razors and sea-boots?

The British Admiralty remained unconvinced, but had to admit that if the alternative theory was correct, and Briggs and Morehouse had decided to make a false claim for salvage, Briggs would actually have lost by the deal – he was part-owner of the ship, and his share of any salvage would have come to a fraction of what he could have made by selling his share in the normal way.

In March 1873 the court was finally forced to admit that it was unable to decide why the *Mary Celeste* had been abandoned, the first time in its history that it had failed to come to a definite conclusion. The *Dei Gratia*'s owners were awarded one-fifth of the value of the *Mary Celeste* and her cargo. The brig herself was returned to her owner, who lost no time in selling her the moment she got back to New York.

During the next eleven years the *Mary Celeste* had many owners, but brought little profit to any of them. Sailors were convinced she was unlucky. Her last owner, Captain Gilman G. Parker, ran her aground on a reef in the West Indies and made a claim for insurance. The insurers became suspicious, and Parker and his associates were brought to trial. At that time the penalty for deliberately scuttling a ship on the high seas was death by hanging; but the judge, mindful of the *Mary Celeste*'s previous record of bad luck, allowed the men to be released on a technicality. Within eight months Captain Parker was dead, one of the associates had gone mad, and another had committed suicide. The *Mary Celeste* herself had been left to break up on the reef.

Over the next decade or so, as no new evidence came to light, interest in the story waned. During the trial, when fraud was still suspected, a careful watch had been kept on the major ports of England and America. But there was no sign of any of the missing crew.

In the year 1882 a twenty-three-year-old newly qualified doctor named Arthur Doyle moved to Southsea, a suburb of Portsmouth, and screwed up his nameplate. And during the long weeks of waiting for patients he whiled away the time writing short stories. It was in the autumn of 1882 that he began a story: "In the month of December 1873, the British ship *Dei Gratia* steered into Gibraltar, having in tow a derelict brigantine *Marie Celeste*, which had been picked up in the latitude 38°40', longitude 70°15' west."

For such a short sentence, this contains a remarkable number of inaccuracies. The year was actually 1872; the *Dei Gratia* did not tow the *Mary Celeste*, the latter came under its own sail; the latitude and longitude are wrong; and the ship was called plain English Mary, not Marie. All the same, when "J. Habakuk Jephson's Statement" was published in the Cornhill magazine in 1884 it caused a sensation, launching Arthur Doyle's career as a writer – he was soon using the name A. Conan Doyle. Most people took it for the truth, and from then on it was widely accepted that the *Mary Celeste* had been taken over by a kind of Black Power leader with a hatred of Whites. Mr Solly Flood, the chief investigator in the *Mary Celeste* case, was so indignant that he sent a telegram to the Central News Agency denouncing. J. Habakuk Jephson as a fraud and a liar. From then on the *Cornhill* was willing to publish most of Conan Doyle's stories at thirty guineas a time instead of the three guineas he had been paid so far.

Doyle's story was the signal for a new interest in the mystery, and over the next few years there were a number of hoax accounts of the last days of the *Mary Celeste*. They told all kinds of stories from straightforward mutinies to mass accidents – such as everyone falling into the sea when a platform made to watch a swimming race gave way, or the finding of another derelict carrying gold bullion, which tempted Captain Briggs to leave his own ship drifting while he escaped in the other one. One author argued that all the crew had been dragged through the ship's portholes at night by a ravenous giant squid, while Charles Fort, the eminent paranormal researcher, suggested the crew had been snatched away by the same strange force that causes rains of frogs and live fish. Fort added, "I have a collection of yarns, by highly individualized liars, or artists who scorned, in any particular, to imitate one another; who told, thirty, forty, or fifty years later, of having been members of this crew." Even today the *Mary Celeste* often sails unsuspectingly into TV serials and Sci-Fi movies to become involved in time warps or attacked by aliens in UFOs.

In fact, a careful study of the facts reveals that the solution of this particular mystery is obvious.

The man most responsible for the perpetuation of the myth about the *Mary Celeste* was Conan Doyle: it was he who insisted that the ship's boats were still intact. This small inaccuracy made an otherwise simple problem virtually insoluble.

In fact, once we know that the boat was missing, we at least know one thing for certain: that the crew abandoned ship, apparently in great haste – the wheel was not lashed, an indication that the ship was abandoned in a hurry. The question then presents itself: what could have caused everyone on board to abandon the ship in such a hurry?

Captain James Briggs, the brother of the *Mary Celeste*'s skipper, was convinced that the clue lay in the last entry in the log, for the morning of 25 November 1872: it stated that the wind had dropped after a night of heavy squalls. James Briggs believed the ship may have become becalmed in the Azores, and started to drift towards the dangerous rocks of Santa Maria Island. The gash-marks found along the side of the *Mary Celeste* – which the British investigators had claimed were deliberately made by the ship's mutinous crew – may have been made when she actually rubbed against a submerged rock, convincing the crew that she was about to sink.

Oliver Deveau proposed that during the storms some water had found its way from between decks into the hold, giving the impression that the ship was leaking.

Another popular explanation is that a waterspout hit the *Mary Celeste*. The atmospheric pressure inside a waterspout is low; this could have caused the hatch-covers to blow open and forced bilge water into the pump well; this would have made it look as if the ship had taken on six to eight feet of water and was sinking fast.

There are basic objections to all these three answers. If the ship scraped dangerous rocks off Santa Maria Island, then the lifeboat would have been close enough to land on the Island. Since no survivors were found and no wreckage from the lifeboat, this seems unlikely.

Oliver Deveau's theory has a great deal more in its favour. There have often been panics at sea. When Captain Cook's *Endeavour* was in difficulties off the coast of eastern Australia the ship's carpenter was sent to take a reading of the water in the hold. He made a mistake, and the resulting hysteria might have ended with the crew leaving the ship if Cook had not been able to control the panic. On another occasion a ship which was carrying a hold full of timber dumped the whole lot into the sea off Newfoundland, before anyone realized that it would be next to impossible to sink a ship full of wood. But it seems unlikely that a captain of Briggs's known efficiency would allow some simple misreading to cause a panic.

The objection to the waterspout theory is that, apart from the open hatches, the ship was completely undamaged. If a waterspout was big enough to cause such a panic, it would surely have caused far more havoc.

In any case, the real mystery is why, if the crew left the *Mary Celeste* in the lifeboat, they made no attempt to get back on board when they saw that the ship was in no danger of sinking.

Only one explanation covers all the facts. Briggs had never shipped crude alcohol before, and being a typical New England puritan, undoubtedly mistrusted it. The change in temperature between New York and the Azores would have caused casks of alcohol to sweat and leak. The night of storms, in which the barrels would have been shaken violently, would have caused vapour to form inside the casks, slowly building up pressure until the lids of two or three blew off. The explosion, though basically harmless, might have blown the hatches off the cargo hold on to the deck in the positions in which Deveau later found them. Convinced that the whole ship was about to explode, Briggs ordered everyone into the lifeboat. In his haste, he failed to take the one simple precaution that would have saved their lives – to secure the lifeboat to the *Mary Celeste* by a few hundred yards of cable. The sea was fairly calm when the boat was lowered, as we know from the last entry in the log, but the evidence of the torn sails indicates that the ship then encountered severe gales. We may conjecture that the rising wind blew the *Mary Celeste* into the distance, while the crew in the lifeboat rowed frantically in a futile effort to catch up. The remainder of the story is tragically obvious.

In Peru, between the Andes and the Pacific, lies the Nazca Plain. It is a vast, flat expanse of sun-baked stones, and from the ground extremely boring. Fly over it however, and what seemed like abstract markings from ground level resolve themselves into complex drawings of a bird, a lizard, a monkey, a spider and many other stylized images. They have been created by moving the dark stones that litter the surface of the desert and revealing the lighter earth beneath. This has been done on a grand scale, some of the "drawings" are over a hundred feet long.

These markings are believed to have been made by the Nazcan Indians, a pre-Inca race, between 100 bc and ad 600. It has been suggested that they correspond to some astronomical alignment, but study has shown that the small extent to which they do could very easily be coincidental. Erich Von Däniken, the God-as-Astronaut theorist believes the lines to be landing strips from alien spacecraft. In his book *Chariots of the Gods?* he shows two parallel lines with a widened area halfway long one of them. This, he puts forward, is a runaway with a flying saucer parking area. The picture is in fact one of the Nazcan birds' legs. The wide area is its knee, a space hardly large enough to park a bicycle in.

Von Däniken does raise an interesting question however. Short of building hot-air balloons the Nazcan Indians could never have been sure that they looked as they intended. One can only conclude that the pictures are designed to be seen by the gods. Whether these gods drove spaceships or not is a matter for conjecture.

WHERE IS THE MONA LISA?

The answer to the above question may seem self-evident: in the Louvre. But the matter is not quite as straightforward as it looks.

The Mona Lisa is better known on the continent of Europe as "La Gioconda", or the smiling woman – the word means the same as the old English "jocund". It was painted, as everyone knows, by the great Italian artist Leonardo, who was born in the little town of Vinci, near Florence, in 1452. Mona Lisa (Mona is short for Madonna) was a young married woman who was about twenty-four when Leonardo met her. She was the wife of a man twenty years her senior, the wealthy Francesco del Giocondo, and when Leonardo started to paint her around 1500 she had just lost a child. Leonardo's biographer Vasari says that her husband had to hire jesters and musicians to make her smile during the early sittings.

For some reason Leonardo became obsessed with her, and went on painting her for several years, always dissatisfied with his work. This has given rise to stories that he was in love with her, and even that she became his mistress; but this seems unlikely. Leonardo was homosexual, and took a poor view of sex, writing with Swiftian disgust: "The act of coitus and the members that serve it are so hideous that, if it were not for the beauty of faces . . . the human species would lose its humanity." Yet there was something about Madonna Lisa that made him strive to capture her expression for at least six years – possibly more. His biographer Antonia Vallentin says she fascinated him more than any other woman he met in his life. He gave the unfinished portrait to Mona Lisa's husband when he left Florence in 1505, but still continued to work on it at intervals when he returned.

In his *Lives of the Painters*, Giorgio Vasari says that Leonardo worked at the Mona Lisa for four years and left it unfinished.

Leonardo da Vinci's painting in the Louvre, Paris. Is it of Mona Lisa?

"This work is now in the possession of Francis, king of France, at Fontainebleau . . ." And this, we assume, is the famous portrait now in the Louvre. Yet this raises a puzzling question. Leonardo gave the portrait to the man who had commissioned it, Mona Lisa's husband, in 1505, and a mere forty or so years later, when Vasari was writing, it is in the possession of Francis I of France. Surely the Giocondo family would not part with a masterpiece so easily? Besides, the Louvre picture is quite obviously finished . . .

There is another interesting clue. In 1584 a historian of art, Giovanni Paolo Lomazzo, published a book on painting, sculpture and architecture, in which he refers to "the Gioconda *and* the Mona Lisa", as if they were two separate paintings. The book is dedicated to Don Carlos Emanuele, the Grand Duke of Savoy, who was a great admirer of Leonardo – so it hardly seems likely that this was a slip of the pen . . .

Two Giocondas? Then where is the other one? And, more important, *who* is this second Gioconda?

The answer to the first question is, oddly enough: in the Louvre. The world-famous painting, which has been reproduced more often than any other painting in history, is almost certainly not the Mona Lisa that we have been talking about.

Then where *is* the painting of the woman who so obsessed Leonardo that he could not finish her portrait? There is evidence to show that this original Mona Lisa was brought from Italy in the mid-eighteenth century, and went into the stately home of a nobleman in Somerset. Just before World War I it was discovered by the art connoisseur Hugh Blaker in Bath, and he picked it up for a few guineas, and took it to his studio in Isleworth. Hence it became known as the Isleworth Mona Lisa. It was bigger than the Louvre painting, and – more important – was unfinished; the background has only been lightly touched in. Blaker was much impressed by it. The girl was younger and prettier than the Louvre Mona Lisa. And Blaker felt that this new Mona Lisa corresponded much more closely to Vasari's description than the Louvre painting. Vasari rhapsodized about its delicate realism:

> The eyes had that lustre and watery sheen which is always seen in real life, and around them were those touches of red and the lashes which cannot be represented without the greatest subtlety . . . The nose with its beautiful nostrils, rosy and tender, seemed to be alive. The opening of the mouth, united by the red of the lips to the flesh tones of the face, seemed not to be coloured, but to be living flesh.

Sir Kenneth Clark, quoting this passage in his book on Leonardo, asks: "Who would recognize the submarine goddess of the Louvre?"

To which Blaker would have replied: "Ah, precisely." But the description *does* fit the Isleworth Mona Lisa.

There is another point that seems to establish beyond all doubt that Blaker's picture is Leonardo's Mona Lisa. The painter Raphael saw it in Leonardo's studio about 1504, and later made a sketch of it. This sketch shows two Grecian columns on either side – columns that can be found in the Isleworth Mona Lisa, but not in the Louvre painting.

Blaker believes that the Isleworth Mona Lisa is a far more beautiful work, and many art experts have agreed with him. It is true that the Louvre painting has many admirers; Walter Pater wrote a celebrated "purple passage" about it in *The Renaissance* beginning "She is older than the rocks among which she sits; like the vampire, she has been dead many times . . .", and W. B. Yeats thought this so beautiful that he divided it into lines of free verse and printed it as a poem in his *Oxford Book of Modern Verse*. On the other hand, the connoisseur Bernard Berenson wrote about it: "What I really saw in the figure of Mona Lisa was the estranging image of woman beyond the reach of my sympathy or the ken of my interest . . . watchful, sly, secure, with a smile of anticipated satisfaction and a pervading air of hostile superiority . . ." He felt the beauty of the Louvre Mona Lisa had been sacrificed to technique. No one could say this of the far more fresh and lively Isleworth Mona Lisa.

But if the lady in the Louvre is not Leonardo's Lisa del Giocondo, then who is she? Here the most important clue is to be found in a document by Antonio Beatis, secretary to the Cardinal of Aragon. When Leonardo went to the court of Francis I in 1517 he was visited by the cardinal, and the secretary noted down the conversation. The cardinal was shown works by Leonardo, including St John, the Madonna with St Anne, and "the portrait of a certain Florentine lady, painted from life at the instance of the late Magnifico Giuliano de Medici . . ."

In her biography of Leonardo, Antonia Vallentin speculates that this work *was* the Mona Lisa, and asks: "Did Giuliano [de Medici] love Mona Lisa in her girlhood . . . did he think with longing of her now she was married to Messer del Giocondo, and had he commissioned Leonardo to paint her portrait?" But this delightful romantic bubble is shattered by a mere consideration of dates. Giuliano de Medici, brother of Lorenzo the Magnificent, master of Florence, was murdered in Florence cathedral in 1478. The plotters – mostly rival bankers – hoped to kill Lorenzo too, but Lorenzo was too quick for them. All this happened in the year before Mona Lisa was born.

Then who *was* the lady that Leonardo painted at the orders of Giuliano de Medici? Almost certainly the answer is Costanza d'Avalos, Giuliano's mistress, a lady of such pleasant disposition that she was known as "the smiling one" – la Gioconda . . .

And so it would seem that the painting in the Louvre has been labelled "the Mona Lisa" by a simple misunderstanding. Its subject is obviously a woman in her thirties not, like Mona Lisa del Giocondo, in her twenties. Leonardo took it with him to France, and it went into the collection of Francis I, and eventually into the Louvre. The unfinished Mona Lisa stayed in Italy, was brought to England, and was purchased by Hugh Blaker in 1914. In 1962 it was purchased for some vast but undisclosed sum – undoubtedly amounting to millions – by a Swiss syndicate headed by the art-collector Dr Henry F. Pulitzer, and Pulitzer has since written a short book, *Where is the Mona Lisa?*, setting out the claims of his own painting to be that of Madonna Lisa del Giocondo. Pulitzer's contention is simple. There are two Giocondas – for Madonna Lisa had a perfect right to call herself by her husband's name, with a feminine ending. But there is only one Mona Lisa. And that is not in the Louvre but in London.

ORFFYREUS AND THE PERPETUAL MOTION MACHINE

The dream of perpetual motion is undoubtedly a delusion. The law of the conservation of energy states that energy cannot be created or destroyed; in other words, you cannot get more energy out of a machine than you put into it. So it is irritating to have to admit that there is one well-authenticated story of a perpetual motion machine that has defied all attempts at explanation. It was invented by a man who called himself Orffyreus, and it is described in the Leipzig *Acta Eruditorum* for 1717.

Its inventor's real name was Johann Ernst Elias Bessler, and he was born in Zittau, Saxony, in 1680. When he decided to choose himself a *nom de guerre* he wrote the alphabet in a circle, then selected the thirteenth letter after each of the letters of Bessler; the result was Orffyre, which he latinized to Orffyreus. Like Leonardo, he seems to have been a man of many talents, and studied theology, medicine and painting as well as mechanics. And in his early thirties he announced that he had discovered the secret of perpetual motion.

Now, perpetual motion *sounds* a practical possibility. Suppose, for example, that you construct an upright wheel, which spins on a well-greased axle. If you stick a very small weight on the top edge of the wheel (say a piece of putty) it will descend by its own weight to the bottom, and will then continue on, through its own momentum, until it comes *very nearly* to the top again. Suppose one could think of some ingenious means to add just that tiny extra push which would carry it over the top, some method of making little weights alter their position on the rim of the wheel, for example . . . But in practice it proves to be impossible without cheating – that is, giving the wheel a tiny extra push.

In 1712 Orffyreus appeared in the town of Gera, in the province of Reuss, and exhibited a "self-moving wheel". It was three feet in diameter and four inches thick. When given the slightest push it started up, then quickly worked itself up to a regular speed. Once in motion it was capable of raising a weight of several pounds. And this in itself is incredible. If an empty spacecraft was drifting through space, far from the influence of any star, it would continue moving in a straight line for ever, because there would be nothing to stop it. (This is Newton's first law of motion.) Similarly, if a wheel was given the slightest spin in empty space, it would go on spinning for ever. But it could not be made to do any "work" – to raise a weight, for example. As soon as its original energy was exhausted, it would stop. Yet according to Orffyreus his wheel could not only keep on spinning for ever, but could also raise weights. This was done by winding a rope round the axis, with a weight attached to it.

Oddly enough, the burghers of Gera do not seem to have been impressed by his demonstrations. It may be simply that they were not sufficiently mechanically minded to realize that he was offering them an invention that could transform the world. (If rediscovered today, his secret would enable us to dispense with coal, oil and atomic energy.) Or it may have been simply that Orffyreus was a singularly irritating person, self-assertive, boastful and dogmatic. At all events, he made far more enemies than friends, and soon had to move on. He left Gera without regret, and moved to Draschwitz, near Leipzig, where in 1713 he constructed a still larger wheel, this one five feet in diameter and six inches in width; it could turn at fifty revolutions a minute and raise a weight of 40lb. Then he moved again to Merseburg, and constructed a wheel six feet in diameter and a foot thick. A number of local "learned men" examined his wheel, agreed that it was not moved by any outer force, and signed a certificate to that effect. But this minor triumph moved Orffyreus's enemies to fury. One published a pamphlet offering Orffyreus a thousand thalers if he could make a wheel revolve in a locked room for a month. Another offered to construct a wheel – admittedly a trick – that would do everything that Orffyreus's wheel could do. And J.G. Borlach of Leipzig published a pamphlet in which he demonstrated (what is undoubtedly true) that a perpetual motion machine is against the laws of nature.

In that same year, 1716, Orffyreus left Merseburg for the small independent state of Hesse-Cassel, in which he was to score his greatest triumph. Here at last his luck seemed to change. The reigning Landgrave (or Count), whose name was Karl, was sufficiently impressed by the homeless inventor to make him a town councillor and offer him rooms in the ducal castle at Weissenstein. And during the year 1717 he constructed at the castle his largest wheel so far, this one being twelve feet in diameter and fourteen inches thick. In spite of its size, it was fairly light-weight. It was described in a letter to Sir Isaac Newton by a Professor   Gravesande of Leyden,

. . . a hollow wheel, or kind of drum . . . covered over

with canvas, to prevent the inside from being seen . . .
I have examined the axles and am firmly persuaded that
nothing from without the wheel in the least contributes
to its motion. When I turned it but gently, it always stood
still as soon as I took away my hand . . .

When set in motion, the wheel revolved twenty-five or twenty-six
times a minute. An "Archimedean screw for raising water" could
be attached to its axle by means of a rope; in that case the speed
dropped to twenty revolutions a minute.

The wheel remained on exhibition in the castle for several months,
and was examined by many learned men, who all concluded that
there could be no deception. Then on 31 October 1717 Orffyreus
was requested to transfer the wheel to another room in the castle
presumably a larger one, "where there were no contiguous walls".
On 12 November the Landgrave and various officials came to look
at the wheel, observed it in motion for a while, then watched as the
doors and windows of the room were tightly sealed, in such a way
that no one could enter without leaving traces behind. Two weeks
later the seals were broken and the room opened; the wheel was still
revolving. The door was resealed, and this time it remained closed
until 4 January 1718. The wheel was still revolving at twenty-six
revolutions per minute.

Deeply impressed, his doubts now laid at rest, the Landgrave
asked Orffyreus how much he wanted for his secret and turned
pale when Orffyreus replied, "Twenty thousand pounds." It was
his greatest invention and his life's work, he reminded them, and
he deserved adequate compensation. The Landgrave and his retinue
of scientists was inclined to agree, but he didn't have that much
money to hand. Baron Fischer, architect to the Emperor of Austria,
pointed out that it should be easy to raise the money in London, and
accordingly wrote to Dr J. T. Desaguliers of the Royal Society. The
arrangement he proposed was that if the movement of the wheel
should prove to be "a perpetual one", then the £20,000 should be
given to the inventor; if not, the money would be returned.

Meanwhile Professor 'sGravesande had made a thorough examination of the axle of the machine, and wrote a report to the effect
that as far as he could see there was no way in which the wheel
could be a fake. Unfortunately, the paranoid inventor suspected
that 'sGravesande was asked to examine the axle in the hope of
discovering the secret without paying for it. Orffyreus exploded.
He locked himself in the room, and smashed the wheel. Then he
wrote a message on the wall, declaring that it was the impertinent
curiosity of 'sGravesande that had provoked him.

And now, regrettably, Orffyreus and his machine vanish into
obscurity. If Orffyreus had lived a century later he would have been
pursued by prying journalists, and we would have a detailed history

of the rest of his life. But these were the days before the invention of newspapers, and all we know is that Orffyreus was rebuilding his machine ten years later, in 1727, and that 'sGravesande had agreed to examine it again. But there is no record that it was ever tested. All we know is that Orffyreus died in 1745, at the age of sixty-five. And his secret, whatever it was, died with him.

The mystery here is surely psychological rather than scientific. If we accept that energy cannot be created or destroyed, then we must conclude that the wheel was a fraud, no matter how well its inventor succeeded in concealing it. Orffyreus, according to one contemporary, had been a clockmaker at some point, and we must assume that he had found some method of concealing a spring mechanism somewhere in the supports. We may assume that other explanations such as that a man was concealed inside it are ruled out by the crucial test in which the machine was left in a locked room for three months.

Yet if we assume that Orffyreus was a fraud, the puzzle remains. What could he hope to gain from it? There was no way in which he could have absconded with the £20,000, for as we can see from Baron Fischer's letter, the money would not even be handed over unless they were first satisfied that he had genuinely discovered the principle of perpetual motion.

It must also be admitted that Orffyreus's character makes it seem unlikely that he was a straightforward swindler. Charm and smoothness are an essential part of the equipment of the confidence man; and while there is no guarantee that paranoia and bad temper are a sign of genius, there is no denying that we find it hard to associate such characteristics with a deliberate confidence trickster. They are more likely to be accompanied by a certain obsessive quality, a conviction of one's own remarkable talents. It is easier to believe that Orffyreus was a self-deceiver than that he was a crook. But could a self-deceiver construct a wheel that would run for three months in a locked room?

On the other hand, let us suppose that Orffyreus was a man with a grudge – a man who was quite certain about his own genius, but who resented his lack of recognition. It *is* conceivable that in a mood of rage and contempt he decided to practise a deliberate swindle, and then use the money to devote the rest of his life to his researches. How could he hope to carry out such a swindle?

A careful study of the case suggests some possible answers. Orffyreus himself published a pamphlet, typically entitled *The Triumphant Orffyrean Perpetual Motion* (1719), in which he offers an exceedingly obscure account of his basic principles. He admits that his wheel depends upon weights, which "constitute the perpetual motion itself, since from them is received the universal movement which they must exercise so long as they remain out of the centre of gravity". These weights, he says, are so placed that they can

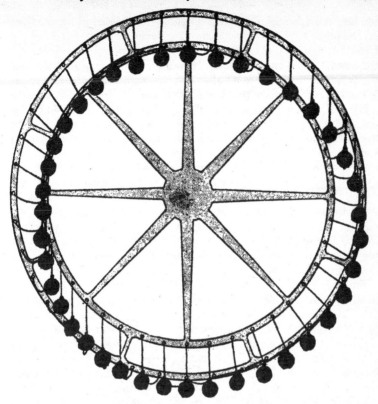

Rupert Gould's drawing of the "overbalancing wheel".

"never obtain equilibrium". Professors who examined his machine described being able to hear the movements of about eight weights, presumably placed on the rim of the wheel. This principle is known as the "overbalancing wheel", and has been the mainstay of inventors who have tried to produce perpetual motion. The basic idea can be seen in Rupert Gould's drawing. If in fact the wheel has two rims, one inside the other, and some ingenious inventor could devise a method for transferring the weights automatically from one rim to another, then the problem of perpetual motion would be solved. As they transfer to the outer rim, they cause it to outweigh the weights on the inner rim on the opposite side, so that side of the wheel descends. As it begins to rise again under its own momentum the "grabs" – or whatever – transfer the weight on to the inner rim, and since they are now closer to the centre, they become in effect lighter than those on the descending outer rim, and rise to the top of the wheel, where they are again transferred to the outer rim. It sounds foolproof.

But the Marquis of Worcester (who originally thought of the idea) overlooked one basic point. The outer rim is of course longer than the inner one, so there are less weights on the descending rim than on the other side. (In Gould's drawing, it can be seen that there are twenty weights on one side of the wheel compared to eighteen on the other.) So the two sides exactly counterbalance one another, and the wheel soon comes to a halt.

But this is not a point that would immediately strike anybody who studied a drawing or model of the overbalancing wheel. And it is conceivable that Orffyreus may have reckoned on this in deceiving the Landgrave and his wise men. We may suppose that he secreted some kind of powerful clockspring inside the supports of his machine, with a cog-wheel that turned the axle. When the time came to hand over his secret he would remove the canvas cover of the wheel and reveal his ingeniously designed "overbalancing wheel". And unless the savants were extremely astute, or had given long consideration to the problem, they would agree that Orffyreus had indeed solved the problem of perpetual motion in an absurdly simple way. And by the time they dismantled the wheel and found the clock-spring mechanism, Orffyreus would be a hundred miles away.

But there is also an objection to this explanation. It is easy to design a modern clock or watch that will run for a year, because the "moving parts" are so light that they can be driven by a tiny battery. But a twelve-foot wheel with weights round the rim would require a great deal more energy: a heavy-duty car battery might do it, but a clock-spring that would drive such a wheel for two months would have to be enormous. There is no obvious room inside Orffyreus's wheel for such a spring. And unless Orffyreus had invented the principle of the dynamo a century and a half before Faraday, there seems to be no other possibility. And so we are left once more with the tantalizing possibility that perhaps Orffyreus *did* stumble upon some simple but profound secret that has eluded all his successors.

PSYCHOMETRY, "TELESCOPE INTO THE PAST"

In the winter of 1921 members of the Metapsychic Institute in Paris met together to test a clairvoyant. Someone produced a letter and asked someone to pass it to her; before it could reach her it was grabbed by a novelist called Pascal Forthunny, who said scathingly: "It can't be difficult to invent something that applies to anybody." He then closed his eyes and pronounced solemnly: "Ah yes, I see a crime, a murder . . ." When he had finished the man who had brought the letter said: "That was written by Henri Landru." Landru was the "Bluebeard" who was then on trial for the murders of eleven women. The sceptic Forthunny had discovered that he possessed the curious ability known as psychometry – the ability to "sense" the history of an object by holding it in the hand.

According to the man who invented the word – an American doctor named Joseph Rodes Buchanan – it is an ability we all possess, although most of us have unconsciously suppressed it. Buchanan – who was a professor of medicine in Kentucky – came to suspect the existence of such a faculty in 1841, when he met a bishop named Leonidas Polk, who claimed that he could always detect brass when he touched it – even in the dark – because it produced a peculiar taste in his mouth. Buchanan was interested in the science known as phrenology – the notion that the "bumps" on our skulls reveal our characters and he was interested to discover that Polk seemed to have a highly developed "bump" of sensibility. So he decided to perform a scientific test on students who had a similar bump. Various metals were wrapped in paper, and Buchanan was delighted to discover that many of his students could detect brass, iron, lead and so on by merely pressing their fingertips against the paper. They could also distinguish substances like salt, sugar, pepper and vinegar.

Buchanan concluded that the answer lay in some "nerve aura" in the fingertips, which can detect different metals exactly as we could distinguish them by touching them with the tip of the tongue. This appeared to be confirmed by his observation that it seemed to work better when the hands are damp with perspiration – for after all, a damp skin is more "sensitive" than a dry skin. But this explanation began to seem inadequate when he discovered that one of his best "sensitives" – a man named Charles Inman – could sense the contents of sealed letters, and the character of the writers. Buchanan's explanation was that the "nerve aura" of the writer had left some kind of trace on the letter, and Inman was able to pick up this trace through his own nerve aura. In other words, Inman's "sensitivity" was abnormally developed, in much the same way as a bloodhound's sense of smell. But that theory also broke down when he discovered that Inman displayed the same insight when presented with photographs – daguerreotypes –᷾ in sealed envelopes. Even the argument that the photograph had been in contact with the "sitter", and had therefore picked up something of his "nerve aura", ceased to be convincing when Buchanan discovered that newspaper photographs worked as well as daguerreotypes.

The professor of geology at Boston University, William Denton, read Buchanan's original paper on psychometry – the word means "soul measurement" – and decided to try it himself. His sister Anne was "highly impressible", and she proved to be an even better psychometrist than Inman; she was not only able to describe the character of letter-writers; she was even able to describe their physical appearance and surroundings.

This led Denton to ask himself whether, if a writer's image and surroundings could be "impressed" on a letter, "why could not rocks receive impressions of surrounding objects, some of which they have been in the immediate neighbourhood of for years". So in 1853 Denton began testing his "sensitives" with geological and archaeological specimens, "and was delighted to find that without possessing any previous knowledge of the specimen, or even seeing it, the history of its time passed before the gaze of the seer like a grand panoramic view." When he handed his sister a piece of volcanic lava from Hawaii, she was shaken to see "an ocean of fire pouring over a precipice and boiling as it pours". Significantly, she also saw the sea with ships on it, and Denton knew that the lava had been ejected during an eruption in 1840, when the American navy had been in Hawaii. A fragment of bone found in a piece of limestone evoked a picture of a prehistoric beach with dinosaurs. A fragment of Indian pottery brought a vision of Red Indians. A meteorite fragment brought visions of empty space, with the stars looking abnormally large and bright. A fragment of rock from Niagara brought a vision of a boiling torrent hurling up spray (which she thought was steam). A piece of stalactite brought an image of pieces of rock hanging down like icicles. To make doubly sure that his sensitives were not somehow picking up unconscious hints or recognizing the specimens, Denton wrapped them in thick paper. He also discovered that when he tried the same specimen a second time – perhaps a month later – it produced the same result, although the picture was never identical.

In one of his most interesting experiments he showed his wife a fragment of Roman tile which came from a villa that had belonged to the orator Cicero. She described a Roman villa and lines of soldiers; she also saw the owner of the villa, a genial, fleshy man with an air of command. Denton was disappointed; Cicero had been tall and thin. But by the time Denton came to write the second volume of *The Soul of Things* he had discovered that the villa had also belonged to the dictator Sulla, and that Sulla *did* fit his wife's description.

Another impressive "hit" was the "vision" induced by a piece of volcanic rock from Pompeii. Mrs Denton had no idea what it was, and was not allowed to see it; but she had a vivid impression of the eruption of Vesuvius and the crowds fleeing from Pompeii. Denton's son Sherman had an even more detailed vision of ancient Pompeii, complete with many archaeological details – such as an image of a boat with a "swan's neck" which proved to be historically accurate.

Denton was immensely excited; he believed that he and Buchanan had discovered a so far unknown human faculty, a kind of "telescope into the past" that would enable us to relive great scenes of history. In effect, everything that had ever happened to the world was preserved on a kind of "newsreel" (although this was not, of course, an image that occurred to Denton) and could be replayed at will.

But while the evidence for the psychometric faculty is undoubtedly beyond dispute, Denton was not aware of how far it can be deceptive. The third volume of *The Soul of Things*, published in 1888, contains "visions" of various planets that we now know to be preposterous. Venus has giant trees like toadstools and animals that sound as if they were invented by Hieronymus Bosch; Mars has a summery temperature (in fact it would be freezing) and is peopled with four-fingered men with blue eyes and yellow hair; Jupiter also has blue-eyed blondes with plaits down to their waists and the ability to float like balloons. Denton's son Sherman (who was responsible for most of these extraordinary descriptions) had clearly developed the faculty that Jung calls "active imagination", and was unable to distinguish it from his genuine psychometric abilities.

What impresses the modern reader about Denton's *Soul of Things* and Buchanan's *Manual of Psychometry* (optimistically sub-titled The Dawn of a New Civilization) is their thoroughly scientific approach. This also impressed their contemporaries at first. Unfortunately, the period when they were conducting their experiments was also the period when the new craze known as Spiritualism was spreading across America and Europe. It had started with curious poltergeist manifestations in the home of the Fox family in New York state in the late 1840s. By 1860 it was a worldwide phenomenon. Scientists were appalled, and most of them dismissed it as sheer delusion. Anything that seemed remotely connected with the "supernatural" became the object of the same scepticism, and the researches of Buchanan and Denton never attracted the attention they deserved. Denton died in 1883, Buchanan in 1900, both in relative obscurity.

The next major experiments in psychometry were made by Dr Gustav Pagenstecher, a German who moved to Mexico City in the 1880s, and who regarded himself as a hard-headed materialist. Some time after World War I, Pagenstecher was treating the insomnia of a patient called Maria Reyes de Zierold by hypnosis. One day, as she lay in a hypnotic trance, she told him that her daughter was listening at the door. Pagenstecher opened the door and found the daughter there. He began testing Maria for paranormal abilities and discovered that while under hypnosis she could share his own sensations; if he put sugar or salt on his tongue she could taste it; if he held a lighted match near his fingers she felt the heat of the flame. Then he began testing her for psychometric abilities. Like Denton's subjects, she could describe where some specimen came from. Holding a sea-shell, she described an underwater scene; holding a piece of meteorite, she described hurtling through space and down through the earth's atmosphere. ("I am horrified! My God!") Dr Walter Franklin Prince, who tested her on behalf of the American Society for Psychical Research, handed her what he thought was a "sea bean" which he had found on the beach. She described a tropical forest. Professional botanists confirmed that the "bean" was a nut from a tree that grew in the tropical forest, and that was often carried down to the sea by the rivers.

Another eminent experimenter of the 1920s was Dr Eugene Osty, director of the Metapsychical Institute at which the novelist Pascal Fortunny correctly identified the letter from the mass murderer Landru. In his classic work *Supernormal Faculties in Man*, Osty described many experiments in psychometry with various "sensitives". In 1921 he was handed a photograph of a sealed glass capsule containing some liquid; it had been found near the great temple at Baalbek. One of his best psychics, a Mme Moral, held the photograph in her hand – it was so blurred it could have been of anything – and said immediately that it reminded her of "a place with dead people", and of one old man in particular. She "saw" a vast place, like an enormous church, then went on to describe the man, who was obviously a high priest. The capsule in the photograph contained the blood of a man who had been sacrificed in some distant land, and had been placed in the priest's grave as a memento.

At the time Osty himself had no idea what the photograph represented, and was surprised when the engineer who had found

Psychic Peter Nelson, USA, performing psychometry experiment, 1984. *Dr Elmar Gruber/Fortean Picture Library.*

it was able to confirm that it had been discovered in a rich tomb in the Bekaa valley.

This story raises again the central problem about psychometry. Buchanan's original hypothesis – that it was simply a matter of "nerve aura", so the psychometrist could be regarded as a kind of human bloodhound – ceases to be plausible if the information can be picked up from a photograph, which could not be expected to retain any kind of "scent". Even Denton's assumption that every object somehow "photographs" its surroundings seems dubious. In that case a piece of Roman pavement could only have "photographed" a limited area, and Mrs Denton's view of Roman legionaries would have been simply of hairy legs towering up above her.

The likeliest hypothesis is that the faculty involved is what is traditionally known as "clairvoyance", a peculiar ability to "know" what is going on in some other place or at some other time. But Bishop Polk's ability to distinguish brass in the dark is obviously not clairvoyance. Here, as in so many other areas of the "paranormal", it is practically impossible to draw neat dividing lines.

Many modern psychometrists – like Gerard Croiset, Peter Hurkos and Suzanne Padfield – have been able use their faculty to help the police solve crimes: Suzanne Padfield was even able to help the Moscow police catch a child-murderer without leaving her home in Dorset.[1] But it is significant that Croiset disliked being called a psychometrist or clairvoyant, and preferred the more ambiguous word "paragnost" – meaning simply the ability to "know" what lies beyond the normal limits of the senses.

Archaeologists in Iraq have found what appears to be an ancient electric battery. The object, dating from roughly 230 bc was found in an excavation of a Parthian village in 1936. It consists of a small vase containing a copper cylinder surrounding an iron rod. Sceptics insist that it is a scroll case. However it cannot be denied that if an acid, such as lemon juice is poured into such a vase, an electric current is created. In fact the current is sufficient to be used to electroplate metal objects suspended in the correct metal solution.

If the battery was indeed used for this purpose it may mean that much of what modern museums classify an ancient gold may only be plate . . .

---

1 See *The Psychic Detectives* by Colin Wilson.

DID ROBIN HOOD REALLY EXIST?

Next to King Arthur, Robin Hood is the most famous of British heroes, and he shares with King Arthur the indignity of having his existence doubted by modern scholarship. The folklorist Lord Raglan concluded that he was really a Celtic god, while in *The God of the Witches* Margaret Murray argues that his name means "*Robin of the Hood*", and that he was probably the devil (or horned god) in ancient witchcraft festivals. Yet there is also convincing evidence that Robin was a real person, and that – as the ballads declare – he plundered the king's deer in Sherwood Forest and had a long-standing feud with the Sheriff of Nottingham.

The first literary reference to Robin Hood occurs in William Langland's *Piers Plowman*, dating from around 1377. Langland makes a priest remark that he could not say his paternoster without making mistakes, but "I know rhymes of Robyn Hood and Randolf Earl of Chester." So there were already ballads of Robin Hood by that date. In 1510 Wynkyn de Worde, one of the earliest printers, brought out *A Lytell Geste of Robyn Hood*, which did for Robin Hood what Malory had done for King Arthur in the middle of the previous century. And by the time he appears in Sir Walter Scott's *Ivanhoe* (1847) Robin had become the boon-companion and ally of Richard the Lion Heart, the heroic outlaw of the woods. All that was needed then was for some folklorist to notice how often Robin Hood's name is associated with folk festivals, like the Hobby Horse ceremony which takes place on May Day in Padstow, Cornwall,[1] to suggest that Robin Hood was really Robin Wood, and that his name is derived from the Norse god Woden . . . In fact he appears as Robin Wood in T.H. White's *Sword in the Stone*, in which he becomes a contemporary of King Arthur, who (if he ever existed) was said to have died about AD 540.

---

1 Actually 8 May, but the date has become displaced over the centuries.

Little John's Grave, Hathersage churchyard, Derbyshire. *Fortean Picture Library*.

Those who assume there is no smoke without fire are inclined to believe that Robin Hood was a real outlaw who at some time lived in Sherwood Forest, and who became so popular during his own lifetime that, like Billy the Kid, he soon became the subject of tales and ballads. Yet it seems unlikely that he was around as early as Richard the Lion Heart (1157–99), or he would surely have been mentioned in manuscripts before *Piers Plowman* two centuries later. In his *Chronicle of Scotland*, written about 1420, Andrew Wyntoun refers to Robin Hood and Little John for the year 1283, which sounds altogether more likely – about a century before *Piers Plowman*.

And where precisely did he operate? One important clue is that there is a small fishing town called Robin Hood's Bay in Yorkshire, not far from Whitby, and that up on the nearby moors there are two tumuli (or barrows) called Robin Hood's Butts. Another is that in medieval England the forest of Barnsdale in Yorkshire joined Sherwood Forest in Nottinghamshire. A sixteenth-century life of Robin Hood among the Sloane Manuscripts says he was born in Locksley, in Yorkshire, about 1160. *The Chronicle of Scotland* associates Robin with "Barnysale" presumably Barnsdale. So the evidence suggests that he was a Yorkshireman.

Later legends declare that he was "Sir Robin of Locksley", or even the Earl of Huntingdon. But it is clear from the earlier ballads that he was a yeoman – a farmer who owns his own land – and that this is partly why he became such a hero: not because he was a nobleman, but because he was a representative of the people. (A small tenant farmer would be only one stage above a landless peasant.)

One of the most important clues to Robin's identity emerged in the mid-nineteenth century, when the Historic Documents Commission was cataloguing thousands of documents which represented eight centuries of British history. It was in 1852 that the antiquary Joseph Hunter claimed that he had stumbled upon a man who sounded as if he might be the original Robin Hood. His name in fact was Robert, and he was the son of Adam Hood, a forester in the service of the Earl de Warenne. (Robin was simply a diminutive of Robert – not, in those days, a name in its own right.) He was born about 1280, and on 25 January 1316 Robert Hood and his wife Matilda paid two shillings for permission to take a piece of the earl's waste ground in "Bickhill" (or Bitch-hill) in Wakefield. It was merely the size of a kitchen garden – thirty feet long by sixteen feet wide. The rent for this was sixpence a year. The Manor Court Roll for 1357 shows a house "formerly the property of Robert Hode" on the site – so by that time Robert Hood was presumably dead.

Now, 1316 was midway through the reign of Edward II, the foppish, homosexual king who was finally murdered – by having a red-hot spit inserted into his entrails – in September 1327. After his coronation (in 1307) he dismissed his father's ministers and judges and made his lover, Piers Gaveston, Earl of Cornwall – to the fury of his barons. It was the most powerful of these, Thomas, Earl of Lancaster, who forced Edward to accept the rule of twenty-eight barons (called Ordainers), and who finally executed Piers Gaveston in 1312. Edward's lack of attention to affairs of state allowed the Scots – against whom his father Edward I had fought so successfully – to throw off their English masters. Edward II was defeated at Bannockburn in 1314, two years before Robert Hood hired the piece of waste ground and set up home with his wife Matilda. So it is understandable that when the Earl of Warenne was ordered by the king to raise a troop to fight the Scots Robert Hood failed to oblige, and the records show that he was accordingly fined. But when a second muster was raised in 1317 Hood's name was not listed among those fined – which led J.W. Walker, a modern historian, to conclude that this time Robert Hood joined the army. Five years later it was the Earl of Lancaster who raised the army, to fight against the king. Again, Hood's name is not among those fined, so it again seems that he answered the summons. Lancaster's army was defeated at Boroughbridge, and Lancaster was captured and beheaded. The quarrel had been about Edward's new favourites, the Despensers, father and son, whom he had been forced to banish; now he was able to recall them.

Many of Lancaster's supporters were declared outlaws, and Walker discovered a document that stated that a "building of five rooms" on Bichhill, Wakefield, was among the property confiscated. Walker believes that this was Robert Hood's home, and that the outlaw now took refuge in the nearby forest of Barnsdale, where he soon became a highly successful robber.

Now, it must be understood that if Robert Hood *was* the legendary Robin, and he took refuge in the forest, living off the deer population, he was risking horrible penalties. When William the Conqueror brought the Normans to England he declared that the forests – which covered a third of the land – were his own property; any peasant who killed deer risked being literally flayed alive. Under William the Saxons suffered as much as countries occupied by the Nazis in World War II. Two and a half centuries later the Normans regarded themselves as Englishmen, and the French language had ceased to be used in England, but the laws were still harsh. The "forest laws" had been mitigated, so a man could no longer have his hands or his lips sliced off for poaching a deer; but the penalty was still a heavy fine, a year's imprisonment, and sureties for his future good behaviour. If he could not find guarantors he had to "abjure the realm" – quit the kingdom for ever.

The battle of Boroughbridge was fought on 16 March 1322, near the Ure river in Yorkshire; dismounted men-at-arms and archers drove back the cavalry, then another royalist army moved up behind the rebels and forced them to surrender. Lancaster was captured and tried; evidence revealed that he had been contemplating an alliance with the king's old enemy Robert the Bruce. Lancaster – the king's cousin – was beheaded. And Robin Hood, deprived of his home, became an outlaw in the king's forest.

But if Walker is correct in identifying Robert Hood of Wakefield as Robin Hood, he was not an outlaw for long. In the spring of the following year the king made a progress through the north of England, reaching York on 1 May. From 16 May to 21 May he stayed at Rothwell, between Wakefield and Leeds, and spent three days hunting at Plumpton Park in Knaresborough Forest. And the *Lytell Geste* makes this visit a part of the story of Robin Hood, describing how the king "came to Plompton Park/ And failed [missed] many of his deer." Where the king was accustomed to seeing herds of deer, now he could find only one deer "that bore any good horn". Which made the king swear by the Trinity "I wish I could lay my hands on Robin Hood":

> I wolde I had Robyn Hode
> With eyen I myght hym se.

So, according to this ballad, one of the foresters suggested that the king should disguise himself as an abbot, riding through the greenwood with a band of monks. The ruse was successful; Robin and his men stopped the "abbot", but recognized him as the king. And the king thereupon found Robin so likable that he invited him to join the royal household as a *vadlet*, a gentleman of the royal bedchamber. The king continued on his travels until February 1324, when he returned to Westminster. The royal household accounts for April record payment of the past month's wages to Robyn Hod and twenty-eight others. The first record of a payment to Robyn Hod is in the previous June. The ballad tells us that after being a servant of the king for somewhat over a year Robin asked the king's permission to return to Barnsdale. And the household accounts for November 1324 record that Robyn Hod, formerly one of the "porteurs" (gentlemen of the bedchamber) had been given five shillings "because he is no longer able to work". The ballad says that Robin asked the king's leave to return to Barnsdale, and was given permission to stay for seven days. But he never returned; instead he regrouped his merry men, and lived on in the greenwood for another twenty-two years. If this is based on fact, then he died about 1346, in his mid-sixties.

The king's fortunes took a downward turn after Robin's departure. He had recalled the banished Despensers, and the younger of the two had become his "favourite" – to the disgust of his queen, who had already had to contend with Piers Gaveston. She was a Frenchwoman, daughter of Philip the Fair. Now she began to take a romantic interest in an unpleasant and ambitious young baron called Roger de Mortimer, who had been thrown into the Tower for his opposition to the Despensers. Queen Isabella became his mistress, and it was probably she who plotted Mortimer's escape. He fled to Paris, and was joined there by Isabella, who was on a mission for the king. They landed at Orwell, in Suffolk, with an army of almost three thousand. When the king heard the news he fled, and was captured, and imprisoned in Berkeley Castle. He was forced to abdicate, and his son (aged fifteen) was crowned Edward III. On the night of 21 September 1327 horrible screams rang through the castle. The next morning it was announced that the king had died "of natural causes". There were no marks on the body, but it is said that his features were still contorted with agony. A chronicle of some thirty years later states that three assassins entered his cell when he was asleep, and held down the upper half of his body with a table. Then a horn was inserted into the anal orifice, and a red-hot iron bar was used to burn out the king's insides.

Mortimer and Isabella ruled England as regents for four years; then the young king asserted himself, had Mortimer seized in Nottingham Castle, and had him executed as a traitor at Tyburn. The loss of her lover almost drove the queen mad. But she was restored to favour, and lived on for another twenty-eight years.

It is of course conceivable that the Robin Hood who lived in Edward's reign had no connection with the legendary outlaw of Sherwood Forest; one reference book (*Who's Who In History*) says that he was alive in 1230, in the reign of Henry III, on the grounds that records show that the Sheriff of Yorkshire sold his possessions in that year (for 32*s* 6*d*) when he became an outlaw; but the same reference book admits that the Robyn Hode of Wakefield is also a good contender. There is something to be said for this earlier dating, for it would give more time for the legend of Robin Hood to spread throughout England. But there is also a great deal to be said for Robin Hood of Wakefield. If he became an outlaw in 1322, as a result of the Lancaster rebellion, then he spent only one year in Sherwood Forest before the king pardoned him. The story of his pardon by the homosexual king certainly rings true – as does his appointment as a gentleman of the bedchamber. It is natural to speculate that he may have found that his duties in the bedchamber involved more than he had bargained for, although at this time the king's favourite was the younger Hugh le Despenser (executed by Mortimer and Isabella in 1326). So he returned to the greenwood, and became a hero of legend. We do not know whether he became the arch-enemy of the Sheriff of Nottingham, but the sheriff – who would be the equivalent of a modern Chief Constable – would have been responsible for law and order in Nottinghamshire and south Yorkshire, and would certainly have resented a band of outlaws who lived off the king's deer. One chronicle states that Robin also had a retreat in what became known as Robin Hood's Bay, and ships in which he could escape to sea. (He is also said to have operated as far afield as Cumberland.) If a concerted attempt had been made to flush him out, it would probably have succeeded. But most of the peasants and tenant farmers would have been on Robin's side. There had been a time when the forests of England were common land, and half-starved peasantry must have felt it was highly unreasonable that thousands of square miles of forest should be reserved for the king's hunting, when the king could not make use of a fraction of that area.

But there could be another reason that Robin was allowed to operate without too much opposition. When he was at court he must surely have met the fourteen-year-old boy who would become Edward III, and Edward would be of exactly the right age to look with admiration on a famous outlaw. This is only speculation, but it could undoubtedly explain why Robin was allowed to become the legendary bane of authority in the last decades of his life.

Authority has its own ways of striking back. According to the Sloane Manuscript, Robin fell ill, and went to his cousin, the Prioress of Kirklees, to be bled – the standard procedure for treating any illness in those days. She decided to avenge the many churchmen he had robbed, and allowed him to bleed to death. Another account says that she betrayed him at the request of her lover, Sir Roger de Doncaster. Still another source states that the man responsible for Robin's death was a monk who was called in to attend him, and who decided that the outlaw would be better dead. He was buried in the grounds of the nunnery, within a bowshot of its walls. Grafton's Chronicle (1562) says he was buried under an inscribed stone, and a century later another chronicle reported that his tomb, with a plain cross on a flat stone, could be seen in the cemetery; in 1665 Dr Nathaniel Johnstone made a drawing of it; Gough's *Sepulchral Monuments* also has an engraving of the tombstone. In the early nineteenth century navvies building a railway broke up the stone – it is said they believed its chips to be a cure for toothache. So the last trace of the real existence of Robin Hood disappeared. But by that time the grave of the prioress had been discovered among the ruins of the nunnery and it bore some resemblance to the tomb of Robin Hood. It also mentioned her name – Elizabeth Stainton.

The real significance of Robin Hood is that he lived in a century when the peasants were beginning to feel an increasing resentment about their condition – a resentment that expressed itself in the revolutionary doctrines of John Ball, and which exploded in the Peasants' Revolt of 1381, only a short time after Robin is first mentioned in print by Langland. The Peasants' Revolt is generally considered to mark the end of the Middle Ages; but it is in the ballads of Robin Hood that we can see that the state of mind known as the Middle Ages is coming to an end.

SYNCHRONICITY OR "MERE COINCIDENCE"?

The *Sunday Times* journalist Godfrey Smith was thinking of writing something about the "saga of lost manuscripts" – Carlyle's manuscript of *The French Revolution*, burnt by a careless maid, T.E. Lawrence's *Seven Pillars of Wisdom*, left in a taxi, Hemingway's suitcase full of early manuscripts, stolen from a train – and decided to call on the literary agent Hilary Rubinstein, a treasure-house of similar stories. But before he could introduce the subject into the conversation a girl sitting with them – the wife of the novelist Nicholas Mosley – mentioned that her husband was upset because he had just had the first 150 pages of his new novel stolen from his car. Smith remarked in his *Sunday Times* column: "We are back in what J.W. Dunne called serial time, and Arthur Koestler called synchronicity, and some of us still call coincidence . . ."

It was Jung in fact who coined the word "synchronicity" for meaningful coincidence. But Arthur Koestler was equally intrigued by the subject, and discussed it in a book called *The Roots of Coincidence* in 1972. In the following year he wrote an article about coincidence in *The Sunday Times* and appealed to readers for examples. Many of these were utilized in his book *The Challenge of Chance* (1973), co-authored by Sir Alister Hardy and Robert Harvie. He begins with a section called "The Library Angel", describing coincidences involved with books. In 1972 Koestler had been asked to write about the chess championship between Boris Spassky and Bobbie Fischer, so he went to the London Library to look up books on chess and books on Iceland. He decided to start with chess and the first book that caught his eye was entitled *Chess in Iceland* by Williard Fiske.

He then tells of how Dame Rebecca West was trying to check up on an episode related by one of the accused in one of the Nuremberg war-crimes trials, and how she discovered to her annoyance that the trials are published in the form of abstracts under arbitrary headings

Carl Jung, the Swiss psychiatrist who coined the word "synchronicity".

and are therefore useless to a researcher. After an hour of fruitless searching she approached a librarian and said: "I can't find it . . .", and casually took a volume off the shelf and opened it. It opened at the page she had been searching for.

This anecdote is particularly interesting because it involved an apparently "random" action, a casual reaching out without logical purpose. The word "synchronicity" was coined by Jung in connection with the *I Ching*, the Chinese *Book of Changes*, which the Chinese consult as an "oracle". The method of "consulting" the *I Ching* consists of throwing down three coins at random half a dozen times and noting whether there are more heads or tails. Two or three tails gives a line with a break in the middle, thus: three heads gives an unbroken line. The six lines, placed on top of one another, form a "hexagram":

The above hexagram is number 58, "The Joyous – Lake", with a "Judgement:": "The Joyous, Success – Perseverance is favourable." But from the logical point of view it is obviously impossible to explain how throwing down coins at random can provide an answer – even if the question has been very clearly and precisely formulated in the mind before the coins are thrown.

The experience of Rebecca West can provide a glimmering of an answer. She was looking for a particular passage. We may assume that some unconscious faculty of "extra-sensory perception" guided her to the right place before she began to speak to the librarian, and then guided her hand as she casually reached out. But could it also cause the book to open in the right place? This would seem to require something more than "ESP", something for which Horace Walpole coined the word "serendipity", "the faculty of making happy and unexpected discoveries by chance". And what of the "chance" that caused the librarian to be standing in the right place at that moment? We have here such a complex situation that it is difficult to conceive of some purely "passive" faculty – a kind of intuition – capable of accounting for it. Unless we wish to fall back on "coincidence", we have to think in terms of some faculty capable to some extent of "engineering" a situation as well as merely taking advantage of it.

And the use of the *I Ching* also seems to presuppose the use of such a faculty in causing the coins to fall in a certain order.

For most of his life Jung was unwilling even to conceive of such a possibility – at least publicly. (He was, in fact, using the *I Ching* as an oracle from the early 1920s.)

In 1944, when he was sixty-eight years old, Jung slipped on an icy road and broke his ankle; this led to a severe heart attack. While hovering between life and death, Jung experienced curious visions, in one of which he was hovering above the earth, out in space, then saw a kind of Hindu temple inside a meteor. "Night after night I floated in a state of purest bliss." He was convinced that if he recovered his doctor would have to die – and in fact the doctor died as Jung started to recover. The result of these strange experiences was that Jung ceased to be concerned about whether his contemporaries regarded him as a mystic rather than a scientist, and he ceased to make a secret of his lifelong interest in "the occult". In 1949 he wrote his influential introduction to Richard Wilhelm's edition of the *I Ching*, in which he speaks about the "acausal connecting principle" called synchronicity; in the following year he wrote his paper *On Synchronicity*, later expanded into a book. Unfortunately, Jung's fundamental premise in both these seminal works is basically nonsensical. Western science, he says, is based on the principle of causality. But modern physics is shaking this principle to its foundations; we now know that natural laws are merely statistical truths, and that therefore we must allow for exceptions. This is, of course, untrue. The philosopher Hume had argued that causality is not a basic law of the universe; a pan of water usually boils when we put it on a fire, but it *might* freeze. Kant later used this argument to demonstrate that the stuff of the universe is basically "mental". We can now see that these arguments were fallacious. It is true that a pan of water might freeze when placed on a fire, if the atmospheric pressure were suddenly increased a thousandfold. But this would not be a defiance of the law of causality, merely a change in some of the basic conditions of the experiment. And by the same argument, we can see that modern physics has *not* demonstrated that the laws of nature are "statistical", and that once in a billion times they might be "broken". A law of nature cannot be broken except for some very good "legal" reason.

So Jung's talk about an "acausal connecting principle" may be dismissed as verbal mystification, designed to throw dust in the eyes of scientists who would otherwise accuse him of becoming superstitious in his old age. The example Jung gives of synchronicity makes this clear. He tells how, on 1 April 1949, they had fish for lunch, and someone mentioned the custom of making an "April fish" (i.e. April fool) of someone. In the afternoon a patient showed him pictures of fish which she had painted. In the evening he was shown a piece of embroidery with fish-like monsters on it. The next morning another patient told him a dream of a fish. At this time Jung was studying the fish symbol in history, and before this string of coincidences began had made a note of a Latin quotation about fish. It is, says Jung, very natural to feel that this is a case of "meaningful coincidence" – i.e. that there is an "a causal connection". But if the coincidence is "meaningful", then there must be a causal connection – even if (as Jung is implying) it is not one that would be recognized by science. Jung is in fact suggesting that there is some hidden connection between the mind and nature.

Jung was not the first to consider this possibility. The Austrian biologist Paul Kammerer – who committed suicide after being accused of faking some of his experiments – was fascinated by odd coincidences, and wrote a book, *The Law of Series*, about it. The book contains a hundred samples of coincidence. For example, in 1915 his wife was reading about a character called Mrs Rohan in a novel; on the tram soon after she saw a man who resembled her friend Prince Rohan; that evening Prince Rohan dropped in to see them. In the tram she had heard someone ask the man who looked like Rohan whether he knew the village of Weissenbach on Lake Attersee; when she got off the tram she walked into a delicatessen shop, and the assistant asked her if she knew Weissenbach on Lake Attersee . . .

Kammerer's theory was that events *do* happen in "clusters", which are natural but not "causal". He thought of it as some unknown mathematical law – a "law of seriality". In short, "absurd" coincidences *are* a law of nature. He spent his days carefully noting all kinds of things – the age, sex and dress of people walking past him in a park or sitting on a tram – and observed the typical "clustering".

Jung offers one of the most amusing examples of "clustering" in his book on synchronicity – it was originally told by the scientist Camille Flammarion in his book *The Unknown*. The poet Emile Deschamps was given a piece of plum pudding by a certain M. Fortgibu when he was at boarding-school – the dish was then almost unknown in France, but Fortgibu had just returned from England. Ten years later Deschamps saw plum pudding in the window of a Paris restaurant and went in to ask if he could have some. He was told that unfortunately the pudding had been ordered by someone else – M. Fortgibu, who was sitting there, and who offered to share it. Years later he attended a party at which there was to be plum pudding, and he told the story about M. Fortgibu. As they sat eating plum pudding the door opened and a servant announced "Monsieur Fortgibu." In walked Fortgibu, who had been invited to another apartment in the same building, and had mistaken the door.

This seems to be a good example of Kammerer's seriality; if there is any "meaning" in the coincidence, it is not apparent. But another example given by Flammarion is a different matter. When he was writing a book a gust of wind carried the pages out of the window;

at the same moment it began to rain. He decided there would be no point in going to get them. A few days later the chapter arrived from his printer. It seemed the porter of the printing office had walked past, seen the pages on the ground, and assumed he had dropped them himself; so he gathered them together, sorted them, and delivered them to the printer. What was the subject of the chapter? The wind . . .

So it would seem there are two types of coincidence: serial "clusterings", which are purely "mechanical", and synchronicities, which might seem to imply that the mind itself has been able to influence the laws of nature – as when Rebecca West snatched the book at random off the shelf.

Koestler gives an even stranger example of synchronicity. The writer Pearl Binder was planning a satirical novel in association with two collaborators. They invented a situation in which camps for the homeless had been set up in Hyde Park. They decided to have a refugee Viennese professor, a brokendown old man with a Hungarian-sounding name – such as Horvath-Nadoly. Two days later they read in the newspaper that a homeless foreign old man had been found wandering alone at night in Hyde Park, and had given his name as Horvath-Nadoly. Here all three collaborators had contributed to the impossible coincidence. So if it is to be regarded as "meaningful" rather than an example of "serial clustering", then it has to be supposed that all three participated in some odd form of telepathy and/or precognition; i.e. that called upon to "invent" a situation at random, their unconscious minds preferred to cheat by supplying them with details about a real person – just as, asked to invent a name on the spur of the moment, we shall probably choose a name we have just seen or heard . . .

This "unconscious" explanation – preferred by Jung – can explain dozens of curious coincidences involving literature. In 1898 a novelist named Morgan Robertson wrote a book about a ship called the *Titan*, "the safest vessel in the world", which hit an iceberg on her maiden voyage across the Atlantic; fourteen years later his story came to life in the tragic maiden voyage of the *Titanic*. Moreover, the editor W.T. Stead had written a story about a ship that sank, and concluded: "This is exactly what might take place, and what will take place, if liners are sent to sea short of boats." Like the liner in Morgan Robertson's novel, the *Titanic* did *not* have enough boats. And W.T. Stead was one of those who drowned.

In 1885 a playwright named Arthur Law wrote a play about a man called Robert Golding, the sole survivor of the shipwreck of a vessel called the *Caroline*. A few days after it was staged, Law read an account of the sinking of a ship called the *Caroline*; the sole survivor was called Robert Golding.

In 1972 a writer named James Rusk published a pornographic novel called *Black Abductor* under a pseudonym; its plot was so similar to the true story of the kidnapping of heiress Patty Hearst in 1974 by the "Symbionese Liberation Army" – even to the name of the victim, Patricia – that the FBI later interrogated Rusk to find if he had been involved in the kidnapping plot. He had not; it was again "pure coincidence".

In the month preceding the Allied invasion of Normandy – D-Day – the *Daily Telegraph* crossword puzzle gave most of the codewords for the operation: Utah, Mulberry, Neptune and Overlord (the last being the name of the whole operation). M15 was called to investigate, but found that the compiler of the crosswords was a schoolmaster named Dawe who had no idea of how the words had come into his head.

To explain "synchronistic" events, Jung was inclined to refer to a phrase of the French psychologist Pierre Janet, *abaissement du niveau mental*, "lowering of the mental threshold", by which Janet meant a certain lowering of the vital forces – such as we experience when we are tired or discouraged and which is the precondition for neurosis. Jung believed that when the mental threshold is lowered "the tone of the unconscious is heightened, thereby creating a gradient for the unconscious to flow towards the conscious". The conscious then comes under the influence of what Jung calls the "archetypes" or "primordial images". These images belong to the "collective unconscious", and might be – for example – of a "great mother", a hero-god, a devil-figure, or an image of incarnate wisdom. Jung thought that when the archetype is activated odd coincidences are likely to happen.

Jung worked out his idea of synchronicity with the aid of the physicist Wolfgang Pauli. Pauli himself seemed to have some odd power of causing coincidences. Whenever he touched some piece of experimental apparatus it tended to break. One day in Göttingen a complicated apparatus for studying atomic events collapsed without warning, and Professor J. Franck is said to have remarked: "Pauli must be around somewhere." He wrote to Pauli, and received a reply saying that at the time of the accident his train had been standing in the station at Göttingen, on its way to Copenhagen. Pauli, understandably, was intrigued by Jung's ideas about synchronicity, and Jung's book on the subject was published together with a paper by Pauli on archetypal ideas in the work of Kepler – Kepler had apparently stumbled on the idea of archetypes three centuries earlier, although he meant something closer to Plato's "ideas". Pauli had created a hypothesis called "the exclusion principle", which says that only one electron at a time can occupy any "planetary orbit" inside an atom. He gave no physical reason for this notion; it simply seemed to him to have a pleasing mathematical symmetry, rather like Avogadro's hypothesis that equal volumes of gases will have equal numbers of molecules. In his own essay on Kepler in *The Encyclopedia of Philosophy*, Koestler tried to show that Kepler had arrived at his correct results about the solar system through completely nonsensical ideas about the Blessed Trinity and other such notions, the implication being that creative minds have some instinct or intuition that *shows* them scientific truths, on some principle of symmetry or beauty, rather than through logical reasoning. And this in itself implies that there is some strange basic affinity between mind and nature, and that mind is not some accidental product that has no "right" to be in the universe. It was this intuition that drew Jung and Pauli together.

More to the point is a passage in the writing of the medieval "magician" Albertus Magnus:

> A certain power to alter things indwells in the human soul and subordinates the other things to her, particularly when she is swept into a great excess of love or hate or the like. When therefore the soul of man falls into a great excess of any passion, it can be proved by experiment that the [excess] binds things together [magically] and alters them in the way it wants. Whoever would learn the secret of doing and undoing these things must know that everyone can influence everything magically if he falls into a great excess.

That is to say, a psychological state can somehow affect the physical world. But Albertus's "great excess" is clearly the opposite of Jung's "lowering of the mental threshold". One is a lowering of vitality, the other an intensification of it.

Some of the concepts of "split-brain physiology" – a science developed after Jung's death in 1961 – may be able to throw a useful light on these problems. The brain is divided into two hemispheres, rather like a walnut. Brain physiology has established that the left cerebral hemisphere is concerned with our conscious objectives – language, logic, calculation – while the right deals with intuition, pattern-recognition and insight. The remarkable discovery made by Roger Sperry was that when the bridge of nerves – called the corpus callosum – which connects the two halves is severed to prevent epilepsy the patient turns into two people. One split-brain patient tried to hit his wife with one hand while the other held it back. The person I call "me" lives in the left hemisphere; the person who lives in the other half – the "intuitive self" – is a stranger. When a female patient was shown an indecent picture with her right brain, she blushed; asked why she was blushing, she replied: "I don't know."

The right-brain "stranger" is an artist; the left-brain "me" is a scientist. There is some interesting evidence that it is this right-brain "stranger" who is involved in so-called "extra-sensory perception" – telepathy, dowsing, "second sight" – and that his main problem is somehow to communicate the things he knows to the logical self, which is too preoccupied in its own practical purposes to pay attention to the "still, small voice" of the "other self".

The "stranger" can at times "take over". When the English boxer Freddie Mills fought Gus Lesnevitch in 1946 he was knocked down in the second round and concussed. He remembered nothing more until he heard the referee announcing the tenth round. But in the intervening seven rounds he had boxed brilliantly against the much heavier Lesnevitch, and was ahead on points. As soon as he "recovered" consciousness he began to lose. His "other self" had taken over when he was knocked down in the second round. Here is an example where a "lowering of the mental threshold" produced positive results.

If, then, we credit the "other person" with some kind of "extra-sensory perception", it would be possible to explain such phenomena as the activities of "the library angel" – for example, how Rebecca West located the trial she was looking for by reaching out casually. It knows where the trial is located, but it cannot communicate its knowledge to the left brain, which is obsessively searching through the catalogues. Then a librarian approaches, and it sees its chance as he stops near the book. She is prompted to go and complain to the librarian – a relatively easy task, since she is seething with exasperation – and then the "other self" reaches out for the book and, with that intuitive skill that we see in great sportsmen, opens it at the right place . . . (It would be interesting to know if Rebecca West reached out with her left hand – for the left side of the body is controlled by the right brain, and vice versa.)

And how does the ESP hypothesis apply to another story told by Rebecca West and quoted by Koestler? Again she was in the London Library, and had asked an assistant for Gounod's Memoirs. As she was waiting she was approached by an American who had recognized her, and who wanted to know if it was true that she possessed some lithographs by the artist Delpeche. She said she did, and they were still talking when the assistant returned with the book. She opened it casually, and found herself looking at a passage in which Gounod describes how kind Delpeche had been to his mother.

Now here, we can see, the chain of coincidences had been set in motion – by her request for the book – before the stranger came and asked her about Delpeche; so we cannot accuse her "other self" of engineering the whole situation. What we *can* suppose is that the "other self" was somehow aware that the Gounod Memoirs contained a reference to the artist they were speaking about at that very moment, and drew her attention to it by causing her to open the book in the right place . . .

Why? One possible answer is self-evident. Modern man has become a "split-brainer"; for the most part, he lives in the left brain.

This means that he is only aware of *half* his identity. Whenever he is reminded of that other half – for example, when music or poetry produce a sudden "warm glow", or when some smell reminds him vividly of childhood – he experiences the strange sense of wild elation that G.K. Chesterton called "absurd good news". The more he feels "trapped" in his left-brain self by fatigue, discouragement, foreboding – the more he actually cuts himself off from that deep inner sense of purpose and well-being. If he had some instant method of re-establishing contact with this inner power – Abraham Maslow called such contacts "peak experiences" – his life would be transformed. It must be irritating for that "other self" to see the left-brain self plunging itself into states of gloom and boredom that are completely unnecessary, and so wasting its life – *both* their lives. So, as a fruitful hypothesis, we might regard "synchronicities" – like the one involving Gounod's Memoirs – as attempts by the "other self" to remind the left-brain personality of its existence, and to rescue it from its sense of "contingency" – the feeling that Proust describes, of feeling "mediocre, accidental, mortal".

There is, unfortunately, another type of synchronicity that cannot be explained on the ESP hypothesis and this is the very type that Jung originally set out to explain. ESP cannot explain how the *I Ching* could produce a "meaningful" answer to a question (if, of course, it actually does so). Common sense tells us that the throwing down of coins can only produce a chance result, *unless* the coins are somehow "interfered with" as they fall. The Chinese believe that the *I Ching* is some kind of living entity – presumably a supernatural one – and we may assume that this entity answers the question by causing the coins to fall in a certain way. The Western psychologist, rejecting the supernatural explanation, can only fall back on the notion that the unconscious mind – the "other self" – can somehow influence the fall of the coins by some form of psychokinesis, "mind over matter". And while this may be more or less satisfactory in explaining how the *I Ching* works, it still fails to explain, for example, the fish synchronicities that Jung found so intriguing: the Latin inscription about a fish, the mention of "April fish", the patient who had painted fish, the embroidery with fish-like monsters, the other patient with the dream of a fish. Psychokinesis can hardly explain this series of coincidences.

This is true also of a type of "cluster" coincidence described by Koestler. A doctor wrote to him commenting that if a patient with some rare and unusual complaint turns up at a surgery, he could be fairly certain that a similar case would turn up later during the same surgery, and that if a patient with a certain name – say, Donnell – should ring him, then another patient called Donnell would be almost certain to turn up at the surgery. Another letter mentioned similar "clusters" of various types: a dentist noting how often he had "runs" of patients with the same kind of extraction problem, an eye specialist noting how often he had runs of patients with the same eye problem, even a typewriter-repairer noticing how often he had runs of the same make of machine for repair, or runs of different machines with the identical problem.

Obviously there can be no "explanation" for such oddities unless a mathematician discovers some completely new law of seriality. But again, we can note that such coincidences tend to produce in us much the same effect as more personal experiences of "serendipity" – a sense that perhaps the universe *is* less meaningless and inscrutable than we assume. And this – as every reader of Jung's book will agree – is what Jung felt about synchronicity. In fact, a hostile critic might object that Jung – who was the son of a parson – is trying to introduce God by the back door. All his attempts to argue in favour of a "scientific" principle of synchronicity are unconvincing because the words "acausal connecting principle" involve a contradiction in terms – unless, that is, he is willing to admit that it is "pure chance", in which case he has undermined his own argument. A coincidence is either "meaningful" or it is not; and if it is meaningful, then it is not a coincidence.

In the last analysis, accepting or rejecting "synchronicity" is a matter of individual temperament. I personally am inclined to accept it because my own experience of "coincidences" inclines me to the belief that they *are* often "meaningful". On the morning when I was about to begin the article on Joan of Arc (*see* page 29), I noticed in my library a bound series of the *International History Magazine*, and decided to spend half an hour looking through it in case it contained material for this book. I opened the first volume at random, and found myself looking at an article on Joan of Arc, whose editorial introduction raised the question of whether she survived her "execution". In fact, the article proved to be useless: the author made no mention of the controversy about the Dame des Armoires. Does this not in itself suggest that the coincidence was "non-meaningful"? Not necessarily. I have cited elsewhere Jacquès Vallee's interesting theory about synchronicity. When he was researching a cult that used the name of the prophet Melchizedek he spent a great deal of time looking up every reference to Melchizedek he could find. In Los Angeles he asked a woman taxi-driver for a receipt: it was signed M. Melchizedek. A check with the Los Angeles telephone directory revealed that there was only one Melchizedek in the whole area.

Vallee points out that there are two ways in which a librarian can store information. One is to place it in alphabetical order on shelves. But computer scientists have discovered that there is a simpler and quicker method. They prefer to store information as it arrives – the equivalent of a librarian putting books on the shelves side by side as they come into the library – and having a keyword or algorithm that will retrieve it. (In a library, the equivalent might be as follows:

as each new book comes into the library, some kind of "beeping" mechanism is attached to its spine; each beeper is adjusted to respond to a certain number code, like a telephone. When the librarian requires a certain book, he dials the number on his pocket beeper, and then goes straight to the book that is beeping.)

Vallee suggests that "the world might be organized more like a randomized data base than a sequential library". It was as if he had stuck on the universal notice-board a note saying; "Wanted, Melchidezeks", and some earnest librarian had said: "How about this one?" "No, that's no good – that's just a taxi driver . . ."

This picture, like Jung's, suggests that there *is* some mutual interaction between the mind and the universe, and that the key to "retrieving information" is to be in the right state of mind: a state of deep interest or excitement: Albertus Magnus's "excess of passion".

Another personal example. I was led to write the present article partly by the "Joan of Arc coincidence", partly by another coincidence that happened a day or two later. I had received in the post a copy of the biography of the American novelist Ayn Rand by Barbara Branden. I was reading this in bed the next day when the post arrived. This included a paperback novel sent to me by an American reader, with a letter enclosed. The letter began: "In Barbara Branden's recent biography of Ayn Rand you are mentioned in a footnote . . ."

Half an hour later, about to go to my study, I noticed a newspaper clipping that my wife had left for me outside the door. I asked her "What's this?", and she said: "It's an article that mentions Hemingway – I thought it might interest you." In fact it was the article about coincidence and lost manuscripts by Godfrey Smith, quoted at the beginning of the present article.

As it happened, I decided not to write the coincidence article immediately; I had planned first of all to write a piece about the disappearance of Mary Rogers. I took Poe's short stories from my bookshelf and opened it at 'The Mystery of Marie Roget'. The opening paragraph reads: 'There are few persons, even among the calmest thinkers, who have not occasionally been startled into a vague yet thrilling half-credence in the supernatural, by *coincidences* of so seemingly marvellous a character that, as mere coincidences, the intellect has been unable to receive them.' It confirmed my decision to write this article.

As if to underline this point, a further coincidence occurred after I had written the preceding sentence, which happened to be at the end of a day's work. About to leave my study, I noticed among an untidy pile of books a title I had no recollection of seeing before: *You Are Sentenced to Life* by W.D. Chesney, published by a private press in California; it was a book about life after death. I had obviously bought it a long time ago and had never – as far as I know – even glanced into it. I decided it was time to remedy this. Later in the afternoon, I spent an hour glancing through it, reading a section here and there; then, just before closing it, I decided to glance at the very end. The top of the last page was headed: ORDER OF MELCHIZEDEK, and was a reprint of a letter from Grace Hooper Pettipher, 'Instructor within the Order of Melchizedek', requesting a copy of another book published by the same press. I doubt whether, in two thousand or so books in my study, there is another reference to Melchizedek; but I had to stumble upon this one after writing about Melchizedek in an article about synchronicity.

It is my own experience that coincidences like this seem to happen when I am in 'good form' – when I am feeling alert, cheerful and optimistic, and not when I am feeling tired, bored or gloomy. This leads me to formulate my own hypothesis about synchronicity as follows. As a writer, I am at my best when I feel alert and purposeful; at these times I feel a sense of 'hidden meanings' lurking behind the apparently impassive face of everyday reality. But this is not true only for writers; it applies to all human beings. We are *all* at our best when the imagination is awake, and we can sense the presence of that 'other self', the intuitive part of us. When we are tired or discouraged we feel 'stranded' in left-brain consciousness. We feel, as William James says, that 'our fires are damped, our draughts are checked'. We can be jarred out of this state by a sudden crisis, or any pleasant stimulus, but more often than not these fail to present themselves. It must be irritating for 'the other self' to find its partner so dull and sluggish, allowing valuable time and opportunity to leak away by default. A 'synchronicity' can snap us into a sudden state of alertness and awareness. And if the 'other self' can, by the use of its peculiar powers, bring about a synchronicity, then there is still time to prevent us from wasting yet another day of our brief lives.

The Melchizedek coincidence seems to me of another kind, designed to confirm that we are on 'the right track'. When in the late 1960s I first turned my attention to the field of the paranormal, and began writing a book called *The Occult*, such coincidences became commonplace. I have described in that book how I needed a reference from some alchemical text. I knew that the book containing the reference was in one of the books facing my desk; but it was towards the end of the day, and I was feeling tired and lazy. Besides, I had forgotten where to find the reference, and my heart sank at the prospect of a fruitless search through half a dozen volumes . . . Conscience finally triumphed and I heaved myself to my feet, crossed the room, and took a book off the shelf. As I did so the next book fell off the shelf; it landed on the floor, open, at the passage I was looking for. And I felt that curious flash of gratitude and delight that we always experience in these moments, as if some invisible guardian angel has politely tendered his help.

Now, a book falling off a shelf and opening at the right page is obviously closer to the procedure of the *I Ching* than, for example, Mrs Kammerer's chain of coincidences about Prince Rohan and Lake Attersee, or Flammarion's story about M. Fortgibu. Yet it seems equally obvious that, in a basic sense, there is a family resemblance between them. The problem arises if we attempt some kind of classification. When Rebecca West reached out and found the right book, this sounds like ESP. But a book falling off a shelf at the right page obviously involves some extra element besides ESP – something closer to psychokinesis. But neither ESP nor psychokinesis can begin to explain Mrs Kammerer's chain of coincidences; and in the case of M. Fortgibu and the plum pudding, it becomes absurd. We seem to be dealing with the mysterious entity that Charles Fort called 'the cosmic joker', and any respectable parapsychologist is bound to draw back in horror at the very idea.

But even if synchronicity declines to fit into any of our scientific theories, this is no reason to refuse to believe in its existence. Science still has no idea of how or why the universe began, of the nature of time, or of what lies beyond the outermost limit of the stars. In fact, science continues to use terms like space, time and motion *as if* they were comprehensible to the human intellect; no one accuses Cantor of being an occultist or mystic because he devised a mathematics of infinity. Science continues to grow and develop in spite of its uneasy metaphysical foundations.

From the purely practical point of view, the chief problem of human existence is individual lack of purpose. In those curious moments of relaxation or sudden happiness that we all experience at intervals, we can *see* that it is stupid to lose purpose and direction, and that if only we could learn to summon this insight *at will*, this fatal tendency to forgetfulness could be permanently eradicated, and life would be transformed. It is obvious in such moments that if we could train ourselves to behave *as if* there were hidden meanings lurking behind the blank face of the present, the problem would be solved. If 'synchronicities' can produce that sense of meaning and purpose, then it is obviously sensible for us to behave *as if* they were meaningful coincidences, and to ignore the question of their scientific validity.

SPONTANEOUS HUMAN COMBUSTION

O n the evening of Sunday 1 July, 1951 Mrs Mary Reeser, aged seventy-seven, seemed slightly depressed as she sat in her overstuffed armchair and smoked a cigarette. At about 9 p.m. her landlady, Mrs Pansy Carpenter, called in to say goodnight. Mrs Reeser showed no disposition to go to bed yet; it was a hot evening in St Petersburg, Florida.

At five the next morning, Mrs Carpenter awoke to a smell of smoke; assuming it was a water pump that had been overheating, she went to the garage and turned it off. She was awakened again at eight by a telegraph boy with a telegram for Mrs Reeser; Mrs Carpenter signed for it and took it up to Mrs Reeser's room. To her surprise, the doorknob was hot. She shouted for help, and two decorators working across the street came in. One of them placed a cloth over the doorknob and turned it; a blast of hot air met him as the door opened. Yet the place seemed empty, and at first they could see no sign of fire. Then they noticed a blackened circle on the carpet where the armchair had stood. Only a few springs now remained. In the midst of them there was a human skull, "charred to the size of a baseball", and a fragment of liver attached to a backbone. There was also a foot encased in a satin slipper; it had been burnt down to the ankle.

Mrs Reeser was a victim of a baffling phenomenon called spontaneous human combustion; there are hundreds of recorded cases. Yet in their standard textbook *Forensic Medicine*, Drs S.A. Smith and F.S. Fiddes assert flatly: "Spontaneous combustion of the human body cannot occur, and no good purpose can be served by discussing it." This is a typical example of the kind of wishful thinking in which scientists are prone to indulge when they confront a fact that falls outside the range of their experience. In the same way the great chemist Lavoisier denied the possibility of meteorites.

The example of Mrs Reeser is worth citing because it is mentioned by Professor John Taylor in his book *Science and the Supernatural*, a book whose chief purpose is to debunk the whole idea of the "paranormal", which, according to Professor Taylor, tends to "crumble to nothing" as it is scientifically appraised. Yet he then proceeds to admit that there are instances that seem "reasonably well validated", and proceeds to cite the case of Mrs Reeser.

Twenty-nine years later, in October 1980, a case of spontaneous combustion was observed at close quarters when a naval airwoman named Jeanna Winchester was driving with a friend, Leslie Scott, along Seaboard Avenue in Jacksonville, Florida. Suddenly, Jeanna Winchester burst into yellow flames, and screamed, "Get me out of here." Her companion tried to beat out the flames with her hands,

Drawing by Phiz for Dicken's *Bleak House* showing an act of spontaneous human combustion.

and the car ran into a telegraph pole. When Jeanna Winchester was examined it was found that twenty per cent of her body was covered with burns. But Jeanna Winchester survived.

Michael Harrison's book on spontaneous combustion, *Fire From Heaven* (1976), cites dozens of cases; they make it clear that the chief mystery of spontaneous combustion is that it seldom spreads beyond the person concerned. On Whit Monday 1725, in Rheims, Nicole Millet, the wife of the landlord of the Lion d'Or, was found burnt to death in an *unburnt* armchair, and her husband was accused of her murder. But a young surgeon, Claude-Nicholas Le Cat, succeeded in persuading the court that spontaneous human combustion *does* occur, and Millet was acquitted – the verdict was that his wife had died "by a visitation of God". The case inspired a Frenchman called Jonas Dupont to gather together all the evidence he could find for spontaneous combustion, which he published in a book *De Incendiis Corporis Humani Spontaneis*, printed in Leyden in 1763.

Another famous case of this period was that of Countess Cornelia di Bandi, of Cesena, aged sixty-two, who was found on the floor of her bedroom by her maid. Her stockinged legs were untouched, and between them lay her head, half burnt. The rest of the body was reduced to ashes, and the air was full of floating soot. The bed was undamaged and the sheets had been thrown back, as if she had got out – perhaps to open a window – and then been quickly consumed as she stood upright, so the head had fallen between the legs. Unlike the wife of innkeeper Millet, the countess had not been a heavy drinker. (One of the most popular theories of spontaneous combustion at this period was that it was due to large quantities of alcohol in the body.)

Two nineteenth-century novelists used spontaneous combustion to dispose of unwanted characters. Captain Marryat borrowed details from a *Times* report of 1832 to describe the death of the mother of his hero Jacob Faithful (in the novel of the same name), who is reduced to "a sort of unctuous pitchy cinder" in her bed. Twenty years later, in 1852, Dickens put an end to his drunken rag-and-bone dealer Krook in *Bleak House* by means of spontaneous combustion – Krook is charred to a cinder that looks like a burnt log. G.H. Lewes, George Eliot's lover, took issue with Dickens and declared that spontaneous combustion was impossible, so in his preface to *Bleak House* Dickens contradicts Lewes and cites thirty examples from press reports. Yet at the end of his article on Krook in *The Dickens Encyclopedia* (1924), Arthur L. Hayward states dogmatically: "The possibility of spontaneous combustion in human beings has been finally disproved." He fails to explain what experiments have "finally disproved" it.

Harrison's book, which gathers together the result of many studies, leaves no possible doubt of the reality of spontaneous

The remains of Dr John Irving Bentley, a possible victim of spontaneous human combustion in northern Pennsylvania, USA, on 5 december 1966. *Larry E Arnold/Fortean Picture Library.*

combustion. But what causes it? At present it must be confessed that the phenomenon baffles medical knowledge. But Harrison offers some interesting clues. He speaks of the researches of an American doctor, Mayne R. Coe junior, who was interested in the subject of telekinesis – mind over matter. Coe was able to move aluminium strips pivoted on the points of needles by moving his hand over them – this was obviously due to some natural physical "magnetism". He began various yoga exercises in an attempt to develop his bioelectricity; sitting one day in an easy-chair, he felt a powerful current passing downward from his head throughout his body; he thought it was of high voltage but low amperage. He suspended a cardboard box from the ceiling on a length of string, and found that he could cause it to move from a distance – when the room was dry, from as much as eight feet. He then charged his body with 35,000 volts DC, using an electric current, and found that he could move the box in exactly the same way. This seemed to prove that he was in fact generating a high voltage current with his mental exercises. He also went up in an aeroplane to an altitude of 21,000 feet, where the air was extremely dry, and produced electric sparks after he had charged his body to 35,000 volts. Coe theorized that this could explain the phenomenon of levitation – when the yogi's body floats off the ground – with the positively charged human body repelling the negatively charged earth.

Harrison also cites cases of human "batteries" and magnets people (usually children) who have developed a powerful electric charge. In 1877 Caroline Clare of London, Ontario, turned into a human magnet, who attracted metal objects and could give a powerful electric shock to as many as twenty people holding hands. She was suffering from adolescent depressions at the time. Frank McKinistry of Joplin, Missouri, developed a magnetic force which caused his feet to stick to the earth. In 1895 fourteen-year-old Jennie Morgan of Sedalia, Missouri, generated a charge sufficient to knock a grown man on his back, and when she touched a pump handle sparks flew from her fingertips. It is also worth noting that many teenagers who became the focus of "poltergeist effects" developed magnetic or electrical properties; in 1846 a French girl named Angélique Cottin became a kind of human electric battery; objects that touched her flew off violently, and a heavy oak loom began to dance when she came near it. On the other hand, Esther Cox, the "focus" of the disturbances at Great Amherst in Nova Scotia, developed a magnetism that made cutlery fly to her and stick fast. It seems that there must be two kinds of charges, positive and negative.

According to Dr Coe, each human muscle cell is a battery, and a cubic inch could develop 400,000 volts. (The inventor Nicola Tesla used to demonstrate that the human body can take immense electrical charges – enough to light up neon tubes – provided the amperage is kept very low.)

But this seems unlikely to explain spontaneous combustion: the whole point of Tesla's experiments was that he did *not* burst into flame. It is high amperage that can cause "burn-ups". (If two 12-volt car batteries are connected by thin wire, the wire will melt; even thick wire becomes hot.) And this could begin to explain why the surroundings of the victim of spontaneous combustion are undamaged; they are non-conductors.

Victims of spontaneous combustion tend to be the old and the young. On 27 August 1938, the twenty-two-year-old Phyllis Newcombe was dancing vigorously in Chelmsford, Essex, when her body glowed with a blue light which turned into flames; she died within minutes. In October of the same year a girl called Maybelle Andrews was dancing in a Soho nightclub with her boyfriend, Billy Clifford, when flames erupted from her back, chest and shoulders. Her boyfriend, who was badly burned trying to put her out, said that there were no flames in the room – the flames seemed to come from the girl herself. She died on the way to hospital. In such cases it seems just conceivable that the activity of dancing built up some kind of static electricity. Michael Harrison even points out that "ritual dancing" is used by primitive tribes to build up emotional tension in religious ceremonies, and suggests that this is what has happened here.

Michael Harrison also points out some curious geographical links. On 13 March 1966 three men were "spontaneously combusted" at the same time. John Greeley, helmsman of the SS *Ulrich*, was burnt to a cinder some miles west of Land's End; George Turner, a lorry-driver, was found burnt at the wheel of his lorry at Upton-by-Chester – the lorry overturned in a ditch; in Nijmegen, Holland, eighteen-year-old Willem ten Bruik died at the wheel of his car. As usual in such cases, the surroundings of all three were undamaged. Harrison points out that the three men were at the points of an equilateral triangle whose sides were 340 miles long. Is it conceivable that the earth itself discharged energy in a triangular pattern?

Another investigator, Larry Arnold, put forward his own theory in the magazine *Frontiers of Science* (January 1982): that so-called "ley lines" – lines of "earth force" may be involved. The man who "discovered" ley lines, Alfred Watkins, noted how frequently places called "Brent" occur on them (brent being an old English form of "burnt"). Other "ley-hunters" have suggested that megalithic stone circles are placed at crucial points on ley lines – often at crossing-points of several leys. It is again interesting to note how many stone circles are associated with the idea of dancing – for example, the Merry Maidens in Cornwall; Stonehenge itself was known as "the Giants' Dance". It has been suggested that ritual dances occurred at these sites, so that the dancers would somehow interact with the earth energy (or "telluric force").

Larry Arnold drew a dozen or so major leys on a map of England, then set out to find if they were associated with mystery fires. He claims that one 400-mile-long "fire-leyne" (as he calls them) passed through five towns where ten mysterious blazes had concurred. He also notes several cases of spontaneous combustion occurring on this "leyne". He cites four cases which occurred on it between 1852 and 1908.

Harrison believes that spontaneous combustion is basically a "mental freak", where the mind somehow influences the body to build up immense charges. The answer could lie in either of the two theories, or in a combination of the two.

THE GREAT TUNGUSKA EXPLOSION

On June 1908 the inhabitants of Nizhne-Karelinsk, a small village in central Siberia, saw a bluish-white streak of fire cut vertically across the sky to the northwest. What began as a bright point of light lengthened over a period of ten minutes until it seemed to split the sky in two. When it reached the ground it shattered to form a monstrous cloud of black smoke. Seconds later there was a terrific roaring detonation that made the buildings tremble. Assuming that the Day of Judgment had arrived, many of the villagers fell on their knees. The reaction was not entirely absurd; in fact, they had witnessed the greatest natural disaster in the earth's recorded history. If the object that caused what is now known as "the Great Siberian Explosion" had arrived a few hours earlier or later it might have landed in more heavily populated regions, and caused millions of deaths.

As it later turned out, the village of Nizhne-Karelinsk had been over 200 miles away from the "impact point", and yet the explosion had been enough to shake debris from their roofs. A Trans-Siberian express train stopped because the driver was convinced that it was derailed, and seismographs in the town of Irkutsk indicated a crash of earthquake proportions. Both the train and the town were over 800 miles from the explosion.

Whatever it was that struck the Tunguska region of the Siberian forestland had exploded with a force never before imagined. Its shockwave travelled around the globe twice before it died out, and its general effect on the weather in the northern hemisphere was far-reaching. During the rest of June it was quite possible to read the small print in the London *Times* at midnight. There were photographs of Stockholm taken at 1 o'clock in the morning by natural light, and a photograph of the Russian town of Navrochat taken at midnight looks like a bright summer afternoon.

For some months the world was treated to spectacular dawns

and sunsets, as impressive as those that had been seen after the great Krakatoa eruption in 1883. From this, as well as the various reports of unusual cloud formations over following months, it is fair to guess that the event had thrown a good deal of dust into the atmosphere, as happens with violent volcanic eruptions and, notably, atomic explosions.

Perhaps the strangest aspect of the Great Siberian Explosion was that no one paid much attention to it. Reports of the falling object were published in Siberian newspapers but did not spread any further. Meteorologists speculated about the strange weather, but no one came close to guessing its real cause.

It was not until the Great War had been fought, and the Russian Revolution had overthrown the tsarist regime that the extraordinary events of that June day finally reached the general public. In 1921, as part of Lenin's general plan to place the USSR at the forefront of world science, the Soviet Academy of Sciences commissioned Leonid Kulik to investigate meteorite falls on Soviet territory. It was Kulik who stumbled upon the few brief reports in ten-year-old Siberian newspapers that finally led him to suspect that something extraordinary had happened in central Siberia in the summer of 1908.

Leonid found the reports confusing and contradictory. None of them seemed to agree quite where the object had exploded. Some even claimed that the "meteor" had later been found. But when his researchers began to collect eyewitness reports of the event Kulik became convinced that whatever had exploded in the Tunguska forest was certainly not a normal meteorite.

These reports described how the ground had opened up to release a great pillar of fire and smoke which burned brighter than the sun. Distant huts were blown down and reindeer herds scattered. A man ploughing in an open field felt his shirt burning on his back, and others described being badly sunburnt on one side of the face but not the other. Many people claimed to have been made temporarily deaf by the noise, or to have suffered long-term effects of shock. Yet, almost unbelievably, not a single person had been killed or seriously injured. Whatever it was that produced the explosion had landed in one of the few places on earth where its catastrophic effect was minimized. A few hours later, and it could have obliterated St Petersburg, London or New York. Even if it had landed in the sea, tidal waves might have destroyed whole coastal regions. That day the human race had escaped the greatest disaster in its history, and had not even been aware of it.

Finally Kulik discovered that a local meteorologist had made an estimate of the point of impact, and in 1927 he was given the necessary backing by the Academy of Sciences to find the point where the "great meteorite" had fallen.

The great Siberian forest is one of the least accessible places on earth. Even today it remains largely unexplored, and there are whole areas that have only ever been surveyed from the air. What settlements there are can be found along the banks of its mighty rivers, some of them miles in width. The winters are ferociously cold, and in the summer the ground becomes boggy, and the air is filled with the hum of mosquitoes. Kulik was faced with an almost impossible task: to travel by horse and raft with no idea of exactly where to look or what to look for.

In March 1927 he set off accompanied by two local guides who had witnessed the event, and after many setbacks arrived on the banks of the Mekirta river in April. The Mekirta is the closest river to the impact point, and in 1927 formed a boundary between untouched forest and almost total devastation.

On that first day Kulik stood on a low hill and surveyed the destruction caused by the Tunguska explosion. For as far as he could see to the north – perhaps a dozen miles – there was not one full-grown tree left standing. Every one had been flattened by the blast, and they lay like a slaughtered regiment, all pointing towards him. Yet it was obvious that what he was looking at was only a fraction of the devastation, since all the trees were facing in the same direction as far as the horizon. The blast must have been far greater than even the wildest reports had suggested.

Kulik wanted to explore the devastation; his two guides were terrified, and refused to go on. So Kulik was forced to return with them, and it was not until June that he managed to return with two new companions.

The expedition followed the line of broken trees for several days until they came to a natural amphitheatre in the hills, and pitched camp there. They spent the next few days surveying the surrounding area, and Kulik reached the conclusion that "the cauldron" as he called it, was the centre of the blast. All around, the fallen trees faced away from it, and yet, incredibly, some trees actually remained standing although stripped and charred, at the very centre of the explosion.

The full extent of the desolation was now apparent; from the river to its central point was a distance of thirty-seven miles. So the blast had flattened more than four thousand square miles of forest.

Still working on the supposition that the explosion had been caused by a large meteorite, Kulik began searching the area for its remains. He thought he had achieved his object when he discovered a number of pits filled with water – he naturally assumed that they had been made by fragments of the exploding meteorite. Yet when the holes were drained they were found to be empty. One even had a tree-stump at the bottom, proving it had not been made by a blast.

Kulik was to make four expeditions to the area of the explosion, and until his death he remained convinced that it had been caused by an unusually large meteorite. Yet he never found the iron or rock fragments that would provide him with the evidence he needed. In fact, he never succeeded in proving that anything had even struck the ground. There was evidence of two blast waves – the original explosion and the ballistic wave – and even of brief flash fire; but there was no crater.

The new evidence only deepened the riddle. An aerial survey in 1938 showed that only 770 square miles of forest had been flattened, and that at the very point where the crater should have been the original trees were still standing. That suggested the vagaries of an exploding bomb, rather than that of the impact of a giant meteor – like the one that made the 600-foot-deep crater at Winslow, Arizona.

Even the way that the object fell to earth was disputed. Over seven hundred eyewitnesses claimed that it changed course as it fell, saying that it was originally moving towards Lake Baikal before it swerved. Falling heavenly bodies have never been known to do this, nor is it possible to explain how it could have happened in terms of physical dynamics.

Another curious puzzle about the explosion was its effect on the trees and insect life in the blast area. Trees that had survived the explosion had either stopped growing, or were shooting up at a greatly accelerated rate. Later studies revealed new species of ants and other insects which are peculiar to the Tunguska blast region.

It was not until some years after Kulik's death in a German prisoner-of-war camp that scientists began to see similarities between the Tunguska event and another even more catastrophic explosion: the destruction of Hiroshima and Nagasaki with thermonuclear devices.

Our knowledge of the atom bomb enables us to clear up many of the mysteries that baffled Kulik. The reason there was no crater was that the explosion confirmed this; at both Nagasaki and Hiroshima, buildings directly beneath the blast remained standing, because the blast spread sideways. Genetic mutations in the flora and fauna around the Japanese cities are like those witnessed in Siberia, while blisters found on dogs and reindeer in the Tunguska area can now be recognized as radiation burns.

Atomic explosions produce disturbances in the earth's magnetic field, and even today the area around the Tunguska explosion has been described as "magnetic chaos". It seems clear that an electro-magnetic "hurricane" of incredible strength has ruptured the earth's magnetic field in this area.

Eyewitness accounts of the cloud produced by the explosion again support the view that it was some kind of atomic device; it had the typical shape of the atomic "mushroom cloud". Unfortunately, the one conclusive piece of evidence for the "atom bomb" theory is lacking: by the time the area's radiation levels were tested, more than fifty years later, they were normal.

Later investigators also learned that Kulik had been mistaken in his theory about the water-filled holes; they were not caused by meteorite fragments but by winter ice forcing its way to the surface through expansion, then melting in summer. Kulik's immense labours to drain the holes had been a waste of time.

Unfortunately, none of the new evidence that has been uncovered by Russian – and even American – expeditions has thrown any light on the cause of the explosion. UFO enthusiasts favour the theory that the object was an alien space craft, powered by atomic motors, which went out of control as it struck the earth's atmosphere. It has even been suggested that such a space craft might have headed towards Lake Baikal because it was in need of fresh water to cool its nuclear reactors; before it could reach its objective the reactors superheated and exploded.

The scientific establishment is naturally inclined to discount this theory as pure fantasy. But some of its own hypotheses seem equally fantastic. A.A. Jackson and M.P. Ryan of the University of Texas have suggested that the explosion was caused by a miniature black hole – a kind of whirlpool in space caused by the total collapse of the particles inside the atom. They calculated that their black hole would have passed straight through the earth and come out on the other side, and the Russians were sufficiently impressed by the theory to research local newspapers in Iceland and Newfoundland for June 1980; but there was no sign of the Tunguska-like catastrophe that should have occurred if Jackson and Ryan were correct.

Other American scientists suggested that the explosion was caused by anti-matter, a hypothetical type of matter whose particles contain the opposite electric charge to those of normal matter. In contact with normal matter, anti-matter would explode and simply disappear. Only atomic radiation would be left behind. But there is even less evidence to support this theory than there is for the black-hole explanation.

Slightly more plausible – but still highly improbable – is the theory of the English scientist Frank Whipple that the earth had been struck by a comet. Astronomers still have no idea where comets originate, or how they are formed. The two chief objections to the comet theory are that it would be unlikely to produce a "nuclear" explosion, and that it would have been observed by astronomers long before it reached the earth. Supporters of the comet theory have pointed out that a comet coming in from the direction of the sun might be very hard to detect, and that the explosion of a comet might produce an effect similar to that of solar flares, which produce radio-activity. But none of the 120 observatories questioned by the Russians have any record of a comet on the trajectory of the Tunguska object.

More recently, it has been pointed out that the Tunguska event took place on 30 June and that on that same day each year the earth's orbit crosses that of a meteor stream called Beta Taurids, producing a "meteor shower". If one of these meteors had been exceptionally large, it could have survived burning up in the earth's atmosphere, and as its super-heated exterior reacted against its frozen interior, it would have shattered like molten glass suddenly plunged into freezing water. If this theory is correct, then it seems that Kulik was right after all. But that only reminds us that Kulik was unable to find the slightest shred of evidence for his theory. Eight decades after it took place, it seems increasingly unlikely that the mystery of the Tunguska explosion will ever be solved.

Does the woolly mammoth still wander the Siberian forests? The last examples are generally thought to have died out ten thousand years ago. Their frozen bodies are discovered from time to time, sometimes in almost perfect condition, locked in ice. More often their tusks are uncovered and sold by the Yakuts or other tribes of the north. It has been estimated that up to 100,000 mammoth tusks have been disinterred in the last three hundred years. There is no doubt that the mammoths so recovered died in antiquity. However modern eyewitness accounts of live mammoths continue to surface.

In 1918 an elderly huntsman told the French consul in Vladivostok of the "chestnut-coloured elephants" that he had once tracked. He had come across a huge trampled path running across the forest, and had decided to follow it. After several days he caught sight of one of the animals responsible. His description exactly matched that of a mammoth: larger than a modern elephant (a beast that the huntsman had never seen) and covered in shaggy chestnut hair.

The Soviet Academy of Science treats the sightings of mammoths as genuine evidence, assigning research staff to investigate them. The argument that such beasts could not remain hidden from modern man does not take into account the vast and relatively unexplored areas of Siberia. There are also the many instances of supposedly extinct creatures being found to still exist, merely shying away from man's presence in their territories: the coelacanth, the okapi, the Chacoan pessary . . .

There may yet be many creatures that we have only succeeded in catching in their fossilized form.

VELIKOVSKY'S COMET

W hen the bulky manuscript of *Worlds in Collision* landed on the desk of a New York editor in 1947 its tattered state left no doubt that it had been rejected many times. All the same, the editor was impressed. According to the author, Immanuel Velikovsky, the earth had been almost destroyed about three and a half thousand years ago by a near-collision with a comet; in the earthquakes and volcanic eruptions that followed, cities were wiped out and whole countries laid waste. It was a fascinating and erudite book, and its author – who was apparently a respectable psychiatrist – had the ability to write a clear and vigorous prose.

The editor cautiously recommended it. His superiors were worried; Macmillans was a reputable publisher with a large textbook list; they could not afford to be accused of encouraging the lunatic fringe. So they compromised, and offered Velikovsky a small advance and a contract that gave them the option to publish, but no guarantee that they would do so. A year later they finally decided to go ahead, and *Worlds in Collision* made its belated appearance on 3 April 1950. Within days it had climbed to the top of the best-seller list. When it appeared in England the following September its reputation had preceded it, so that it sold out its first impression even before publication. But by that time Macmillans' doubts had been justified; the denunciations of the book were so violent that they were forced into retreat, and *Worlds in Collision* had to be passed on to another publisher. By then Velikovsky had become one of the most famous and most vilified men in America.

Who was this controversial psychiatrist who also seemed to be an expert on astronomy, geology and world history? Immanuel Velikovsky was a Russian Jew, born in Vitebsk in June 1895, who had studied mathematics in Moscow. He went on to study medicine, qualifying in 1921, then studied psychiatry in Vienna with Freud's pupil Stekel. In 1924 he moved to Palestine to practise, and became increasingly interested in Biblical archaeology. The turning-point in his career was a reading of Freud's *Moses and Monotheism* (1937). In this book Freud proposes that Moses was not a Jew but an Egyptian, and that he was a follower of the monotheistic religion of the Pharaoh Akhnaton, the king who replaced the host of Egyptian gods with one single sun god. Freud proposed that Moses fled from Egypt after the death of Akhnaton (probably murdered) and imposed his religion on the Jews.

The obvious historical objection to this theory is that Moses is supposed to have lived about a century after the death, of Akhnaton; but Freud contested this view, and moved fearlessly into the arena of historical research. Dazzled by his boldness, Velikovsky decided to do the same. His researches into Egyptian, Greek and Near Eastern history soon convinced him that much of the accepted dating is hopelessly wrong. But they led him to an even more unorthodox conclusion: that the pharaoh Akhnaton was none other than the legendary Oedipus of Greek myth, and that the story arose out of the fact that Akhnaton had murdered his father and married his mother.

Velikovsky went on to construct a theory beside which even Freud's heterodox views seemed conservative; that the various events that accompanied the plagues of Egypt – the crossing of the Red Sea, the destruction of the Egyptian armies by floods, the manna that fell from heaven – were the outcome of some great cosmic upheaval. And at this point Velikovsky came across exactly what he was looking for: a papyrus written by an Egyptian sage called Ipuwer, which contained an account of events that sounded strangely like the Bible story in Exodus.

In 1939 Velikovsky moved to the United States, and continued his researches in its libraries. What precisely *was* the "great catastrophe"? The Austrian Hanns Hoerbiger had put forward the theory that the earth has had several moons, and that the collapse of one of these moons on the earth caused the great floods and upheavals recorded in the Bible and in other ancient documents. But Velikovsky came to reject the Hoerbiger theory. There was a far more exciting clue. Before the second millennium BC – and even later – the planet Venus was not grouped by ancient astronomers with the other planets. That might have been because it was so close to the sun that they mistook it for a star – in fact, it is called the morning star. But what if it was because Venus was not in its present position at that time? Velikovsky found tantalizing references in old documents to something that sounded like a near-collision of a comet with the earth. In legends from Greece to Mexico he found suggestions that this catastrophe was somehow linked with Venus. Only one thing puzzled him deeply: that other legends seemed to link the catastrophe with Zeus, the father of the gods, also known as Jupiter. He finally reconciled these stories by reaching the astonishing conclusion that Venus was "born out of" Jupiter – forced out by a gigantic explosion. Venus began as a comet, and passed so close to Mars that it was dragged out of its orbit; then it came close to earth, causing the Biblical catastrophes; then it finally settled down near the sun as the planet Venus.

It sounds like pure lunacy; but Velikovsky argued it with formidable erudition. And, unlike the usual crank, he spent a great deal of time searching for scientific evidence. He needed, for example, a spectroscopic analysis of the atmospheres of Mars and Venus, and he decided to approach the eminent astronomer Harlow Shapley. Shapley had himself become a figure of controversy in 1919 when he announced his conclusion that our solar system is not – as had previously been believed – at the centre of the Milky Way, but somewhere much closer to its edge; perhaps it was the blow to human self-esteem that caused the opposition. At all events, Velikovsky seems to have reasoned that Shapley might be sympathetic to his own heterodox ideas. Shapley was polite, but said he was too busy to read *Worlds in Collision*; he asked a colleague, a sociologist named Horace Kallen, if he would read it first. Kallen did so, and was excited; he told Shapley that it seemed a serious and worthwhile book, and that even if it should prove to be nonsense, it was still a bold and fascinating thesis. The Macmillan editor agreed, and Velikovsky got his contract.

Three months before its publication, in January 1950, a preview of *Worlds in Collision* appeared in *Harper's* magazine, and aroused widespread interest. Shapley's reaction was curious. He wrote Macmillans a letter saying that he had heard that they had decided *not* to publish the book after all, and that he was greatly relieved; he had discussed it with various scientists, and they were all astonished that Macmillan should venture into "the Black Arts".

Macmillans replied defensively that the book was not supposed to be hard science, but was a controversial theory that scholars ought to know about. Shapley replied tartly that Velikovsky was "complete nonsense", and that when he had introduced himself to Shapley in a New York hotel Shapley had looked around to see if he had his keeper with him. The book, he said, was "quite possibly intellectually fraudulent", a legpull designed to make money, and if Macmillans insisted on publishing it, then they had better drop Shapley from their list.

Macmillans ignored this attempt at blackmail, and published the book in April. No doubt they were astonished to find that they had a best-seller on their hands. America has a vast audience of "fundamentalists" – people who believe that every word of the Bible is literally true, and are delighted to read anything that seems to offer scientific support for this view. (The same audience made Werner Keller's *The Bible as History* a best-seller in 1956.) Now they rushed to buy this book that seemed to prove that the parting of the Red Sea and the destruction of the walls of Jericho had really taken place. So did thousands of ordinary intelligent readers who simply enjoyed an adventure in speculative thought.

Scientists did not share this open-mindedness. One exception was Gordon Atwater, chairman of the astronomy department at New York's Museum of Natural History; he published a review urging that scientists ought to be willing to consider the book without prejudice; the review resulted in his dismissal. James Putnam, the editor who accepted *Worlds in Collision*, was dismissed from Macmillan. Professors deluged Macmillan with letters threatening to boycott their textbooks unless *Worlds in Collision* was withdrawn. Macmillans failed to show the same courage that had led them to ignore similar veiled threats from Shapley; they passed on Velikovsky to the Doubleday corporation, who had no textbook department to worry about, and who were probably unable to believe their luck in being handed such a profitable piece of intellectual merchandise. Fred Whipple, Shapley's successor at Harvard, wrote to Doubleday[1] telling them that if they persisted in publishing Velikovsky, he wanted them to take his own book *Earth, Moon and Planets* off their list. (Twenty years later, he denied in print ever writing such a letter.)

Velikovsky himself was rather bewildered by the sheer violence of the reactions; it had taken him thirty years to develop his theory, and he had expected controversy; but this amounted to persecution. He was willing to admit that he could be wrong about the nature of the catastrophe; but the historical records showed that *something* had taken place. Why couldn't they admit that, and *then* criticize his theory, instead of treating him as a madman? The only thing to do was to go on collecting more evidence.

And more evidence was produced in intimidating quantities during the remaining twenty-nine years of Velikovsky's life; he died on 17 November 1979, at the age of eighty-four. In 1955 came *Earth in Upheaval*, in many ways his best book, presenting the scientific evidence for great catastrophes. But again it outraged scientists – this time biologists – by suggesting that there are serious inadequacies in Darwin's theory of "gradual evolution", and arguing that a better explanation would be the effect of radiation due to "catastrophes" on the genes. Then came four books in a series that Velikovsky chose to call *Ages in Chaos*, whose main thesis is that historians of the ancient world have made a basic mistake in their dating, and that a period of about six or seven centuries needs to be dropped from the chronological record. In Velikovsky's dating, Queen Hatshepsut, generally assumed to have lived about 1500 BC, becomes a contemporary of Solomon more than four centuries later (in fact, Velikovsky identifies her with the Queen of Sheba), while

1 In fact, to the Doubleday subsidiary, Blakiston.

the pharaoh Rameses II – assumed to live around 1250 BC – becomes a contemporary of Nebuchadnezzar more than six centuries later. The great invasion of barbarians known as the Sea Peoples, usually dated about 1200 BC, is placed by Velikovsky in the middle of the fourth century BC, about the time of the death of Plato. The arguments contained in *Ages in Chaos* (1953), *Oedipus and Akhnaton* (1960), *Peoples of the Sea* (1977) and *Rameses II and his Time* (1978) are of interest to historians rather than to scientists, but, like the earlier works, are totally absorbing to read. Two other projected volumes, *The Dark Age in Greece* and *The Assyrian Conquest*, have not so far been published. But a third volume of the *Worlds in Collision* series, *Mankind in Amnesia*, appeared posthumously in 1982. It expands a short section in *Worlds in Collision* arguing that catastrophic events produce a kind of collective amnesia. It is his most Freudian book, but it reveals that he never lost that curious ability to produce a state of intellectual excitement in the reader, even when his arguments seem most outrageous.

How far does Velikovsky deserve to be taken seriously? Should he be regarded as another Freud, or merely as another Erich von Däniken? It must be admitted that the basic thesis of *Worlds in Collision* sounds preposterous: that various Biblical events, like the parting of the Red Sea and the fall of the walls of Jericho, can be explained in terms of an astronomical catastrophe. But it is possible to entertain doubts about this aspect of Velikovsky's thesis without dismissing the most important part of his theory: that Venus may be far younger than the rest of the solar system. Moreover, whether or not Velikovsky is correct about the origin of Venus, there can be no doubt whatever that many of his controversial insights have been confirmed. Astronomers object that Jupiter was not likely to be the source of a "comet" because it is too cold and inactive. However, a standard textbook of astronomy – Skilling and Richardson (1947) states "From the fact that Jupiter is 5.2 times as far from the source of heat as is the earth, it can be seen that it should receive only $1/5.2^2$, or $1/27$ as much heat as does the earth. The temperature that a planet should have as the result of this much heat is very low – in the neighbourhood of $-140°C$." But space probes have since revealed that the surface temperature on Jupiter is around $-150°C$, and that its surface is extremely turbulent, with immense explosions. The same textbook of astronomy states that the temperature on the surface of Venus "may be as high as boiling water". Velikovsky argued that it should be much higher, since Venus is so "young" in astronomical terms. Mariner 2 revealed that the temperature on the surface of Venus is about 900°C. It also revealed the curious fact that Venus rotates backward as compared to all the other planets, an oddity that seems incomprehensible if it was formed at the same time and evolved through the same process.

Russian space probes also revealed that Venus has violent electrical storms. Velikovsky had argued that the planets have powerful magnetic fields, and that therefore a close brush between the earth and a "comet" would produce quite definite effects. The discovery of the Van Allen belts around the earth supported Velikovsky's view. There also seem to be close links between the rotation of Venus and Earth – Venus turns the same face to earth at each inferior conjunction, which could have come about through an interlocking of their magnetic fields. In the 1950s Velikovsky's assertion about electromagnetic fields in space was treated with contempt – in *Fads and Fallacies in the Name of Science*, Martin Gardner remarked dismissively that Velikovsky had invented forces capable of doing whatever he wanted them to do. His electromagnetic theory also led Velikovsky to predict that Jupiter would be found to emit radio waves, and that the sun would have an extremely powerful magnetic field. One critic (D. Menzel) retorted that Velikovsky's model of the sun would require an impossible charge of 10^{19} volts. Since then, Jupiter *has* been found to emit radio waves, while the sun's electrical potential has been calculated at about 10^{19} volts. It could be said that many of Velikovsky's theories are now an accepted part of astrophysics except, of course, that no one acknowledges that Velikovsky was the first one to formulate them.

Another matter on which Velikovsky seems to have been proved correct is the question of the reversal of the earth's magnetic poles. When molten volcanic rocks cool, or when clay or brick is baked, the magnetic minerals in it are magnetized in the direction of the earth's magnetic field. At the turn of the century Giuseppe Folgerhaiter examined Etruscan vases, looking for minor magnetic variations, and was astonished to find that there seemed to have been a complete reversal of the magnetic field around the eighth century BC. Scientists explained his findings by declaring that the pots must have been fired upside down. But in 1906 Bernard Brunhes found the same complete reversal in certain volcanic rocks. Further research revealed that there had been at least nine such reversals in the past 3.6 million years. No one could make any plausible suggestion as to why this had happened. Velikovsky's suggestion was that it was due to the close approach of other celestial bodies, and that the earth's brush with Venus should have produced such a reversal. His critics replied that there have been no reversals in the past half-million years or so. But since then two more have been discovered – one 28,000 years ago, the other about 12500 BC, and one of Velikovsky's bitterest opponents, Harold Urey, has come to admit that the "celestial body" theory is the likeliest explanation of pole-reversal. Yet so far the crucial piece of evidence – volcanic rock revealing a reversal about 1450 BC has not been forthcoming.

Those who regard Velikovsky as an innovator comparable to Freud should also be prepared to admit that he had many of

Freud's faults – particularly a tendency to jump to bold and unorthodox conclusions, and then to stick by them with a certain rigid dogmatism. Yet it must also be admitted that whether or not his Venus theory proves to be ultimately correct, his "guesses" have often been amazingly accurate. Like Kepler, who came to all the right conclusions about the solar system for all the wrong reasons (including the belief that it is somehow modelled on the Holy Trinity), Velikovsky seems to possess the intuitive genius of all great innovators. Even one of his most dismissive critics, Carl Sagan, admits: "I find the concatenation of legends which Velikovsky has accumulated stunning . . . If twenty per cent of the legendary concordances . . . are real, there is something important to be explained."

"THE MOST MYSTERIOUS MANUSCRIPT IN THE WORLD"

The Voynich Manuscript

It was in 1912 that an American dealer in rare books, Wilfred Voynich, heard of a mysterious work that had been discovered in an old chest in the Jesuit school of Mondragone, in Frascati, Italy, and succeeded in buying it for an undisclosed sum. It was an octavo volume, six by nine inches, with 204 pages; it had originally another 28 pages, but these are lost. It is written in cipher, which at first glance looks like ordinary medieval writing. And the pages are covered with strange little drawings of female nudes, astronomical diagrams, and all kinds of strange plants in many colours.

There was a letter accompanying the manuscript, dated 19 August 1666, and written by Joannes Marcus Marci, the rector of Prague University. It was addressed to the famous Jesuit scholar Athanasius Kircher – remembered today mainly for some interesting experiments in animal hypnosis – and stated that the book had been bought for 600 ducats by the Holy Roman Emperor Rudolf II of Prague. Kircher was an expert on cryptography, having published a book on the subject in 1663, in which he claimed to have solved the riddle of hieroglyphics. This in itself may be taken to indicate that Kircher was inclined to indulge in wishful thinking, since we know that it would be another century and a half before Champollion succeeded in reading hieroglyphics. Kircher had apparently already attempted to decipher a few pages of the book, sent to him by its previous owner, who had devoted his whole life to trying to decode it. Now he sent him the whole manuscript.

We do not know how the manuscript came to be in Prague, but the likeliest possibility is that it was taken there from England by the famous Elizabethan "magician" Dr John Dee, who went there in 1584; one writer speculates that Dee may have obtained it from the Duke of Northumberland, who had pillaged monasteries at the behest of Henry VIII. The English writer Sir Thomas Browne said later that Dee's son Arthur had spoken about "a book containing nothing but hieroglyphics" which he had studied in Prague. Marci believed the mysterious book to be by the thirteenth-century monk and scientist Roger Bacon.

The Voynich manuscript (as it came to be known) is a baffling mystery because it *looks* so straightforward; with its drawings of plants it looks like an ordinary medieval "herbal", a book describing how to extract healing drugs from plants. One would expect astronomical or astrological diagrams in a herbal, because the plants were often supposed to be gathered by the full moon, or when the stars or planets were in a certain position.

Kircher obviously had no success with the manuscript; he finally deposited it in the Jesuit College in Rome, whence it came into the hands of the Jesuits of Frascati.

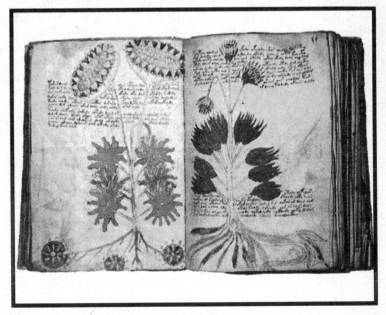

Two pages from the Voynich manuscript. For years cryptologists have tried to unravel its secrets – without success.

Voynich was fairly certain that the manuscript would not remain a mystery once modern scholars had a chance to study it. So he distributed photostats to anyone who was interested. The first problem, of course, was to determine what language it was in – Latin, Middle English, perhaps even Langue d'Oc. This should have been an easy task, since the plants were labelled, albeit in some sort of code. But most of the plants proved to be imaginary. Certain constellations could be recognized among the astronomical diagrams but again, it proved impossible to translate their names out of code. Cryptanalysts tried the familiar method of looking for the most frequent symbols and equating them with the most commonly used letters of the alphabet; they had no difficulty recognizing 29 individual letters or symbols, but every attempt to translate these into a known language was a failure. What made it so infuriating was that the writing didn't *look* like a code; it looked as if someone had sat down and written it as fluently as his mother tongue. Many scholars, cryptanalysts, linguists, astronomers, experts on Bacon, offered to help; the Vatican Library offered to throw open its archives to the researchers. Still the manuscript refused to yield up its secret – or even one of its secrets.

Then in 1921 a professor of philosophy from the University of Pennsylvania, William Romaine Newbold, announced that he had solved the code; he explained his discovery before a meeting of the American Philosophical Society in Philadelphia. What he had done, he explained, was to start by translating the symbols into Roman letters, reducing them in the process from 29 to 17. Using the Latin *conmuto* (or *commuto*: to change) as a key word, he then went on to produce no less than four more versions of the text, the last of which was (according to Newbold) a straightforward Latin text mixed up into anagrams. These merely had to be unscrambled and the result was a scientific treatise which revealed that Roger Bacon was one of the greatest intellects of all time.

This had, of course, always been suspected. It was Bacon who had inspired Columbus to seek out America by a passage in his *Opus Majus* in which he suggested that the Indies could be reached by sailing westward from Spain. In the days of alchemy and a dogmatic and muddled science derived from Aristotle, Bacon advocated learning from nature by experiment and observation, and was thrown into prison for his pains. In rejecting the authority of Aristotle he was also by implication rejecting the authority of the Church. In his *City of God*, St Augustine had warned Christians to shun science and intellectual inquiry as a danger to salvation. Roger Bacon, like his Elizabethan namesake Francis, could see that such an attitude was tantamount to intellectual suicide. Yet when all this is said, it has to be admitted that Bacon was very much a man of his time, and that the *Opus Majus* is full of statements that a modern scientist would regard as gross errors and superstitions.

But if Newbold was correct, Bacon was one of the greatest scientists before Newton. He had made a microscope and examined biological cells and spermatozoa – these were the tadpole-drawings in the margins – and had made a telescope long before Galileo; he had even recognized the Andromeda nebula as a spiral galaxy. Newbold translated a caption to what he claimed to be a sketch of the nebula: "In a concave mirror I saw a star in the form of a snail . . . between the navel of Pegasus, the girdle of Andromeda and the head of Cassiopeia." (It is known that Bacon understood how to use a concave mirror as a burning-glass.) Newbold declared that he had no idea of what he would find by looking in the region indicated, and was surprised to find that the "snail" was the Andromeda nebula.

But in *The Codebreakers* cipher expert David Kahn has pointed out one of the basic flaws in Newbold's system. Newbold's method depended on "doubling up" the letters of a word, so that, for example, "oritur" became or-ri-it-tu-ur, and this text was solved with the aid of the key word "conmuto" and the addition of a q. But how would this process be carried out in reverse – in other words, when Bacon was turning his original text into a cipher? Kahn says: "Many one-way ciphers have been devised; it is possible to put messages into cipher, but not to get them back out. Newbold's seemed to be the only example extant of the reverse situation."

Newbold died in 1926, only sixty years old; two years later his friend Roland G. Kent published the results of Newbold's labours in *The Cipher of Roger Bacon*. It was widely accepted – for example, by the eminent cultural historian Étienne Gilson.

But one scholar who had been studying Newbold's system was far from convinced. He was Dr John M. Manly, a philologist who headed the department of English at Chicago University, and who had become assistant to the great Herbert Osborne Yardley – described as the greatest codebreaker in history – when US Military Intelligence set up a cryptanalysis department in 1917. Manly had produced the definitive edition of Chaucer in eight volumes, comparing more than eighty versions of the medieval manuscript of the *Canterbury Tales*. One of his most remarkable feats was the deciphering of a letter found in the baggage of a German spy named Lothar Witzke, who was captured in Nogales, Mexico, in 1918. In three days of non-stop application Manly had solved the twelve-step official transposition cipher, with multiple horizontal shiftings of three and four letter groups finally laid out in a vertical transcription. In a military court he was able to read aloud a message from the German minister in Mexico beginning: "The bearer of this is a subject of the empire who travels as a Russian under the name of Pablo Waberski. He is a German secret agent . . ." It was the spy's death warrant (although President Wilson commuted it to life imprisonment).

Now Manly studied Newbold's *Cipher of Roger Bacon*, and concluded that in spite of his undoubted integrity, Newbold had been deceiving himself. The weak point of the cipher was the anagramming process. Most sentences can be anagrammed into a dozen other sentences, a method by which admirers of Francis Bacon have had no difficulty proving that he wrote the plays of Shakespeare. With a sentence involving more than a hundred letters, there is simply no way of guaranteeing that some particular rearrangement provides the only solution – David Kahn points out that the words "Hail Mary, full of grace, the Lord is with thee" can be anagrammed in thousands of different ways.

Newbold had also made certain "shorthand signs" a basic part of his system of interpretation. When Manly looked at these through a powerful magnifying glass he found out that they were not "shorthand" at all, only places where the ink had peeled off the vellum. By the time he had pointed out dozens of cases in which Newbold had allowed his interpretation to be influenced by his own twentieth-century assumptions, Manly had totally demolished Newbold's claim to have solved "the cipher of Roger Bacon".

Since that time, 1931, there have been many attempts to decipher the Voynich manuscript. In 1933 a cancer specialist, Dr Leonell C. Strong, published his own fragments of translation, and proved to his own satisfaction that the work was a herbal by an English scholar, Anthony Ascham; he even published a recipe for a contraceptive which apparently works. But Strong failed to explain the method by which he arrived at his translations, so they have never achieved wide acceptance.

William F. Friedman, who organized a whole group of specialists to work on the problem in the last year of World War II, was frustrated by the end of the war and the disbandment of his group. But Friedman pointed out that the Voynich manuscript differs from other codes in one basic respect. The inventor of a code attempts to frustrate would-be cryptanalysts by trying to remove repetitions that would give him away (for example, a repeated group of three words would almost certainly be "and" or "the"). The Voynich manuscript actually has far more repetitions than an ordinary text. This led Friedman to hypothesize that the text is in some artificial language which, because of a need for simplicity, would inevitably have more repetitions than a highly complex "natural" language. But this presupposes that Roger Bacon (or whoever wrote the manuscript) was so anxious to conceal his meaning that he went to far greater lengths than even a code-expert would consider reasonable. And for a thirteenth-century monk, who had little reason to fear code-breakers, this seems unlikely . . .

And this, of course, is the very heart of the mystery. We do not know when the manuscript was written, or by whom, or in what language, but even if we knew the answers to these questions it is difficult to think of any good reason for inventing such a baffling code. The earliest ciphers in the Vatican archive date from 1326 (when Roger Bacon was a boy) and these are merely "coded" names relating to the struggle between Ghibellines and Guelphs. These were respectively supporters of the Holy Roman Emperor and the Pope; the Ghibellines are called Egyptians and the Guelphs Children of Israel. (It is easy to guess what side the inventor of the code was on.) The earliest Western "substitution" cipher dates from 1401. The first treatise on codes, the *Polygraphia* of Johannes Trithemius, was not printed until 1518, two years after the death of its author. So it is hard to imagine why Roger Bacon or anyone within a century of his death should have gone to so much trouble to invent a code of such apparent sophistication when something much simpler would have sufficed.

Kahn offers one clue to why the author of a herbal (which is what the Voynich manuscript looks most like) should want to conceal his meaning when he speaks of one of the earliest encipherments, a tiny cuneiform tablet dating from about 1500 BC. "It contains the earliest known formula for the making of glazes for pottery. The scribe, jealously guarding his professional secret, used cuneiform signs . . . in their least common values." The author of the Voynich manuscript may have been a highly skilled professional herbalist who wrote down his secrets for his own use and those of his pupils, and was determined to keep them out of the hands of rivals.

This view would have struck the antiquarian bookseller Hans Kraus as altogether too commonplace. When Ethel Voynich died at the age of ninety-six, in 1960, Kraus purchased the manuscript from her executors and put it up for sale at $160,000; he explained that he thought that it could contain information that might provide new insights into the record of man, and that if it could be deciphered it might be worth a million dollars. No one took it at that price, and Kraus finally gave it to Yale University in 1969, where it now lies, awaiting the inspiration of some master-cryptographer.

chapter nineteen

CROP CIRCLES – UFOs WHIRLWINDS OR HOAXERS?

On 15th August 1980, The *Wiltshire Times* carried an oddlie report concerning apparently wanton vandalism of a field of oats near Westbury in Wiltshire. The owner of the field, John Scull, had found his oats crushed to the ground in three separate areas all within sight of the famous White Horse of Westbury, the hillside figure cut into the chalk. It seemed obvious to Scull that the crops had been damaged by people rather than natural phenomena since the areas were identical in size and shape; almost perfect circles, sixty feet in diameter.

It was noted that the circles had apparently been produced manually rather than mechanically; since there was no sign that any kind of machinery had been moved through the field. In fact there seemed to be no evidence of *anything* crossing the field; the circles were surrounded by undamaged oats, with no paths that would indicate intruders. One speculation was that the vandals had used stilts.

Close examination of the flattened cereal revealed that all the circles had not been made at the same time – in fact, that the damage had been spread over a period of two or three months, probably between May and the end of July. The edges to the circles were sharply defined, and all the grain within the circle was flattened in the same direction, creating a clockwise swirling effect around the centre. None of the oats had been cut – merely flattened. The effect might have been produced by a very tall and strong man standing in the centre and swinging a heavy weight around on a long piece of rope . . .

Dr Terence Meaden, an atmospheric physicist from nearby Bradford-on-Avon – and a senior member of the Tornado and

Storm Research Organization (TORRO) –, suggested that the effect had been produced by a summer whirlwind. Such wind effects are not uncommon on open farmland. But Dr Meaden had to admit that he had never seen or heard of a whirlwind creating exact circles. Whirlwinds tend to scud-about randomly, pausing for only a few seconds in any one place – so one might expect a random pathway through the crop with only occasionally wider areas of damage to field.

Another interesting fact was also noted by Ian Mrzyglod, editor of the anomaly magazine *The PROBE Report*. The "centre point" on all three circles was in fact off centre by as much as four feet. The swirling patterns around them were therefore oval, not circular. This seemed to contradict the vandal theory – vandals would hardly go to the trouble of creating precise ellipses. It also made Meaden's whirlwind explanation seem less plausible.

Almost exactly a year later on August 19th 1981, another three circle formation appeared in wheat below Cheesefoot Head, near Winchester in Hampshire. These circles had been created at the same time and, unlike the widely dispersed circles in Wiltshire, were in close formation – one circle sixty feet across with two twenty-five foot circles on either side. The sides of the circles had the same precise edges, and again the swirl of the flattened plants was slightly off centre, creating an ellipse. Again there were no paths through the corn to indicate intruders.

The new evidence seemed to undermine the natural-causes theory. Instead of a neat, stationary whirlwind creating only one circle, Meaden now had to argue the existence of an atmospheric disturbance that "hopscotched" across the landscape, and produced circles of different sizes – instead of the identical ones that might be expected from a whirlwind. Meaden suggested that perhaps peculiarities of terrain created this effect – the field in question was on a concave, "punchbowl" slope and this might indeed have caused the vortex to "jump".

There were a few isolated reports of incidents in 1982, but they were unspectacular and excited little attention. As if to make up for it, a series of five-circle phenomena began in 1983, one of them again at Bratton, close to the White Horse of Westbury. These made it clear that whirlwinds could not explain the circles, for they consisted of one large circle with four smaller ones spaced around it like the number-5 on a dice. More "quintuplets" appeared at Cley Hill, near Warminster – a town that, in earlier years, had had more than its share of "Flying Saucer" sightings – and in a field below Ridgeway near Wantage in Oxfordshire. Quintuplets were no longer freaks, but were virtually the norm.

Now the national press began to cover the phenomena. The British press often refer to the summer as the "silly season" because – for some odd reason – there is often a shortage of good news stories in the hot months of the year, so newspapers tend to supply the deficiency by blowing up trivia into major news stories. Crop circles answered the need perfectly, with the result that the British public soon became familiar with the strange circle formations. UFO enthusiasts appeared on television explaining their view that the phenomena could only be explained by Flying Saucers. Sceptics preferred the notion of fraud.

This view seemed to be confirmed when a second "quintuplet" found at Bratton turned out to be a hoax sponsored by the *Daily Mirror*; a family called Shepherd had been paid to duplicate the other Bratton circles. They did this by entering the field upon stilts and trampling the crops underfoot. But, significantly, the hoax was quickly detected by the editor of an anomaly magazine, *The Fortean Times*, Bob Rickard, who noted the tell-tale signs of human intruders which had not been present in earlier circles, and the fact that the edges of the circles were so rough and imprecise. The aim of the hoax was to embarrass the competing tabloid *The Daily Express*, which had originally scooped the crop circle story.

During the next two years the number of circles increased, as did their complexity. There were crop circles with "rings" around them – flattened pathways several feet wide, that ran around the outer edge in a neat circle – some were even found with two or three such parameters. At the same time the quintuplet formations and "singletons" also continued to appear.

It began to look as if whoever – or whatever – was creating the circles took pleasure in taunting the investigators. When believers in the whirlwind theory pointed out the "swirling" had so far been clockwise, a circle promptly appeared that was anti-clockwise. When it was suggested that a hoaxer might be making the circles with the use of a helicopter, a crop circle was found directly beneath a power line. And when an aerial photographer named Busty Taylor, was flying home after photographing crop circles, and mentioned that he would like to see a formation in the shape of a celtic cross, a celtic cross appeared the next day in the field they had been flying over. And, as if to rule out all possibility that natural causes could be responsible, one "sextuplet" in Hampshire in 1990 had key-like objects sticking out of the sides of three circles, producing an impression like ancient pictograms. Another crop "pattern" of 1990 (at Chilcomb) seemed to represent a kind of chemical retort with a long neck, with four rectangles neatly spaced on either side of it, making nonsense of Meaden's insistence that the circles are caused by "natural atmospheric forces."

Rickard brought together a number of eye-witness descriptions of the actual appearance of circles.

"Suddenly the grass began to sway before our eyes and laid itself flat in a clockwise spiral . . . A perfect circle was completed in less than half a minute, all the time accompanied by a high-pitched humming sound . . . My attention was drawn to a "wave" coming through the heads of the cereal crop in a straight line . . . The agency, though invisible, behaved like a solid object . . . When we reached the spot where the circles had been, we were suddenly caught up in a terrific whirlwind . . . [The dog] went wild . . . There was a rushing sound and a rumble . . . then suddenly everything was still . . . It was uncanny . . . The dawn chorus stopped; the sky darkened . . ."

The high pitched humming sound may be significant. It was noted on another occasion, on June 16, 1991, when a seventy-five foot circle (with a "bullseye" at the centre) appeared on Bolberry Down, near Salcombe in Devon. A local radio ham named Lew Dilling was tuned into a regular frequency when strange high pitched bips and clicks emerged. He recognised the sounds as the same as others that had been heard in connection with other crop circle incidents. "The signals were so powerful", said Dilling, "that you could hear them in the background of Radio Moscow and Voice of America – and they would normally swamp everything."

The landlord of the local pub, Sean Hassall, learned of the crop circle indirectly when his spaniel went berserk and began tearing up the carpet, doing considerable damage.

The farmer, Dudley Stidson, was alerted to the circle by two walkers. He went to the six acre hay field and found the huge circle in the centre. But this one differed from many such circles in that the hay was burnt, as if someone had put a huge hot-ring on it. Stidson emphasised that there was no sign of intrusion in the field, such as trampled wheat.

Another local farmer, Peter Goodall, found a sixty foot circle in his winter wheat (at Matford Barton) at the same time.

A few days before these incidents, a Japanese professor had announced that he had solved the crop circle mystery. Professor Yoshihiko Ohtsuki, of Tokyo's Waseda University, had created an "elastic plasma" fireball – a very strong form of ionised air – in the laboratory. When the fireball touched a plate covered with aluminium powder, it created beautiful circles and rings in the powder. Ohtsuki suggested that plasma fireballs are created by atmospheric conditions, and that they would flatten the crops as they descended towards the ground. This certainly sounds as if it could be the solution of the mystery – until we remember the crop circles with rectangles, or key-like objects sticking out of the side. Another objection is that fireballs are usually about the size of footballs, and are clearly visible. Surely a fireball with a seventy-five foot diameter would be visible for many miles? And why were no fireballs seen by witnesses cited by Rickard, who simply saw the corn being flattened in a clockwise circle?

Another recent suggestion is that an excess of fertiliser will cause the corn to shoot up much faster than that which surrounds it, but that it then "collapses" and lies flat. Here there are two objections: why a farmer should spray an excess of fertiliser in a circle – or some even more complicated design – and why the corn should "collapse" in a clockwise direction . . .

In a symposium called *The Crop Circle Enigma* (1990), John Michell has made the important suggestion that the crop circles have a meaning, and that "the meaning . . . is to be found in the way people are affected by them." He goes on: "Jung discerned the meaning of UFOs as agents and portents of changes in human thought patterns, and that function has been clearly inherited by crop circles."

In order to understand this fully, we have to bear in mind Jung's concept of "synchronicity" or "meaningful coincidence." His view is basically that "meaningful coincidences" are somehow *created* by the unconscious mind – probably with the intention of jarring the conscious mind into a keener state of perception. Preposterous synchronicities imbue us with a powerful sense that there *is* a hidden meaning behind everyday reality. Certain pessimistically-inclined writers – such as Shakespeare and Thomas Hardy – have taken the view that accidents and disasters indicate a kind of malevolent intelligence behind life. Jung's view is that synchronicities produce a sense of a benevolent intelligence behind life. He suggested at one point that the UFO phenomenon was an example of what he called "projection" – that is, of a physical effect somehow produced by the unconscious mind – in fact, by the "collective unconscious."

What Michell is suggesting, in effect, is that the crop circle phenomenon has the same purpose. Yet to say, as he does, that the crop circles have a "meaning" could also imply that some "other intelligence" is trying to influence human thought patterns. This is an idea that has been current since the earliest UFO sightings in the late 1940s, and was popularised by Arthur C. Clarke in the film script of *2001 – A Space Odyssey*: the notion that "higher intelligences" have been involved in the evolution of the human brain.

The logical objection to this is that the "make" man evolve is a contradiction in terms; evolution is due to an *inner* drive. Presumably a higher intelligence would recognise this better than we do. Yet it is also true that intelligence evolves through a sense of curiosity, of mystery, and that such apparent absurdities as flying saucers and crop circles certainly qualify as mysteries.

Michell concludes by quoting Jung's words that UFOs are "signs of great changes to come which are compatible with the end of an era." And whether or not Jung was correct, there can be no doubt that the UFO phenomenon has played an enormous part in the transformation of human consciousness from the narrow scientific materialism of the first half of the 20th century to the far more open-minded attitude of its second half. Whether or not they prove to have a "natural" explanation, this may be the ultimate significance of the crop circles in the history of the late 20th century.

In 1992, two men confessed to having made the crop circles as a hoax, using a long board on a pivot. Most experts have dismissed this as a possible explanation – the difference between genuine circles and hoaxes being fairly easy to detect. Even if some circles had been made by the two hoaxers, it would have been impossible for two men to have made all of them. Tests to be conducted by zoologist Rupert Sheldrake – who has offered a prize for the best "fake" crop circle – may throw further light on the problem. For the moment, it remains stubbornly intractable.

CULTS AND FANATICS

COLIN WILSON
with
Damon and Rowan Wilson

MIRACLES SOMETIMES HAPPEN

*T*here is no way in which we can dismiss the idea that certain people
  can perform "miracles". And if that is true, then we cannot dismiss
all "messiahs" as fakes. Perhaps they are people who sense that human
beings possess extraordinary powers, and realize that the best way to
develop them is to try to live the "religious life", and to persuade as
many of their fellow creatures as possible to do the same thing. There
are even cases where the powers of such poeple seem to live on after
their death, as in the odd case of the Deacon of Paris.

Saint Joseph of Copertino and the Deacon of Paris demonstrate that
miracles can happen. What seems stranger still is that the "miracle
worker" need not be a genuine saint. Grigory Rasputin, the man who
has been described as the "evil messiah" of pre-revolutionary Russia,
was a bewildering mixture of saint and sinner.

The Day of Judgement According to William Miller

On 22 October, 1843, crowds of men and women gathered on a
hilltop in Massachussetts, led by their prophet William Miller.
In the previous year, Miller, a farmer and an ardent student
of the *Book of Daniel*, had arrived at the conclusion that the
end of the world was at hand, and that Christ was about to
return to earth. One man tied a pair of turkey wings to his

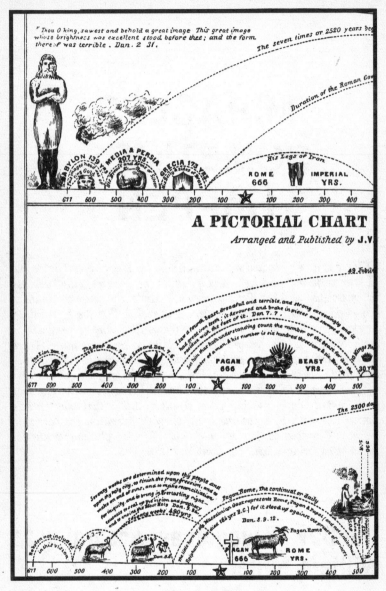

A Millerite chart of the visions and prophecies of Daniel.

shoulders and climbed a tree to be ready for his ascent into heaven; unfortunately, he fell down and broke his arm. Other disciples carried umbrellas to aid the flight. One woman had tied herself to her trunk so that it would accompany her as she sailed upward.

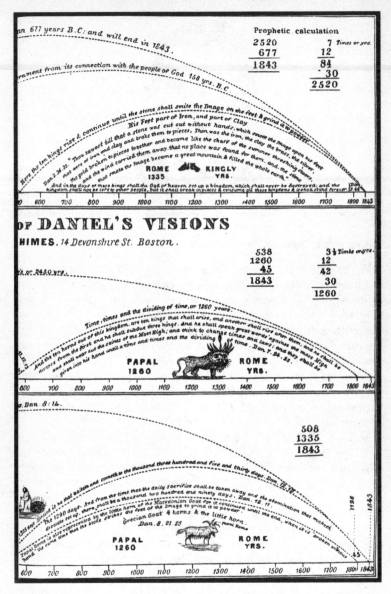

an 677 years B.C.; and will end in 1843.

Prophetic calculation

2520	7 Times or yrs.
677	12
1843	84
	30
	2520

ernment from its connection with the people of God 158 yrs. B.C.

Here the ten kings rise & continue until the stone shall smite the Image on the feet & grind it to powers

His Feet part of Iron, and part of Clay

" Thou sawest till that a stone was cut out without hands, which smote the Image upon his feet

Dan 2.34.35. that were of iron and clay and brake them to pieces, Then was the iron, the clay the brass, the silver

the gold broken to pieces together and became like the chaff of the summer threshing floor,

and the wind carried them away, that no place was found for them, and the stone

and that smote the Image became a great mountain & filled the whole earth.

ROME   KINGLY
1335   YRS.

And in the days of these kings shall the God of heaven set up a kingdom, which shall never be destroyed; and the
kingdom shall not be left to other people, but it shall break in pieces & consume all these kingdoms & it shall stand forever. Dan. 2.44.

0   600   700   800   900   1000   1100   1200   1300   1400   1500   1600   1700   1800 1843

OF **DANIEL'S VISIONS**

HIMES. 14 Devonshire St. Boston.

or 2450 yrs.

538	3½ Times or yrs.
1260	12
45	42
1843	30
	1260

Time, times and the dividing of time, or 1260 years

And the ten horns out of this kingdom, are ten kings that shall arise, and another shall rise after them; and he shall be

diverse from the first and he shall subdue three kings. And he shall speak great words against the most High,

and shall wear out the saints of the Most High; and think to change times and laws: and they shall be

given into his hand until a time and times and the dividing of time. Dan 7. 24. 25.

PAPAL   ROME
1260   YRS.

600   700   800   900   1000   1100   1200   1300   1400   1500   1600   1700   1800 1843

s. Dan. 8.14.

| 508 |
| 1335 |
| 1843 |

And Unto me and cometh to the thousand three hundred and five and thirty days. Dan. 12.12.

The 1290 days, And from the time that the daily sacrifice shall be taken away and the abomination that maketh

desolate set up, there shall be a thousand two hundred and ninety days. Dan. 12. 11.

is also represented by the little horn of the Macedonian Goat for it continued until the end, when it is broken without

Grecian Goat 4 horns & the little horn
Dan. 8. 21. 25.

hand the same time that the stone strikes the feet of the Image to grind it to powder.

PAPAL   ROME
1260   YRS.

600   700   800   900   1000   1100   1200   1300   1400   1500   1600   1700   1800 1843

One Millerite met the writer Ralph Waldo Emerson walking with his friend Theodore Parker, and asked them if they did not realize the world was about to end. "That doesn't affect me", said Parker, "I live in Boston."

William Miller, leader of the "Millerites".

When midnight passed with no sign of Armageddon, the disciples ruefully went home. One farmer had given his farm to his son – who was a non-believer, and who now declined to give it back. Most of the others had sold all they had. In this moment of depression, Miller suddenly had an inspiration: his calculations had been based on the Christian year, and no doubt he should have used the Jewish year. That would make the date of Armageddon the following 22 March. On that date, his followers once more gathered for the last Trump. Still nothing happened. One man wrote sadly: "Still in the cold world! No deliverance – the Lord did not come."

Miller's 50,000 followers soon dwindled to a small band of "true believers". Miller himself was not among them; he admitted sorrowfully that he had made his mistake through pride and fanticism. Another follower made an even more penetrating comment, which might be regarded as the epitaph of any number of "messiahs": "We were deluded by mere human influence, which we mistook for the Spirit of God." Miller died five years later, a deeply chastened man, who recognized that he had been wasting his time in his Biblical calculations. Few other messiahs have possessed his honesty.

In fact, very few had his opportunity, for a large proportion of them have died ignominiously. In 1172, an unnamed prophet from the Yemen was dragged in front of the Caliph, who demanded proof that he was a messenger from God. "That is easy", replied the prophet, "Cut off my head and I shall return to life." "That would indeed be a sign", said the Caliph, "and if you can do as you say, I will become your follower." Whereupon he signalled to his headsman. The head of the prophet rolled on the floor, and – predictably – the messiah failed to keep his promise.

The word messiah means "anointed" in Hebrew, and refers to the Jewish belief that King David will one day return and lead his people to victory. (Christ means the same thing in Greek.) The prophet Isaiah announced triumphantly that "unto us a child is born", and that the Messiah would take the "government upon his shoulders". Isaiah was writing roughly around 700 BC, after the Assyrians had conquered Israel and led its people (including the mythical "lost tribes") into exile. Ever since then, certain men have become possessed of the conviction that they are the promised Messiah, and ordered their disciples to follow them to victory and kingship. None has so far succeeded.

In the first millennium, it was widely believed that the year AD 1,000 would mark the end of the world. It failed to materialize, but there was plenty of war and bloodshed – the Crusades, for example – to encourage the believers to feel that the end was nigh. The rollcall of those who – like William Miller – have announced the end of the world is impressive, as we shall see in this book.

Women have also been among these prophets of the new Millennium, and a few have shown even greater fanaticism than their male counterparts. Perhaps the most gruesome example is the German prophetess Margaret Peter.

The Crucifix of Margaret Peter

In the week after Easter, 1823, a horrible ceremony took place in a house in Wildisbuch, on the German-Swiss border. A twenty-nine year old woman named Margaret Peter, who was regarded as a holy woman by her disciples, announced that she had decided that she had to be crucified if Satan was to be defeated. Her sister Elizabeth immediately begged to be allowed to take her place. To demonstrate her sincerity, she picked up a mallet and struck herself on the head with it. Margaret then shouted: "It has been revealed to me that Elizabeth shall sacrifice herself", and she hit her sister on the head with a hammer. Then the remaining ten people in the room – including Margaret's other brothers and sisters – proceeded to beat Elizabeth with crowbars, hammers and wedges. "Don't worry", Margaret shouted, "I will raise her from the dead." One tremendous blow finally shattered Elizabeth's skull.

"Now *I* must die", Margaret told them. "You must crucify me." Following her sister's example, she picked up a hammer and hit herself on the head, then ordered the others to make a cross out of loose floorboards. When it was ready, she sent her sister Susanna downstairs to fetch nails. When Susanna returned, Margaret was lying on the floor on the cross. "Nail me to it", she ordered. "Don't be afraid. I will rise in three days." Two followers obediently nailed her elbows to the cross. The sight of the blood made them hesitate, and one was sick. Margaret encouraged them. "I feel no pain. Go on. Drive a nail through my heart." They drove nails through both her breasts, and a girl called Ursula tried to drive a knife through her heart. It bent against one of her ribs. Her brother Conrad, unable to stand the sight any longer, picked up a hammer and smashed in her skull.

The ten remaining disciples then went to eat their midday meal. They were exhausted but had no doubt that Margaret and Elizabeth would be among them again in three days time. The deaths had taken place on Saturday; that meant Margaret and Elizabeth were due to arise on Tuesday.

But as the disciples sat around the battered corpses on Tuesday morning, no sign of life answered their prayers. Meanwhile, the local pastor, who had heard about the "sacrifice" from another disciple, called in the police. (He had known about the deaths for two days, but felt he had to give Margaret time to make good her promise.) The disciples were arrested, and taken to prison. They were tried in Zurich that December, and were all sentenced to varying prison terms.

The Death of Joanna Southcott

Sometimes, the prophet – or prophetess – loses faith at the last moment, but even when that happens, the disciples remain immune to doubt. When the English prophetess Joanna Southcott lay on her deathbed in 1814, she suddenly announced to her dismayed followers that her life's work now appeared a delusion. Although Joanna was a virgin, she had been convinced that she was about to give birth to the "child" foretold by Isaiah.

And when one of her followers reminded her that she was carrying the Messiah (called Shiloh) in her womb, Joanna's tears suddenly changed to smiles.

After her death a few days later, her followers kept her body warm for three days as she had instructed them – then summoned a small army of medical men to remove the Christ child from her womb. The smell of putrefying flesh filled the room as the surgeon made the first incision, and some of the disciples hastily lit pipes to cover the smell. But when the womb was opened, there was obviously no baby there.

"Damn me", said a doctor, "if the child is not *gone*." These words filled the disciples with new hope. Obviously, he meant that the child *had* been there, but had now been transferred to heaven. And even today, there are a small number of followers of Joanna Southcott – they call themselves the Panacea Society – who believe that when her mysterious box is opened – a box supposed to contain her secret writings – all sin and wickedness in the world will suddenly disappear.

It is tempting to dismiss all these prophets and would-be saints as frauds or madmen. But that would undoubtedly be a mistake. Consider, for example, the strange case of Joseph of Copertino.

Joanna Southcott.

The flying Capuchin monk Guiseppe Desa.

The Flying Monk

Giuseppe Desa was born in Apulia, Italy, in 1603, a strange, sickly boy who became known as "Open Mouth" because his mouth usually hung open; one commentator remarks that "he was not far from what today we should call a state of feeble-mindedness"; a bishop described him as *idiota* (although the word meant innocent rather than idiotic). He was subject to "ecstasies" and, even as a teenager, given to ascetic self-torments that undermined his health. At the age of seventeen he was accepted into the Capuchin order, but dismissed eight months later because of total inability to concentrate. Not long after, the order of Conventuals near Copertino accepted him as a stable boy, and at twenty-two he became a Franciscan priest. He continued to starve and flagellate himself, acquiring a reputation for holiness. Then one day, in the midst of his prayers after mass, he floated off the ground and landed on the altar in a state of ecstasy. He was unburned by candle flames, and flew back to his previous place.

Sent to see the Pope, he was again seized by such rapture that he rose in the air. His flying fits seem to have been always associated with the state that the Hindus called *samadhi*, ecstasy. His levitations ceased for two years when a hostile superior went out of his way to humiliate and persecute him; but after a holiday in Rome as the guest of the superior of the order, and an enthusiastic reception by the people of Assisi, he regained his good spirits and sailed fifteen yards to embrace the image of the Virgin on the altar.

He seems to have been a curious but simple case; floating in the air when in a state of delight seems to have been his sole accomplishment. The ecstasy did not have to be religious; on one occasion, when shepherds were playing their pipes in church on Christmas Eve, he began to dance for sheer joy, then flew on to the high altar, without knocking over any of the burning candles. Oddly enough, Saint Joseph could control his flights. On one occasion, when he had flown past lamps and ornaments that blocked the way to the altar, his superior called him back, and he flew back to the place he had vacated. When a fellow monk remarked on the beauty of the sky, he shrieked and flew to the top of a nearby tree. He was also able to lift heavy weights; one story tells of how he raised a wooden cross that ten workmen were struggling to place in position, and flew with it to

436

the hole that had been prepared for it. He was also able to make others float; he cured a demented nobleman by seizing his hair and flying into the air with him, remaining there a quarter of an hour, according to his biographer; on another occasion, he seized a local priest by the hand, and after dancing around with him, they both flew, hand in hand. When on his deathbed, at the age of sixty, the doctor in attendance observed, as he cauterized a septic leg, that Fr Joseph was floating in the air six inches above the chair. He died saying that he could hear the sounds and smell the scents of paradise.

What are we to make of such phenomena? It would be convenient if we could dismiss the whole thing as a pack of lies or as mass hysteria or hypnosis. We can certainly dismiss ninety-five per cent of the miracles attributed to the saints in this way without a twinge of conscience. (A typical example: St Dunstan of Glastonbury is reported to have changed the position of the church by pushing it.) But the evidence cannot be dismissed; it is overwhelming. His feats were witnessed by kings, dukes and philosophers (or at least one philosopher – Leibnitz). When his

---

Flying saucer cults exist all around the world. Most hold the view put forward in Erich Von Däniken's book *The Chariots of the Gods*?: that the human concept of "God" was created when we were visited by alien beings at some stage in our pre-history.

UFOs reached the public consciousness during the late 1940s. A spate of sightings seemed to loose a tidal wave of stories involving abduction by aliens and mysterious landings. Throughout the Fifties pulp science fiction publications pushed the idea of mysterious alien races that hang around in earth's upper atmosphere planning our downfall. Strange mutilations of cattle in Texas were ascribed to them. More recently a series of "corn circles", bizarre asymmetric patterns composed of crushed crops were said to be produced by their landings.

Believers in the UFO conspiracy maintain that witnesses to alien activities are visited by the mysterious Men In Black. These black-suited officials advise the witness to keep quiet about the sighting. Whether these are aliens in disguise or agents of government covert operations is not known – perhaps they are both.

The spiritual side of saucer cults tends to focus on the higher knowledge of alien beings conquering famine and war. Some believe that life on earth was "seeded" here millions of years ago by aliens, and that they will soon return to see how their experiment has gone. This idea actually forms the basis of obscure-but-popular film "*2001 – A Space Odyssey*".

canonization was suggested, the Church started an investigation into his flights, and hundreds of depositions were taken. He became a saint a hundred and four years after his death.

The Miracles of Saint-Médard

The strange events that took place in the little Paris churchyard of Saint-Médard between 1727 and 1732 sound so incredible, so preposterous, that the modern reader is tempted to dismiss them as pure invention. This would be a mistake, for an impressive mass of documents, including accounts by doctors, magistrates and other respectable public figures, attests to their genuineness. The miracles undoubtedly took place. But no doctor, philosopher or scientist has even begun to explain them.

They began with the burial of François de Pâris, the Deacon of Paris, in May 1727. François was only thirty-seven years old, yet he was revered as a holy man, with powers of healing. He was a follower of Bishop Cornelius Jansen, who taught that men can be saved only by divine grace, not by their own efforts. The Deacon had no doubt whatever that his own healing powers came from God.

Great crowds followed his coffin, many weeping. It was laid in a tomb behind the high altar of Saint-Médard. Then the congregation filed past, laying their flowers on the corpse. A father supported his son, a cripple, as he leaned over the coffin. Suddenly, the child went into convulsions; he seemed to be having a fit. Several people helped to drag him, writhing, to a quiet corner of the church. Suddenly the convulsions stopped. The boy opened his eyes, looking around in bewilderment, and then slowly stood up. A look of incredulous joy crossed his face; then to the astonishment of the spectators he began to dance up and down, singing and laughing. His father found it impossible to believe, for the boy was using his withered right leg, which had virtually no muscles. Later it was claimed that the leg had become as strong and normal as the other.

The news spread. Within hours cripples, lepers, hunchbacks and blind men were rushing to the church. At first few "respectable" people believed the stories of miraculous cures – the majority of the Deacon's followers were poor people. The rich preferred to leave their spiritual affairs in the hands of the Jesuits, who were more cultivated and worldly. But it soon became clear that ignorance and credulity could not be used as a blanket explanation for all the stories of marvels. Deformed limbs, it was said, were being straightened; hideous growths and cancers were disappearing without trace; horrible sores and wounds were healing instantly.

The Jesuits declared that the miracles were either a fraud or the work of the Devil; the result was that most of the better-off people in Paris flatly refused to believe that anything unusual was taking place in the churchyard of Saint-Médard. But a few men of intellect were drawn by curiosity, and they invariably returned from the churchyard profoundly shaken. Sometimes they recorded their testimony in print: some, such as one Philippe Hecquet, attempted to explain the events by natural causes. Others, such as the Benedictine Bernard Louis de la Taste, attacked the people who performed the miracles on theological grounds, but were unable to expose any deception or error by them, or any error on the part of the witnesses. The accumulation of written testimony was such that David Hume, one of the greatest of philosophers, wrote in *An enquiry concerning human understanding* (1758):

> There surely never was a greater number of miracles ascribed to one person . . . But what is more extraordinary; many of the miracles were immediately proved upon the spot, before judges of unquestioned integrity, attested by witnesses of credit and distinction, in a learned age . . . Where shall we find such a number of circumstances, agreeing to the corroboration of one fact?

One of those who investigated happenings was a lawyer named Louis Adrien de Paige. When he told his friend, the magistrate Louis-Basile Carré de Montgéron, what he had seen the magistrate assured him patronizingly that he had been taken in by conjuring tricks – the kind of "miracles" performed by tricksters at fairgrounds. But he finally agreed to go with Paige to the churchyard, if only for the pleasure of pointing out how the lawyer had been deceived. They went there on the morning of 7 September 1731. And de Montgéron left the churchyard a changed man – he even endured prison rather than deny what he had seen that day.

The first thing the magistrate saw when he entered the

churchyard was a number of women writhing on the ground, twisting themselves into the most startling shapes, sometimes bending backward until the backs of their heads touched their heels. These ladies were all wearing a long cloth undergarment that fastened around the ankles. M. Paige explained that this was now obligatory for all women who wished to avail themselves of the Deacon's miraculous powers. In the early days, when women had stood on their heads or bent their bodies convulsively, prurient young men had begun to frequent the churchyard to view the spectacle.

However, there was no lack of male devotees of the deceased Abbé to assist in the activities of the churchyard. Montgéron was shocked to see that some of the women and girls were being sadistically beaten – at least, that is what at first appeared to be going on. Men were striking them with heavy pieces of wood and iron. Other women lay on the ground, apparently crushed under immensely heavy weights. One girl was naked to the waist: a man was gripping her nipples with a pair of iron tongs and twisting them violently. Paige explained that none of these women felt any pain; on the contrary, many begged for more blows. And an incredible number of them were cured of deformities or diseases by this violent treatment.

In another part of the churchyard, they saw an attractive pink-cheeked girl of about nineteen, who was sitting at a trestle table and eating. That seemed normal enough until Montgéron looked more closely at the food on the plate, and realized from its appearance as well as from the smell that reached him that it was human excrement. In between mouthfuls of this sickening fare she drank a yellow liquid, which Paige explained was urine. The girl had come to the churchyard to be cured of what we would now call a neurosis: she had to wash her hands hundreds of times a day, and was so fastidious about her food that she would taste nothing that had been touched by another human hand. The Deacon had indeed cured her. Within days she was eating excrement and drinking urine, and did so with every sign of enjoyment. Such cases might not be remarkable in asylums; but what was more extraordinary – indeed, preposterous – was that after one of these meals she opened her mouth as if to be sick, and milk came pouring out. Monsieur Paige had collected a cupful; it was apparently perfectly ordinary cow's milk.

After staggering away from the eater of excrement, Montgéron had to endure a worse ordeal. In another part of the churchyard a number of women had volunteered to cleanse suppurating wounds and boils by sucking them clean. Trying hard to prevent himself vomiting, Montgéron watched as someone unwound a dirty bandage from the leg of a small girl; the smell was horrible. The leg was a festering mass of sores, some so deep that the bone was visible. The woman who had volunteered to clean it was one of the *convulsionnaires* – she had been miraculously cured and converted by her bodily contortions, and God had now chosen her to demonstrate how easily human beings' disgust can be overcome. Yet even she blenched as she saw and smelt the gangrened leg. She cast her eyes up to heaven, prayed silently for a moment, then bent her head and began to lap, swallowing the septic matter. When she moved her face farther down the child's leg Montgéron could see that the wound was now clean. Paige assured him that the girl would almost certainly be cured when the treatment was complete.

What Montgéron saw next finally shattered his resistance and convinced him that he was witnessing something of profound significance. A sixteen-year-old girl named Gabrielle Moler had arrived, and the interest she excited made Montgéron aware that, even among this crowd of miraculous freaks, she was a celebrity. She removed her cloak and lay on the ground, her skirt modestly round her ankles. Four men, each holding a pointed iron bar, stood over her. When the girl smiled at them they lunged down at her, driving their rods into her stomach. Montgéron had to be restrained from interfering as the rods went through the girl's dress and into her stomach. He looked for signs of blood staining her dress. But none came, and the girl looked calm and serene. Next the bars were jammed under her chin, forcing her head back. It seemed inevitable that they would penetrate through to her mouth; yet when the points were removed the flesh was unbroken. The men took up sharp-edged shovels, placed them against a breast, and then pushed with all their might; the girl went on smiling gently. The breast, trapped between shovels, should have been cut off, but it seemed impervious to the assault. Then the cutting edge of a shovel was placed against her throat, and the man wielding it did his best to cut off her head; he did not seem to be able even to dent her neck.

Dazed, Montgéron watched as the girl was beaten with a great iron truncheon shaped like a pestle. A stone weighing half a hundredweight (25 kilograms) was raised above her body and dropped repeatedly from a height of several feet. Finally, Montgéron watched her kneel in front of a blazing fire, and plunge her head into it. He could feel the heat from where he stood; yet her hair and eyebrows were not even singed. When she picked up a blazing chunk of coal and proceeded to eat it Montgéron could stand no more and left.

But he went back repeatedly, until he had enough materials for the first volume of an amazing book. He presented it to the king, Louis XV, who was so shocked and indignant that he had Montgéron thrown into prison. Yet Montgéron felt he had to "bear witness", and was to publish two more volumes following his release, full of precise scientific testimony concerning the miracles.

In the year following Montgéron's imprisonment, 1732, the Paris authorities decided that the scandal was becoming unbearable and closed down the churchyard. But the *convulsionnaires* had discovered that they could perform their miracles anywhere, and they continued for many years. A hardened sceptic, the scientist La Condamine, was as startled as Montgéron when, in 1759, he watched a girl named Sister Françoise being crucified on a wooden cross, nailed by the hands and feet over a period of several hours, and stabbed in the side with a spear. He noticed that all this obviously hurt the girl, and her wounds bled when the nails were removed; but she seemed none the worse for an ordeal that would have killed most people.

So what can we say of the miracles from the standpoint of the twentieth century? Some writers believe it was a kind of self-hypnosis. But while this could explain the excrement-eater and the woman who sucked festering wounds, it is less plausible in explaining Gabrielle Moler's feats of endurance. These remind us rather of descriptions of ceremonies of dervishes and fakirs: for example, J.G. Bennett in his autobiography *Witness* describes watching a dervish ritual in which a razor-sharp sword was placed across the belly of a naked man, and two heavy men jumped up and down on it – all without even marking the flesh. What seems to be at work here is some power of "mind over matter", deeper than mere hypnosis, which is not yet understood but obviously merits serious attention.

It would be absurd to stop looking for scientific explanations of the miracles of Saint-Médard. But let us not in the meantime deceive ourselves by accepting superficial "sceptical" explanations.

Some groups believe that the Great Pyramid in Egypt had encoded within its measurements many great truths. Christian sects have maintained that it was not the Egyptians who built it at all but the Israelites. According to this theory the internal passageways of the Pyramid, measured in the correct units, are a three dimensional model of the history of the world up to Christ's birth. On a more secular level, twice the length of the base of the Pyramid divided by its height, again in the correct units, is supposed to approximate to *pi*. It is difficult to verify these statements as the nature of the correct units is a matter of conjecture, and the actual size of the Pyramid in any units is still problematic.

The Anglo-Israelite fundamentalist sect took the argument a stage further. Not only was the Pyramid not built by the Egptians; it was also not entirely correct to say the Israelites built it. According to the Anglo-Israelites the Anglo-Saxon races of Britain and America were the only true tribe of Israel remaining. It was they who had built the Pyramid, as a warning that the world would end and that Christ would return on 20 August, 1953. When the date passed without significant upheaval, the Anglo-Israelites began to formulate the theory that the message of the Pyramid was not literal, but a religious metaphor . . .

Rasputin, "the Holy Sinner"

Grigory Rasputin's body was taken from the frozen river Neva, in Petrograd, on 1 January, 1917. He had been murdered three days before, and was one of the most notorious figures in Russia. Now that he was dead, he would become a legend all over the world – a symbol of evil, cunning, and lust. If ever you see a magazine story entitled "Rasputin, the Mad Monk", you can be sure it will be full of lurid details of how Rasputin spent his days in drunken carousing, his nights in sexual debauchery; how he deceived the Tsar and Tsarina into thinking he was a miracle worker; how he was the evil genius who brought about the Russian Revolution and the downfall of the Romanov dynasty. It is all untrue. Yet it makes such a good story that there is little chance that Rasputin will ever receive justice. The truth about him is that he really was a miracle worker and a man of strange powers. He was certainly no saint – very few magicians are – and tales of his heavy drinking and sexual prowess are undoubtedly based on fact. But he was no diabolical schemer.

Rasputin.

Rasputin was born in the village of Pokrovskoe in 1870. His father was a fairly well-to-do peasant. As a young man, Rasputin had a reputation for wildness until he visited a monastery and spent four months there in prayer and meditation. For the remainder of his life, he was obsessed by religion. He married at nineteen and became a prosperous carter. Then the call came again; he left his family and took to the road as a kind of wandering monk. When eventually he returned, he was a changed man, exuding an extraordinarily powerful magnetism. The young people of his village were fascinated by him. He converted one room in his house into a church, and it was always full. The local priest became envious of his following, however, and Rasputin was forced to leave home again.

Rasputin had always possessed the gift of second sight. One day during his childhood this gift had revealed to him the identity of a peasant who had stolen a horse and hidden it in a barn. Now, on his second round of travels, he also began to develop extraordinary healing powers. He would kneel by the beds of the sick and pray; then he would lay hands on them, and cure many of them. When he came to St Petersburgh, probably late in 1903, he already had a reputation as a wonder worker. Soon he was accepted in aristocratic society in spite of his rough peasant manners.

It was in 1907 that he suddenly became the power behind the throne. Three years before, Tsarina Alexandra had given birth to a longed-for heir to the throne, Prince Alexei. But it was soon apparent that Alexei had inherited haemophilia, a disease that prevents the blood from clotting, and from which a victim may bleed to death even with a small cut. At the age of three the prince fell and bruised himself so severely that an internal haemorrhage developed. He lay in a fever for days, and doctors despaired of his life. Then the Tsarina recalled the man of God she had met two years earlier, and sent for Rasputin. As soon as he came in he said calmly: "Do not worry the child. He will be all right." He laid his hand on the boy's forehead, sat down on the edge of the bed, and began to talk to him in a quiet voice. Then he knelt and prayed. In a few minutes the boy was in a deep and peaceful sleep, and the crisis was over.

Henceforward the Tsarina felt a powerful emotional dependence on Rasputin – a dependence nourished by the thinly veiled hostility with which Alexandra, a German, was treated at court. Rasputin's homely strength brought her a feeling of security. The Tsar also began to confide in Rasputin, who became a man of influence at court. Nicholas II was a poor ruler, not so much

Rasputin surrounded by the adoring ladies of the Russian court.

cruel as weak, and too indecisive to stem the rising tide of social discontent. His opponents began to believe that Rasputin was responsible for some of the Tsar's reactionary policies, and a host of powerful enemies began to gather. On several occasions the Tsar had to give way to the pressure and order Rasputin to leave the city. On one such occasion, the young prince fell and hurt himself again. For several days he tossed in agony, until he seemed too weak to survive. The Tsarina dispatched a telegram to Rasputin, and he telegraphed back: "The illness is not as dangerous as it seems." From the moment it was received, the prince began to recover.

World War I brought political revolution and military catastrophe to Russia. Its outbreak was marked by a strange coincidence: Rasputin was stabbed by a madwoman at precisely the same moment as the Archduke Franz Ferdinand was shot at Sarajevo. Rasputin hated war, and might have been able to dissuade the Tsar from leading Russia into the conflict. But he was in bed recovering from his stab wound when the moment of decision came.

Rasputin's end was planned by conspirators in the last days of 1916. He was lured to a cellar by Prince Felix Yussupov, a man he trusted. After feeding him poisoned cakes, Yussupov shot him in the back; then Rasputin was beaten with an iron bar. Such was his immense vitality that he was still alive when the murderers dropped him through the hole in the ice into the Neva. Among his papers was found a strange testament addressed to the Tsar. It stated that he had a strong feeling he would die by violence before January 1, 1917, and that if he were killed by peasants, the Tsar would reign for many years to come; but, if he were killed by aristocrats – as he was – then "none of your children or relations will remain alive for more than two years". He was right. The Tsar and his family were all murdered in July 1918 – an amazing example, among many, of Rasputin's gift of precognition.

The lesson is simple: many messiahs are deluded, but it would be a mistake to dismiss them all as madmen.

WAITING FOR THE WARRIOR-KING

*A*lthough many of the great mystics spent their lives as members of the Church, they did not believe that the Church was essential for "salvation". Man can know God directly, without the need for priests and sacraments. Some of them – like the thirteenth century mystic Meister Eckhart – came dangerously close to being excommunicated, or even burned at the stake. (Eckhart was tried for heresy but died before he was condemned – which he was.)

It was only one step from this belief that man has direct access to God to the belief that there is no such thing as sin. If man is truly free, then he has choice, and if he chooses to reject the idea that something is sinful – for example, sexual promiscuity or incest – no authority has a right to tell him he is a sinner. Preachers of this doctrine were known as Brethren of the Free Spirit.

Was Jesus a Messiah?

The answer to that question may seem obvious, for his followers certainly regarded him as *the* Messiah. But did Jesus agree with them? The answer is: probably not. When his disciple Peter told him: "They call you the Christ, the Messiah", Jesus advised him to be silent. The claim obviously embarrassed him.

Why? Because, as we have seen, the Jewish craving for a Messiah arose out of the longing for someone to lead them to victory. After the Assyrian invasion, the Jews became a conquered people, oppressed by a series of more powerful nations: the Seleucids (descendants of Alexander the Great), the Babylonians, the Egyptians, the Romans. For the same reason, the British of a thousand years later came to believe firmly that King Arthur would return to throw off the foreign yoke. Jesus had no desire to be regarded as a military commander, which is what the word Messiah originally implied.

What is difficult for modern Christians to grasp is that Jesus was only one of many Hebrew prophets who were believed to be the Messiah; the historian Josephus mentions several of them. He regarded them all as charlatans and agitators. Christians later changed Josephus's text, in which Jesus is described as a small man with a hunched back and a half-bald head, to read: "six feet tall, well grown, with a venerable face, handsome nose . . . curly hair the colour of unripe hazel nuts . . .", and various other details that transform the unpreposessing little man into the early Christian equivalent of a film star. So all the writings about Jesus have to be treated with great caution; the later Christians were quite unscrupulous in changing anything that disagreed with their own image of "the Messiah".

But if Jesus declined to be regarded as a military leader, why did anyone pay any attention to him? The answer is that he announced that the end of the world was about to take place, and that this would happen *within the lifetime of people then alive*. This is why he told them to take no thought for the morrow, and that God would provide. The world would soon be ending.

It is also important to understand that it was the Jews themselves, not their Roman conquerors, who disliked Jesus. The Sadducees, who loved Greek culture and disbelieved in life after death, thought him an uncultivated fanatic. The Pharisees, who regarded themselves as the guardians of the Law, reacted angrily to Jesus's attacks on them as narrow-minded and old-fashioned. The Zealots wanted to see the Romans conquered and thrown out of Palestine, and had no patience with a Messiah who preached peace and love. While Jesus was wandering around the countryside preaching in the open air, no one worried about him. But when he rode into Jerusalem on a donkey (fulfilling the prophesy of Isaiah) and was greeted with enthusiasm by the people, the Jewish establishment became alarmed. And when Jesus threw the money changers out of the temple, they saw the writing on the wall, and had him arrested. The arrest had to take place in a garden at night to avoid causing trouble.

Of the four Gospels, only one, that of John, claims to be that of an eyewitness. When Jesus is taken before Caiaphas, the high priest asks him about his teachings, and Jesus tells him to ask those who have heard him – to the indignation of the high priest's servant, who slaps his face and tells him not to be impertinent. It is in the other three Gospels – by writers who do not claim to have known him – that Jesus answers the question about whether he is the son of God by replying that he is "Son of Man" who will sit on the right hand of God.

In John's account, Pilate asks him if he is the king of the Jews, and Jesus replies that his kingdom is not of this world – meaning, in effect, that Pilate should not imagine he is claiming any political leadership. "I have come into the world to bear witness to the truth." There is certainly nothing here about claiming to be the Messiah.

To Pilate's disgust, the Jews then demanded Jesus's execution, declining to allow him to be pardoned in honour of Passover. And so Jesus died, like so many other messiahs and political agitators, by crucifixion.

How, then, did Christianity go on to conquer the world? The answer lies partly in the many stories of miracles that circulated about Jesus – including the story that he had risen from the dead. A Jewish sect called the Messianists (or Nasoraeans) believed that Jesus would return and lead them against the Romans. At this point, a convert to Christianity named Paul produced a strange and mystical new version of Jesus's teaching that seemed to have very little to do with anything Jesus had actually said. Paul declared that Jesus was the Son of God (which Jesus had denied) who had been sent to redeem Man from the sin of Adam, and that anyone who believed in Jesus was "saved". In fact, Jesus had preached salvation through the efforts of the individual, and insisted that the Kingdom of God is within everybody. But since there was still a widespread belief that the End of the World would occur within a year or so, Paul's version of the Christian message was a powerful incentive to belief. The Messianists regarded such a notion as absurd and blasphemous, and since they were politically stronger than Paul's Christians, it looked as if their version would triumph.

However, as it happened, the Messianists were among those wiped out by Titus, the son of the Roman emperor Vespasian, who was sent to put down the latest rebellion. He did more than that; he destroyed the Temple and carried its treasures back to Rome. Paul's "Christians" were so widely scattered that they were relatively immune from massacre. And so, by a historical accident, Paul's version of Christianity became the official version, and the "vicarious atonement" – the notion that

Jesus died on the cross to redeem man from the sin of Adam – became the basis of the religion that went on to conquer the world.

By the year AD 100 it was obvious that the world was not going to end within the lifetime of Jesus's contemporaries, and that Jesus, like so many other messiahs, had quite simply been wrong. But by that time, Christianity was too powerful to die out. It was now a political force, the focus of all the dissatisfaction of the underdogs and victims of Roman brutality. The belief now spread that the end of the world would occur in the year AD 1000. And, as we have seen, there was so much violence, pestilence and bloodshed around that time that the believers had no doubt that the end was just around the corner.

Simon Bar Kochba

But even before the millennium, there were plenty of messiahs. In AD 132 a Jewish revolutionary named Simon Bar Kochba led a revolt against the Romans in Judaea when he learned that the Emperor Hadrian intended to build a temple dedicated to Jupiter on the site of the temple that had been destroyed by Titus. A celebrated student of the Talmud, (the Jewish book of law) Rabbi Akiva, told Simon Bar Kochba: "You are the Messiah." And Bar Kochba behaved exactly as a Jewish Messiah was expected to behave (and as Jesus had failed to behave); he seized town and villages from the Romans, had his own head stamped on the coinage, and built fortresses. But he stood no real chance against the Romans, with their highly trained troops. It took Julius Severus three and a half years to destroy the rebels, and in that time he destroyed fifty fortresses and 985 villages, and killed over half a million people. Since Bar Kochba's men were guerillas, and guerillas survive by being supported by sympathizers, Severus set out to kill all the sympathizers. He finally killed Bar Kochba himself in the fortress of Bethar, and renamed Jerusalem Aelia Capitolana. So one more Messiah was proved to be mortal after all. The Jews were so shattered by this defeat that there were no more Jewish messiahs for many centuries.

Moses of Crete

In about AD 435 an unnamed messiah from Crete, who called himself Moses, announced that, like his predecessor, he would lead his followers back to the Promised Land, causing the sea to part for them so they could walk on the bottom. Hundreds of followers gathered on the seashore, and Moses raised his arms and ordered the sea to separate. Then he shouted the order to march into the waves. They obeyed him, but the sea ignored his order, and many of his followers were drowned. Moses may have been drowned with them; at all events, he disappeared.

The Christ of Gevaudon

In AD 591, an unnamed messiah began to wander around France. This man had apparently had a nervous breakdown after being surrounded by a swarm of flies in a forest; he recovered after two years and became a preacher, clad himself in animal skins, and wandered down through Arles to the district of Gevaudon in the Cevennes (noted later for a famous case of a werewolf). He declared he was Christ, had a companion called Mary, and healed the sick by touching them. (As we have seen in the case of Rasputin, this may be a natural gift.) His followers were mostly the very poor, and they often waylaid travellers (most of whom would be rich) and seized their money. The Messiah redistributed it to the poor. His army of 3,000 became so powerful that most towns lost no time in acknowledging him as the Christ.

Before he arrived at the cathedral city of La Puy he quartered his army in neighbouring halls and churches, and sent messengers to announce his coming to Bishop Aurelius. When these messengers appeared in front of the bishop stark naked and turned somersaults, he decided it was time to end the career of this dangerous and disrespectful rebel. He sent his men to meet him, apparently to welcome him, and as one of them bowed down as if to kiss the Messiah's knees, they grabbed him and dragged him to the ground, his companions rushed forward and hacked the Messiah to pieces. With their "Christ" dead, the rebellious followers soon dispersed. Mary was apparently tortured until she revealed the "diabolic devices" that had given the Messiah his power – St Gregory of Tours, who recounts the story, naturally assumed that it was all the Devil's work. But he also records that the Messiah's followers continued to believe in him to the day they died, and to maintain that he was the Christ.

The inhabitants of the Melanesian islands in the Pacific have, since their first contact with western travellers, developed the so-called "cargo cults". Cargo refers in the islanders' pidgin to goods of any kind given by visitors.

First contact occurred with the arrival of the Russian Count Nikolai Miklouho-Maclay in 1871. He was received as a god, due to the incredible nature of his transport, a Russian frigate, and his gifts, which were amazing to a culture that was still in the Stone Age. German traders and Christian missionaries only served to reinforce the natives awe and faith. The basic tenets of the religion became set: visitors who give "cargo" are good, those who do not are evil, as they withhold what are seen as spiritual gifts.

In 1940 the Americans built a military base on the Melanesian island of Tanna in the southern New Hebrides. Cargo planes zoomed in and out leaving radios, canned beer and other western necessities. The natives observed the American service men in uniform, and wishing to bring more planes and enjoy similar luxuries they improvised uniforms and spoke into empty beer cans, as they had seen the Americans speak into microphones.

What began as adoration and emulation soon turned to dissatisfaction as their rituals failed to get the desired response. The faith changed its nature, becoming a conviction that the present western presence on the island was of the wrong kind. Soon a messiah would come to give the natives what the Americans refused to give them. John Frum or Jonfrum was the name that the natives gave this messiah, although the reason is not clear. Some say that Frum is a corruption of broom, to sweep away the white man. Others put forward the simpler explanation that the name is derived from "John from America". He is described as a small man with bleached hair, a high-pitched voice and a coat with shiny buttons.

The cult persists in many different forms on each of the remote Melanesian islands. What began as simple worship of westerners has developed into an entire liberation theology in a very short time: John Frum will one day arrive and hand over all of the "cargo" to the natives, while getting rid of the westerners. After that the islanders would live on as normal, only richer and happier than before.

A century and a half later, about 742, a messiah called Aldebert, who came from Soissons, announced that he was a saint; his followers built chapels for him which he named after himself. He claimed to own a letter from Jesus himself. Pope Zachary was so worried about "Saint" Aldebert's influence that he tried hard to capture him, and, when that failed, excommunicated him. Adelbert went on for at least two more years, and seems to have died of natural causes.

Eudo de Stella

Three centuries later, another messiah called Eon or Eudo de Stella was less lucky. He gathered hordes of disciples in Britanny, and organized his followers into a Church with archbishops and bishops. Unlike Jesus of Nazareth, he had no hesitation in declaring that he was the son of God. AD 1144 was a good year for a messiah to acquire followers, for an appalling winter caused multitudes to starve. Eon's followers lived in the forest, and ravaged the countryside, living mainly by plunder. But in 1148, he was finally taken prisoner by soldiers of the Archbishop of Rouen, and imprisoned in a tower, where he was starved to death. His followers refused to renounce him, and the "bishops" and "archbishops" were burned alive in the now traditional Christian spirit.

Tanchelm

One of the most remarkable messiahs of the twelfth century, Tanchelm of Antwerp, was already dead by then. He seems to have started his career as a monk, then become a diplomat working for Count Robert of Flanders, trying to persuade the Pope to hand over some of Utrecht to Count Robert. The Pope refused, and when Count Robert died, Tanchelm's career as a diplomat came to an end. He became a wandering preacher, making his headquarters in Antwerp.

Tanchelm seems to have possessed what all messiahs possess:

tremendous powers as a preacher and orator. We also have to remember that a large part of his audience would be ignorant peasants who had never heard a really good preacher. As Tanchelm addressed them in the open fields, dressed as a monk, the audiences reacted like modern teenagers to a pop idol. He denounced the Church for its corruption, and told them that if the sacraments were administered by sinful priests, they would fail to work. So many were convinced that the churches were soon empty. And when Tanchelm told his followers not to pay taxes to the church (called tithes), they were delighted to follow his advice.

Was Tanchelm a charlatan, or did he really believe he was a messiah? He certainly felt that he had a right to live like a king. He dressed magnificently, and was always surrounded by a large retinue, including twelve men who were supposed to be the twelve disciples. One day he announced that he would become betrothed to the Virgin Mary, and held a ceremony in which he and a sacred statue were joined together in front of a vast crowd, who offered their jewellery as an engagement present.

With so many followers, the Church could do nothing about him; he held Utrecht, Antwerp and large areas of the country-side. Finally, about AD 1115, he was killed – like the Messiah of Gevaudon – by treachery, being stabbed by a priest who had been allowed to approach him. But his influence remained as powerful as ever, and it took another "miracle worker", Norbert of Xanten (who was regarded with favour by the Church) to finally "de-convert" his followers in Antwerp and restore power to the Church.

Rebellion, Mysticism and Sex.

How did these "messiahs" become so powerful? To begin with, all of them had the gift of preaching. But it was more than that. The Christian Church, which began as a poor and persecuted organization whose leaders were thrown to the lions, suddenly became the official religion of Rome in AD 313, under the Emperor Constantine. As soon as they gained power, the Christians began to behave far worse than their enemies, destroying pagan temples, burning heretics, and squabbling amongst themselves.

In effect, the Church became the supreme dictator. And the poor, ordered to go to church every Sunday, groaning under heavy taxes and forced to pay to have their sins forgiven, became increasingly disenchanted with their spiritual masters. But there was nothing they could do; the Church exerted the same iron grip as the Nazis in Germany or the Communists in Stalin's Russia.

This is why rebel messiahs found an eager audience. Like Jesus, they attacked the establishment and declared that the "law" was less important than the spirit. Besides, there had always been a strong tradition of Mysticism in the Church. Mystics were men who had experienced moments of overwhelming joy and illumination in which they felt they had seen God. The mystics taught that every man has a divine spark, and that therefore, in a sense, every man is God – or contains a fragment of God. They also believed that all Nature is an expression of God – in fact some (called Pantheists) believed that Nature *is* God. One of the greatest of the early mystics, Dionysius the Areopagite (around AD 500) taught that God is a kind of emptiness or darkness, and can only be reached by recognizing that God is *not* knowledge or power or eternity, or anything else that the mind can grasp. God is beyond all words and ideas.

The Wife Who Lost her Ring

One popular story of the Middle Ages was about a rich merchant whose wife began to spend a great deal of time in church. When her husband heard rumours that the church consisted of believers in the Free Spirit, he decided to follow her one day. Wearing a disguise he walked behind her into an underground cavern where – to his surprise – the service began with a dance, in which everyone chose his or her partner. After that, the congregation ate food and drank wine. The husband began to understand why his wife preferred this to the local Catholic church; the service was better.

When the priest stood up, he announced that all human beings are free, and that provided they lived in the spirit of the Lord, they could do what they liked. "We must become one with God." Then he took a young girl and led her to the altar. The two of them removed their clothes. Then the priest turned to the congregation and told them to do the same. "This is the Virgin Mary and I am Jesus. Now do as we do." The girl lay down on the altar, and the priest lay on top of her and, in full view of the congregation, commenced an act of intercourse. Then the congregation each seized his dancing partner, and lay down on the floor.

In the chaos that followed, the wife did not notice as her husband took hold of her hand and pulled off her wedding ring; she was totally absorbed in her partner. Realizing that no one was paying any attention to him, the husband slipped away.

When his wife returned home, he asked her angrily how she dared to give herself to another man, even in the name of religion. She indignantly denied everything, demanding whether, as the wife of a wealthy merchant, he thought she would behave like a prostitute. But when the husband asked her what had happened to her wedding ring, she went pale. Then, as he held it out to her, she realized that he had seen everything, and burst into tears.

The wife was beaten until she bled, but she was more fortunate than the others, who were arrested by inquisitors and burnt at the stake.

The story may or may not have happened, but such congregations actually existed. They came into existence soon after the year AD 1200, and soon spread across Europe. The Free Spirit movement declared that God is within us all, and that therefore the Church is unnecessary – in fact, it is the Whore of Babylon. The great poets are as 'holy' as the Bible. Sex *must* be an acceptable way of worshipping God, since it brings such a sense of divine illumination. In his book *The Black Death*, Johanne Nohls gives this account of the Brethren:

> "The bas reliefs . . . in French churches . . . represent erotic scenes. In the Cathedral of Alby a fresco even depicts sodomites engaged in sexual intercourse. Homosexuality was also well known in parts of Germany, as is proved by the trials of the Beghards and Beguins in the fourteenth century, particularly in the confessions of the brethren Johannes and Albert of Brünn, which are preserved in the Greifswald manuscript. From these it is evident that the Brethren of the Free Mind did not regard homosexuality as sinful. 'And if one brother desires to commit sodomy with a male, he should do so without let or hindrance

and without any feeling of sin, as otherwise he would not be a Brother of the Free Mind.'"

In a Munich manuscript, we read: "And when they go to confession and come together and he preaches to them, he takes the one who is the most beautiful among them and does to her all according to his will, and they extinguish the light and fall one upon the other, a man upon a man, and a woman upon a woman, just as it comes about. Everyone must see with his own eyes how his wife or daughter is abused by others, for they assert that no one can commit sin below his girdle. That is their belief."

Other curious doctrines, "such as that incest is permissible, even when practised on the altar, that no one has the right to refuse consent, that Christ risen from the dead had intercourse with Magdalena, etc., all indicate the deterioration and confusion of moral ideas caused by the great plagues, particularly that of 1348"

In short, according to the Brethren of the Free Spirit, every man is his own messiah.

Sex with a Stranger

The Church did its best to stamp out these beliefs by sword and fire, but it still took three centuries. And even when the Free Spirits had been wiped out, the ideas continued to exert influence. Around 1550, a man named Klaus Ludwig, who lived in Mulhausen in Germany, formed a church in which members were initiated by having sex with a stranger. Like so many messiahs, Ludwig said he was Christ, the son of God, and that these things had been revealed to him. The sacrament was another name for sex. Man was bread and woman was wine, and when they made love, this was Holy Communion. Children born out such communion were holy. And the members of his congregation could not be killed. His sermons ended with the words "Be fruitful and multiply", and the congregation made haste to undress and do their best to obey.

Ludwig taught that sexual desire is the prompting of the

Holy Spirit, so that if a man feels desire for any woman, he should regard it as a message from God. If, of course, the woman happened to be a member of Ludwig's "Chriesterung" (or Bloodfriends), then it was her duty to help him obey the will of the Lord, even if she was another man's wife.

Ludwig told the Bloodfriends to observe great secrecy and to behave like other people. But no doubt some of his congregation were eager to make converts of husbands with attractive wives. Like the congregation in the medieval story, the Bloodfriends were found out and put on trial, although Ludwig himself escaped. One member of the Council of Twelve Judges admitted that he had celebrated Holy Communion with sixteen different women. Three Bloodfriends were executed, and the others were re-converted to a more conventional form of Christianity.

Sabbatai Zevi

One of the most remarkable of all the "messiahs" was a Turkish Jew named Sabbatai Zevi (pronounced Shabtight Svy), who at one point seemed about to become one of the most powerful kings in Europe.

Sabbatai was the son of a wealthy merchant of Smyrna (now Izmir) on the coast of Turkey. Born in 1626, he was always of a deeply religious disposition; he spent hours in prayer, and at the age of sixteen, decided to observe a permanent fast, which lasted for six years. He permitted himself to be married to a girl whom his parents chose, but the marriage was never consummated, and she divorced him. The same thing happened to a second wife. He was what would nowadays be called a manic depressive, experiencing periods of immense joy and elation, followed by days of suicidal gloom.

In 1648, when Sabbatai was twenty-two a great tragedy occurred across the sea in Poland. The fierce Cossacks of the Ukraine rose against the Polish landlords. The Russians and Poles had traditionally been enemies – in 1618 the Poles had even tried to put a Pole on the throne of Russia. The Russians and the Poles both wanted the rich Ukraine. A Cossack leader called Bogdan Khmelnitsky invaded Poland and challenged the Polish army. He also set out to destroy the Jews.

Poland's Jews had been servants of the rich landlords whom

the Cossacks hated, and they were massacred in vast numbers. All the usual atrocities of massacre were committed – children hacked to pieces in their mothers' arms, pregnant women sliced open, old men disembowelled, girls raped before their husbands. One girl who had been forcibly married to a Cossack chose a cunning method of suicide: she told him that she had magic powers, and could not be harmed by a sword; if he didn't believe her, he should try running his sword through her. He did as she asked, and killed her.

A hundred thousand Jews died in this seventeenth century holocaust. Thousands of others fled the country, and many went to Turkey, where there were already wealthy Jewish communities.

When Sabbatai Zevi heard about these massacres he was appalled. Overwhelmed by a desperate desire to do something for his people, he suddenly became convinced he was the Messiah who would lead them back to the Holy Land. And he began his mission by doing something that horrified his orthodox fellow Jews – he stood up in the synagogue and pronounced the name of Jehovah (or Jahweh), which Jews regard as too sacred to speak. (Instead they called it Adonai.)

Like all messiahs, he soon collected a small band of followers who believed every word he said. His fellow orthodox Jews found this menacing, and banished him when he was twenty-five. In the Turkish town of Salonika (now Thessaloniki, and a part of Greece) he gained even more converts. But even his followers were often puzzled by his strange behaviour. On one occasion he went around carrying a basket of fish, explaining that it represented the Age of Pisces, when Jews would be released from bondage. And on another occasion he shocked the rabbis by inviting them to a feast, then taking a Scroll of the Law in his arms as if it were a woman, and carrying it to a marriage canopy that he had set up; this symbolic marriage of the Messiah and the Law shocked the orthodox so much that he was expelled from Salonika.

At the age of thirty-six, surrounded by disciples (who supported him in style) he moved to Jerusalem. There he was seen by a young man who was to become his John the Baptist or St Paul, the son of a Jewish scholar named Nathan Ashkenazi, who was deeply impressed when he saw Sabbatai in the street, but was too young and shy to approach him. It was at this time that Sabbatai found himself a bride, a Polish girl named Sarah, who had escaped the pogrom, become a courtesan (or high class tart), and developed a strange conviction that she was destined to be the bride of the Messiah. The story has it that Sabbatai heard about the beautiful courtesan and send twelve of his disciples to Leghorn, in Italy, to bring her to him. They were married in March 1664.

In the following year, Sabbatai finally met Nathan, who was now twenty-two (Sabbatai was nearly forty), and allowed himself to be convinced that it was time to announce to the whole world – and not merely to his disciples – that he was the Messiah.

The news spread throughout Palestine. But when Sabbatai rode seven times around the city of Jerusalem, then went to present himself to the rabbis as their new master, he met with violent hostility, and another order of banishment. Sabbatai now decided to return to the city of his birth, Smyrna. Meanwhile, his St Paul was writing letters to Jewish communities all over Europe announcing that the Messiah had come. These letters were read aloud in synagogues, and thousands of Jews were suddenly filled with hope that the Day of Judgement had at last arrived. In Amsterdam, another Jewish centre, crowds danced in the streets. In London, Samuel Pepys recorded that Jews were placing ten to one bets that Sabbatai would soon be acknowledged as the King of the World.

Not all Jews shared this enthusiasm; the orthodox were appalled, for the doctinres preached by Sabbatai were horribly similar to those preached by the Brethren of the Free Spirit. "The forbidden" was now allowed, which included incest and promiscuity. The Sabbataians (as they were called) shocked their neighbours by walking around naked at a time when nakedness was regarded as a sin. In the Jewish religion, as in Mohammedanism, women were kept strictly apart. Sabbatai told them they were men's equals and should mix freely with their fellow worshippers. Divorce or infidelity was no reason for a woman to be excluded from full participation in religious rites. Was not the Messiah himself married to a woman who admitted to having been a whore?

Not that Sabbatai's followers were inclined to sexual self indulgence. They took pride in mortifying the flesh, scourging and starving themselves, rolling naked in the snow, even burying themselves in the earth so only their heads stuck out. It was a frenzy of religious ecstasy, all based on the belief that the Millennium was about to arrive.

Now Sabbatai made the mistake that was to dismay all his followers and bring an abrupt end to his career. He decided to go to Constantinople, the Turkish capital, a journey of fourteen days by sea. When the news reached Constantinople, it caused the same wild scenes of rejoicing that had been seen in other European capitals. There was a general feeling that the Day of Judgement was at hand, and that Sabbatai's arrival would finally restore the Jews to the glory they had enjoyed under King David.

The Sultan, the young Mehmet IV, was understandably alarmed. Enemies of Sabbatai informed his Grand Vizier, Ahmed Koprulu, that the Messiah was a charlatan who wanted the Sultan's throne. If Sabbatai had heard about this, he might have felt complimented. The people of Constantinople were prepared to welcome him as the people of Jerusalem had welcomed Jesus Christ, and the secular authorities thought he wanted to become king. History was repeating itself. His reply, of course, would be: "My kingdom is not of this world."

But the parallel with Jesus should also have warned him that he would soon be under arrest. In fact, the boat had only just docked – after a painful journey of thirty six days – when Mehmet's soldiers came on board and carried him off to jail.

He was luckier than his messianic predecessor. Wealthy followers greased enough palms to make sure he was not put to death. Instead, he was installed in the castle of Abydos, in Gallipoli, and allowed to continue to live in style, with a succession of distinguished visitors. Unfortunately, one of these was a paranoid old man named Nehemiah ha-Kolen, a Polish scholar who wanted to argue with Sabbatai about the Kabbalah, the Jewish mystical system. He was determined to prove Sabbatai an imposter, or at least, compel him to acknowledge himself, Nehemiah, as an equal. Sabbatai stood up for himself, and probably allowed Nehemiah to see that he regarded him as a bilious and envious old neurotic. Nehemiah hastened away to denounce him to the Sultan as a revolutionary who had admitted that he hoped to usurp the throne. In September 1666, Sabbatai was brought before Sultan Mehmet, and ordered to convert to Islam or die on the spot. Faced with his supreme opportunity for martyrdom, Sabbatai behaved as unpredictably as ever. He promptly removed his Jewish skullcap and accepted a turban instead. He also accepted a new name: Azis Mehmet Effendi. His wife converted too, becoming known as Fatima Radini. The Sultan then granted him a comfortable sinecure as keeper of the palace gates, which carried a generous pension.

Sabbatai, it seemed, had simply abandoned his conviction that he was sent to save the world. He chose comfort – even though he secretly continued to practice Judaism. In public he was a good Mohammedan. But his followers knew better: they realized that this was another of his inexplicable actions.

Unfortunately, he was still subject to these extraordinary swings of mood, in one of which he divorced Sarah – although he took her back gain as soon as he was normal. And he also continued to preach sexual freedom. In due course, these views caused the Sultan embarrassment, and six years after his conversion, Sabbatai was arrested again. This time he was banished to a remote village in Albania, Dulcigno, where he lived on for another four years. Sarah predeceased him in 1674, and he married again. He still had manic moods in which he declared he was the Messiah, but no one paid any attention.

Oddly enough, his "John the Baptist" Nehemiah continued to love and revere him as the Messiah, as did thousands of followers, who regarded his conversion as yet another of his strange god-like actions – rather like those of the Japanese Zen masters who suddenly kick a pupil downstairs. Sabbatai was the only messiah known to history who was able to have it both ways – to proclaim himself a charlatan, and still continue to retain the devotion of his followers. He was the last of the great Jewish Messiahs.

These are only a small cross-section of the messiahs who have appeared since the crucifixion of Jesus of Nazareth. Readers who want a fuller account should read read Jack Gratus's *The False Messiahs* or Norman Cohn's *The Pursuit of the Millennium*, where they will find a wide array of amazing and colourful figures. This chapter, unfortunately, has run out of space.

There was a widespread belief in England in the late Middle Ages that the British were the descendants of Trojans who fled from Asia Minor after the fall of Troy. The Romans, in fact, believed that they were descendants of the Trojan prince Aeneas, who came to Italy after the fall of Troy. (Virgil described the wanderings of Aeneas after Troy in the *Aeneid*.)

Around AD 1140 Geoffrey of Monmouth published his immensely popular *History of the Kings of Britain*, which is largely about King Arthur and Merlin. But it begins by describing how Aeneas's great grandson Brutus (or Brute) was forced to flee from Italy after he accidentally killed his father when hunting. After various adventures, Brutus came to the island of Albion – inhabited then only by a few giants – and changed its name to Britain, after his own name. Geoffrey's book was accepted as reliable history even down to Elizabethan times.